Exploring Christian Holiness

Volume 2

The Historical Development

Volume 1

THE BIBLICAL FOUNDATIONS

by W. T. Purkiser, Ph.D.

Volume 2

THE HISTORICAL DEVELOPMENT

by Paul M. Bassett, Ph.D., and

William M. Greathouse, M.A., D.D.

Volume 3

THE THEOLOGICAL FORMULATION

by Richard S. Taylor, Th.D.

EXPLORING CHRISTIAN HOLINESS

Volume 2
The Historical Development

by
Paul M. Bassett, Ph.D., and
William M. Greathouse, M.A., D.D.

BEACON HILL PRESS OF KANSAS CITY
Kansas City, Missouri

ISBN: 0-8341-0926-3
0-8341-0842-9 (Set)

Printed in the United States of America

10 9 8 7 6 5 4 3 2

Contents

Section II.

From Wesley to the American Holiness Movement

by William M. Greathouse

Foreword

John Wesley is the principal forebear of what is commonly called the "Holiness Movement." Although he was obviously not the originator of the doctrine of Christian perfection (as he chose to call it), he was the one who retrieved from theological limbo this biblical truth so positively enunciated in the Scriptures but so greatly neglected since apostolic days.

It is recognized, also, that Wesley did not come forth with a full-blown doctrinal statement that comprehended all aspects of holiness belief and practice. Indeed it remained for such associates as John Fletcher and Adam Clarke to "fine tune" the doctrinal structure, even introducing some nuances not found in Wesley's writings or only lightly alluded to by him. The matter of "Spirit baptism" is among the most crucial of such extensions. Certainly they did much to clarify the practical matters of secondness and how to obtain entire sanctification, since Wesley's emphasis had been upon the experience itself.

Nor has the elaboration of holiness doctrine ceased. As various concepts and interpretations have been added, and aberrations introduced, splinter groups have proliferated, each emphasizing some specific point or points of belief or conduct. The result has been some confusion and even contradiction among groups that claim a common Wesleyan ancestry.

The consequent need for a comprehensive and definitive summation of the doctrine of holiness or entire sanctification has long been recognized. Although numerous competent works have been written on the subject, it appears that no complete study of all aspects of the doctrine has ever been attempted before. The publishers have undertaken this task with some sense of obligation, representing as they do the largest extant holiness body. But there has also been a sensitivity to the variant interpretations of equally knowledgeable and devoted believers who share our doctrinal heritage. These resultant volumes are neither a polemic nor a studied attempt to establish consensus. Rather they simply present an in-depth study of the three areas that form the foundation of holiness theology—Scripture, history, and doctrine.

The writers of this work are highly respected scholars and exponents of the truth of holiness. Although all are members of the Church of the Nazarene, this is in no sense a sectarian presentation. Indeed it is the hope of the publishers that this work may stand as the best possible statement of holiness doctrine to which the broad spectrum of "holiness people" can heartily subscribe.

—The Publishers

Preface

The purpose of this second volume of *Exploring Christian Holiness* is to trace the historical development of the experience, life, and doctrine of holiness through the centuries of Christian history. The first volume by Dr. W. T. Purkiser surveys the biblical foundations of holiness. The third volume by Dr. Richard S. Taylor presents a contemporary theological formulation of the teaching.

George Croft Cell declared that it was John Wesley who "restored the neglected doctrine of holiness to its merited position in the Protestant understanding of Christianity." Wesley did indeed formulate the doctrine in its essentials as understood within historic Methodism and the modern holiness movement, yet he but recovered a truth clearly taught in the Scriptures and given expression in one form or another in the intervening centuries.

Although the light of holiness often flickered and sometimes seemed almost to go out, the truth remained a part of the experience, liturgy, life, and thought of the Church from apostolic days onward. In the first half of this volume Dr. Paul Bassett tells this thrilling story. From a great company of both ancient and medieval witnesses he chooses those he regards as providing a background for Wesley's doctrine. His treatment reveals how the truth of Christian perfection, which in the New Testament is synthesized with that of entire sanctification, began early a separate development of its own. He has therefore chosen to deal with the subject under the rubric of "Entire Sanctification."

John Wesley reunited the biblical truths of perfection and sanctification. Historically, his doctrine has usually been known as "Christian Perfection," the term I have chosen for the teaching. Beginning with Wesley's associates, John Fletcher and Adam Clarke, some aspects of the truth not clearly enunciated in Wesley's writings were introduced, and in the works of the standard Wesleyan theologians of both Britain and America, the doctrine found creative, fresh expressions. Yet in every instance the developments remained within the parameters of the classical Wesleyan teaching.

In the 19th-century holiness movement, the doctrine was given a more pragmatic cast. Along with a much stronger emphasis on the critical nature of "the second blessing," a different understanding of the baptism with the Holy Spirit was introduced. The result was a new shape and tenor of the doctrine. The final chapters trace these interesting developments and, it is hoped, reveal something of the dynamism of modern holiness teaching as it seeks to interact honestly with Scripture, experience, and the Wesleyan tradition.

—WILLIAM M. GREATHOUSE

SECTION I

From the Apostolic Fathers to Early Protestantism

by Paul M. Bassett

1

The Significance of Historical Study

Historians often dislike defending the significance of what they do. And, with equal frequence, those who call upon them to make a defense have difficulty knowing when a valid response has been given—the demand for satisfaction being sometimes as strong as the demand for truth. But the question of the value of "doing history" is a good one anyway: "What difference does it make where an idea or an account of an event has been or where it comes from?" In terms specific to this book, the question is, "What difference does this historical path of the doctrine of entire sanctification make?" Why study that path? Why not satisfy ourselves with biblical and theological studies of the doctrine?

These questions cannot be answered in full, nor to everyone's satisfaction, in the space allotted. But perhaps a few trailblazes can be established that will aid in the appreciation of the doctrine and aid also in understanding it.

I. The Authority of Tradition

As Protestants, we accept Scripture as the sole authority for faith and practice. "Sole authority" in this case means final and ultimate authority. There is no other authority standing alongside the Bible.

Nonetheless, few Protestants would deny to other forms of authority limited jurisdiction so long as they be kept clearly subservient to the Bible. Especially important in this regard is tradition, the Christian practice of the past. Mainstream Christianity has kept in touch with its past, even in the contemporary clamor for the new. Why is this? Why is tradition so important to Christianity?

The answer to this question is deceptively simple. For all of its fracturing and splintering, for all of its bickering between parties, Christianity senses a unity beyond the differences, and it yearns to express it. Often in the face of obstacles they have themselves very carefully placed, two millennia of Christians have still sought the unity of the Church.

This unity has at least two dimensions: unity with one's own contemporaries in the faith, and unity with the long line of witnesses to the same grace of God in Christ Jesus. Roman Catholicism, through its practices of praying through the saints and praying for those believed to be in Purgatory, expresses historical unity more explicitly than Protestantism does, but Protestantism is not one whit less conscientious in maintaining its ties to the past. "He is a Calvinist," "She is an Episcopalian," "They are Mennonites"—these declarations of theological allegiance entail long histories. Most Protestants also continue to celebrate two great symbols of Christian unity, baptism and Communion. And most Protestants would say that they are aligned with the long past of Christianity in this conviction, that the Bible is still their standard for faith and practice.

Among both Roman Catholics and Protestants,[1] then, there are many expressions of this deep desire that is of the very nature of the faith itself. We must remain true to the past. Legend and mythology ultimately do not suffice. The doctrine of the Incarnation itself keeps alive the awareness that the Church's past is one of flesh and blood, not of mere ideas, abstractions, and pious tales. Who, then, were our spiritual ancestors, and are we keeping faith

---

1. Also to be included in our thinking along these lines are the various branches of Eastern Christianity—what is today known as Eastern Orthodoxy. Nothing is said of them in the text at this point because they have had scant impact upon the Western world in modern times. In the historical development of the doctrine of entire sanctification, nonetheless, Eastern Christianity's contribution has been enormous.

with them? Loyalty to them has historically been viewed as loyalty to the faith itself. It is in the context of such ideas and questions as these, and under their influence, that tradition has undeniable authority, however problematic it may be.

Then, too, Christian faith is radically historical. Basic to our faith are *events,* events that transpired in the time and space that we know. And at the center of our faith stands a Person, not an idea nor an ideal. To be sure, that Person taught ideas and ideals, but they did not make *Him* important. Rather, He made *them* important.

At its best, Christianity has measured all of its notions, practices, and plans by *His* person and work. Prayer, for instance, is not made better merely by being literarily sound nor by expressing philosophical or even spiritual profundities. Prayer is a person-to-person interchange, however much it may be guided by literary, philosophical, religious, or other ideas or ideals.

The great guarantee that Christianity is radically historical, and that this historicity has to do with the profoundly personal, is Christ Jesus. His was an earthly birthdate and His an earthly date of death. Bethlehem, His birthplace, is still a bit of earthly real estate, as is Mt. Calvary, where He died. And it is precisely what happened there that our faith rests upon. Apart from what happened in the specific geographical spot called Palestine in the very specific time period during the reigns of Augustus and Tiberius, Roman emperors, there would be no Christian faith.

And through the ages, Christianity has spread by means of passing on its contagion. Preservation and dissemination of the Bible alone, or of some good ideas, would not have done the work. The faith has demanded a faithful people, and one aspect of their faithfulness has been the yearning to "infect" others. This matter of being contagious, of infecting, of handing down, is precisely what the early Church meant by "tradition." Its words are *traditio,* in the Latin-speaking West, and *parádōsis,* in the Greek-speaking East. And they mean just this: "handing on." Passing on not just content, not just propositions or theological declarations, then, but a way of life itself, a way of life that included the "contamination" of others; this was the meaning of tradition. And by understanding that this is what it meant, we can see why tradition had such authority, and still has it, and why the study of history is far more significant than it at first appears to be.

II. Christian Perfection and Entire Sanctification

But what do the authority of tradition and the need to study the history of a doctrine have to do with the topic to which this book is devoted? Only this: If the doctrine of entire sanctification is a new doctrine, a doctrine not grounded in the long history of the Christian faith and its practice, it is not to be accepted as valid and not to be held as authentically Christian.

Of course, we shall not be so foolish as to expect everyone at all times to have expressed it the same way. Further, we may expect some additional development of this doctrine as there has been development of most others. For example, the precise theological description of what is meant by saying that Jesus Christ is both divine and human, though it was part of the Christian confession of faith from the very beginning, was completed only in A.D. 680 and even then not to everyone's satisfaction. Just so will we see widely varying expressions concerning the nature of the Christian life and precisely what grace can do with it and for it. There will be both clarification and obscuration along the historical path of this and almost any doctrine. But again, if the doctrine and practice are not there in some form, approved among the people of God, we must be immediately suspicious of the teaching.

Here, we must enter a word of caution. The history of the idea of Christian perfection and the history of the doctrine of entire sanctification are not the same. Generally, the history of the doctrine of entire sanctification lies within the boundaries of the history of the broader idea of Christian perfection, but there are critical moments when it does not, as we shall see. The two doctrines belong together, but they have not always been kept connected, much to the impoverishment of both of them.

So it is that while the work of such authors as Garrigou-Lagrange, Pourrat, Windisch, and, especially, Flew, supplies an indispensable groundwork for the study that you are about to read, the present essay does not cover the same territory again. The authors named, the incomparable *Dictionnaire de spiritualité,* and the scholarly journal *La Vie spirituelle* offer careful and often profound researches and insights into the historical course of the idea of perfection, and the careful student of the narrower route of the doctrine of entire sanctification must peruse them.[2] But the history

2. R. Garrigou-Lagrange, *Perfection chrétienne et contemplation,* 2 vols. (Paris, 1923); P. Pourrat, *La Spiritualité chrétienne,* 4 vols. (Paris, 1918-28); H. Windisch,

presented in this present essay will be narrower still and will need more critical study, for it traverses new territory in interpretation. It is a history of the doctrine of entire sanctification.

The doctrine of entire sanctification is more elusive than the idea of Christian perfection in the history of the faith. Perfection is a persistent and pervasive notion, not especially difficult to identify and describe. Wide variation in expression and entanglement in other concerns, both theological and practical, make entire sanctification more difficult to find and to delimit. But we shall see that it, too, is a persistent and pervasive theme in Christian thought and practice.

At this point, then, we must establish a working definition of both terms, but the reader must beware that these are working definitions, definitions that the historian uses in his investigations, definitions sufficiently supple to allow for many ways of saying the same thing. Many systematic or constructive theologians should be able to say of these definitions, "Yes, my own technical definitions will fit here." But they would not wish to state matters so broadly in their technical work.

Christian perfection, doctrinally identified, is that idea which includes the following notions: that the Christian is called to some sort of perfection of spirit or attitude or motive or even action in this life; that this perfection is more or less dependent upon the work of the Holy Spirit in the Christian believer; that the ideal is Christlikeness and is usually cast in terms of perfect love.

Entire sanctification is that doctrine which includes those notions stated as aspects of the doctrine of Christian perfection and in addition includes the following: That in the life of the believer there comes a moment when the believer actually does love God with all of the heart and soul, mind and strength, and neighbor as self; that this moment marks the beginning of a qualitatively different relationship with God and neighbor than that which existed previously, even though the person experiencing this moment was

---

Taufe und Sunde im altesten Christentum bis auf Origines (Leipzig, 1908); R. Newton Flew, *The Idea of Perfection, an Historical Study of the Christian Ideal for the Present Life* (London: Oxford University Press, 1934). One should also mention that the immense literature on Christian mysticism and monasticism contains frequent reference to the idea of Christian perfection. The best way into these areas is the still incomplete but monumental *Dictionnaire de spiritualité* (Paris, 1937—), now about halfway done in nearly 60 vols. Regrettably, it is not in English. *La Vie spirituelle* is published in Paris.

certainly a believer previously; that while this moment sees the believer perfected, it is also the beginning of a process of perfecting in love; that both the initiating moment and the process are always and in all ways dependent upon the grace of God in Christ; that integral to this moment and to the ensuing process is cleansing from sin.

III. Overcoming History with History: Preservation, Change, and Creative Appropriation in Historical Theology

From a Christian point of view, it is incorrect to treat the past as nothing more than a reliquary or as a collection of curious but now useless data. It is incorrect because it is precisely from the past that we understand our present. Our name, "Christian," may from time to time undergo shifts in denotation, most of them brought on by cultural change; but the connotation of that name remains constant, and one mark of authentic Christianity has been its perpetual desire to remain true to its own past. This desire has created a twofold problem: (1) the discovery of the past, with due regard for the fact that perceptions of the past have often been as important to Christianity's self-understanding as the "actual" past has been; and (2) the temptation to exploit the past in selfish and self-preserving ways.

A very telling verse in Isaiah says, "There shall come a voice from behind you saying, 'This is the way; walk in it'" (30:21). This verse and the continual reminders to remember that are found throughout the Bible say much about the role of history in Christian thinking. Someone has said that the analogy for the Christian understanding of history is that of the rower of a small boat who sits facing rearward. In order to steer a straight course, he chooses some landmark behind the boat and keeps aligned with it as he proceeds toward his destination.

The scholarly way to say this is to note that we overcome history with history. History is the great guarantee that God keeps His promises, but more, it is the landmark by which the Church moves toward her future. That future, of course, is the return of her Lord. So steering back into the past is quite inappropriate. Attempting to reenter the past is futile. The precise nature of the future is quite unknown. The past and God's promises for the future are all that the Church has to steer by. And it is her faith that her history and the promises made to her are sufficient compass.

So we treasure doctrinal statements and formulations from the past and use them to guide us into the future. But if the movement of history is genuine movement, if change is really more than an illusion, if people really are important and different as individuals, we may expect the past to be perceived differently as a function of time and circumstance. And, therefore, the past will serve differently, depending upon time and circumstance.

Are there, then, no fixed points in the interpretation or perception of God's great acts in history? There are. The basic fixed point is Scripture, which is the basic witness to those utterly indispensable events upon which the faith is predicated. It is the chosen instrument of the Holy Spirit for guiding God's people—that is how the Church has historically seen it. So all is not relative.

Scripture itself helps us overcome history with history. In the case of Martin Luther, for example, the long theological tradition, or at least a considerable segment of it, had come to say that one must make himself worthy to receive God's justifying grace. But Scripture said that such grace is God's free gift and that grace subsequently makes people worthy of final salvation. Scripture had once been thus understood by Augustine and many others. Luther picked up their note and found it verified in the Bible, or found them verified by the Bible, and by drawing on both Scripture and the tradition that included Augustine and was even older than medieval catholicism, overcame history with history.

Also involved here is what the great German historical theologian Adolph Harnack called the "creative appropriation of history." History is kaleidoscopic. The value of a given event to our present circumstances changes as it is thrown into new light. Of course, there is a temptation to pick and to choose from history only in terms of present need. But this temptation must be resisted. Any specific event has its own context, immediate and larger, and to wrench it free of that context for some special present use is to distort it.

Then, too, we must confess that we know little of the historical context of our own present and nothing of the context that the future will form for it. Moreover, the only appropriate use of the past is to use it to keep us in line with the past. So, for instance, one would not follow Wesley merely because he fits some perceived needs of one's time, but because Wesley met perceived needs of his own time. He serves to keep one aligned with a particular past within the wider Christian tradition. But not everything that he said or did helps even the person who wants to align with him, and through him with the longer past. So one may appropriate that which does elicit alignment and in creativity apply it to one's own time precisely in order to keep in line with the great past. The remainder of Wesley's thought is not necessarily rejected but is in humility held in abeyance.

In studying the history of the doctrine of entire sanctification, then, we shall be showing where the alignment lies in the history of Christian thought. Sometimes the very words will line up, but not usually. To expect verbal congruity would be to overlook human differences in perception and contextual dissimilarities as well.

Of course, to seek and to presume to find similarity in meaning apart from verbal agreement is a tricky business. But the sources are there for all to peruse, and such perusal is in itself part of overcoming history with history and of creatively appropriating the past. So what follows is both an analysis of the sources and an invitation to all to make their own researches in the interest of truth, for the sake of the Church.[3]

---

3. In order to encourage the student who may wish to pursue further study of any of the many and complex issues we but touch upon in the following chapters, we have attempted to provide good, basic bibliographic leads. Sources in foreign languages are not listed for pedantic purposes but to meet our aim in helpfulness. It should be said here as well that all translations from sources are those of this author unless otherwise noted.

2

Entire Sanctification in the First Five Christian Centuries

The idea of Christian perfection has remained alive, if not robust, from the days of the apostles until the present. The relationship between Christian perfection and entire sanctification, delineated in terms of our earlier working definition, has also remained alive but usually has suffered precarious health. Sometimes it has been limited to sources not usually drawn upon by the historian of doctrine.

In our study, we will be compelled to keen awareness of their relationship at every step, though limitations of space will call upon us to fall back upon representative expressions rather than to develop a full historical tracing.

What happened, then, to the doctrines of Christian perfection and entire sanctification in the two or three centuries after the passing of the apostles? Most significantly, they became separated, theologically. And, for the most part, they remained separated until the time of John Wesley. In what follows, we will see something of the process of separation, but our primary interest will be in those cases in which the two were maintained in tandem.

I. The Witness of the Apostolic Fathers

Historians of doctrine have customarily distinguished two groups of Christian theologians in the century or so following the deaths of the original apostles: the Apostolic Fathers and the Apologists. The Apostolic Fathers include (1) the letters of Ignatius, bishop of Antioch, who was martyred in either A.D. 98 or 117; (2) a letter sent about A.D. 98 to the Corinthian congregation from the Roman congregation, entitled "I Clement," for tradition assigned its authorship to Clement, who may have been bishop of Rome; (3) a sermon entitled "II Clement," attributed to the same Clement but probably of later origin (about A.D. 150); (4) the *Shepherd of Hermas,* written before A.D. 150, a series of visions recorded by Hermas, a Roman writer and possible brother to an early bishop of Rome; (5) the *Didache* or *Teaching of the Twelve Apostles,* written no later than A.D. 120, with parts of it being probably much earlier, which is a manual of church instruction probably of Syrian origin; and (6) the *Epistle of Barnabas,* a treatise on the Christian understanding of the Old Testament, written probably before A.D. 110. The *Epistle to Diognetus,* a defense of Christian practices with a sermon attached, is usually counted with the Apostolic Fathers, but its late date, surely after A.D. 161, and its apologetic purpose make it different from them. It is anonymous.[1]

The Apologists were those who sought to defend early Christianity from its enemies, especially from its intellectual antagonists. Most of their writings were in the form of tracts to various important persons, usually government figures, pleading for those persons to gain a true perspective on the faith. Most important among the Apologists was Justin, a Gentile living in Palestine and teaching philosophy. He wrote an apology plus an appendix, and a dialogue with a Jew. These are now known as his *First Apology, Second Apology,* and *Dialogue with Trypho,* respectively. All were written between A.D. 150 and 165.

---

1. A useful critical Greek text of the Apostolic Fathers, with an English translation on facing pages, is Kirsopp Lake, ed., *The Apostolic Fathers,* 2 vols. (New York: Macmillan, 1925-30). There is no *extended* commentary on the Apostolic Fathers in English. For general commentary, see G. Bardy, *La vie spirituelle d'après les Pères des trois premiers siècles* (Paris, 1935) and *La Théologie de l'Église de s. Clement a s. Irene* (Paris, 1945). For an excellent translation and more limited commentary, see Robert M. Grant, ed., *The Apostolic Fathers: A New Translation and Commentary* (New York: T. Nelson, 1964—). At present, this work is incomplete.

Aristides, probably a Greek philosopher, wrote his *Apology* about A.D. 140. Tatian, an Assyrian, a pupil of Justin who may later have fallen into heresy, wrote *Discourse to the Greeks* about A.D. 150. Athenagoras, an Athenian philosopher, wrote *A Plea for the Christians* in the late 170s. Some 15 to 20 years later, Theophilus, bishop of Antioch (Syria), wrote a defense of Christianity now known simply as *To Autolycus.* Also included among the Apologists are two anonymous works of uncertain date (but written not later than A.D. 180), *Discourse to the Greeks* and *Hortatory Address to the Greeks.* Then, too, as we have already mentioned, the *Epistle to Diognetus* is more properly included with the Apologists than with the Apostolic Fathers.[2]

These writers, both the Apostolic Fathers and the Apologists, have often been understood by modern scholars as having a less vibrant faith, and a less authentically Christian faith, than the apostles. They have usually been described as somehow having debased or cheapened or alloyed genuine Christianity by importing into it Greek philosophy and Graeco-Roman ethical patterns and beliefs.[3]

Having adopted the typical modern analysis of the faith of those postapostolic days, such students of Christian perfection as R. Newton Flew have assumed that if the note of perfection be

---

2. The best critical text of the Apologists under a single title is J. C. Th. Otto, *Corpus Apologeticarum Christianorum Saeculi Secundi,* 9 vols., 1st ed. (Jena, 1847-72); vols. 1-5, 3rd ed. (Jena, 1876-81). The third edition is preferred. Useful English translations are found in A. C. Coxe, ed., *The Ante-Nicene Fathers . . . ,* vols. I, II, IX (American reprint; Grand Rapids: Wm. B. Eerdmans, 1978-79). There are no commentaries on the entire corpus of the Apologists. Their works have each been studied in separate monographs in depth. However, cf. Bardy, *La vie spirituelle,* for useful general introduction and for a more extended specialized study, cf. A. Peuch, *Les apologistes grecs du 2e siècle de nôtre ère* (Paris, 1912).

3. E.g., A. C. McGiffert, following the lead of the great Adolph Harnack, says: "[The Apostolic Fathers] all represent the same general type of Christianity, a type very different from Paul's. They agreed with him . . . in recognizing the God of the Jews as their God and the Jewish Scriptures as their Scriptures. But whereas to him Christianity appeared under the guise of a mystery-religion, in which salvation is secured by union with a dying and risen Lord, to them it appeared rather as a moral system based on divine sanctions, a religion similar to the Judaism of the dispersion but stripped of all racial and national features. It was as a law that these Christians chiefly thought of Christianity. Of Paul's notion of Christian liberty there is no trace in their writings" (*A History of Christian Thought,* vol. I: *Early and Eastern* [New York: C. Scribner's Sons, 1932], 48-69). If the Apostolic Fathers be taken literally and without consideration of their purposes and contexts, McGiffert is absolutely correct. But the rising authority of Paul's writings themselves in the second century would suggest that the Apostolic Fathers must not be taken as if they were at-

found in that period, it existed in spite of the attitudes prevalent in the Church at large. But the evidence would seem to tell another story. The evidence would point to a firm retention of perfection, perfection in love, as the attainable Christian ideal. But it would point to increasing concern to translate this perfection into various forms of activity and to describe it in these terms while at the same time—and here is an important theological problem—slowly but surely cutting perfection loose from its theological and experiential moorings in the doctrine of sanctification.

The Apostolic Fathers and the Apologists did not, in the nature of things, attempt to explicate all of Christian faith. They wrote in response to specific problems and situations. In this, they did as the biblical writers, especially Paul, Peter, James, and Jude, had done. And as we do not expect to read the whole gospel in Paul, not even in the entire collection of his letters, neither do we expect to find an Ignatius nor the *Didache* laying the entire Christian faith before us.

Just as Paul had done, each Apostolic Father and each Apologist writes from a specific context. And fundamental to that context in each case is the fact that the writer belongs to the worshiping Christian community. Each is taking for granted a great deal about Christian theology and the Christian community's practice of the faith.

Whatever these sources may say, then, concerning perfection or sanctification must not be taken as a complete exposition. Nor do we have a complete exposition by adding their works together. However, it seems valid to say that whatever they did write would

---

tempting to declare the whole truth. The very process of collecting the New Testament shows that they were aware of theological issues beyond those appearing in their own work. Then, too, the profound significance of the sacraments and the sacramental context to the works of those writers would cast McGiffert's assertion into doubt.

Also cf. Flew, *Idea of Perfection,* 45 ff. Typical of his assumptions concerning the postapostolic period is the following: "Granted that the New Testament ideals have suffered transformation or eclipse, what vestiges are traceable?" (p. 118). Another example: "The teaching of St. Paul is not understood, although the person of the apostle is surrounded by great reverence and affection. The righteousness which is of the law comes back as the goal of man's striving and with it comes a tendency to distinguish between degrees of good works" (p. 120). Flew is here drawing upon Friedrich Loofs (1858-1928), a German historian of doctrine who was of liberal sympathies although he did maintain that Jesus was divine as well as human and that the Jesus of the Gospels and the Jesus presented by Paul were the same.

have been understood and generally approved by the Church at large, which would understand it in its own broader context of thought and worship.

All of this is to say that whatever we read of perfection and sanctification in the Apostolic Fathers and Apologists is not written in spite of the supposed fact that the Church was moving away from its original faith, nor is it evidence itself of decay. Rather, it is written as expressive of what the Church actually believed, though not of its total spirituality. The Apostolic Fathers and Apologists may have been unique in their modes of expression, but they were not unique in their faith. Not unique, but selective in their written expression of it.

What, then, did they write concerning perfection and sanctification?

A. Ignatius of Antioch: Example of the Problematic

For Ignatius of Antioch (d. A.D. 98 or 117), the essence of Christian salvation is union with God by way of God's having become man in Christ.[4] That which brings us into union with God is union with Christ.[5] The goal of this union is Christlikeness, and it appears that Ignatius believes this to be a goal for this life, insofar as it is attainable here; and it is a goal for that life which is to come. He continually insists that Christ's resurrection was of both spirit and flesh (cf. *Smyrnaeans* xii.2) and in doing so several times implies that Christ's resurrection in the flesh does indeed give us Christlikeness even while we are in the flesh, for He is our life.[6] The principal means for accomplishing our union with Christ, and thus with the Father, is the Lord's Supper.[7]

Arthur Cushman McGiffert, whose findings are similar to those just presented, goes on to say, however: "Though [Ignatius] thus agreed with Paul and John in interpreting the Christian life in

---

4. This is the meaning of his frequent phrase "attain to God" (e.g., *Ephesians* xii.2; *Magnesians* xiv.1; *Trallians* xii.2), among other phrases.

5. E.g., *Smyrnaeans* i.1—iv.2. Ignatius' principal target in this passage is Docetism, i.e., the view that Christ, being divine, could not truly suffer, but only appeared to do so. Also cf. iii.1.

6. E.g., *Ephesians* iii.2; iv.2; viii.1-2, and ix.1-2; *Trallians* xi.2. Ignatius also uses frequently the near-technical phrase of Paul, "in Christ." E.g., *Ephesians* xi.1; xx.2; *Trallians* ix.2.

7. E.g., *Philadelphians* iv.1; *Ephesians* xx.2.

mystical terms and in emphasizing the Christian's oneness with Christ, he apparently did not draw their conclusion that the Christian life is perfectly holy and free from sin." McGiffert continues: "[Ignatius] must have found Paul's heroic belief (that the Christian cannot sin) difficult to say the least."[8]

In the first place (to respond to McGiffert), Paul did not believe that the Christian cannot sin. Nor did he and John believe "that the Christian life is perfectly holy and free from sin." Paul believed that the Christian need not sin and ought not to sin. And Paul and John both recognize sin in believers. What they do insist on is that the norm for Christians is a life free of *willful* sin, as has been shown earlier in the first volume of this work.

With this latter view Ignatius is clearly in accord, as his letter to the Ephesians testifies:

> None of these things (e.g., the knowledge that spiritual strength is gained by corporate worship) is foreign to you if you possess perfect faith and love toward Jesus Christ, which are the origin and fulness [beginning and end] of life; for the beginning is faith and the end is love, and when the two are joined together in unity there is God; and all else honorable and beseeming follows. 2. No one who professes faith sins, nor does one who has gotten love hate.[9]

It seems quite clear that Ignatius of Antioch holds to a concept of Christian perfection that is compatible with (if not identical to) those of Paul and John. But what is the precise relationship of Ignatius' understanding of Christian perfection to his understanding of sanctification? Here we are completely stymied. There is no direct evidence with which we may work, nor even material from which inferences may be drawn. Ignatius simply does not write of the way in which one enters upon the way of perfection nor of the strictly theological side of the idea.

---

8. McGiffert, *History of Christian Thought,* 1:41.

9. *Ephesians* xiv.1-2. McGiffert cites the last sentence here quoted and passes it off as "nothing more than the expression of a pious hope or a warning to hypocrites" (ibid., 41). His judgment seems to fly in the face of other evidence similar to the cited passage. See, for instance, *Ephesians* viii.1-2: "Let none therefore deceive you, as indeed you have not been deceived, but are entirely God's. You really do live according to God, the proof being that no strife has set upon you to torture you. I am dedicated to your purposes and devoted to you Ephesians and to your Church, which is eternally noteworthy. (2) The carnal cannot do spiritual things; the spiritual cannot do carnal things, just as faith is incapable of acts of faithlessness and faithlessness of acts of faith. Yet even your fleshly deeds are spiritual, for you do all things in Jesus Christ."

Ignatius' concern in his letters is the unity of the Church. And in being both theological and practical about it, he underlines the role and position of the bishop in that unity. The link in unity is love. The love of Christ for the believer and the Church, and the love of the believer for Christ and for fellow believers. Here it is that the doctrine of perfection is significant. The perfection of which Ignatius writes is a perfection of love that issues in a perfection in practice.[10]

Further, it is the Holy Spirit who joins the machinery of redemption to the life of the believer. Ignatius' language is quite striking in this regard.

> I have learned, however, that some from elsewhere having evil teachings have stayed among you. But you did not allow them to sow it among you. You plugged your ears so as not to receive what they sow, being as it were, stones of the Father's temple, readied for the construction work of God our Father, carried up to the heights by the Jesus Christ's machine, the cross, using as a rope the Holy Spirit. Moreover, your windlass is your faith and love is the road which brings one up to God. 2. So, fellow-travellers are you all; God-bearers, temple-bearers, Christ-bearers, holiness-bearers, in every way adorned with commandments of Jesus Christ. This I share in joy, for it has been granted to me to speak to you by way of my writing, and to rejoice with you, that you love nothing in a fleshly way, but that you love only in God's way.[11]

Other than this reference, and another in which Ignatius claims personal inspiration from the Spirit (*Philadelphians* vii.1-2), he is silent concerning the work of the Spirit in the individual believer. Nor has he much to say of the Spirit's work in the Church at large.[12] But again, the question is: How much ought we to expect

---

10. E.g., the salutation in *Romans;* also *Smyrnaeans* vii.1-2; *Philadelphians* ix.2. Examples are legion.

11. *Ephesians* ix.1-2. This passage is rich in nuances in its original language. For instance, in speaking of the believers' being "carried up to the heights," the verb "carried up" has deep connections with the NT, especially with Jesus' bringing the disciples to the Mount of Transfiguration (Matt. 17:1), with Jesus' own ascension to the Father (Luke 24:51), with Jesus' having carried our sins to the Cross (Heb. 7:27; 1 Pet. 2:24), with our sacrifice of praise to God (Heb. 13:15), and most especially with Peter's word: "You also, as living stones, are being built up as a spiritual house for a holy priesthood, to offer up spiritual sacrifices acceptable to God through Jesus Christ" (1 Pet. 2:5, NASB). The last phrase in the original is difficult to translate, so I have paraphrased it. It is of a piece with the closing phrase of the previous paragraph (i.e., *Ephesians* viii.2), which translates with relative ease.

12. E.g., *Ephesians* xvii.2, where "the gift which the Lord has truly sent" seems to be the Spirit.

Ignatius to say of the Spirit given the issue with which his letters deal? "Very little," seems to be the best reply. And yet, what little he does say indicates a profound interest in the Spirit as the divine agent who activates and applies the benefits of redemption within the Church. By logical extension, then, the Spirit would be the agent of the perfection in love of which Ignatius speaks. Yet, there is no word of the Spirit as sanctifier or agent of sanctification, and still no word of the theological character of perfection.

We sum up our study of Ignatius of Antioch by asserting that while he clearly advocates perfection, perfection in love, as the Christian norm for this life, he says nothing of how one enters upon this perfection, nothing of its relation (whether theological or experiential) to justification, and nothing of its connection with the notion of sanctification, although he does relate it to the work of the Holy Spirit. He either was able to take such connections for granted or they did not occur to him. Or, if they did occur to him, they seemed relatively unimportant in meeting the task at hand.

We shall see in our study of early liturgies that it is likely that he took them for granted, but for now, we move on to study the doctrine of perfection in another Apostolic "Father," the *Shepherd of Hermas.*

B. The *Shepherd of Hermas:* Perfection as Norm; Repentance as Necessity

Regrettably, there is insufficient space to investigate in this book the doctrine of perfection of all of the Apostolic Fathers, for each is slightly different from the other, though all reflect upon a common theological-experiential root. We chose to investigate the *Epistles of Ignatius* because of their intensely practical concern. They thus have some kinship to *I Clement,* Polycarp's *Epistle to the Philippians,* the *Martyrdom of Polycarp,* and (more remotely) the *Epistle of Barnabas.*

In turning to the *Shepherd of Hermas* (pre A.D. 150) we find ourselves examining an apocalyptic work, yet a work meant to be applicable to wide ranges of Christian behavior. Its immediate concern is the question of the spiritual status of those who sin after baptism. It works with the doctrine of repentance in the face of a widely held opinion that the baptized can live without sin and the corollary concept that any who sin after baptism are beyond hope of forgiveness. It was accounted by many in the early Church as a canonical book, that is, as a book on a par in authority with the four Gospels and the letters of Paul (among other works).[13]

In the *Shepherd of Hermas* we find in the foreground the doctrine of the Holy Spirit, if it indeed can be called a "doctrine" at that time. What the *Shepherd* seems to do is to reflect upon the life of the Church in the context of the Church's own confession of faith. This confession, by the time of the writing of the *Shepherd,* includes in its creedal expression the belief that Christ "was born of the Holy Spirit and the Virgin Mary" and belief "in the Holy Spirit."[14]

Also integral to the Church's belief in that period was a conviction, already noted, that the baptized Christian can live without sin and forfeits all hope of salvation if he does sin. That is to say, the expectation was that the baptized were perfect, at least at the point of righteous living. It is in the context of the expectation of perfection in practice, then, that the *Shepherd* speaks of the work of the Holy Spirit.

Perhaps before proceeding further, the reader should be warned of two points at which there appears to be confusion in the *Shepherd's* understanding of the Spirit—a confusion probably induced by unclear symbolism in the worship of the Church and by the fact that the doctrine of the Holy Spirit was still in a very elementary stage even by the mid-second century. These two points are: (1) the *Shepherd's* apparent belief that the preexistent Christ (that is, the Word before He became man) was "the Holy Spirit,"[15] and (2) the apparent belief in a sort of collective character

---

13. References to the *Shepherd of Hermas* are usually made in the following form (which conforms to the three divisions of the work itself): (1) *Visions,* of which there are four, to which is added the introduction to the *Mandates,* cited as if it were the fifth vision. The *Visions* speak of the necessity for repentance. (2) *Mandates,* 12 of them. The *Mandates* speak of the life the penitent must lead. (3) *Similitudes* or *Parables,* 10 in number, which present a doctrine of repentance.

14. This would be the so-called Old Roman Symbol, a creedal statement probably developed for use in the rite of baptism. It is known to have had fixed form no later than A.D. 140 in the Church at Rome. While there are more detailed discussions of this creed or symbol, and some that are less concerned to prove a particular point of view, an easily accessible and very illuminating discussion of it is found in Adolph Harnack, *History of Dogma,* trans. from third German ed. (1900) by Neil Buchanan (New York: Dover, n.d.), 1:157-59, n. 6.

15. Cf. *Similitudes* V.vi.5-8. Also, *Similitudes* IX.i.1. The confusion of divine names and roles is quite common throughout the entire work, reflecting on the fact that Christian theology was far from fixed even a century after the Resurrection. See, for instance, *Vision* III.iii.5, where God the Father is the foundation of the Church, and *Similitudes* IX.xiv.4, where the "Name of the Son of God" is said to be that foundation.

for the Holy Spirit (that is, that the Holy Spirit is a composite of such "holy spirits" as faith, purity, truth, and love).[16] Nonetheless, the *Shepherd* presents a consistent idea of the work of the Spirit in the context of the expectation of purity and perfection.

The expectation is purity and perfection, but the reality, according to the *Shepherd,* is quite otherwise. First, there is the matter of appearing to act in righteousness when the intentions are quite evil and selfish.[17] Then in Book III of *Visions* come the problems of those sinning who wish to repent (v.5), the hypocrites (vi.1), those who backslide (vi.2), those who bear malice secretly (vi.3), those who "live righteously for the most part but have some degree of wickedness" (vi.4), the wealthy Christians who are inconstant under pressure (vi.5-7), the double-minded (vii.2), the apostates (vii.2), and the spiritually fickle (vii.3). For all of these there is restoration if they repent, although their place will not be as "honorable" as it previously was, and that place will be attainable only after and through temporal suffering (vii.5-6). Yet, repentance will bring renewal and rejoicing, strength and powerful faith (xii.—xiii.).

So it is that the *Shepherd* argues for the possibility of repentance for the baptized who have sinned, and yet maintains the norm of sinlessness.[18] He also demonstrates the fact that whether it should have been or not, sinlessness had come to be a matter of external conformity to certain mores and folkways. The motive behind such conformity was counted as unimportant by all too many—even by some ecclesiastical officials.[19] Worse, these careless-hearted officials were among the most adamant in insisting that for those who sinned after baptism there was no hope.[20]

Into this situation the angel of repentance must be admitted.

---

16. Cf. *Similitudes* IX.xiii.1-7. Throughout the *Similitudes* the Holy Spirit and the "maidens" seem quite interchangeable.

17. *Visions* I.i.4-9. It seems good to mention here that the *Shepherd* continually works with sinfulness at the level of the attitude and motivation. A tendency developed among some scholars, such as McGiffert, to imply that such works as the *Shepherd* were really lapsing back into a theology of legalism and works-righteousness because of their practical advices. Flew picks this notion up (e.g., *Idea of Perfection,* 120) as evidence of a declension or decay in the purity of the faith in the postapostolic period.

18. This is found expressed in several ways in the *Visions.* Its clearest expression is in *Mandates* IV.iii.1-7.

19. E.g., *Visions* II.ii.6; also *Mandates* II.iii.1-7.

20. This attitude or perspective is part of the double-mindedness against which Hermas is warned throughout the visions (e.g., *Visions* IV.ii).

With a nice touch of irony, the *Shepherd* now writes of the life of all penitents, and of how those who believe there is no repentance possible after baptism must repent. Again, he is not insisting that the norm or expectation be lowered; he only writes to comfort those despairing baptized who had sinned and believed there was no hope of repentance. He seeks to show that those who were declaring the hopelessness of those who had sinned needed, and could find, repentance and hope for themselves. The *Shepherd* was later said to lower the Church's standard of morality, and in some sense this was true.

Many read with joy that there was yet hope for them but did not pay heed to the *Shepherd's* continuing demand that sinlessness be the norm. As has already been noted, the *Shepherd* was considered by many to be a canonical book until the sixth century (and later), so that ironically, its popularity and authority no doubt contributed to the belief that perfection was not the norm, but only the ideal. It worked its desired effect with respect to giving hope to the believers who sinned after baptism. It was taken amiss in that its fundamental commitment to perfection was overlooked.

Here is a clear example of the *Shepherd's* commitment both to perfection and to hope for the sinning baptized:

> Said I, "Sir, I have heard from some teachers that beyond the repentance we were given when we went down into the water and received remission of our former sins, there is no second repentance." He said to me, "You have heard correctly, because that is so. He who has received remission of sin ought never to sin again, but rather to live in purity. But since you are clearly asking about the whole matter, I shall explain further to you without giving excuse to those who in the future shall believe nor to those who already believe on the Lord: Those who already believe or will believe in the future have no such repentance of sins, but do have remission of their former sin. Yet, for those who were called before these days, the Lord did appoint repentance. For the Lord knows the heart, and knowing everything ahead of time he knew human weakness and the devil's subtlety—that he will do some evil to God's servants, and do them mischief—the Lord, being merciful, had mercy on his creation, and thus established this repentance. And to me was given its control. But," said he, "I tell you that if, after that great and holy calling, a man be tempted by the devil and sin, he has one repentance. But if he sin and repent repeatedly, this repentance is of no use for that man, for he shall live only barely." I said to him, "I came to life when I heard these matters accurately from you, for I know that if I do not add again to my

sins, I shall be saved." He said, "You will be saved, and so will all who do these things" (*Mandates* IV.iii.1-7).

This demand for purity, and the expectation that it is the normal condition of the Church, is reinforced time and again in the third section of the *Shepherd,* the *Similitudes* or *Parables.* Especially telling in this regard is the parable of the building of the tower, which is the Church.[21]

In the second century there had not yet grown up the distinction between the authentic or "real" Church and the institution calling itself the Church. The real Church was the "visible" Church, the "visible" Church was the real Church. So it is that the *Shepherd,* insisting on the purity of the Church, speaks of stones once in it being removed from it and of stones being thrown from the Church (*Similitudes* IX.xviii.3). He also speaks of those who, because their repentance is slow and incomplete, are disallowed a place in the tower, though not a place in the wall that is around it.[22]

It is in the *Similitudes* also that the *Shepherd* relates clearly the work of the Holy Spirit and the purity and perfection of the Church as well as of the individual believer, although we must call to attention again the flexibility of the concept of Holy Spirit in the work. Especially important are the fruits of the Spirit in the work of building the Church and in maintaining its purity and perfection (IX.xv.2). They are personalized as maidens who yearn to associate with the believer (IX.xi.1-9). But never are they considered separately. Always they act in concert and are a unity and together clothe the believer (IX.ii.3-5; iii.4—iv.1).

> "And what are these maidens?" "They are holy spirits," said he [the shepherd]. "Except he be clothed in them with their clothing, a man can in no other way be found in the kingdom of God. For if you receive only the name but do not receive the clothing from them, you will not be benefited at all, for these maidens are the powers of the Son of God. If you bear the name but do not bear his power, you shall be bearing his name in vain" (*Similitudes* IX.xiii.1-2).

Nonetheless, we do not find in the *Shepherd* a clear doctrine of sanctification nor a clear exposition of its relation to the perfection and purity for which he continually calls. How much "right" we have to expect such clarity is in question, of course, since the *Shepherd* has other purposes in mind in his work.

---

21. *Similitudes* VIII (passim); also, cf. IX.xviii.3-4; X.i.1-3; X.iii.1-5.

22. Cf. esp. *Similitudes* VIII.vii.3; also VIII.vi.6.

What is quite clear is the expectation that purity or perfection, both ethical and motivational, is expected of the Church and of each believer. It is not merely an ideal; it is the norm. And this norm is fulfilled by the work of the "holy spirits," that is, the fruit of the Holy Spirit. The very insistence upon repentance may be seen under this rubric.

It is highly unlikely that either Ignatius or Hermas could have written of perfection and purity as he did without some underlying doctrine of sanctification, without some basic understanding of how one enters into purity and perfection. It is to the probable source of that understanding that we shall turn in our next section. But first we would note that this very practice of speaking of perfection apart from the personal and theological dynamics of it is quite possibly a major source of the complete separation of the two concepts throughout the late classical and medieval periods. It should be noted that the Church had to work more and more with these concepts without acquaintance with the Jewish or even Graeco-Roman ethical heritage. Thus the idea of perfection was externalized and put in terms of pious practices. The doctrine of sanctification was made increasingly to refer to a strictly theological process.

By the time of Augustine (354-430), it was possible to speak of being holy quite apart from being pure or perfect. One was holy because he belonged to Christ and the Church and Christ's holiness covered his utter lack of holiness. And perfection came to refer principally to renunciation of material goods, physical desires, and yearnings for status.

We shall say something later of how this developed. For the moment, let us look at the evidence concerning the doctrine of sanctification in the period of the Apostolic Fathers.

II. Symbolic Expression: Entire Sanctification in Early Liturgies

At the very center of being a Christian, in the earliest Church, was worship. Corporate celebration, not debate nor even intellectual explication, marked the way theologically for those primitive Christians. Even the theologians were principally worshipers and understood authentic worship to transcend their academic exercise—*but not to exclude it.*

Within the worship of the early Church no activities were more important than the rites denoting entrance into the faith and the continuing grace of God in Christ in redemption. Entrance or initiation was marked by baptism; the continuance of redemptive grace by the Lord's Supper.

These rituals were called "mysteries" and "symbols." They were mysteries not because they hid anything or were obscure in meaning but because of their very simplicity and commonness. They utilized everyday "stuff" like water and bread and wine, which was taken over by the Holy Spirit to reveal the very heart of God's purposes. The mystery was in the capacity of the common to carry such profoundly uncommon meaning.

The term *symbol* was used by the early Church in a way quite different from our modern use of it. We believe that a symbol stands for or represents something, but is itself an abstraction from the thing symbolized. In the early Church, in fact in much of the Graeco-Roman world, a symbol was not an abstraction at all but was a way into the very essence of a thing or an event or an idea. The symbol participated, as it were, in the character of the thing or event or idea as authentically as the thing or event or idea itself did.

Baptism was the symbol of repentance and of the washing away of sin in the early Church. It was also a symbol of the burial and resurrection of Christ. This means that participation in the rite itself involves one in the very reality of repentance and cleansing, of burial and resurrection. It is not an abstraction, but a way into the reality; not a testimony, in our sense, but a saving moment. Here is how Justin Martyr (d. about 165), who taught in both Palestine and Rome, describes baptism:

> I shall explain how we dedicated ourselves to God and how we were new-made through Christ, for should I omit this, I might seem to be insincere in this explication of the faith. Those who are persuaded and believe to be true the things that we teach and who promise to live according to them, they are enabled, are taught to pray and with fasting to ask God for forgiveness of their past sins. We pray and fast with them. This done, they are led by us to a place where there is water, and in the manner in which we were regenerated they are regenerated, for at that time they are washed in the water in the name of God the Master and Father of all, and of our Savior Jesus Christ, and of the Holy Spirit. This is in keeping with what Christ said: "Unless you be born again you shall not enter into the kingdom of heaven."

> Now it is quite clear that those who have already been born cannot reenter the wombs of those who bore them. Yet, my previous citation from Isaiah the prophet did indicate how those who have sinned and repent shall escape from their sins: "Wash yourselves, be clean, take away evil doing from your souls. Learn to do good. Be an advocate for the orphan. Defend the widow's cause. Come and let us reason together, says the Lord. For though your sins be as scarlet, I shall make them as white as snow. If you will not listen to me, the sword will eat you up, for the mouth of the Lord has spoken these things."
>
> We learned this reason for baptism from the apostles: at our first birth, we came forth of necessity, apart from our knowledge, from the moist seed of the intercourse of our parents with each other; we grew up in bad habits and in evil doing; yet, so that we should not remain children of such mere necessity and ignorance but instead become children of our free choice and knowledge, and so that we might obtain remission of the sins we have already committed—the name of God, the Father and Master of all, is named over him who has chosen to be new-born and has repented of his sinful deeds. . . . This washing is called Illumination, since they who learn these things are inwardly illumined. The illuminated one is also washed in the name of Jesus Christ, who was crucified under Pontius Pilate, and in the name of the Holy Spirit, who foretold all about Jesus through the prophets (*Apology* I.61).

Irenaeus, a mid-second century bishop in Gaul, though a native of Asia Minor, also wrote of his understanding of baptism as follows:

> Now, here is what faith does for us, according to the tradition reaching us from the elders, disciples and apostles. First of all, it admonishes us to remember that we have received baptism for the remission of sins in the name of God the Father, and in the name of Jesus Christ, the Son of God, who became incarnate and died and was raised, and in the name of the Holy Spirit of God. Further, this baptism is the seal of eternal life and is rebirth unto God so that we be no more children of mortals but of the eternal and everlasting God.[23]

We do not wish to belabor the point, but it is useful to our purpose to show, as clearly as possible, just what was believed concerning baptism throughout the Church in the second century (and in all probability in the previous century as well). Justin represents both Palestine and Rome, Irenaeus both Asia Minor and Gaul (France). Clement of Alexandria represents both Greece, his home,

---

23. Irenaeus, *Proof of the Apostolic Preaching,* 3.

and Egypt, where he was a presbyter in the great Church in that seaport and ancient center of learning. He died no later than 215.

> Is Christ perfected by the washing (of John's baptism) and is he sanctified by the descent of the Spirit? Yes! The same things also take place in our case, for whom the Lord became the pattern. Being baptized, we are illumined; being illumined we are made sons; being made sons we are perfected; being perfected we are made immortal. . . . This work [i.e., baptism] is variously called "a gift of grace," "illumination," "perfection," and "washing." It is the washing through which we are cleansed of our sins; the grace-gift by which the penalties for our sins are removed; the illumination through which the divine is clearly seen. . . . Instruction leads to faith, and faith, together with baptism, is trained by the Holy Spirit. . . . We who have repented of our sins, renounced our faults, and are purified by baptism run back to the eternal light, as children to their father (*Paedagogos* i.6.25.3—26.2; 30.2; 32.1).

What is clear in each of these passages is the understanding that regeneration *takes place in* baptism, but there is a vast difference between insisting that baptism is the means of regeneration or the moment in which regeneration is effected and saying that baptism regenerates. Referring to baptism in terms like those in John 3:5, Eph. 5:25-26, and Heb. 10:22, the early Christians would say that the very act of baptism is itself part of the total act of salvation. "No baptism, no salvation," they would say. "No symbol, no reality," and they would repeat our Lord's command that the Church baptize.

The New Testament is not clear as to whether Christian baptism is different from "John's Baptism" or from "the baptism of repentance" (cf. Mark 1:4; Acts 13:24; 18:25). It does record 12 specific instances of Christian baptism on or after Pentecost.[24] There may have been some baptizing in Jesus' name alone at first, especially among believing Jews (for example, Acts 8:16; 19:5; Rom. 6:3), but the evidence seems to be overwhelming on the side of a trinitarian baptismal formula as the usual form. That is to say, the believer was baptized "in the name of the Father, and of the Son, and of the Holy Ghost." This form was understood to have been commanded by our Lord (Matt. 28:19).

The connection of baptism with the Father and with the Son is self-evident. What may not be so clear is its relationship to the

---

24. Acts 2:41; 8:12; 8:13; 8:38; 9:18; 10:47-48; 16:15; 16:33; 18:8; 19:5; 1 Cor. 1:14; 1:16.

Holy Spirit. In fact, baptism symbolized the work of the Spirit, and it was the work of the Spirit that made baptism effective. Tertullian (d. no later than 230), a native of Carthage, North Africa (near present-day Bône, Algeria), and the first of the great Latin-writing Christian scholars, records the early Church's view on the matter in responding to some critics of the rite.

Tertullian says that just as in the first creation the Spirit of God "moved over the waters," making them fit for God's own purposes, so Christians invoke the Spirit's presence upon the waters of baptism to sanctify them to the Father's purposes again. And as the waters are sanctified, so are they used to sanctify. Baptism, says Tertullian, does not give the gift of the presence of the Spirit in fullness, but it makes one ready for that presence. So it is that immediately following baptism itself, and as part of the rite, "we are anointed all over with consecrated oil . . . then the hand is laid on us, while the Holy Spirit is invoked and invited by way of a blessing. . . . Then, down over the body thus cleansed and consecrated there comes, from the Father, the Holy Spirit."[25]

What is clear here, and important to understanding the doctrine of entire sanctification, is the distinction between the actual act of baptizing and the actual act of receiving the Holy Spirit in His fullness. Cyprian, writing a generation later than Tertullian, but believing himself to be free of the slightest hint of novelty, makes the same point even more clearly in several letters. In an epistle in which he responds to the question of the validity of heretical baptism, he says: "Those who are baptized in the Church are brought before the bishops of the Church, then by way of our prayers and the laying on of our hands they receive the Holy Spirit and are made perfect by the Lord's seal."[26]

On the other hand, the distinction in symbolism must not mask the intimate relationship between the two acts. The early Christian could not think of baptism without thinking of the gift of the fullness of the Spirit, or perfection, as well. The baptismal act itself ("going into the water") was most especially related to the remission of sins. But already in the beginning, our Lord had con-

---

25. *On Baptism,* 4-8. The entire passage, too long to be cited here, should be read. Actually, Tertullian's clearest statement on baptism is in his treatise *Against Marcion.* There he noted four basic "gifts" of baptism: remission of sins, deliverance from death, regeneration, and the bestowing of the Spirit (cf. *Against Marcion* I.xxviii.2).

26. Cyprian, *Letters* 73.9. See also 63.8 and 70.2, where the same point is made.

nected remission of sins with the giving of the Holy Spirit (John 20:21-23). So, the whole baptismal liturgy, which was meant to symbolize the appropriation of our complete redemption, included first the symbol of remission, then the symbol of the gift of the Spirit.

The whole ritual (that is, the celebration of both parts) is considered in the early Church as an illumination of the mind,[27] the new creation or new birth,[28] the sealing to eternal life of the soul that remains faithful to the end,[29] the restoration of the divine image in us,[30] sanctification and deification,[31] and the process of making "Christs" of believers.[32]

These are powerful claims, and the Church occasionally had to explain or defend them. In its explanations and defenses, the double ritual is often called by one name, baptism, as in Cyprian, *Letters* 63.8. But it was more often than not made clear that the claims applied only in part to the first part of the ritual, the actual baptizing (see Tertullian, *On Baptism* 6). It was understood that highly significant aspects of the claims rested in the second act of the drama, as it were: the anointing with oil and the laying on of hands. These further acts symbolized and precipitated the coming of the Spirit in fullness upon the believer, a coming for which only water baptism (the "washing of regeneration") could prepare him.

These separate ritual acts, the second part of the drama, so intimately related to the baptism with water, were believed to symbolize the "baptism of (with) the Holy Spirit."[33] The term itself, however, is used on occasion to refer also to the entire double

---

27. Justin Martyr, *Apology* I.61; Cyprian, *To Donatus,* 4; Cyril of Jerusalem, *Catechetical Lectures* xvi.16.

28. E.g., Justin Martyr, *Apology* I.61; Cyprian, *To Donatus,* 4; Ambrose, *On the Holy Spirit* i.6; ii.1-5.

29. Cyril of Jerusalem, *Catechetical Lectures* iv.16; xvii.35-36; Didymus the Blind, *On the Holy Spirit,* 34-37.

30. Cyril of Jerusalem, *Commentary on Joel* ii.28; *Commentary on Nahum* ii.2.

31. Athanasius, *Letters to Serapion* i.25; Gregory of Nazianzus, *Orations* v.29; John of Damascus, *On the Orthodox Faith,* c. 13.

32. Methodius, *Banquet of the Ten Virgins* (Symposium) viii.8; Cyril of Jerusalem, *Catechetical Lectures* xxii.1.

33. Pseudo-Cyprian, *On Rebaptism* ii.; Cyril of Jerusalem, *Mystagogical Lectures* iii. This is also the point of much of Cyprian's correspondence (e.g., *Letters* 72.1; 73.9).

ritual.[34] Further, the entire ritual was believed necessary to the validation of the claims of either part.[35]

How conscious was the early Church of the theological implications, and experiential implications, of its baptismal liturgy? Did it intend, by this two-part liturgy, to express two intimately related but theologically distinct "works of grace"? Certainly their sensitivity to symbol, a sensitivity shared by the cultures around them, would seem to argue so. But we need to look at the documentary evidence.[36]

We do know that at least in the West, and at least by the end of the second century (but probably much earlier), the baptismal liturgy was nearly uniform. Hippolytus (d. by 235), a Greek-speaking presbyter in Rome, gives us a well-developed outline of that liturgy in his work, *The Apostolic Tradition.* He perceived it in four parts: prebaptism, baptism, laying on of hands, eucharist.

First was the prebaptismal liturgy, with the blessing of the water and a prayer that the sanctifying power of the Spirit might come upon it to give the rite the power to confer spiritual blessing. (This connection with the Spirit explains the preference for *running* water.) This was followed by the candidate's disrobing, the symbolism being that of coming into earthly life naked and leaving it that way and that of disclaiming this world's goods. Then came a

---

34. E.g., Cyprian, *Letters* 63.8. Tertullian is interesting here. He says, "The waters are made the sacrament of sanctification by the invoking of God's presence. Immediately, the Spirit descends from heaven, and resting on the waters, sanctifies them himself. In turn, since they are sanctified they drink in the power to sanctify" (*On Baptism,* 4). But Tertullian also speaks of the coming of the Holy Spirit into the believer by anointing and by the imposition of hands rather than in baptism itself. Cf. *On Baptism,* 8.1. Even the pseudo-Cyprian, who does deflate the value of actual baptism to heighten the value of the imposition of hands, insists that both are necessary.

35. This is the force of Firmilian's argument as he writes Cyprian in support of the latter's stand on heretical baptism. Cyprian had argued that the heretics, already baptized in their own conventicles, could not be received into the Church merely by the laying on of hands, since the laying on of hands was of a piece with baptism. (Cf. e.g., Cyprian, *Letters* 73 and 74. Firmilian's letter is found among Cyprian's as number 75.) But while Cyprian argues for the intimacy of relationship between the two parts of the baptismal liturgy, a council over which he presided also refers to them as two sacraments, apparently with his approval. Cf. Cyprian, *Letters* 72.1, for Cyprian's own willingness to call the one double ritual two sacraments.

36. Also valuable, though at times mutually contradictory, are several histories of doctrine. Especially useful and careful are J. N. D. Kelly, *Early Christian Doctrines* (rev. ed.; New York: Harper and Row, 1978), 207-11; and Jaroslav Pelikan, *The Christian Tradition,* Vol. I: *The Emergence of the Catholic Tradition (100-600)* (Chicago: University of Chicago Press, 1971), 163-66.

solemn renunciation of Satan (in some liturgies this was accompanied by a ceremonial expectoration). This was a moment of great seriousness and danger in some liturgies, for Satan would be directly addressed: "I renounce you, Satan; and all service to you." Finally in the prebaptismal liturgy came an anointing with the oil of exorcism. This drove away all of Satan's minions and delivered the candidate from their power. Now he or she was ready for presentation to Christ.

Baptism proper was preceded by the confession of faith, sometimes with a series of questions and answers. This was followed by triple immersion in the name of each of the persons of the Trinity, and the baptism proper was concluded by an anointing of the candidate with the oil of thanksgiving.

After the baptizand had dried and clothed himself, he was led to the assembly for the postbaptismal liturgy. Here, hands were laid on him and he was given a *second* anointing. (Yet a third anointing, the anointing of thanksgiving, was understood to be in another category from this anointing and the anointing of exorcism, both theologically and liturgically.) The presiding officer placed his hand on the baptizand's head, prayed, poured oil on the new Christian's head, and "signed" him with the sign of the Cross.

At the close of this part of the liturgy came the kiss of peace and then the newly baptized celebrated Communion with the Church for the first time.[37]

Tertullian also mentions a second anointing, speaking of the act of baptism itself as being a restoration that prepares the baptizand for the receiving of the Holy Spirit.[38] He is emphatic in distinguishing between the two parts of the ritual.[39] Hippolytus' order is not perfectly clear, but the anointing of the postbaptismal part of the liturgy seems analogous to that of the prebaptismal part. In the prebaptismal order, the anointing *brings* the Holy Spirit; the postbaptismal anointing symbolizes the Spirit's *filling* the baptizand. In the first there is exorcism, in the second invocation.

---

37. Hippolytus, *Apostolic Tradition,* 22.

38. Tertullian, *On Baptism,* 4-8 (esp. 6).

39. Ibid., 6: "Not that we receive the Holy Spirit in the water, but after being restored in the water we are prepared by an angel for the Holy Spirit."

Cyprian clearly distinguishes the two acts of the liturgy on purpose, as we have seen. And by the middle of the third century, the theology supporting the distinction is complete, as can be seen by the pseudo-Cyprianic *On Rebaptism.* This tract is actually an attack on the position of Cyprian with respect to the rebaptism of heretics. Cyprian argued for rebaptism. The pseudo-Cyprian, not a heretic himself, argues that the laying on of hands is sufficient if the heretic had already been baptized by use of the trinitarian formula. To argue thus, he does devalue the actual rite of baptizing, calling it "a lame, incomplete mystery of faith," using as proof texts Acts 8:14-17; 9:17-19; and 19:4-7. However, he in no way denies its necessity. He sees the laying on of hands, the second act of the baptismal ritual, as completing the first. It is called Spirit-baptism or spiritual baptism since it bestows the Spirit.[40]

What the evidence seems to show is a very early practicing of a twofold ritual in baptism for which the theology became increasingly clear. By the mid-third century, that theology was rather well fixed in the West, if not in the East as well.[41] What was symbolized by the mid-second century, if not much earlier, had full intellectual articulation a century later. God's grace was seen to grant two essential boons: regeneration and the presence of the Holy Spirit in His fullness to direct the regenerate one in a holy walk. The baptismal liturgy would seem to show not only a distinction between the two but also an insistence that they were intimately related. Certainly the explications of the Fathers, from late in the second century onward, show both sides of this.

Further, in spite of some ambiguity in language that calls the entire rite baptism and assigns sanctification to it, as a whole, it does not seem far afield to say that given the usual language of the Church in describing the work of the Holy Spirit, the special association of that Spirit with the second part of the ritual would make it more especially the moment of sanctification.[42] And "entire sanctification" at that (if it be proper to be a bit anachronistic), for one

---

40. Pseudo-Cyprian, *On Rebaptism* ii.5-6. (This work is difficult to find. G. Rauschen edited it in vol. 11 of the *Florilegium Patristicum* [Bonn, 1916].) Also cf. pseudo-Cyprian, *Against the Jews* x.79-82.

41. We will investigate the thought of the Eastern fathers, Clement of Alexandria and Gregory of Nyssa, separately. See following sections.

42. E.g., Tertullian, *On Baptism,* 10.5-6. Also cf. Hippolytus, *Commentary on Daniel* (fragment), 4.59.

is from that time on part of a Church that assumed, as we have seen, that the practiced norm was spiritual purity, no less.

Let us turn our attention, then, to the Fathers of the Eastern wing of the early Church, for it was they who thought and wrote about Christian perfection in the theological mode.

III. The Beginnings of Systematic Exposition

A. Irenaeus: Sanctification Versus Escape

Irenaeus (d. about 200), a native of Asia Minor who became bishop of Lyons, in what is now southern France, comes closest to producing a systematic theology of any of the Christians writing in the second century. His principal work, *Against Heresies,*[43] is remarkable for its synthesis of fidelity to the tradition, including what is now called the New Testament, and genuine creativity. Of course, this is not the place to review his entire theology. Instead, we confine ourselves to those elements of it that bear upon the history of the doctrine of entire sanctification.

Negatively speaking, Irenaeus' principal aim is the refutation of Gnosticism, especially those forms of it that denied or in any way depreciated the Incarnation by claiming that divinity could not (would not) assume human flesh. Irenaeus' counterattack is upon two lines: (1) If there is no real Incarnation, there is no salvation.[44] Moreover, (2) not only is there an authentic divinity-becoming-flesh but there is also a flesh-becoming-divinity.[45] In fact, the latter is the reason for the former. So potent and profound is the unity of deity and humanity brought about in Christ Jesus

---

43. Also called the *Refutation of Gnosis* or, simply, *Refutation.* English translations: *Ante-Nicene Fathers,* vol. 1; *Library of Christian Classics,* vol. 1.

44. E.g., *Against Heresies* iii.18.6: "He [Christ] warred and he won. Now, he was man doing battle for our progenitors, by his obedience utterly abolishing disobedience. For he tied up the strong man, freed the feeble, and by destroying sin endowed his creation with salvation." Another example is found in v. 14.2: "However, now the saving word has become that which really did exist—man who had perished."

45. The word that Irenaeus uses is *eikōn,* which allows the reader to think of some quality more intimate than Godlikeness but not so intimate as being God himself. Perhaps it helps to try to sense the difference between "God" and "god." For example, Irenaeus says (*Against Heresies* iv.38.4): "We were not made gods at the beginning, but first men, then, finally, gods." Also cf. iv.20.5-6.

that believers united to Him are united also to the very Father.[46] By a process of maturation-education—the Greeks called it *paideia* —the believer is actually transformed to deity in his essential character, though not in his physical, intellective, or affective capacities.[47] This deity is that which is seen inherent in Jesus Christ.[48]

The agent of this work, which Irenaeus most often calls perfection, is the Holy Spirit. The Father is the Creator of both the original Adam and of the new creature in Christ;[49] the Word is the revealer,[50] and by His identification with the believer at every stage of development He makes each of the stages holy (that is, not simply a sort of way-station but in itself a full participant in deity).[51] Bringing this work along to its culmination is the Spirit, and the work itself is the great culmination of the plan and labors of the Father and of the Son in the believer.[52]

More specifically, the Spirit is to "fit us for God," to make all believers to be one in Christ Jesus, and to enlighten the whole world.[53] But the Spirit does not work in independence from the

---

46. *Against Heresies* v.16.2: "For in the past, it was truly said that man was made in the image of God; but it was not demonstrated. The Word, in whose image man had been created, was still invisible then. And that is why man easily lost the likeness. But when the Word of God was made flesh, both points were established in fact. He manifested the authentic image by becoming just that; and he restored the likeness by conjoining it, making man like the Father by means of the visible Word."

47. *Against Heresies* iii.29.2: "The Gnostics have despised God, esteeming him to be of little value because out of his love he disclosed himself to human beings—not, of course, in his substance and greatness, but by his acting *within* us." Also see iv.38.2-4. On the difference between God and man, cf. iv.11.2.

48. *Against Heresies* iv.20.6-7. Also cf. iv.6.3-7.

49. E.g., *Against Heresies* i.10.1. This is Irenaeus' noteworthy commentary-summation of the creed.

50. *Against Heresies* iv.6.3-7: "The Father has disclosed himself through the Word become visible and tangible, even if all do not believe in him. Nonetheless, all have seen the Father in the Son. The Father of the Son is invisible, but the Son of the Father is visible" (iv.6.6).

51. *Against Heresies* ii.22.4: "[He was] made an infant for infants, he sanctified infancy; a child among children, he sanctified childhood; . . . a young man among young men, becoming their example, he sanctified them to the Lord. So also, he was a mature man among older men, so that he might be a fitting teacher for everyone; not merely at the point of revealing the truth but also at the point of this stage in life he sanctified the older men and became an example to them as well."

52. *Against Heresies* iii.17.1.

53. *Against Heresies* iii.17.2. Also cf. v.1.2.

Son. In fact, the Father gives the Spirit to the Son so that the Spirit can be communicated to believers.

> The Father bears both the creation and his Word, and the Word borne by the Father gives the Spirit to all, which is as the Father wills. . . . The Father is above all. He it is who is the head of Christ. The Word is through all. He it is who is the head of the Church. The Spirit is in us all. He it is who is the living water which the Lord gives to all who with true faith love him and believe in him (*Against Heresies* v.18.2).

Irenaeus' interpretation of the parable of the Good Samaritan, mixed with use of others of Jesus' metaphors, beautifully tells how Christ, who is that Samaritan, supplies the Spirit to the individual believer. Christ, the Good Samaritan, finding our human nature robbed and injured, in pity bound up our wounds and "left it (that is, that human nature) to the solicitude of the Holy Spirit, donating two of the King's coins that we might by way of that Spirit receive the image and superscription of the Father and the Son; making the coin entrusted to us to bear fruit, counting upon the Lord for its multiplication" (ibid., iii.17.3).

In other passages where he works with the presence of the Spirit with the believer, Irenaeus indicates that only where the Spirit is can there be either authentic life or authentic humanity.

> That which was made by the Father's hands was not one part of man, but man himself—in the likeness of God. "Soul" or "spirit" may be one part of man, but they cannot be man as such. The complete man is the mixture and union of the soul, receiving the Spirit from the Father, mingled with the flesh, which was formed in the image of God (ibid., v.6.1).[54]

In fact, Irenaeus parallels the giving of authentic life by the Spirit with God's having breathed life into Adam at the beginning—a life that was lost, of course, in the Fall.[55]

All of this said, however, it must be noted that Irenaeus believes that the perfecting work of the Spirit is confined to the Church, that is, to believers in community. So it is that he responds to those Gnostics who either deny need of the Church because of

---

54. Some terms here need explanation. Usually, but not always, Irenaeus distinguished between the "image" of God and the "likeness" of God. The "image" usually referred to the body, not so much as a mere corporal something as the material form in which the "likeness" dwelt. The "likeness" is precisely the gift of the Spirit. The word translated "complete" here is interpreted "perfect" in some other translations. The Latin is "perfectus," the Greek was probably *teleios*.

55. *Against Heresies* v.12.2.

their supposedly immediate access to God or deprecate the Church as an institution and therefore as a material attempt to enclose the Spirit. He says that to reject the Church is to "defraud" oneself of the Spirit. "For where the Church is, there, too, is the Spirit of God. Where the Spirit of God is, there is the Church and every kind of grace, for the Spirit is truth" (ibid., iii.24.1). Further, rejection of the Spirit is rejection of Christ. It is to refuse to drink from "the sparkling spring that flows from the body of Christ." This is probably a reference to both Baptism and Eucharist, both of which are thus instruments of the Spirit in His work of perfecting believers.[56]

Two things must be noted here, then, in the light of Irenaeus' conviction of the link between Spirit and Church. Since the Spirit is indeed the perfecter, that perfecting work takes place within the Church. That is to say, one does not perfect oneself in order to become a true member of the Church, nor is the Spirit engaged in perfecting nonbelievers that they may merit inheritance in the Kingdom. Perfection is for believers. For Irenaeus, however, this perfection is not completed when one is converted or baptized, nor is it imputed.

It should also be noted that Irenaeus develops his understanding from within the context of the preaching and the sacraments of the Church. He is a minister who must celebrate and teach the meaning of the Church's rites. It is most likely that on these matters his thought was in great part formed by the existing symbols. It is also likely that his understanding of the baptismal ritual would closely parallel that of his contemporary, Tertullian, whose tract on baptism was to become the standard discourse on the meaning of that sacrament.

This is to say that Irenaeus would have connected to baptism his idea of the work of the Spirit as the agent of perfection. Baptism is the point at which the Spirit comes in fullness to do His perfecting work. Irenaeus, who was clearly a traditionalist in such matters, probably also understood baptism as expressing a "secondness" and an "instantaneity" with respect to the Spirit's coming upon the baptizand in fullness. But there are some problems with asserting this with much certainty.

In the context of baptism, Irenaeus says: "By baptism our bodies receive unity (with God) and the life incorruptible; our souls

---

56. Cf., e.g., *Against Heresies* v.2.3.

receive it by the Spirit. Both are thus necessary and through them we obtain the life of God." This certainly sounds as if sanctification, or perfection, is in some sense completed at baptism—an idea that would not be at all unusual given the symbolism of the second part of the rite. Further, the illustration Irenaeus uses in this passage is that of the Samaritan woman, who was given "an internal springing up of life eternal." "This is the gift which the Lord has received from his Father and which he accords to those who are united to him" (ibid., iii.17.2). Again, there is expressed here a certain sense of a completed work, although it must be admitted that the passage need not be read that way.

But what is one to make of the following rather long passage?

> The perfect man, as we have shown, is made up of three elements: flesh, soul and spirit. The one who saves and gives form is the Spirit. The flesh is that which is united and formed. Between the two, the soul, which presently adheres to the Spirit, is lifted up by the Spirit. Anon, they yield to the flesh, falling to earthly desires. . . . All those who fear God, who believe the coming of his Son, who, by faith establish the Spirit of God in their hearts, deserve to be called pure, spiritual, alive unto God. For they have the Spirit of the Father, who purifies man and arouses him to the life of God. For if, according to the testimony of the Lord, the flesh is weak, according to the testimony of the same Lord, the Spirit is prompt. And he can perfect all of that which he possesses. If then a man employs like a goad the promptitude of the Spirit to the infirmity of the flesh, it is inevitable that that which is strong gains victory over that which is feeble. The infirmity of the flesh may be absorbed by the force of the Spirit. And such a man will no longer be carnal but spiritual, thanks to the communion of the Spirit. So it is that the martyrs expressed their testimony and defied death—not according to the weakness of the flesh, but according to the promptitude of the Spirit. The infirmity of the flesh, now absorbed, manifested the power of the Spirit; and in turn, the Spirit, absorbing the infirmity, possessed the flesh as its inheritance. The authentically living man is made up of two elements (i.e., Spirit and flesh). "Living," thanks to the participation of the Spirit; "man" by reason of being in the flesh (ibid., v.9.1-2).[57]

---

57. The apparent inconsistency between the opening line, where the perfect man is said to be composed of three elements, and the closing, which speaks of two, is a matter of Irenaeus' rapidly shifting his perspective. In the first line, he is responding to those Gnostics who try to distinguish flesh, soul, and spirit as three distinct types of human being. Irenaeus befuddles this point of view by saying that far from being the element that intelligently distinguishes and separates itself from

Again, the language is not unequivocal, but it certainly would allow an interpretation asserting a fundamental perfection here and now. The assertion of some scholars that this passage *proves* that Irenaeus held to a gradual perfection is certainly not sustained here.

Another evidence of Irenaeus' commitment to a belief in some kind of perfection before that ultimate glorification is attained may be seen in his understanding of the difference between man as truly man and man as merely an animated being. He grounds the difference in the "effusion of the Spirit," surely an allusion to the baptismal rite.

> By the effusion of the Spirit, man becomes spiritual and perfect. This is what brings him to the image and likeness of God. But if the Spirit be not united to the soul of a man, that man is imperfect. He remains sensual and carnal. He surely has in his flesh the image of God, but he has not received the likeness by the Spirit (ibid., v.6.1).

There seems to be sufficient, if not conclusive, evidence that Irenaeus sees some sort of perfection as having been given by the work of the Spirit at the outset of the Christian life, but given to the one already declared a believer. For, finally, whatever may be said of some general operations of the Spirit in the world, the Spirit's essential and principal work is within the Church: "For where the Church is, there, too, is the Spirit of God. Where the Spirit of God is, there is the Church and every kind of grace, for the Spirit is truth" (ibid., iii.24.1). And at the Spirit's coming, at Pentecost, that Spirit's presence in individual believers was manifested in their various gifts. But more important than the gifts was the fact that these were now "spiritual men" (ibid., v.6.1.).

Nonetheless, Irenaeus insists that spiritual perfection lies in the future.

> At present, we receive a partial participation in the life of the Spirit of God, in order to perfect us, in order to prepare us for incorruptibility. And little by little it habituates us to know and to bear God. This is what the Apostle calls an earnest, for it is one part of the glory which God has promised us.

---

the others, it is precisely the spirit, through the Spirit, that unites and gives shape to the body itself—a thing thought impossible and abhorrent by the Gnostics. In the second case, Irenaeus' perspective is quite Pauline and biblical as he responds to those (perhaps Christians) who question whether spirit and flesh can ever really dwell together in harmony.

Still, as a contrapuntal note, the great bishop adds:

> This earnest, which dwells in us, already makes us spiritual persons, already the mortal element is absorbed by immortality. . . . If then, already through having received this earnest we cry, "Abba, Father," what will it be when, risen, we see him face to face? When all the members, flocking together, shall chant the hymn of triumph in honor of him who has raised them from the dead, of him who has endowed them with life eternal? For if the Earnest already makes him shout, "Abba, Father," knowing man and assimilating him, what will be the full grace of that Spirit, who is given to men by God? He shall make us like him. He will make us perfect according to the will of the Father. He will make man in the image and likeness of God (ibid., v.8.1).

What we have in Irenaeus, then, is what we have in the New Testament—the exciting tension between the "already" and the "not yet." In time, as the Church realistically faced up to its weaknesses and failures, it was to mute the note of the "already" or to limit it to a few of God's "athletes." But as late as Irenaeus, the word is still clear: *there is a consummation of perfection awaiting us in this life.* Even here, thanks to the Father's gift of the Spirit through the Son, we do know the Spirit in fullness and are already made perfect as part of the work of God's great earnest.

B. Clement of Alexandria: Entire Sanctification as Essential to Authentic Humanness

In this section we meet one of the most fertile and powerful minds in the history of Christianity. Clement was from Alexandria, Egypt, although he was probably born in Athens. He died before 220. Together with Origen, he made the theological school at Alexandria noteworthy as a place of deep reflection upon the Christian faith.[58]

---

58. The best critical edition of Clement's work is O. Stählin and L. Früchtel, *Die grieschischen christlichen Schriftsteller der ersten drei Jahrhunderte: Clemens Alexandrinus,* 4 vols. (Berlin, 1905-60). The most readily available English translation of all of his works under one title is in volume II, *The Ante-Nicene Fathers.* The most useful study of Clement's life and work in English is R. B. Tollinton, *Clement of Alexandria: A Study in Christian Liberalism,* 2 vols. (London: Williams and Norgate, 1914). The standard study, to date, is E. de Faye, *Clément d'Alexandrie* (2nd ed.; Paris, 1906). Also to be consulted is Jean Daniélou, *Message évangélique et culture héllènistique aux IIe et IIIe siècles* (Paris, 1961), passim. Fortunately, this work has been translated into English by John Austin Baker under the title *Gospel Message and Hellenistic Culture,* vol. II: *A History of Early Christian Doctrine before the Council of Nicea* (London: Darton, Longman & Todd; Philadelphia: Westminster, 1973). We use the Greek titles, transliterated, in our notes because they are the usual titles used.

Clement and Origen, Clement's successor as principal teacher in Alexandria's great Christian catechetical school, have been called "Christian Platonists," but the title is not quite true to fact. It was given to them by two or three generations of modern scholars who believed that early Christianity was increasingly impregnated and shaped by Hellenistic philosophy, especially by Platonism. These scholars mistook the profound acquaintance with Greek thought that Clement and Origen demonstrated for accommodation to it. To be sure, the two Alexandrians do not escape its influence, but they were much more critical of it and discriminating in their use of it than those two or three generations of modern scholars recognized. Generally, scholars on either side of the time line of those who spoke and wrote of Clement and Origen as "Platonists" have seen the two as being well within the Christian tradition, as it had developed to that time, and as utilizing pagan thought usually in a very guarded way.

The present section will be written from this latter perspective, so it will be at odds with what R. Newton Flew and others have written about the doctrine of Christian perfection in the writings of the Alexandrian fathers.

As a way into an understanding of Clement's thought, let us consider his concept of what theologians call the "natural man." That is, human nature in the abstract, apart from either sinfulness or the operations of saving grace. "Natural man" is, of course, an abstraction helpful to study but no living being exists apart from sinfulness or the operations of saving grace.

Clement believed that human nature consists of several elements or components, and, depending upon the purpose at hand, he utilizes several lists of them. Conscious of the symbolism of the number 3, he gives Plato's inventory (passion, desire, and thought), Aristotle's (perception, intellect, desire), and Paul's (body, soul, and spirit).[59] But Clement more commonly uses, or assumes, a list of 10, 9 of them found in Stoic literature and 1 obviously Christian addition: the 5 senses, the faculties of speech and re-

---

59. These lists occur frequently, see for example *Stromateis* iii.10.68, for use of both Plato's and Paul's lists. See *Paedagogos* iii.1.2. for a use of Aristotle's. *Stromateis* is also sometimes called *Miscellanies* and *Paedagogos* is called either *The Instructor* or *(Christ) The Educator.*

production, the "animal soul," the "rational soul," and the Holy Spirit.[60]

Classical thought tended to account the body as of little or no value, or even to assign it negative value as a source of deflection from concern with higher, more spiritual affairs. Basic to the kind of Platonism studied in Clement's Alexandria, and to Gnosticism, which was threatening Christianity, was the belief that the human body is evil and that salvation is therefore found in some sort of escape from it. While Clement has keen regard for physical discipline with a spiritual purpose,[61] he will have nothing to do with a view of human nature that disparages the body.

> Those who deprecate the material creation and who disparage the body do so in error. They do not see that man was created upright in stature so that he could contemplate heaven. Further, the very organization of the senses aims [them] at knowing, and the members and parts are arranged for good, not mere sensuality. This is why this earthy house comes to be able to take in the soul—the soul, so precious to God. It is considered to be worthy of the Holy Spirit, who sanctifies both soul and body once the body has been perfected by that restoration which is the work of the Savior (*Stromateis* iv.26.136).[62]

Irenaeus had said that the body is the image of God, an idea of Semitic origin. Clement disagrees.[63] But he also rebuts those who say that it is the Holy Spirit who is the image of God, meaning thereby to demean the body or to deprive it of spiritual value.[64] So, for instance, he says, "The Word of God is percipient *[noetos]*, and we see this characteristic imaged in man alone" (ibid., vi.9.72).

Agreeing with Irenaeus, over against Tatian (a second-century Bible scholar who fell into heresy) or the Gnostics, Clement believes that all, converted or unconverted, have the image of God. But rather than thinking of it in terms of the body, Clement locates it in the mind, not as a faculty or capacity but as a relationship—a relationship to "the divine and royal Logos, who is the image of

---

60. *Stromateis* vi.16.135.

61. E.g., *Stromateis* vi.12.100; iii.10.55-59.

62. Cf., *Stromateis* iii.17.104, for Clement's critique of a Julius Cassian, not the early Christian monk, who has doubts about the goodness of the human body.

63. In *Stromateis* vi.14.112 he even calls the idea "impious."

64. E.g., Tatian, *Oration*, 15.

God." "The human mind is the image of this image" (ibid., v.14.94).[65]

But as elevated as the status of the mind is, Clement insists that man is not truly man without one more component, as it were. While all other components are in some sense natural to man, including the "image of God," that which makes him authentic man is the presence of the Holy Spirit, and the Holy Spirit comes and joins himself to man only as a divine gift.[66] So, while Clement holds a high view of human nature as it was originally created, he is not about to grant that *any* individual was *created* spiritual. That would be to fall into the Gnostics' error.

On the other hand, neither is he going to accept the Gnostics' view that insofar as any man is material, earthy, or physical, he is incapable of salvation. Nor will he accept the view that man was originally a divine nature who fell from perfection. Rather, he seeks to preserve two Christian tenets: (1) that man was a special creation, not simply another facet of nature nor yet some divine emanation, and (2) that being man is good, even if man is not created perfect in the sense of being created spiritually complete.

The Gnostics, who did not believe that God created man, for the sake of argument insisted that if God had created man, He would have created him perfect. Clement responds to them from the perspective of man's moral freedom. As *man,* he *is* created perfect, but he is not God, after all.[67] The one thing that created man lacks is the likeness of God; this is brought by the gift of the presence of the Holy Spirit. But because human nature in itself is good and is in the image of God (that is, capable of moral percep-

---

65. Also see *Protrepticus* (also called *Exhortation to the Heathen* or *Exhortation to the Greeks)* x.98.4. Clement is not entirely consistent in his language when he talks about the human being in the image of God. He notes of course that Scripture speaks of the human being "in the image and likeness of God." Are "image" and "likeness" two words for the same thing, or are they quite distinct? When Clement uses both terms together, he distinguishes clearly between them. So, in *Protrepticus* xii.120.4, all are said to be in the image of God, but only Christians are in God's likeness. (Also cf. ibid., 122.) In *Paedagogos* i.12.98, Clement says that only Christ is fully in both the "image and likeness of God," that the human being is "only in the image." By imitating Christ, one receives the likeness added to the image one already possesses (cf. *Paedagogos* i.3.9).

66. Cf. *Stromateis* ii.8.49; v.13.88; vi.16.135.

67. *Stromateis* iv.23.150 reads: "As far as his physical form is concerned, Adam was created perfect because he lacked none of the distinctive characteristics of the idea and form of man. So, in the act of coming to be he received perfection; and it was in his power to become an adult, being justified by obedience."

tion), it has both the freedom and the responsibility to acquire virtue. "God wills to save us by means of ourselves. It is the nature of the soul to be self-moving" (ibid., vi.12.96).[68]

If it is "the nature of the soul to be self-moving," it may move either toward evil or good, but its truest inclination is godliness, that is, to move toward virtue, toward perfect obedience to the will of God. How is it, then, that humankind is so sinful?

Clement describes it this way:

> The first man gamboled about in Paradise with naive freedom, for he was the child of God. But he fell victim to pleasure, allegorically signified by the serpent, who crawls about on its belly nourishing itself on earthly wickedness—fuel for the flames. So [Adam] was, in that childhood, seduced by lusts, and he grew old in disobedience, dishonoring God by disobeying the Father. Such was the ascendancy of pleasure.
>
> So man, once free by reason of childlike simplicity, was discovered to be fettered by sins (*Protrepticus* xi.111).

Now it must be noted that Clement does not work with the question of how the sin of Adam and Eve becomes the origin of continuing human sinfulness. He has no doctrine of "original sin" in the formal sense. In fact, there are passages where he seems to deny that subsequent generations are implicated in Adam's sin and guilt. In a fragment of his commentary on Jude, preserved for us in a Latin translation, Clement indicates that our sinfulness may be a matter of the imitation of Adam: "'Woe to them!' says Jude, 'for they have gone the way of Cain.' And so we too lie under Adam's sin through similarity of sin."[69]

These two and other indications from the theology of Clement seem to show him believing that humanity's continuing and universal sinfulness is empirically or existentially known. It is not simply a matter for faith, declared to be true even in the face of evidence that can be read several ways. Finally, the Fall belongs to Adam alone, except as the human race has mimed him. The sinfulness of the rest of humanity is a matter of fact, not simply a matter of faith.

Here, Clement seems to be on shaky ground, for historical Christianity had never yet tried to prove the doctrine of the Fall

---

68. In saying that God wills to save us by means of ourselves, Clement is not advocating a works-righteousness, but is insisting that salvation, while totally a work of grace, is not wrought altogether in spite of what we are nor outside of what we are.

69. E.g., *Stromateis* iii.16.100; iv.25.160.

and original sin by appeals to experience. But it must be recalled that the historical-theological context of Clement's work is the threat of Gnosticism—Gnosticism with its ultimate disparaging of the body and with its denial that the human will is authentically free. This disparaging and denial finally destroy any genuine sense of moral responsibility. As Clement sees it, such a position is totally unacceptable. So it may be that in order to counteract Gnosticism, he has overemphasized the element of individual moral responsibility and the freedom of the will and the goodness of the created human being that these imply. Nonetheless, he does grant great significance to the Fall, as we shall see.

It seems clear enough that Clement sees disobedience as the heart of sinfulness, with surrender to "pleasure" or sensuality as its principal expression—at least in the case of Adam and Eve.[70] A basic effect of that first disobedience was the disordering of human nature. "At the moment that the first man sinned and disobeyed God, he became beast-like, lacking reason, as Scripture says. Rightly then is he from that moment onward regarded as irrational and likened to the animals" (*Paedagogos* i.13.101).

"Likened to animals," for Clement, means "allowing the animal nature, the passions (anger and desire), to dominate the reason." Reason is not lost, but it is commandeered when it should be commanding. The Fall has turned man's control system upside down, as it were. But this inversion, brought on by disobedience and maintained by disobedience, does not destroy our freedom to choose good or evil.[71] If it did, the term *disobedience* would be morally empty. Here he notes the irony in the name *Eve.* It means "life," but she brought disorder: "She became responsible for the succession of those who were born and then fell into sin. But since each of us is righteous or disobedient through his own doing, she is the mother of the righteous as well as unrighteous" (*Stromateis* iii.9.65).

This same concern to retain the idea of personal moral responsibility is seen in Clement's comment upon Ps. 51:5, where David

---

70. Clement says that Adam and Eve disobeyed in that they had sexual intercourse before God gave them leave to do so. (Cf. *Protrepticus* xi.111 and *Stromateis* iii.17.103.) Clement is arguing against the Gnostic view, adopted by many orthodox Christians as well, that marriage is wrong (or at least gravely to be questioned) and sexual indulgence of any kind, even in marriage, is to be strictly avoided.

71. E.g., *Stromateis* iii.9; iv.24; vi.12.

speaks of being born in sin and conceived in unrighteousness: "But even if he was conceived in sin, he was not (at birth) in sin himself. Nor is he sin in himself" (ibid., iii.16.100).

Is it possible that some have escaped the disordering effect of the Fall and have not imitated the disobedience of Adam and Eve? Clement denies the possibility emphatically: "Continual sinning is natural and common to all" (*Paedagogos* iii.12.302). The Fall was morally ruinous and none are exempt from its effects.[72]

But while the Fall ruined all humankind, there is a remedy, a remedy available in this life and for this life. While Clement retains the typical Christian hope for the life to come, he also retains what some Christians already by his time were losing; that is, confidence that deliverance from sin and sinfulness is not deferred but may be a present reality for the believer.

> So man [in consequence of the Fall], once free by reason of childlike simplicity, was discovered to be fettered by sins. But the Lord once again purposed to loose him from his bonds. So, clothing himself with the bonds of flesh (ah, divine mystery), he vanquished the serpent and enslaved Tyrant Death. Then, most marvellous of all, the very one who had erred through pleasure and was fettered by corruption was shown to be free again by his outstretched hands.[73]

Salvation, for Clement, overcomes even here the moral ruin brought about by the Fall. It restores the believer to a life of complete obedience to the will of God, even while he is still on earth. Clement counters stoutly the Gnostic claim that the path to obedience and to overcoming the Fall lies in escaping the body with its desires and needs. He denies their contention that the culmination of salvation comes when the believer's soul is absorbed into the Godhead itself.

Instead, Clement argues that there is no humanly contrived path to moral restoration nor to perfect obedience. These are gifts given by God, of His grace.[74] To be sure, there is maturation in that

---

72. In *Stromateis* iii.16.100, Clement works with the question of the inevitability of the sinfulness of every individual. He points out that infants, even before their birth, are in close association with their mothers. Since the mother is inevitably already a sinner (from the chain reaching back to Eve), sinfulness inevitably tinges all that she does; so even though the child is pure in creation, he will inevitably be corrupted through maternal influence.

73. *Protrepticus* xi.111. The phrase "outstretched hands" refers to the Cross.

74. E.g., *Protrepticus* xi. This is the point of this entire chapter, which is quite moving.

restoration and in obedience, but this is by way of continuing manifestation of what is given at the beginning, not development toward salvation.[75]

He does speak of man's becoming God.[76] But he does so in the language of the mystery of the Incarnation, of God's having become man, not in the philosophical or everyday languages of metaphysics, logic, or sense-experience. So, just as God becomes man without being absorbed into humanity, so man becomes God without being absorbed into the Godhead.

At the heart of this restoration is perfect obedience, which in turn is a consequence of our having received immortality.

> "For he who loves his life shall lose it, and he who loses his life shall find it," this latter only as we unite our mortality to God's immortality. God's will is that we know God, and this knowledge imparts immortality. So, the one who, agreeing with the declaration of the need for repentance, knows his life to be sinful will lose it. He will lose it as far as sin is concerned, wrenching it away. Yet in losing it, he will find it, in conformity with the rebirth of obedience in faith—a circumstance in which one dies to sin. This, then, is what it is to "find one's life," to "know one's self" (*Stromateis* iv.6.27).

This "rebirth of obedience in faith" is accomplished by the work of Christ and under the guidance of the Holy Spirit.[77] As a part of it, the believer, spiritually immature though he be, is granted perfection: "Straightway upon being regenerated, we attained to that perfection after which we had aspired, for we were illuminated, which is to know God. The one who knows the Perfect cannot be imperfect" (*Paedagogos* i.6). Clement will go on to speak of another sort of perfection, one gained by maturation in spiritual insight, but it is this present perfection that we must study more closely.

It is clear that this perfection is instantaneously received, and it appears to be given subsequent to regeneration. What is its character?

Clement disputes the Gnostic disparaging of the body, and even of man as a creature, and goes on in the other direction to speak of the true gnostic (the perfectly disciplined and enlightened Christian). He even suggests that there are two classes of Chris-

---

75. E.g., *Stromateis* i.6.

76. E.g., *Protrepticus* i.8.4.

77. E.g., *Protrepticus* xi.111; xii.120; *Paedagogos* i.5; i.11.

tians. Yet he does not believe the Christian gnostic to be essentially different from any other Christian nor to possess any "basic equipment" not given to all other Christians. More particularly, every believer is granted the Holy Spirit. This presence makes him complete. It restores in the believer the likeness of God. It is precisely this presence and likeness that the unbeliever lacks. And it is precisely this presence and likeness that make the human being to be truly human.[78]

Clement's contribution to the doctrine of entire sanctification, then, lies in his insistence that we have a moral responsibility for our own spirituality. God gives us great gifts, but they are given in the context of human freedom. And, of course, the greatest of the gifts is the Holy Spirit, whose presence makes us complete, restores us in the likeness of God, and makes us truly free. Far from saying that an increase in holiness decreases one's humanness (a Gnostic notion), Clement sees such increase as making us more truly human as we were intended to be human.

It might be said, then, that Clement's notion of Christian perfection is one that emphasizes that it is the perfection of Christians, of human beings, and that therefore it must always be thought of in relative terms, in terms of limitation. On the other hand, neither is any Christian so spiritually limited as to be shut out of the possibility of such perfection. It is not an experience limited to a certain elite. The Holy Spirit is granted to every believer, and that gracious gift opens the way to the sanctification of all who possess it.

C. Origen of Alexandria: Sanctification as Cosmic Phenomenon

From our vantage point, Origen appears to be one of the most attractive figures in all of the history of Christianity, both personally and intellectually. But his life was full of suffering at the hands of powerful ecclesiastical enemies, to say nothing of his persecution and finally his execution at the hands of the government about A.D. 254. What is more, while some of his views were suspect even during his lifetime, his memory suffered the ultimate humiliation for a Christian when he was declared a heretic. First it was by a synod in his own town of Alexandria a century and a half

78. *Stromateis* ii.8.49.

after his death; then by an emperor in A.D. 543; and again by the General Church Council of Constantinople in A.D. 553.

To be sure, Origen did present some rather unusual ideas, but he seems to have done this in the spirit of the teacher propounding, not in the spirit of the preacher proclaiming. And, those views for which he was condemned touched upon matters far from settled in the Church in his own day. But such is the nature of Christianity—she never has the luxury of an abstract existence. Always, she exists in very concrete circumstances, responding to very "real" needs and questions so that one generation's speculations appear to a later one as foolish, or worse. And one generation's heroes become the "fall guys" of the next. Such processes are not right, not at all. But they are typical. And Origen was caught up by them.[79]

Our interest, of course, is not in Origen's thought in general but in his understanding of Christian perfection and, most especially, entire sanctification. As in the case of Clement, our best method is to begin with his understanding of human nature in the abstract, then to proceed to his account of the Fall and human sinfulness. Then we will present his view of redemption and regeneration and his concept of the broadest possibility of grace for the Christian in this life.[80]

---

79. There are few biographies of Origen and equally few full scale studies of his theology, although there are many more specialized studies of particular aspects of his thought. Charles Bigg, *The Christian Platonists of Alexandria* (Oxford: Clarendon Press, 1886), is the classic study in English, but it must be used with caution because of its overstatement of the influence of Platonism on the method and content of Origen's work. To balance this, see Jean Daniélou (Walter Mitchell, trans.), *Origen* (New York: Sheed and Ward, 1955); E. de Faye (Fred Rothwell, trans.), *Origen and His Work* (New York: Columbia University Press, 1926); and K. O. Weber, *Origenes, der Neuplatoniker* (Munich, 1962).

80. A complete edition of Origen's work is in J. P. Migne, *Patrologia Graeca,* vols. XI-XVIII (Paris, 1857). The best critical edition, albeit at present incomplete, is in Otto Stählin, *Die grieschischen christlichen Schriftsteller der ersten drei Jahrhunderte: Origenes,* vols. I-XII (Berlin, 1899-1959). The *Patrologia Graeca* is usually abbreviated MPG; *Die grieschischen christlichen Schriftsteller* is usually abbreviated GCS. G. W. Butterworth, *Origen: On First Principles* (New York: Harper and Row, 1936), is an excellent translation of *De principiis.* The Harper Torchbook Edition (New York: Harper and Row, 1966) of this translation carries a very useful introduction by Henri de Lubac. J. E. L. Oulton and Henry Chadwick, *Alexandrian Christianity,* vol. II: "Library of Christian Classics" (Philadelphia: Westminster Press, 1954), has introductions to, bibliographies for, and translations of *De oratione (On Prayer), Exhortatio ad martyrium (Exhortation to Martyrdom),* and *Dialektos (Dialogue with Heraclides).* R. P. Lawson, *The Song of Songs: Commentary and Homilies,* vol. 26: "Ancient Christian Writers" (Westminster, Md.: Newman Press, 1957), is a translation of *Commen-*

Who, then, does Origen perceive the human being to be? The story of humankind begins with the creation of the universe. Not with the creation of the physical character of the universe (which was to come later), but with the creation of the spiritual character of the universe. Created at that time were rational spirits. These rational spirits were free in will, otherwise rationality would mean nothing. Furthermore, since God who created them is perfect, they were created perfect; and since God's perfection includes or implies justice, they were created equal in their freedom.[81]

At this point, however, we must understand that when Origen speaks of the creation of the spiritual universe, or, rather, of the creation of the spiritual character of the universe, he is speaking only by analogy. That character of the universe did not come into being at some past moment. It has existed eternally. This has been so, Origen reasons, because God is, by definition, creative and creating. So, since He has always been God, there has always been creating or creation. And since His fundamental creating or creation is most like himself—that is, it is both personal and spiritual—there have forever been personal spirits, rational and free just as He is personal, spiritual, rational, and free.[82]

Originally, these spirits were alike, insofar as each was free in will and thus rational. And it was intended that they would use their freedom and rationality to come to ever closer communion with their Creator.[83] But being free proved detrimental to all of them except to the spirit of Christ.[84] They abused their freedom and rationality and fell into sin. So now the basic equality of the spirits was destroyed.

Some remained relatively untouched by the abuse of freedom

---

tarius in Cantica Canticorum. Henry Chadwick, *Origen: Contra Celsum* (Cambridge: Cambridge University Press, 1953), is a translation of the work called in English *Against Celsus.* J. J. O'Meara, *Origen: Treatises on Prayer and Martyrdom,* vol. 19: "Ancient Christian Writers" (Westminster, Md.: Newman Press, 1954), is a translation of *De oratione* and *Exhortatio ad martyrium.* It is usual to use the Latin abbreviations to the titles when referring to Origen's works, though he, of course, wrote in Greek. As in all sections of this book that are this author's responsibility, translations are his own except where otherwise noted.

81. *De principiis* I.7.1; III.5; II.9.3,6.

82. *De principiis* II.1.2-3,10; II.9.6.

83. *De principiis* I.3.8.

84. *De principiis* I.8.3.; II.9.2. According to Origen, the Fall occurred when the spirits fell into torpor and slothfulness in the preservation of the good, "standing aloof from all the best and caring little for it" (II.9.3).

and rationality. They chose virtue and did not take part in the Fall. These were given the privilege of eternal communion with God. The purest, and the only one absolutely untouched, was the spirit of Jesus; the rest of them we know as angels, good angels. At the other extreme are those spirits whose rebellion was total. They yearned for evil alone. These, then, became the demons.

Between the angels and the demons were the spirits who were to become human beings. Neither perfectly virtuous nor totally evil, their ranks varied in degree of fallenness.[85] It was for these that the physical world was created.[86] Here they would be placed in material bodies and taught to discern good and evil, and to follow after good. So the material world was created for humanity's sake, as a disciplinary colony, that eventually each fallen spirit might be saved.[87]

Here we must understand the basic simplicity of Origen's thought, reflecting back upon his concept of what humanity was before the Fall and upon his concept of the Fall itself, while anticipating his view of redemption. His thought is simple, in that it rests upon but two pillars: divine love and human freedom.[88] As the Fall resulted from the rejection of divine love through the abuse of (human) freedom, so redemption will come as divine love restores and purifies that abused freedom. It will be complete when humankind is once again totally free (and rational), equal again to the good spirits—in a sense, equal to Christ himself, though this is not absolutely attainable. After all, Christ's spirit never fell. (The thoughtful reader can see here a powerful extension of Irenaeus' idea of recapitulation.)

It is through Christ, of course, that this redemption-restoration is accomplished. The Christ that the believer knows, Jesus of Nazareth, was a unity of the divine Son of God (that personal being within the Godhead who is the Godhead's agent in creation and in revelation—the Logos) and the preexistent spirit of Jesus, unitedly incarnated in the historical human person, Jesus of Nazareth.[89]

---

85. *De principiis* I.8.1.
86. *De principiis* I.8.1; III.5.4-6.
87. *De principiis* II.1-4; III.4.5.
88. *De principiis* I.8.3; III.5.6.
89. *De principiis* II.6.3-4.

But believers will differ in their need for the actual historicity of Jesus Christ. Origen is firm in his confidence that God was incarnate in Jesus of Nazareth and that His incarnation, passion, death, and resurrection were absolutely necessary to salvation. Here, he is thoroughly orthodox. But he also believes that behind the historical fact stand many ranges of spiritual understanding and appropriation.

At the most elementary distance are those believers who see in the historical fact of Christ the payment of a ransom to Satan, which effects their deliverance. To these believers, Christ is the Physician who heals the sick, the Shepherd who finds the lost sheep and defends and feeds the flock, and the Redeemer who rescues us from the clutches of Satan and his minions.[90]

The aim of the believer, however, should be to advance beyond this history-bound level to the range of gnosis, to the perspective where all is understood spiritually. Here we find an often overlooked point in Origen's thought. It is clear that *all* can and must pass from range to higher range in this life, but some do naturally begin with broader vistas than others.[91] To the mature, or "spiritual," or gnostic believer, the contact is not so much with Jesus of Nazareth as with the Logos, with the totally divine nature of Christ, who is Wisdom and Reason to that believer—the Revealer of the mysteries of God.[92]

What perfection would be under this scheme is quite clear: it is restoration to the freedom that desires only the Good (that is, only God) and to the rationality that identifies with God/Good through free submission and likeness to Christ the Logos.

> The end is like the beginning. As the end of all things is a unity, so is the beginning. As the many come to one end, so the beginning became many. And the varieties and differences that came out of the beginning are recalled to the one end by the goodness of God, by submission to Christ, by the unity of the

---

90. E.g., *Contra Celsum* III.61-62.

91. To a charge that the difference between creatures is unjust, Origen would respond that as preexistent souls all were equal. The differences arose as a consequence of their respective use and abuse of their equal freedom and rationality. So the differences existent upon earth among humans, at the point of spiritual understanding, are not of God's doing, but of our own. The good news is that God again is actively seeking to bring even the most history-bound human back to full freedom and rationality (and spirituality)—that is, to equality. Cf. *De principiis* II.9.6; I.6.3; IV.3.10.

92. *De principiis* I.1.7; also see *De oratione* xx.2.

Holy Spirit—back to the beginning, by "bowing the knee at Jesus' name" and thus declaring their submission (*De principiis* I.6.2).

Such is perfection for Origen, a restoration to freedom and rationality that identifies us with the freedom and rationality of God himself, all of it made possible through the person and work of Christ. But what is the relationship of this perfection to sanctification? Here, in Origen's thought, we take a giant step in the separation of the two.

More typical of Origen than the word *sanctification* is the word *purification,* but they would seem usually to refer to the same spiritual experience. And, as with most of the early Fathers of the Church, this purification or sanctification is given at baptism, for it is there that sin is forgiven and (more to our point) the Holy Spirit bestowed. In fact, as Pelikan says, "The most distinctive gift of baptism was the gift of the Holy Spirit."[93]

On the other hand, while Origen clearly claims purification for the baptizand and the gift of the fullness of the Spirit,[94] he also makes it clear that the new "pneumatic" (his name for one full of the Spirit, but not an unequivocated term) now must consecrate the rest of a lifetime to realizing or making manifest what has been received in baptism. In fact, baptism does not guarantee salvation—one may be "baptized unto damnation."[95] It must be more than an outward rite. It must be received by faith and spelled out ethically. Only then does it become true baptism. In other words, the purification received at baptism can be frittered away. Sanctification can be forfeited.

Origen's proposed remedy for postbaptismal sin is quite curious, and of great interest to the contemporary holiness movement because of its language. He speaks of a baptism of fire (usually by martyrdom), which occurs just before the believer enters "Paradise."[96] Scholars disagree concerning what Origen believed about the precise moment in which this second baptism takes place—

---

93. Pelikan, *Christian Tradition,* 1:165. Also see *De principiis* I.3.2; *in Luc. hom.* xxi.; *in Matt. comm.* xv.23. Unfortunately, there are no published English translations of either the 39 homilies on Luke (which exist only in a Latin edition by Jerome) or the commentary on Matthew (which is also only partial, as are most of Origen's surviving works).

94. *Hom. in Levitic.,* 6.2. No English translation.

95. *Hom. in Ezek.,* 6.5. No English translation.

96. *Hom. in Jer.,* 2.3; *in Luc. hom.* xxiv.; xxvi. No English translation.

whether it is effective in and on this life or not. But what is obvious is its purificatory nature. It cleanses from all sin and it is the culminating act of the Spirit in the drama of redemption insofar as the drama takes place on earth. It seems to be a sort of entire sanctification for those who backslide by postbaptismal sin from the sanctification (certainly complete) granted at baptism.

Whatever may be the meaning of the "baptism of fire" (beyond what we have already suggested), Origen speaks of yet another baptism—the "baptism of martyrdom"[97]—comparing it to the baptism "with water and the Spirit." It may be that this baptism is the same as the "baptism of fire," for in both cases Origen connects them with the remission of postbaptismal sin and with purification. But the identification is not certain.

Nonetheless, whether or not the "baptism of fire" and the "baptism of martyrdom" be equivalent, what is clear is Origen's concern to declare the possibility of spiritual purity in this life. In fact, it is more than a possibility; it is a necessity, even to the point that he supplies, as it were, a sort of "second chance" entire sanctification.

For Origen, it is the martyr who is the true Christian.[98] Such is the very point of his *Exhortation to Martyrdom.* But who is a true martyr? From much the same perspective that keeps him from seeing the ritual of baptism (water baptism) as the true "washing of regeneration" except as it is accompanied by faith and a commitment to a lifelong existential explication of its meaning, Origen sees martyrdom as a spirit of faithful witness to the gospel. It may well entail death, but it is not simply that death itself.[99]

So, the sanctification brought by either water baptism or the "baptism of martyrdom" (perhaps the "baptism of fire") issues in a life (or even physical death) in which the will of the believer and the will of God, and of Christ, are identical.[100] Here, Origen ponders Christ's prayer in Gethsemane—that the cup pass from Him if it be the Father's will.

But two other aspects of this life of sanctification must be noted before we close the section. First, attention must be drawn to Origen's understanding that at the base of Christian experience is

---

97. E.g., *Exhortatio ad martyrium,* 30.

98. *Exhortatio ad martyrium,* 34-39.

99. *Exhortatio ad martyrium,* 11-15.

100. *Exhortatio ad martyrium,* 28-30; also see *De oratione* xxvi.1-6.

gnosis, knowing. This knowing is not mere intellection, but knowledge of God himself (and thus of divine profundities). This is revealed by God himself as a revelation of himself; it is a knowledge that transforms and makes us evangelical. It is a knowledge that "begets children," Origen says.[101] It is a grasp of rationality, true reason—of the *logos* itself.[102]

With this point of view, Origen voids any Christianity that is only, or principally, emotional or even ethical. And since the gnosis is the knowing of a Person and is grace-given, he voids the mere intellectualism of some and the claims to salvation by esoteric revelation made by others.[103] The life of the true and fully "baptized" believer is characterized by a "Christian love of learning"—learning the very mind of God himself. But, of course, one can never really plumb its depths, however great the loving yearning to do so.[104]

The second aspect of Origen's understanding of the life of sanctification that must be mentioned is its cosmic character. In moving the authentic Christian life beyond doctrine, ritual, feeling, and ethics—though not excluding these—to the true gnosis (knowledge or knowing), Origen seeks to make it of a piece with the very life of God himself, who is all in all. In the ultimate sense, of course, this is impossible as long as we remain "in the body," but through true baptism we have already become what we finally shall be, as far as essential spirituality is concerned.[105] Now, what we finally are to be is, in the truest sense, a mystery; but we know that through Christ, and by the work of the Holy Spirit, we shall be "rendered capable of receiving God; then God will be to [us] 'all in all.'"[106]

> I myself think that when it is said that God is "all in all," it means that he is all things in each individual. And he will be all things in such a way that the rational mind, purified of all the dregs of its vices and utterly cleared of every cloud of wick-

---

101. *Exhortatio ad martyrium,* 14-16.

102. *Exhortatio ad martyrium,* 11, 13-14.

103. *Exhortatio ad martyrium,* 13. Origen is not opposed to esoteric interpretation of Scripture, but he will allow no validity nor saving authority to anything beyond the Rule of Faith. Cf. *De principiis,* Pref. 3-8; III.3.2.

104. *Exhortatio ad martyrium,* 14; *De principiis* IV.3.14-15.

105. *De principiis* III.6.1-2. Also cf. *De oratione* xxii.1-5 with *De principiis* II.6.1-9.

106. *De principiis* III.6, passim, but esp. III.6.9.

> edness, can feel or understand or think will be all God and that the mind will no longer be conscious of anything besides or other than God, but will think God and see God and hold God and God will be the mode and measure of its every movement; and in this way God will be all to it. For there will no longer be any contrast of good and evil, since evil nowhere exists; for God, whom evil never approaches, is then all things to it; nor will one who is always in the good and to whom God is all things desire any longer to eat of the tree of the knowledge of good and evil.[107]

It is in this way that the process of sanctification is made cosmic. It involves each of the Persons of the Trinity, into the life of which the believer is taken. It is part of that grand work of re-creation and restoration of the entire universe that has been put into effect by the earthly work of Christ. Further, far from being a "Jesus and me" experience, the believer's "baptism of martyrdom" serves evangelically. That is, in line with the effect of Christ's death, "the baptism of martyrdom may also, thanks to the ministry of those who suffer it, bring purification to many" (*Exhortatio ad martyrium* 30).

Seldom has the doctrine of sanctification been cast with such grandeur as it has by Origen. While he does seem to separate perfection from sanctification, making the former the culmination of the latter and available only in the life to come (at least this is usually so in his writings), there is a purity or perfection of yearning, at least, possible in this life. And, while we must be careful not to assign to Origen a taxonomy of the process of salvation that is more clear-cut than he would allow for, it does not seem unfair to say that he did see sanctification as a distinct activity of divine grace—that is, distinct from justification. And he did see it as being given to the believer in a moment distinct from the moment in which justification was given. But there are three, or perhaps just two, such moments: the second "act" of the ritual of water baptism and the baptism of fire or the baptism of martyrdom.

The cosmic note was never picked up with any enthusiasm or depth of understanding in the subsequent history of Christian thought, for it was read in the context of the general suspicion of Origen and consigned either to the pantheistic or Platonic camps. Its genuinely Christian character was hidden by the readers' prejudices.

---

107. *De principiis* III.6.3. This is essentially Butterworth's translation.

For a century after the death of Origen, the theological preoccupation of the Church was with the nature of Christ and of the Trinity. The question of the nature of Christian experience was preempted. Only with Augustine would it rise with vigor again in the West and but a generation earlier in the East.

IV. The Formative Period

The fourth century was exceptionally difficult for the Christian Church. As it opened, the Roman government was executing its fiercest official persecution of the Christians; as it closed, Christianity was attempting to adjust to being the official religion of the Roman Empire. As it opened, the Church was aquiver with theological controversy, especially concerning what it meant to say—that Christ was both human and divine; as the century closed, the argument was, if anything, hotter and there had even been a Christian bishop executed for heresy by a Christian government after trial before a church court.[108]

But for all of the doctrinal turmoil and in spite of the temptation to arrogance on the part of churchmen who were now also civic "somebodies," deep spirituality had not left the Church. Her resources in piety were apparently as plentiful in A.D. 400 as in A.D. 300. There was still a deep and obvious chasm between Christian and pagan in moral practice and in spiritual commitment.[109]

Not a little of the spiritual vitality of Christianity in the later decades of the fourth century must be credited to the religious movement that later yet crystallized as monasticism.[110] It began

---

108. The bishop was Priscillian of Avila; the date was probably A.D. 385 or 386; the place was Trier in Gaul (France). The best account of this sordid affair is that of Henry Chadwick, *Priscillian of Avila: The Occult and the Charismatic in the Early Church* (London: Oxford University Press, 1976). His suggestion that the shrine to St. James at Santiago de Compostela in northwestern Spain was originally a shrine to Priscillian needs further investigation, however.

109. A favorite hypothesis of those who would reform the church by taking it back to its "primitive" faith and practice is that a deep spiritual decline set upon Christianity from the moment (in A.D. 312) that the Emperor Constantine legalized the faith and entered the path of making allies and then partners of Church and State. The peculiar problems and temptations posed by the new situation after A.D. 312 are to be seriously considered. They did have great effect. But the data show no general spiritual decline in the Church through the fourth century.

110. On early monasticism in general, cf. Owen Chadwick (ed.), *Western Asceticism,* vol. XII: "Library of Christian Classics" (Philadelphia: Westminster, 1958); H. B. Workman, *The Evolution of the Monastic Ideal* (2nd ed.; London: SPCK, 1927;

late in the third century, principally in Egypt and Palestine, and gained marked momentum in the fourth, encouraged by even broader popular Christian support as an ideal expression of the faith. It was both a protest against the encroachment of the world upon the Church and a positive response to the invitation of Scripture and tradition to a radically renunciatory faith. As such, asceticism was understood to be an enterprise undertaken by some in behalf of all—the specialists in prayer, meditation, and renunciation serving representatively, even vicariously. Their contemplations were not to be privately edifying personal exercises but were to be regimens whose results would redound to the spiritual health of the whole Church. The ascetics' gifts were understood as the Spirit's boon to the whole Body of Christ.

There was, therefore, a lot of coming and going. Either the ascetic periodically came back to the more usual Christian community to teach and to counsel, or some of the community would set out to see the ascetic, some of them to stay and others to return enlightened.

It is not quite proper to call the fourth-century ascetics "monks" nor to call their communities "monasteries." Those terms fit better a century or so later. Better to call them ascetics, which means "exercisers" or "those in rigorous training." Or call them "God's athletes," a name attached to them then. Or call them "contemplatives," a term describing what they saw themselves as doing.

Care must be taken to understand what "contemplation" was. It was not a matter of sitting about, growing emaciated, awaiting a special revelation. There was reflection—upon Scripture and other Christian writings, and upon "the mysteries," the great sacraments by means of which the Church celebrated the work of Christ on her behalf. And there was action—the contemplative often returning to teach and to do good works. It is readily apparent that this reflection and action were formed and directed by the Christian community and its spiritual resources. The ascetic might be a "solitary" (another name given them), but "solitary" did not mean "private" nor "individualistic." His faith, so he and everyone else understood, was the faith of the Church.

Reprint, Boston: Beacon, 1962). These works will guide the reader to the principal primary sources.

True, there were excesses, absurdities, and pious frauds among even the earliest ascetics. But these were neither normative nor usual. Unfortunately, our present-day activist mentality, especially in its Protestant expressions, has tended to report and to assume the worst, or at least to study the most bizarre concerning early asceticism. In doing so, it has lost much of its awareness of the sensitivity of the early (and medieval) Church to the call to Christian holiness—to perfection. In the next few pages, an attempt will be made to remedy (of course, only in small part) that situation.[111]

A. Macarius the Egyptian: Entire Sanctification in the Ascetic Mode

It is almost certain, now, that the works entitled (in English) *The Fifty Spiritual Homilies of St. Macarius the Egyptian* were not written by Macarius. They do seem, however, to be from his era (he lived from about A.D. 300 to 390), are certainly ascetic in tone, and are from his native land, Egypt.[112] Following tradition, therefore, we shall call them by his name, but only as a convenience.

---

111. A very important series on the idea of perfection among early Christian ascetics who were influenced by Philo Judaeus was published by Walter Volker. The series includes *Das Vollkommenheitsideal des Origenes* (Tübingen, 1931); *Fortschritt und Vollendung bei Philo von Alexandrien* (Tübingen, 1938); *Die Vollkommenheitslehre des Clemens Alexandrinus in ihren geschichtlichen Zusammhängen* in *Theologische Zeitschrift* (Basel, 1947), 15-40; *Gregor von Nyssa als Mystiker* (Wiesbaden, 1955); *Der Wahre Gnostiker nach Clemens Alexandrinus* (Berlin, 1952). Also on the "must consult" list for future study should be included P. Pourrat, *Christian Spirituality* (London, 1924); F. Vernet, *La spiritualité médiévale* (Paris, 1929); and the indispensable *Dictionnaire de spiritualité ascétique et mystique* (Paris, 1937 et seq.).

112. Their Greek title is *Homiliai Pneumatikai.* The most readily available text is in J. P. Migne's *Patrologia Graeca* (MPG), vol. XXXIV. The best text is the critical edition done by H. Dorries, E. Klostermann, M. Kroeger, *Die funfzig geistlichen Homilien des Makarios* (Leipzig, 1964). An English translation based on the MPG text was produced by A. J. Mason under the title *Fifty Spiritual Homilies of St. Macarius the Egyptian* (Oxford: Oxford University Press, 1921) and reissued with a biography of Macarius and a summary of his teachings by Ivan Michailovich Kontzevich under the title *Fifty Spiritual Homilies, St. Macarius the Great* (Willits, Calif.: Eastern Orthodox Books, 1974). John Wesley published extracts in English from some of the sermons in vol. 1 of his *Christian Library,* but seems to be following a different order from the MPG edition. Numbering in the present essay will follow the MPG edition (and Dorries, et al.) and the translations are the author's own from the critical text.

The best brief discussion of the matter of the content of "Macarius'" work and the best extensive bibliography on both content and the critical problems are in Berthold Altaner and Alfred Stuiber, *Patrologie: Leben, Schriften und Lehre der Kir-*

Not all of the homilies give clue as to their intended audience, but those that do are quite clearly geared to a congregation of ascetics.[113] More important to us, in considering the doctrine of entire sanctification contained in them, is the fact that those that are genuine homilies—some are rather lectures of a sort—reflect a context of Christian worship.[114] A good, clear example of this is found in *Homily* XIII, where Macarius clearly grounds spiritual life in the reception of the eucharistic bread and wine.

> When a man gives that which is innermost in him—his mind, his thoughts—to God, keeping himself stayed on God and holding steady, not wandering away, then the Lord judges him to be worthy, holier and more pure; fit to receive the mysteries. And He gives him the food of heaven and spiritual drink (*Homily* XIII.1).[115]

Baptism is almost taken for granted as the rite of entrance into the heavenly kingdom.[116] But it is quite significant to our present study that Macarius refers from time to time to the Christians' having been anointed with oil (which, as we have seen, is part of the baptismal ritual), and that this gives to the believers "rank," making them kings.[117] And even more significant, and more frequent, are the references to the Christian's vestment with the "divine and heavenly raiment."[118] This is almost certainly a reflection upon the meaning of the symbol of vesting the baptizand as he came up out of the water at baptism.

Now cleansed, the new Christian was robed in a clean, white garment in a ceremony accompanied by the reading of such passages as Rom. 13:14: "Put on the Lord Jesus Christ." This robing was accompanied as well by a symbolic anointing, signifying the coming of the Holy Spirit upon the believer. Macarius does not

---

chenväter (Freiburg, Basle, 1978), 264-65, 601. Werner Jaeger, *Two Rediscovered Works of Ancient Christian Literature: Gregory of Nyssa and Macarius* (Leiden: E. J. Brill, 1954), 37-47, 145-62, 208-30, has helpful and extended discussion of the issues, especially as they bear on the so-called "Great Letter" of Macarius.

113. E.g., *Homily* III, as an example of a homily clearly indicating that the audience or congregation is ascetic.

114. As a rule of thumb, the homilies that proceed in question-and-answer form are not true homilies, though we cannot categorically assert that they were delivered apart from the context of divine worship. Cf., for example, Homilies VI, VII, VIII, and XI.

115. Also see *Homily* XXVII.17.

116. E.g., *Homily* XV.14; XX.3; XXXII.4.

117. E.g., *Homily* XV.35.

118. E.g., *Homily* XX.1; XXXII.1-2 ff.

miss the symbolism. He refers to the reality in which it participates as "the divine and heavenly raiment, which is the power of the Holy Spirit" (*Homily* XX.1).

As we noted earlier, this anointing was apparently the point of the filling with the Holy Spirit, the moment of entire sanctification, liturgically expressed. No matter how much growth in grace lay in the future, here was the Christian's essential purification, his perfection in righteousness. Entire sanctification and Christian perfection were held together, but also separated. Christian perfection was understood as relative perfection, so there could (and should) be growth in grace, growth in perfection. Macarius reflects this tradition but goes on to emphasize the later reaches of perfection and of the "filling with the Holy Ghost." His emphasis is so strong as to imply that beyond the sanctification and perfection liturgically signified, there is a deeper and more complete sanctifying and perfecting work of grace.[119] It is precisely to this later work that the *Fifty Homilies* call Macarius' readers.

The significance of this insight is immense. For one thing, it removes entire sanctification from the ritual and places it well within the living of the Christian life. It is presented as an experience arrived at only as one has developed some Christian maturity and self-understanding. In *Homily* XIX, Macarius puts it in negative terms, telling his readers of the reluctance of the heart and its disinclination to follow Christian discipline. But he insists that the discipline must be maintained until the Lord "shows mercy upon him, and rescues him from his enemies and from indwelling sin, filling him with the Holy Ghost." Positively, the new experience enables the believer "to do all of the Lord's commandments in truth [really, it is the Lord doing his own commandments], without coercion or struggle, now bringing forth in purity the fruits of the Spirit" (*Homily* XIX.2).

Another significant effect of Macarius' insight into the nature of entire sanctification is his removing it from its liturgical expression and putting it within the living of the Christian life as a consequence of discipline, maturity, and self-understanding. In doing so, he returns it to the possibility of its New Testament expression, where it is truly a matter of a tension between an "already" and a "not yet." This was certainly *intended* in the liturgical symbolism.

---

119. *Homily* XIX.1-2.

The entire sanctification/Christian perfection received there was clearly to be understood as preliminary or introductory, as empowerment, as pointing to a life of growth in grace, even perfection itself.

By the late fourth century, however, perhaps as a reflection of a pessimistic mood that prevailed throughout the culture, that interpretation of the symbolism was displaced, more so in the Western branch of the Church than in the Eastern, but neither escaped.

Now, the second part of the baptismal ritual was often believed to express primarily the coming and presence of the Spirit to strengthen or fortify the believer. In fact, little by little, the second part of the ritual was separated from the first and referred to as confirmation (*confirmatio,* which means affirmation, strengthening, encouragement). The note of purification or sanctification or perfection was not lost but it was muted, especially in the West.[120] The emphasis fell on the "not yet."

Baptism-confirmation was seen as entry into the Church.[121] And the Church, now much more institutional than ever before, makes way in its theology and in its disciplinary processes for believers who are self-consciously both saints and sinners. The Church admits its sinfulness as it had not earlier. That is, it comes to confess it as a matter of course.

This radical change is seen as it clearly manifests itself in the theology of Augustine. One of the marks of the true Church is its holiness. But this cannot mean the perfection in righteousness of its members. Rather, the holiness of the Church consists solely in the holiness of the Head of the Church, Christ Jesus, with or to whom the members are united.[122] This holiness in union is cele-

---

120. E.g., Augustine, *Enarratio 26 in psalm 2:2;* Synod of Orange I (441), canon 2 (Mansi VI.435); Faustus of Riez (d. 490/500), *Homil. in Pentecost,* cf. L. A. van Buchem, *L'homélie pseudo eusébienne de Pentecôte* (Nijmegen, 1967). The note of perfection is kept strong in the East: e.g., Cyril of Alexandria, *Comm. in Joel,* 32; Dionysius pseudo-Areopagite *De eccl. hierarch.* IV.3, 11. Eastern sources speaking in terms of strengthening include Serapion of Thmuis (d. 280), *Euchologium,* 25.2 (in F. X. Funk, *Didascalia et constitutiones apostolorum,* vol. 2 [1950]). In all cases, the basic interpretation was that this rite (or part of the baptismal rite) bestowed the Holy Spirit. The differences have to do with why the Spirit is bestowed, and even there the answers differ only in emphasis, not in the elements involved.

121. E.g., Cyril of Jerusalem, *Catachetical Lectures,* 21.5; Augustine, *Enarratio 26 in psalm 2:2,* and *Homil.,* 351.12; Synod of Laodicea (prob. 363), canon 48 (Mansi II.571).

122. The notion that the four marks of the true church are unity, holiness, universality, and apostolicity was probably quite common in the early fourth cen-

brated, proclaimed, and maintained not through the ethical life of the members but through the sacraments of the Church, especially the Eucharist.[123] And rather than talk about the presence of the Spirit in the believer, the emphasis now falls on the presence of the Spirit in the Church.[124] To speak of the entire sanctification or perfection of a believer in this life is almost out of the question.[125]

Macarius swims against this stream and begins with the assumption that while the sacraments are surely means of grace, they and the Christian life itself are to be understood in the light of Scripture. The late fourth century Church in the West, with Ambrose of Milan and Augustine in the vanguard, tended to interpret Scripture in the light of the lives of the Christians about them (and in the light of their own experience). They defined who was Christian and who was not in terms of participation or nonparticipation in the sacraments.[126] The East, too, tended to reflect this point of view, but the older perspective remained. Thus Macarius' position was in many ways representative of the Christianity of the centuries before the deep change caused by Constantine's conversion.

Macarius' insight into the nature of entire sanctification and Christian perfection as they relate to the liturgy was not without

---

tury. It was made official dogma by the Council of Constantinople (A.D. 381). Cf. Augustine, *Enarratio 1 in psalm 30:4*. "Many Christians there are, but only one Christ. The Christians themselves along with their head form one Christ, because he has ascended to heaven. But it is not as if he were one and we many; rather, we the many are one in him. So there is but one man, Christ, who consists of head and body" *(Enarratio in psalm 127.3)*.

123. E.g., Augustine, *Epistle*, 187.20; *Serm.*, 354.4.

124. Late fourth-century discussions of the second part of the baptismal rite tend to be quite concerned with the precise role of the bishops in relation to that of the presbyters and to how it is that these ecclesiastics have the authority to pass on the Spirit rather than to what this does to and for the believer. The ritual itself, not its effects, takes center stage. Cf., for instance, *Apostolic Constitutions*, 3.16, 3-4. And, of course, see such works as Augustine's *De baptismo contra Donatistan* and the *Contra epistolam Parmeniani*, both anti-Donatist pieces. The Donatist controversy often focused on the nature of the relationship of baptism to piety.

125. We shall consider Augustine in more depth later. Here, cf. *Enarratio in psalm 38.13; De doctrina christ* i.38, 43; *Retractions* i.19.

126. Augustine's thought here is very complex and ambivalent. His doctrines of grace, election, and predestination must be held in tension with his doctrines of church and sacraments. The true "Church" can never be defined solely as the institution calling itself "the Church," but neither can the true Church be defined totally apart from that institution. Being an authentic Christian, then, is not necessarily to be identified with the institution called "the Church," but neither can one be an authentic Christian totally apart from what that institution in essence is. Cf., for instance, *De baptismo* v.38-39.

danger. He sees them as lying beyond the sacramental symbolism and in some sense dependent upon experiencing the fully Christian life as one develops maturity and self-understanding. In so doing, he runs the risk of teaching that entire sanctification and Christian perfection come as a consequence of certain good works or attitudes or that they are to be maintained and evaluated by means of good works. This, in fact, is basically what "perfection" came to mean in later monasticism. It became a deadly legalism.

But Macarius is very conscious of the traps and seeks to avoid them. His understanding is that an authentic experience of entire sanctification is totally and at every moment dependent upon the presence of Christ and His work, and the believer must totally and at every moment submit to Christ in love. The fruits of such an experience can be faked or counterfeit forms of them may arise of purely human striving. So it cannot be the fruits that are the *sine qua non,* but only the presence of Christ in the person of the Holy Spirit totally loved and reigning unhindered.[127]

It has already been noted several times that entire sanctification, in Macarius' view, may come only after one has walked a while as a Christian and has come to some self-understanding, some awareness of the depth of sin and of the double-mindedness that sin has engendered. The question naturally arises, "Why does God not do the entire work at the very beginning?" Why is a *second* work necessary?

Macarius recognized that all sin could be cleansed away "and a man made perfect in the span of an hour." But God does not work thus. Rather He gives grace "only in part" at first, "in order to test the man's resolve—whether he keep full-fledged his love toward God, not submitting in anything to the evil one, but yielding himself up entirely and integrally to grace." In this way, one in freedom invites grace into the deepest recesses of character, recesses of which one knows and learns only after conversion. Such opening of the heart is not for selfish purposes but because one keenly senses how loving God must be to come so fully and graciously to "such an immense range of inner wickedness" (*Homily* XLI.1-3).

---

127. E.g., *Homily* XVII.1; *Homily* XXXVIII entire; *Homily* XXVI.182-6. In the latter citation, from paragraph 21 onward, Macarius works with the question "Such fruits as love, faith and prayer can issue from our human nature. How do such fruits differ when they issue from spirituality?" Also see *Homily* XLV.7, where Macarius speaks of coming to dissatisfaction with even the greatest gifts of grace and yearning instead for union with "the heavenly Bridegroom."

So, entire sanctification is, for Macarius, a distinct work of grace, necessarily subsequent to conversion, but it is also totally dependent upon it.[128] Life as a converted person should bring increasing awareness of three factors: (1) the depth and pervasiveness of sin in the human character;[129] (2) the command and promise of God that all sin be cleansed away by the Holy Spirit;[130] and (3) the fact that this can and should be done in this life by a definite commitment to it on the part of both the Spirit and the believer.[131] It is not reached by growth in grace alone, for growth in grace prior to entire sanctification is also growth in the awareness of one's distance from all that is being commanded and offered.[132] It is certainly not reached by ethical discipline, though failure to enter upon such discipline will not only shut the door on the kind of maturity and self-awareness necessary to precipitate the leap into the arms of the sanctifying Spirit, as it were; it will also lead to the rescinding of conversion, the surcease of regeneration.[133]

---

128. Cf. *Homily* XIX.1-3. This highly significant passage begins thus: "He who yearns to come to the Lord, to be found worthy of life eternal, to become Christ's lodging, to be filled with the Holy Spirit, in order to be able to bear the fruits of the Spirit and fulfil Christ's commandments purely and without fault, must begin by unwaveringly believing the Lord, surrendering himself altogether to the Lord's commands, renouncing the world totally—these things so that his entire intellective process be occupied about nothing mundane." After going into detail concerning such discipline, Macarius then declares, "Then the Lord, seeing such resolve and diligence—how [this seeker] obliges himself to remembrance of the Lord, ever compelling his heart, whether it will or no, to what is good, to humility, meekness, and charity, how he steers it by coercion to the best of his ability—demonstrates mercy upon him. He delivers him from his enemies and from indwelling sin, filling him with the Holy Spirit. So, afterward, he does all of the Lord's commandments with authenticity, without compulsion or drudgery. Or, rather, the Lord does his own commandments in him, and then the man bears purely the fruits of the Spirit."

129. E.g., *Homily* X, passim; *Homily* XI.14; *Homily* XX, passim; and esp. *Homily* XXV.

130. E.g., *Homily* IV.26; *Homily* XX.8. In both of these passages, but especially in the first, the argument runs: "If God has done such a marvelous work in rescuing us from the grasp of unrighteousness in our conversion, how much more firmly may we believe him to deliver us from the power of sin completely, in this life." The biblical reference in both is to Luke 11:13: "If you, then, bad as you are, know how to give your children what is good for them, how much more will the heavenly Father give the Holy Spirit to those who ask him!" (NEB).

131. *Homily* XIX.7-8.

132. Cf. n. 27. Macarius continually warns against spiritual pride, so that both those on the road to entire sanctification and those having received it must be constantly aware of their feelings. Humility is to be the hallmark of both sorts. Cf. *Homily* XXVI.11-26 and *Homily* XXVII.5-7.

133. E.g., *Homily* XIX.6; *Homily* XXVI.25.

Entire sanctification is an act of divine grace, and while it has an ethical dimension, especially at the point of a fundamental transformation of motives from egocentrism to pure love, it is not essentially ethical but religious. It is not basically behavioral but relational, as touching communion with both God and humankind.[134] In this way, Macarius preserves the twofold nature of entire sanctification, that is, its character as both an act and a process admitting of growth. Were it solely ethical or behavioral, one could reach an absolute perfection at certain points (for example, abstention from fornication) but perhaps never reach it at others (such as in almsgiving). But, according to Macarius, it is religious. That is, it has to do with love toward God and neighbor. And while such love can and will grow as the relationships take on depth, and while ethical or behavioral expression of it will continually expand and improve, it is necessary to see (so Macarius) that the very basis for growth and improvement must be a *pure* heart, not a divided one; *perfect love,* not double-mindedness.

Macarius is quite sensitive to what has come to be noted as the difference between purity and maturity. Here, two human gifts, both of them suffering the consequences of the fall of Adam, play critical roles: human nature (that is, those capacities and limitations with which we were born and which have been shaped by our environments) and the freedom of the human will.

The possibilities of grace for humankind are of the highest order and are so because originally humankind was created by God himself for divine fellowship.

> Beloved, do not take lightly the spiritual quality of the soul. The immortal soul is a precious vessel. Consider the magnificence of the heavens and of the earth! Yet God was not content with them, but only with you. Consider your dignity, your nobility—that the Lord himself, in person, not just angels, came to your aid. You, lost, he came to recall. You, wounded, he came to restore to you the original configuration of the pure Adam. You see, master was man, from the sky above to things beneath. He was capable of discerning his real feelings. He had no interchange with devils. He was pure from sin. He was the very image and likeness of God. But by the transgression he was lost. He was wounded. To death was he brought. Satan has darkened his mind. On the one hand, this is true. But on the other, he lives, he discerns. And he has a will.

---

134. Cf., for instance, *Homily* XVII.15. Most of this homily is dedicated to this theme. Also see *Homily* XXVI.21.

> Question. When the Holy Spirit comes, isn't natural desire rooted out with the sinful nature?
>
> I have earlier said that sin is rooted out and one recovers the original configuration of pure Adam. Humankind, however, thanks to the Spirit's power and to spiritual regeneration, not only measures up to the first Adam, but is made greater than he. Man is deified (*Homily* XXVI.1).

Here is an astounding claim! So Macarius raises the possibility that if this is true, perhaps it is because Satan is somehow being limited. And he answers that this is indeed the case. Satan is not omnipotent. God constrains him and forces him to direct even his power so that it may strengthen, not overthrow, the Christian.[135]

Still, the claims presented by Macarius are stupendous, even if we may rest assured that Satan's power is limited. What of the limitations of being human? Do they not hold us back from being made "greater than Adam," from being "deified"?

Not at all. In the *first* place, the "limitations" of being human allow the Christian's witness to refer directly to the grace of God. Any good that comes of that Christian will have to be seen as being of God, coming as it does from the context of obvious weaknesses.

Second, God's purpose is not to coerce people to follow Him, but to woo them to follow freely, in love. So rather than produce miracles that compel, He works through humanity and His miracles allow room for either faith or unbelief.

Third (and here Macarius works from the LXX translation of Job 1:11 and 2:5, which [perhaps ironically] says "bless" where our versions say "curse"), it is precisely because the Christian recognizes his vulnerability that he relies totally on God. Satan duped Adam because the one thing Adam did not know by experience was his own vulnerability. Now Satan misjudges, thinking that by increasing the level or number of temptations he will bring the Christian down. But the Christian sees the strategy only in terms of the need to be more acutely aware of his weakness and more open to the delivering grace of God.

Fourth, the "limitation" of human nature finally proves to be an embarrassment to Satan, for Satan "desires" us and tries his worst and is still bested even by the Christian with severest limitations. "Satan is ashamed and rueful." He got to do just what he desired, by divine permission, and still he failed.[136]

---

135. *Homily* XXVI.3-4.

136. *Homily* XXVI.5-8. Also cf. *Homily* XXVII.8.

Here, then, is a victory that more than matches the defeat in Eden. And it is gained by learning the mastery of dependence, the "advantage," as it were, of human limitations.[137] Purity is granted at the point of recognizing and accepting total dependence, human limitation.[138] Maturity develops as one learns to express the fruits of the Spirit within that dependence.[139]

Basic to Macarius' position is a confidence in the freedom of the human will. One does not accept the idea of total dependence, especially spiritual dependence, because one is somehow forced into it. The acceptance of human limitation in spiritual understanding is not coerced. We are at no point forced to obey God. This holds true whether we stand inside the Kingdom or outside.[140] God has granted us "the power of will either to agree with the Spirit or to grieve him" (*Homily* XXVII.13). It is precisely this freedom that makes sinfulness so tragic, temptation so fierce, and righteousness so glorious.[141]

While the entirely sanctified Christian will express that sanctification ethically and behaviorally, according to Macarius, the basic goal will not be ethical or behavioral perfection. Christlikeness,[142] or, as Macarius sometimes puts it, likeness to the Spirit or the image of the Spirit,[143] that is the only aim of the authentic Christian.

We have taken some extra space in the discussion of "Macarius" for several reasons. First, this collection of sermons marks a clear break from the developing tendency to think of sanctification principally in sacramental and churchly terms rather than in experiential and personal terms. In the longer run of the Middle Ages, especially in the Western branch of Christianity, but in the Eastern as well, the sacramental and churchly emphasis would prevail. But Macarius' position, as we shall see, was not completely obscured. In fact, it resurfaced in full vigor in Pietism and within

---

137. *Homily* XXVI.14-17.

138. *Homily* XXVI.18-20. Also cf. *Homily* XXVII.3-4.

139. *Homily* XXVI.21-26. Also cf. *Homily* XXVII.5-7.

140. Cf. *Homily* XXVII.9-12. Also cf. *Homily* XV.16, 36, 40.

141. *Homily* XXVII.18-23. Also cf. *Homily* XV.35-38.

142. E.g., *Homily* XV.38; *Homily* XXVI.26 (the Mason translation does not make sufficiently clear what is clearly intended by the text, that Macarius is not accusing his hearers of spiritual slothfulness but exhorting them to Christlikeness); *Homily* XXX.4-5.

143. E.g., *Homily* XXX.3; *Homily* XLVI.5.

Anglicanism, and those two streams conjoined with new force in the life and thought of John Wesley, whom we shall later study.

We must delay getting to the 18th century for some time, however, for the intervening doctrinal history must be outlined in order for us to understand that century so critical for our own theological development.

Joining Macarius, then, as an influence in the formation of Wesley's understanding of entire sanctification are several other persons and perspectives even from Macarius' fourth century. One of these is Gregory of Nyssa.

B. Gregory of Nyssa: Entire Sanctification in the Hellenistic Mode

Gregory of Nyssa (c. 330-94),[144] roughly a contemporary of "Macarius the Egyptian" and an older contemporary of Augustine of Hippo, is considered one of the principal teachers of the Church by Eastern Orthodox believers even today. Deeply educated in the great classical tradition of Greece and for a time perhaps even committed to it in revolt against the rusticity and feisty dogmatism of all too many Christians, Gregory brought to the faith a combination of intellect and heart that it had not seen since Origen. Along with his brother, Basil, and their mutual friend, Gregory of Nazianzus, the three are known as the Cappadocian Fathers. Cappadocia is in what is now called Turkey.

Our interest in Gregory is in his contribution to the history of the doctrine of entire sanctification. To be sure, in Gregory's thought this doctrine is a subdivision of the doctrine of perfection.

---

144. There is no extended biography of Gregory in English. The best biography available is E. Moutsoulas, *Gregori ho Nysses* (Athens, 1970). Cf., however, Jean Daniélou, "Le mariage de S. Grégoire de Nyssa et la chronologie de sa vie," *Revue des Études augustiniennes* (1958), 71-78; "S. Grégoire de Nyssa à travers les lettres de s. Basile et de s. Grégoire de Nazianzen," *Vigiliae Christianae* (1965), 31-41. T. A. Goggin, *The Times of St. Gregory of Nyssa as Reflected in His Letters and the "Contra Eunomium"* (Washington, D.C.: Catholic University of America, 1947), does give some sense of the historical context for Gregory's life and work.

The most commonly available edition of Gregory of Nyssa's works is MPG, XLIV-XLVI. A much better critical edition is W. Jaeger and H. Langerbeck, *Gregorii Nysseni Opera,* vol. i ff. (Leiden: E. J. Brill, 1921 ff. Still in process.). Some works have been edited and printed separately, most notably, for our purposes, Jean Daniélou ed., *Vie de Moise,* is in *Sources chrétiennes* (Paris, 1955) and W. Jaeger, J. P. Cavarnos, V. Woods Callahan, eds., *Gregorii Nysseni Opera,* vol. viii.1 *(Opera ascetica)* (Leiden: E. J. Brill, 1952), esp. the tract "De perfectione."

But we shall not here retrace the ground of the wider doctrine except where it bears directly on the narrower issue at hand.[145]

What we shall find in Gregory is a much more theologically and philosophically careful and complex statement of what we have already seen in "Macarius." And because it was so much more careful and complex, it has had wider currency and greater effect than Macarius'.

At the outset of our discussion of Gregory's understanding of entire sanctification, let's look at his definition of Christian perfection.

> My dear friend, so you have earnestly asked me to write out an exposition of the life of perfection for you! And your clear purpose is that if you should find what you seek in my presentation, you will apply the grace revealed by my words to your own life.
>
> Well, in both of these matters, I see difficulty, for either to delineate perfection or to manifest it in my own life is, I feel, beyond my capabilities. And I doubt that I am alone in this. Many great men would confess the impossibility of attaining such a goal—even men superior in virtue. Yet, I shall write down more clearly what I mean by perfection, for I do not wish to leave the impression of having fear where there is none—as the Psalmist says.
>
> First, then, we recall that when we speak of the perfection of things which can be measured, things our senses know, "perfection" always implies definite limits. An example: When we speak of extension, whether that extension be continuous or discrete, we are speaking of limits. Every measurement of quantity presupposes its own limits. For example, when you think about the cubit or the number ten, you see that they have a beginning and an end—and that is what is meant by their "perfection."[146]
>
> Now, when we think about virtue, we know from the Apostle that "perfection" means perfection without limits. As

145. For specific studies in Gregory's understanding of perfection, see D. L. Balas, *Metousia Theou: Man's Participation in God's Perfection According to St. Gregory of Nyssa* (Rome, 1966); R. Heine, *Perfection in the Virtuous Life: A Study in the Relationship Between Edification and Polemical Theology in Gregory of Nyssa's "De Vita Moysis"* (Cambridge, 1975); W. Jaeger, et al., "De perfectione" in *Gregorii Nysseni Opera,* vii.1 *(Opera ascetica)* (Leiden: E. J. Brill, 1952). An English translation of the latter tract is in Virginia Callahan (trans. and ed.) *St. Gregory of Nyssa: Ascetical Works,* vol. 58: "Fathers of the Christian Church" (Washington: Catholic University of America, 1966).

146. "Extension" refers to something's occupying space. The "extension" of a parked car would be discrete. The extension of a moving car would be continuous (in common sense terms, at least). Both have definite limits.

> the holy Apostle saw it, one who is great and deep in spirit constantly reaches ahead to the future in following the path of virtue. He felt that stopping in his course was dangerous. And this was so because every good is by nature unlimited. It is limited only when its contrary is present, in the way that life has its limit at death and light at darkness. So, only where its opposite sets in does total goodness cease. Thus, just as death begins where life ends, one enters the path of evil by stopping on the path of virtue.
>
> Now you can see that I was not in error when I said it was impossible to define perfection, for I have shown that virtue simply cannot be contained within boundaries.
>
> Now let me explain why it is impossible for those who pursue virtue ever to reach perfection. The ruling and highest Good is the divine nature itself. It is goodness itself. Whatever perfection can be conceived of a nature like that we assign to Him—we call Him that, we say He *is* that.
>
> We have already shown that vice is the only limiter to virtue. Now, the divine nature excludes anything contrary to itself. So it follows that the divine nature (which is Good itself) is seen to be without boundary, without limit.
>
> Because God is infinite virtue, the soul pursuing virtue actually participates in God himself. Since the desire of those who have come to know the highest good is to share in it completely—share in this limitless good—their desire must extend as far as the goodness extends. So, their desire and the goodness they desire are limitless. That is why it is utterly impossible to attain perfection. As I've said, the only "limitation" to virtue is that it has no limits. How can one reach a boundary that doesn't exist?
>
> Nonetheless, though my argument has shown that we cannot reach our goal, we must not, no matter what, neglect the divine command: "Be perfect as your Father in heaven is perfect." For while we may not be able to attain completely the sovereign and ultimate good, it is still utterly desirable at least to share in it—as the wise do.
>
> So, we bend every effort to come as close as we can to the perfection possible for us, to possess as much of it as we can, to avoid falling utterly short. After all, it may be that human perfection lies precisely in this—constant growth in the good.[147]

In speaking of perfection as a human possibility, Gregory has hinted that perhaps it is precisely the fact that we can grow, and grow, and grow some more in grace that constitutes our perfection.

---

147. *De vita Moysis* (Daniélou, ed., i.3-10; MPG, XLIV.300-01). The translation is the present author's own, following Daniélou's edition.

That is, we are limitless, and thus perfect, at the point of the possibility of spiritual growth.

Gregory deals with this very thing in his work *On Christian Perfection,*[148] possibly in response to a critique from those influenced by the philosophic tradition of Plato. The critique claimed that growth implies change ("mutability," they called it), and mutability implies imperfection, at least imperfection in what we're changing from. If we were perfect, said they, we would need no change, nor desire change. Some even said we would be incapable of change if we were perfect.

The fact that we are indeed mutable, that we do indeed change, is proof that we are not perfect. As they saw it, only God is changeless, so only God is perfect. Of course, their God had nothing to do with human beings, at least not directly, for to enter into and leave and modify relationships with humans would require change and thus imperfection. But God is, by definition, perfect.

What Gregory saw was the fact that for Christianity the issue was not a metaphysical one—not something about the nature of God. And while he certainly did use philosophical language in resolving it, he treated it as a spiritual issue.

Gregory refounded the notions of "good" and "virtue" in a personal God who relates himself to persons and made goodness and virtue precisely what He *is* rather than retaining them as abstract qualities that God *has.* He was thus able to see in our mutability a good rather than an evil. Goodness and virtue have no boundaries, no limits in themselves. God has no limits. So God *is* goodness and virtue. God is perfect, so goodness and virtue are perfect. Insofar as the Christian is in God, he is in goodness and virtue without limit; he is in perfection. Moreover, the Christian is maturing and growing in goodness and virtue, maturing and growing *without limit* in goodness and virtue (for they are limitless by nature). This limitless possibility, then, is the Christian's perfection.

> What my essay has shown, then, is that what seems so frightening—the mutability of our nature—can in fact be a wing for our flight toward even higher matters. In fact, were we not responsive to change for the better, it would be a hardship.

---

148. *De perfectione* or *De perfecta Christiani forma,* in W. Jaeger, J. P. Cavarnos, V. Woods Callahan, eds., *Gregorii Nysseni Opera,* viii.1 *(Opera ascetica)* (Leiden, 1952), 143-214.

> So, we should not be distraught when we think about this proclivity that is in our very nature [i.e., the tendency to change]. Rather, let us change in such a way that we continually develop in the direction of that which is better, as those being "transformed from glory to glory." Let us always be improving, ever becoming more perfect through daily maturation, but never coming to any boundary to perfection. For such perfection lies in our never halting our growth in good, never circumscribing our perfection by boundaries.[149]

Gregory had also to counteract another pagan idea (one that many Christians had accepted). That is the notion that our mutability arises out of our dissatisfaction with ourselves, others, and things as they are. Gregory readily admits that this is indeed the source of much of the change we know. In fact, it is of the very essence of being a created being and not the Creator.[150] But Gregory insisted that this kind of change is really cyclic, that it comes round and round again; the dissatisfaction being momentarily assuaged, sooner or later it rises again and the process of seeking to remedy it is renewed.[151] So it is that this apparent process of change is in reality lack of change. Motion it is; change it is not, for the individual finds himself often back at "Go."

There is another sort of mutability, however, that arises out of the deepest sort of satisfaction with the spiritual life as it is. "In fact, the choicest characteristic of our changeableness is the possibility for growth in good. This ability to improve increasingly transforms the soul . . . into the divine likeness."[152]

This is the change "from glory to glory" spoken of by the apostle Paul. We move from perfection to perfection, but any ultimate perfection in the sense of a static condition is impossible, even undesirable, precisely because this perfection is perfection in goodness and virtue. And these, by definition, have no boundaries, so their limits are unreachable. Yet the Christian is deeply satisfied at every stage of the way, for it is God himself, pure and perfect

---

149. This argument is developed most clearly in *De perfectione*, MPG, XLVI.285.

150. *The Great Catechetical Discourse* 21 (MPG, XLV.57) (this work bears the Latin title *Oratio catechetica magna*); *De vita Moysis* (Daniélou, ed.), ii.2-3 (MPG, XLIV.328), et al.

151. E.g., *De vita Moysis* (Daniélou, ed.), ii.60-61 (MPG, XLIV.344).

152. *De perfectione* (W. Jaeger, et al., eds., 213.14-214.6; cf. MPG, XLVI.285).

good and virtue, in whom he lives and moves and has his being.[153] "Indeed, the Only-Begotten, by Whom all things were made, is himself the 'place' for the runner; by his own declaration, he is the very 'Way' and the 'Rock' for the well-founded, the 'Abode' for those taking their rest."[154]

Typical of early Christianity, Gregory of Nyssa sees this process of increasing perfection beginning at baptism[155] and being sustained by the Eucharist.[156] His baptismal imagery is rich and among the figures developed is baptism as the waters of the mystically interpreted Jordan, which flow back to heaven and to Christ, its source, carrying the baptized in its current.[157] Baptism applies to the individual what Christ's death and resurrection did for all—His death purified human nature; His resurrection restored humanity.[158] And, again, we see Gregory's consistent emphasis on the Christian life as being both dynamic and perfect (that is, without limit as to growth in love) at any given moment.

> The true meaning of seeing God is this—never to have the desire satisfied. But fastening our gaze on that which helps us to see, we must always keep alive the yearning to see more and more. So it is that no limit can be set to our progress toward God. In the first place, no limit can be placed upon the beautiful. In the second place, there is no sense of satisfaction that can halt our desire for the beautiful.[159]

Given such an idea of progress and satisfaction yet dissatisfaction, who may enter onto this path and how? Is this path begun with baptism, and if so, in what sense?

For Gregory, each stage is a "glory," each a "perfection," and

---

153. E.g., *Commentary on the Canticle of Canticles,* sermon 5 (MPG, XLIV.873-76); *On the Soul and Resurrection (Dialogus de anima et resurrectione)* (MPG, XLVI.105).

154. The basic reflection here is on Exod. 33:20-23. *De vita Moysis* (Daniélou, ed.), ii.249 (MPG, XLIV.408).

155. Gregory wrote two sermons on baptism, both of them bearing this basic message. Cf. *On the Baptism of Christ* (MPG, XLVI.577-600); and *Against Those Who Put Off Baptism* (MPG, XLVI.416-32).

156. E.g., *Commentary on the Canticle of Canticles,* sermon 10 (MPG, XLIV. 989-92). We do not propose here to review Gregory's rich eucharistic theology, but it is helpful to note that it seems to reflect three major themes: Eucharist as sacrifice, as the fulfillment of the eschatological meal prophesied in the Old Testament, and as the remedy for mortality.

157. Cf. *Against Those Who Put Off Baptism* (MPG, XLVI.420-21).

158. *Great Catechetical Discourse* 35 (MPG, XLV.89).

159. *De vita Moysis* (Daniélou, ed.), ii.219-39; (cf. MPG, XLVI.397-405).

each a new beginning.[160] And sin is, in fact, a refusal to develop, to follow the path of penetrating even deeper into our own souls where God is to be found. Becoming attached to some past stage, though it was in its own sense perfect, is spiritually lethal.[161]

We can say, then, that for Gregory perfection both begins and is accomplished at baptism, and it is constantly being accomplished and begun again in this life. It may cease in one of two ways: (1) we may die and go to be with the Lord, where there continues to be growth in perfection but of a somewhat different sort from that experienced here;[162] or (2) we may refuse the lure of new beginnings, new resurrections, new knowledge of ourselves and of the divine Goodness, allowing this world—even the very best of its ways—to capture our affection.

"Know thyself," Gregory cautions. But here he does not make Socrates' point, anticipating that we can come to full self-knowledge in some positive sense. Rather, true self-knowledge is to come at last to know that at our very center is not ourselves but God; not the capacity to make this world our "oyster," as it were, but the capacity to express our true grandeur—the fact that we are God's image and that He pervades our whole being.[163]

Gregory's doctrine of entire sanctification holds that at every stage in the Christian life, the believer is wholly purified from sin provided that believer yearns for and is willing to enter upon further growth.[164] And, in this sense, while the believer is indeed always pure, so is he always in need of forgiveness and the exercise of a penitent spirit.[165] But we must not see the movement from stage to stage as a solely human endeavor. Sanctification is not, for Gregory, a matter of self-purification. Not even the yearnings to

---

160. E.g., *Comm. on Cant.*, sermon 9 (MPG, XLIV.940-41); *Adv. Eunom.* 2 (MPG, XLV.940-41); *Comm. on Cant.*, sermon 6 (MPG, XLIV.885-88).

161. E.g., *Comm. on Cant.*, sermon 5 (MPG, XLIV.865-81), esp. 868-72: "'But it is not enough for you to arise from sin,' he says. 'You must also move ahead in goodness and *finish the course* of perfection.'"

162. *Comm. on Cant.*, sermon 8 (MPG, XLIV.940-41): "Thus he [Paul] instructs us, it seems to me, that the graces we receive at every point in our continual participation in the blessed nature of Good are exceedingly great. But beyond our immediate reach lies an infinite path. This is the continuing experience of those who genuinely share in the divine Goodness. And they will forever enjoy an ever greater participation in grace throughout eternity."

163. *Comm. on Cant.*, sermon 2 (MPG, XLIV.804-08).

164. *Comm. on Cant.*, sermon 12 (MPG, XLIV.1029-37).

165. *Comm. on Cant.*, sermon 12 (MPG, XLIV.1016-24).

move onward toward God may be said to be our own in the final analysis.

Sanctification is totally dependent, from beginning to end (or better: from old beginning to new beginning), on the gracious activity of God in Christ.[166] Gregory reversed a trend in Christian thought that was concerned to show all change as bad and really quite contrary to the nature of God. He was convinced that God is the author of change and that it can be absolutely good.[167]

Gregory held this quite high view of the nature of the Christian's spirituality in the face of several increasingly potent tendencies. By the middle third of the fourth century, a strong current was ready to deny any authentic entire sanctification to the believer except as Christ's holiness might be imputed to that believer. Here, the sacraments of the Church were seen as the principal vehicles of imputation. Gregory holds out for an authentic sanctification of the believer in which the believer is *made* righteous, not merely *declared* righteous.

But another opinion currently held was that while growth in grace was preferable to spiritual stagnation, the nature of salvation (especially as it was mediated through the sacraments) was such that it was not necessary. Gregory sees stagnation and the refusal to grow in grace as sinful. Yet another developing opinion declared that there were degrees of sanctity, that some Christians were indeed holier than others. Gregory agrees that some Christians may be more enlightened than others or more mature than others, but all true Christians are perfect. That is to say, perfection is to be measured by no standard but the loving yearning to grow in grace.

One other opinion threw the weight of achieving holiness on the work of the believer, thus putting the definition of holiness in terms of the worthiness of the believer to be saved. Gregory's definition of holiness is in terms of the recognition of the paradox of attainment and new beginning, all as a consequence of one's already being a recipient of the gift of salvation—the original perfection.

---

166. E.g., *Comm. on Cant.,* sermon 13 (MPG, XLIV.1045-48). While Gregory continually exhorts the reader to press onward (better: inward), he continually sets this in the context of God's having descended to us—in Christ and in the Spirit.

167. *On Perfection* (MPG, XLVI.285); *Comm. in Psalm* 3 (MPG, XLIV.460); ibid., 4 (MPG, XLIV.500); *De vita Moysis* (Daniélou, ed.), ii.243-44 (MPG, XLIV.407); *Great Catechetical Discourse* 21 (MPG, XLV.57-60).

So it is that Gregory responds with remarkable breadth to a number of trends that arose out of the intense pressures put upon the Church in the fourth century, chief of which was the tendency to give up, to surrender, the ever and again realized idealism of the holy life. The "real world" the Church faced in that period had scant patience for such idealism. It saw its Golden Age as being in the past, as lost forever. And to a degree of which it should have been ashamed, much of the Church agreed, and saw itself in the same terms.

Macarius, and the early monastic enterprise generally, agreed with this gloomy analysis and left the world, if not the Church, to pray for its restoration, or for the Second Coming, or for forgiveness. Gregory (among others) simply refused to accept analysis or description as prognosis. He could not believe that the great days of the Church, nor of the individual believer, lay behind. He was no Pollyanna, but his works ring with the optimism of grace.

C. Augustine of Hippo: Entire Sanctification in the Latin Mode

For an example of a doctrine of entire sanctification forged in the less hopeful mode of which we wrote earlier, we turn to the West and to Augustine of Hippo in particular.[168] This moves us on over into the first third of the fifth century, which was even grayer in outlook than the fourth.

Emperor Theodosius made Christianity the official religion of the Empire in 391, but paganism, spent as it was, did not simply roll over and die. In fact, the sheer decency of some of the pagan aristocracy stood in sharp contrast to the contentiousness of all too many Christian bishops. For example, it was a group of bishops who saw to the condemnation (and execution by the State in 385) of Priscillian, bishop of Abula (Avila), whose only real "heresy" was rigid disciplinary demands.

---

168. Augustine does not lack excellent studies of his life and work. Among the very best is Gustav Bardy, *Saint Augustine: L'homme et l'ouvre* (7th ed.; Paris, 1954). A solid English biography is Peter Brown, *Augustine of Hippo: A Biography* (Berkeley, Calif.: University of California, 1967). Nearly indispensable to the English reading student of Augustine's thought is Roy Battenhouse (ed.), *A Companion to the Study of St. Augustine* (New York: Oxford University Press, 1955). For bibliography, see Altaner and Stuiber, *Patrologie* 412-49, 636-40. His works may be found in adequate and better translation in NPNF, LCC, FC, etc. Also see Eugène Portalié, trans. by R. J. Bastian, *A Guide to the Thought of Saint Augustine* (Chicago: University of Chicago Press, 1960).

But in the eyes of the government, even more serious than paganism's dying kicks and Christian fractiousness was the increasing power of the Germanic tribes to the West. By 410, they held the Iberian Peninsula and Gaul and had even sent a raiding party to sack Rome itself. As Augustine lay dying in Hippo, North Africa, in 430, the Vandals were at the very gates of that town.

Within another half-century, the government in Constantinople faced reality in the West and named Theodoric, the Ostrogothic king, imperial agent there. To be sure, most of the Germanic folk wanted only to inherit the Empire, not to destroy it. But they could not inherit without change, and change was already apparent to Augustine in his adult years.

The religious context, too, was unsettled. Christianity boiled with controversy in the West. Priscillian's was one case. Earlier, scores of lives were lost in riots in Rome surrounding the election of Damasus as pope (366). Then came Pelagianism atop the already troubled scene created by controversy with the Manichaeans and the Donatists.

In such a confused and chaotic situation, the Pelagians seemed to many to preach utter nonsense, for they told the people, who saw themselves as victims of ineluctable forces, that human beings have morally free wills and therefore moral responsibility. And as for the rather popular talk about original sin as a necessary inheritance from Adam and the unremediable source of all moral foulness, the Pelagians said this was only a proclivity to imitate and adopt the sins and bad habits of our forefathers. Salvation, said certain Pelagians, is a matter of doing good, for which we need divine aid; and it is a matter of breaking the hold of that imitative, adoptive behavior.[169]

The Manichaeans were dualists, believing that two kingdoms are the source of all that is and that these kingdoms strive most

---

169. On Pelagianism see T. Bohlin, *Die Theologie des Pelagius und ihre Genesis* (Uppsala/Wiesbaden, 1957); G. Bonner, *Augustine and Modern Research on Pelagianism* (Villanova, Pa.: Villanova University Press, 1972); R. F. Evans, *Pelagius: Inquiries and Reappraisals* (New York: Seabury, 1968); J. Ferguson, *Pelagius: A Historical and Theological Study* (Cambridge: W. Heffer, 1957); G. de Plinval, *Pélage: ses écrits, sa vie et sa réforme* (Lausanne, 1943); G. de Plinval, *Essai sur le style et la langue de Pélage* (Freiburg, Switz., 1947); S. Prete, *Pelagio e il Pelagianesimo* (Brescia, 1961). The works of Pelagius are in *MPL Supplementum,* 1:1101-1704. The best edition of the works is by A. Souter, *Pelagius' Expositions of 13 Epistles of St. Paul* ("Texts and Studies," 9, 2) (London: Oxford University Press, 1922-26). R. F. Evans has translated some letters into English in *Four Letters of Pelagius* (New York: Seabury, 1968).

obviously (with the most at stake) in man. The human soul comes from the Kingdom of Light, of true spirit. The human body has the soul imprisoned and is of the Kingdom of Darkness, as is all that is material. Salvation is a matter of freeing the soul from the prison house of the body; of making life truly, wholly, and only spiritual.[170] The Manichaeans usually made no claim to being Christian, only an alternative to Christianity.

The Donatists were Christian rigorists and moralists, mostly North African. They had no beliefs that differed from those of the Church catholic but had separated themselves from it in the early 300s over the questions of how and when to readmit to the Church persons who had yielded to persecution, and whether sacraments celebrated by clergy who had once lapsed were valid.[171]

These three positions, then, posed a grave threat to authentic Christianity as Augustine understood it—*Pelagianism* to the Christian understanding of salvation, *Manichaeism* to its understanding of creation and man, and *Donatism* to its understanding of the Church with her hierarchy and sacraments. There were other tides to be stemmed as well, but these were the principal ones, and Augustine felt obligated to respond to them all, not with the cool calculation of the broker of abstractions but as the shepherd of a Christian flock threatened by wolves.

These three contexts must be kept in mind in any study of Augustine's thought: (1) a crumbling social structure; (2) a doctrinally and organizationally beleaguered church; and (3) a deep sense of personal responsibility. Augustine's thought can be very subtle, very complex, very profound, but it is seldom abstract. Real situations are pressing his intellect. His model is the scholar-bishop-man-of-affairs Ambrose. With this example in mind and

---

170. There is as yet no extensive, source-based study of Manichaeism in English. There are excellent studies in French and German: F. Decret, *Aspects du Manichéisme dans l'Afrique Romaine* (Paris, 1970); H. C. Peuch, *Le Manichéisme, son fondateur, su doctrine* (2nd ed.; Paris, 1967); G. Widengren (ed.), *Der Manichaismus* (Darmstadt, 1977). The texts have been collected in an edition by A. Adam, *Texte zum Manichaismus,* vol. 178 of "Kleine Texte für Vorlesungen und Übungen" (2nd ed.; Berlin, 1969).

171. On the Donatists, see W. H. C. Frend, *The Donatist Church: A Movement of Protest in Roman North Africa* (2nd ed.; Oxford: Clarendon Press, 1971); E. Tengstrom, *Donatisten und Katholiken: soziale, wirtschaftliche und politische Aspekte einer nordafrickanischen kirchenspaltung,* vol. 18: "Studia Graeca et Latina Gothoburgensia" (Stockholm, 1964).

on this anvil he forged his understanding of Christian perfection with its concomitant idea of sanctification.

Like Gregory of Nyssa, Augustine is certain that we meet God most truly and in the most revolutionary fashion within ourselves. He is not met, however, as a God who is totally encompassed by our own spirit. He is both immanent and transcendent. "You were more inward to me than my most inward part, and higher than my highest" (*Confessions* iii.11).[172]

Augustine attempts to describe in several passages just what is the nature of that "You" whom he discovers deep within and yet transcending all. He does so with a mixture of philosophical and religious language as his "method" is also a mixture.

> Now, having been advised by them [the "books of the Platonists"] to return into myself, I went into my very inmost self with you as my Guide. I went in, and with the eye of my soul, I saw above that same eye, above my mind, the Unchangeable Light (*Conf.* vii.16).
>
> Step by step I was led upward, from bodies to the soul which uses the bodily senses to perceive. From thence I was led to the soul's inward faculty, to which the bodily senses report external things. (This is the limit of the intelligence of animals.) Then was I led on to the reasoning faculty, which assesses the knowledge received by the bodily senses. But then this faculty too was transformed and lifted itself up to its own self-understanding (intelligence) and withdrew its thinking from experience, abstracting itself from the contradictory garble of sense images so that it might discover the nature of the light that bathed it when it protested that the unchangeable is doubtless preferrable to the changeable. Now it knew that Unchangeable. And thus with the flash of one trembling glance it arrived at That Which Is. At last, I there saw your "invisible things understood by the things that are made," but I could not gaze for long. My weakness retaliated. I was relegated to ordinary experience and bear with me but a loving memory and a longing for what I had perceived by odor, as it were, but was yet able to feed upon (*Conf.* vii.23).

This experience is perhaps from Augustine's preconversion period. At least it falls thus in the order of the *Confessions.* But as the now Christian Augustine recounts it in his "spiritual auto-

---

172. The Confessions were written between A.D. 397 and 401. They therefore show nothing of the effects of the Pelagian controversy on Augustine's thought. This is important to remember, for certain passages in the *Confessions* seem almost to contradict Augustine's later, more pessimistic view of what grace can do in an individual's life.

biography," it is obvious that he still approves it and holds it to be something of a norm for the Christian life as well.[173] How, then, does he bridge the gap between pagan philosophical ecstasy and Christian spiritual-nuptial union? And, what relationship does Augustine see between holiness, perfection, and sanctification? In a way, these are modern questions, not Augustine's. So we must go back and lay the foundation in a way that allows Augustine to respond on his own terms.

To understand Augustine, and our own heritage, on these matters, let's begin by considering Augustine's understanding of who the human being is in a "natural" state, that is, who one is apart from the work of grace.[174]

Prior to the time of Augustine, the Church's thinkers had confronted at every turn pagan understandings of human nature and the world. These placed so much power in the hands of fate or chance, the stars or the gods, nature or some vaguely defined cosmic forces, that human moral responsibility was barely conceivable.[175] Or, where human nature was taken seriously, it was primarily a matter of advising that the truly moral person adjusts to whatever fate, chance, stars, gods, nature, or cosmic forces "decreed."[176] Even among Christians, very much aware of their appar-

---

173. Passages like it abound in Augustine's writing. E.g., *Conf.*, ix.23-25; *Enarrationes in Psalmos xli.* The best critical text of the *Enarrationes* is in vols. 38-40 of the *Corpus Christianorum* (E. Dekkers, J. Fraipont, eds.) (Tournhout, 1956). The best English translation is by S. Hegbin and F. Corrigan (eds. and trans.), *St. Augustine on the Psalms,* 2 vols. (Westminster, Md.: Newman Press, 1960-61). A complete edition was done by an anonymous translator and J. Tweed, *Expositions on the Book of Psalms* by S. Augustine, Bishop of Hippo in "A Library of Fathers of the Holy Catholic Church," 6 vols. (Oxford: John Henry Parker, 1847-57).

174. For excellent secondary source discussions of this matter, cf. Erich Dinkler, *Die Anthropologie Augustins* (Stuttgart, 1934); Heinrich Karpp, *Probleme altchristlicher Anthropologie: Biblische Anthropologie und philosophische Psychologie bei den kirchenvatern des dritten Jahrhunderts* (Gutersloh, 1950); Jaroslav Pelikan, *The Christian Tradition,* vol. 1: "The Emergence of the Catholic Tradition (100-600)" (Chicago: University of Chicago Press, 1971), 278-331; Otto Scheel, *Die Anshauung Augustins über Christi Person und sein Werk* (Tübingen, 1901); Norman P. Williams, *The Ideas of the Fall and of Original Sin, a Historical and Critical Study* (London: Longmans Green, 1927).

175. For an excellent, source-based discussion of this matter, cf. Charles Norris Cochrane, *Christianity and Classical Culture: A Study of Thought and Action from Augustus to Augustine* (London and New York: Oxford University Press, 1944).

176. This was generally the position of both the Stoics and the Epicureans. For a Stoic exposition of the notion, cf. Marcus Aurelius Antoninus, *Meditations.* (Perhaps the most helpful and readily available edition with translation is that of C. R. Haines in the "Loeb Classical Library" [Cambridge, Mass.: Harvard University,

ent helplessness in the face of the unchangeable course of history, some fell to the temptation to believe thus. More often, the Christian was tempted to believe in both historical inevitability and the necessity for morality.[177]

Generally, Christian thinkers urged the community to be morally responsible on the basis of a concept (later a doctrine) of free will.[178] But it is very important here to note the direction of the development of this doctrine. There was no argument from free will to moral responsibility; rather it ran from moral responsibility to free will. The Scriptures commanded certain existential expressions of moral responsibility, therefore (Christians reasoned) we must be created with a free will. We do have the freedom to sin or not to sin. Otherwise, commandments either to do good or to refrain from evil would be fatuous.

But why do human beings use that freedom to sin? Why is it so seldom used in the unadulterated doing of good? Here was a question that was ripening at just about the same time as the Church's understanding of what it meant to say that Jesus Christ was both very God of very God and very man of very man. It was especially the declaration of His humanity that bore heavily on their consideration of the question: Why do we sin?

Sins, deeds, and attitudes committed and taken in violation of divine commandments could be forgiven. This the Christians knew from experience. But why did they arise in the first place, and why is human freedom used to perpetuate and rationalize and create them when that same freedom could be mustered to avoid them? Is this sin*ful*ness part of what it means to be human? These questions nagged with increasing importunity for four centuries when little by little the responses emerged, one from the confes-

---

1924].) For an Epicurean expression, cf. Titus Lucretius Carus, *On the Nature of Things.* (Probably the best translation of this work, known in Latin as *De natura rerum,* is C. Bailey, *On the Nature of Things* [Oxford: Clarendon Press, 1936].) For a work comparing and contrasting the two schools, cf. R. D. Hicks, *Stoic and Epicurean* (New York: C. Scribner's Sons, 1910)—very old but still quite useful.

177. For source-based discussion of this complex issue, cf. A. Harnack, *History of Dogma,* 3:241-54.

178. For a review of the early Church's understandings of freedom of the will, compare Origen, *De principiis* III; Augustine, *De libero arbitrio* (On the Freedom of the Will), which was written A.D. 388-95, and *De gratia et libero arbitrio* (On Grace and Free Will) written in A.D. 426-27; and John Cassian (a contemporary of Augustine's), *Collationes patrum* (Conferences).

sion of faith (and Scripture), the other from the practice of the Church.

The Gospels of Matthew and Luke both asserted that Jesus Christ was virgin-born and the confessions of faith, the creeds, had carried that note along. Luke 1:35 gives a reason for the Virgin Birth: "Therefore the child to be born of thee will be called holy, the Son of God." Here, then, Christ's holiness and the Virgin Birth were connected. But only slowly did the notion develop—and that in the face of certain cultural factors—that if the Virgin Birth guaranteed Christ's holiness (that is, His sin*less*ness), then the fact that we are not virgin-born guarantees our sin*ful*ness.[179] This was backed up, then, by such passages as Ps. 51:5: "Behold I was born in iniquity and in sin did my mother conceive me."

The next step was to connect our sin*ful*ness (since we are not virgin-born) with the very act of being conceived.[180] From the beginning, or nearly that far back, certain rigorists had argued that a spouse and children were at least a hindrance to full Christian commitment, if not sources of worldliness. And they were saying this in a period in which human sexuality was quite debased in the culture at large.[181] So a development in the direction of tying sinfulness to what appeared to any high-minded person, pagan or Christian or Jew, to be an easily and often abused human appetite is perfectly understandable, however ludicrous it may appear to be in retrospect. In effect, this sort of thinking came to attach inevitability to sinfulness. To be human was always and ever to be sinful and that sinfulness was most clearly expressed in sexuality.

This point of view, linking sinfulness and sexuality, was not undebated,[182] but by Augustine's time it was very widely accepted.

---

179. Cf. Hans von Campenhausen, trans. by Frank Clarke, *The Virgin Birth in the Theology of the Ancient Church* (Naperville, Ill.: Alec Allenson, 1964). Also, cf. Ambrose, *Explanatio super Psalmos XII* (Exposition of the Psalms), 37:5 for a specific example.

180. E.g., Augustine, *Contra duas epistolas Pelagianorum* (Against Two Epistles of the Pelagians) iv.11.29.

181. On classical understandings of human sexuality, cf. W. E. H. Lecky, *History of European morals from Augustus to Charlemagne* (3rd ed. rev.; New York: D. Appleton, 1879), vol. I, passim. Also see Lydia Stöcker, *Die Frau in der alten Kirche* (Tübingen, 1907), and L. Zacharnack, *Der Drenst der Frau in den ersten Jahrhunderten der christlichen Kirche* (Göttingen, 1902).

182. E.g., the great debate between Augustine and the Pelagian, Julian of Eclanum. Cf. Augustine, *Contra Julianum* (Against Julian) and, more specifically, *Contra secundam Juliani responsionem opus imperfectum* (Incomplete Work Against

Augustine himself propagated it in such a way that it stuck with Western Christianity. And to it had been added the effects of Adam's sin in Eden. The New Testament (Paul, to be precise) had talked about how sin had entered the human race through one person and thus had passed on to all (Romans 5). Now it came to be believed that only by being virgin-born was it possible to escape that inheritance from Adam. The question of how sinfulness was handed on had no universally agreed upon response. But there was no doubt that its root was Adam and that it infected the entire human race.[183]

The other factor that helped to fix the Church's response to the question: Why do we sin? was infant baptism.[184] When and where and how the practice began is a complete mystery that has produced many and varied guesses. The early Church itself was of a divided mind over it. Passages such as Matt. 18:1-4; Mark 10:13-16; 1 Cor. 7:14; and Eph. 6:1-4 are cited in favor of the practice by the very earliest Church, but they are not conclusive and were not used in proof of the practice until long after it had become widespread.

Perhaps the earliest evidence is from Irenaeus, whom we have already met and who stoutly opposed novelty in doctrine and practice, writing between A.D. 180 and 185.[185] Perhaps just a bit later, Tertullian writes of the practice from North Africa. He is opposed to it and hints that it is a relatively new practice.[186] In about 215, Hippolytus of Rome in his *Apostolic Tradition* (21.3-5) writes as if the practice were of long standing and without question. Yet another 10 years, more or less, and the great Alexandrian, Origen, writes of it as an apostolic practice and links it to the remission of sins. And, with his characteristic honesty, he raises the question:

Julian). For a thoughtful survey, see D. S. Bailey, *The Sexual Relation in Christian Thought* (New York: Harper, 1959).

183. For good, source-based survey, see Williams, *Ideas of the Fall and of Original Sin.* Also, cf. Karl Rahner, "Sünde als Gnadenverlust in der frühchristlichen Literatur," *Zeitschrift für katholische Theologie* 60 (1936), 471-510, and John S. Romanides, *tō propatrikon hamartia* (Athens, 1957). The latter work presents findings concerning points of view on original sin not like that of Augustine.

184. Cf. Joachim Jeremias, *Infant Baptism in the First Four Centuries,* trans. by David Cairns (Philadelphia: Westminster, 1960) and *The Origins of Infant Baptism,* Vol. I trans. by Dorothea M. Barton; "Studies in Historical Theology" (Naperville, Ill.: Alec Allenson, 1963).

185. *Adversus haeresis* II.22.4.

186. *De baptismo,* 18.5.

"Of what sins are they guilty?"[187] He then reasons in reverse: If infant baptism (an apostolic practice) is for the remission of sins, then, no matter what reason may urge, the infant must still be guilty of sin.[188]

Here, as Pelikan points out, is an irony.[189] Tertullian, who fully believed in the sinfulness of infants, was opposed to baptizing them. Origen, who had questions about the sinfulness of infants, believed they must be baptized. Important to us in the present investigation is the fact that the practice of infant baptism was well on its way to becoming a formative factor in the later doctrine of original sin. And it is in the context bounded by this practice, with its attendant theological influence, and by the confessional stance dealt with previously, that Augustine forges the theological understanding that will dominate Western Christian thought until the late 19th century.

In your Bible and mine, Rom. 5:12 (a foundational verse in Augustine's understanding of the human character) reads something like this: "So, it was through one man that sin entered the world, and through sin death. So death came upon the entire human race because all have sinned." Such a translation is true to the best Greek manuscripts. But Augustine's Latin Bible drew from more questionable manuscripts and said: "Sin entered the world and death through sin. So death spread to all through one in whom all sinned." The phrase "in whom all sinned" is the nub of Augustine's understanding of human nature. Sin and death have come to all from Adam because he is the parent of all. When he sinned, we all sinned.[190]

Our translations simply state it as a fact that all have sinned. No theory whatsoever is offered as to how sin begins with Adam—how he is related to our sinning. Adam sinned; all have sinned. But in Augustine's Bible there is a theory of sorts. All are in Adam: Adam sinned; all have sinned. In our Bibles, we are all seen to be *like* Adam. In Augustine's Bible, we are all seen to be *in* Adam. Of

---

187. *In Luc. hom.*, 14.5; *Hom. in Levitic.*, 8.3; *In Rom. comm.*, 5.9. The quotation is from *Hom. in Levitic.*, 8.3.

188. *In Luc. hom.*, 14.5.

189. *Christian Tradition*, 1:291. I have utilized, but not followed entirely, the presentation of Pelikan in developing this section.

190. *De peccatorum meritis et remissione* (On the Merits and the Remission of Sins) i.15.19-20. Hereinafter, this work is abbreviated as *De pecc. merit.*

course, the human situation is the same either way—however it happened, all have sinned. But Augustine's theory came to grip the West and affect even the way in which the Bible was read. It persisted long after the Bible was being translated from manuscripts that did not support the translation given in his Bible.

Now Augustine had to reconcile the fact that to be human is to be sinful with the Christian confession that God created humanity and that His creation is good. The reconciliation would be especially difficult since Augustine saw sin transmitted from generation to generation through the very process by which we are conceived.[191]

Augustine believed that Adam was created with the ability not to sin and not to die. He believed that Adam could have done either (that is, he could have sinned and he could have died) but that he was created with the ability to avoid both.[192] At the same time, remaining sinless and alive would have to have been an option freely chosen. Adam was not created in such a way that he *must* remain sinless or alive, nor in such a way that he *must* sin or die. Of course, had Adam chosen to remain sinless and alive he would have retained authentic existence, he would have been truly "of God." Choosing sin (and thus death as well) would be to lose authentic existence.[193]

Adam made the latter choice. He fell. He refused to obey God (that is, to recognize that God is God), and to that degree and in that way he became inauthentic; he had no genuine existence. Setting himself up as the one to be obeyed instead of the sovereign God, he established an illusion—an illusion that he willed to call reality. He gave himself over to the pursuit of nothingness, to "vanity," as if it were reality. Here was the ultimate sinfulness, to pursue nothing as if it were all. This Adam did, and because humanity is his progeny, it too participated in what he did. And ever since, the human race, universally, has expressed in its own pride and willful disobedience to divine command its approving kinship to Adam, leaving it without excuse.[194]

---

191. E.g., *De pecc. merit.* i.9.10. He is writing theology here, not biology.

192. E.g., *De correptione et gratia* (On Rebuke and Grace), 12.33; *De civitate dei* (City of God) xiv.26.

193. Cf. *De duabus animabus contra Manichaeos* (On Two Souls against the Manicheans), 9.

194. E.g., *De civitate dei* xiv.11.

The body becomes the principal vehicle in the pursuit of the illusion. It is not evil in itself. But it becomes the chief excuse for the pursuit of nothingness ("We do have physical needs, you know.") as well as the principal instrument in that pursuit. So the body is seen by Augustine as the very locus of the transmission of sinfulness from generation to generation. And the very act by which bodies conceive bodies comes very close to being the great sin, according to Augustine. Only the Bible's affirmation of the physical world as a divine creation, and the Church's reliance upon the Bible, and trust in its authority hold him back from this extreme position.[195]

Nonetheless, the fall into sin and the continuing sinfulness of the human race could not entirely destroy the image of God in mankind. The Fall totally corrupted the original creation, but it could not make any authentic new creation.[196] And while the body appeared to Augustine to have been almost completely corrupted, or at least helpless before the power of the downward pull of the yearning for the illusion, there remained life (however truncated and diminished), the senses, and the rational mind.[197] It is not human nature that is disgraced. Nor is it abolished.[198] But it is badly distorted and abused and in need of healing. Of course, it cannot heal itself. It may be restored only by the Redeemer-Creator.[199] And of this restoration it may even be given foretastes from time to time where it accepts the grace to be open to them. The passage cited above is a description of one such moment of foretaste, a foretaste granted even before Christian baptism.

This foretaste and any subsequent healing must come from resources far richer and more powerful than any provided by human nature. Certainly they must exceed the power of human free will, for since the Fall that power has been good only for sinning. We choose sinning and its illusion of reality quite freely, with little or no sense of coercion, and are pleased to pretend that at least we are happy in it. It does not bother us, at least not profoundly, that we cannot choose the good, for that is not what we want. Only the occasional regret for the consequences of our evil disturbs us, but

---

195. E.g., *De pecc. merit.* i.15.19-20.

196. E.g., *De gratia Christi* (On the Grace of Christ), 19.20.

197. *Contra Faustum Manichaeum* (Against Faustus the Manichee), 24.2; *De natura et gratia* (On Nature and Grace), 3.3.

198. E.g., *De peccati originali* (On Original Sin), 40.46.

199. Cf. *De doctrina christiana* (On Christian Doctrine), 1.14.13.

not the evil itself. Not only are we unable to save ourselves, but we are unwilling to do so as well. So says Augustine.

It is Christ, of course, who is that grace, that healing and healer, that power to save and that will to do it.

> The traditional picture of Christ as the physician and of salvation as divine healing was incorporated into Augustine's doctrine of grace. . . . This grace was not based upon any preceding merit or works of man; for man could not love God unless God first loved him. The love of God shed abroad, or grace, brought it about "not only that we learn to know what ought to be done, but also that we do what we have learned." Grace, then, preceded and followed man's life of love: preceded it in order that we might be healed, followed it that we might become healthy and strong.[200]

Now, what is entailed in that healing? What is the nature of our healing and of our growth in spiritual health and strength? Here, Augustine was caught in some controversies that elicited responses more negative than definitive. He tells us more, sometimes, about what that healing cannot entail than about what it does involve and accomplish. We must, then, examine the backdrop of what Augustine will say and allow our examination to help us understand what he is not saying as well.

One of the controversies that shaped Augustine's way of explaining theological matters was with the Donatists, a large group of North African Christians whose answer to the question concerning the nature of the Church was: "The true Church is the fellowship of authentic, perfect saints with a priesthood free of any stain of apostasy." The Church could be holy, and thus the only true Church, only if her members were holy. The priestly structure especially must be holy. Generally, *holy* meant "without taint of apostasy." More personal forms of piety were secondary to doctrinal fidelity, especially in times of persecution.

Holiness, brought to the believer by the coming of the Holy Spirit, was believed by the Donatists to be given at the believer's baptism. This was why it was so necessary to have a holy priesthood. Only a holy priesthood would be honored by the Holy Spirit in its administration of baptism; only a holy priesthood would be fit to pass on the presence of the Holy Spirit with His gifts. Ordination would likewise demand holiness on the part of the one or-

---

200. Pelikan, *Christian Tradition,* 1:301-02.

daining, and only holy hands could administer grace through the Lord's Supper.

So, among the Donatists, the very means of grace were destroyed as means of grace if celebrated by an unholy priest, for the sacraments must bring the Spirit and holiness to the recipients. At the same time, the recipients must be morally fit to receive them. In a sense, they must be sanctified to receive sanctification and holy to receive holiness; the exception, of course, being baptism. A sort of moral perfection, brought about by catechesis and the guidance of the clergy in preparation for the reception of baptism, was required of the adult candidate for baptism. But babies were exempt from this requirement; so holiness did not always precede baptism.

While the concern of the Donatists for the moral and doctrinal purity of the Church must be applauded (with due recognition for their inconsistencies) and imitated or even bettered, their theological error must be avoided. They came to believe that it is holiness that brings grace, that purity begets sanctification (that is, the presence of the Spirit), that only where there is spiritual perfection is there the true Church. Their concern persuaded them to invert the order of salvation. And it made of the Church a spiritually elitist society made up of saints only. No wonder Augustine twits them by saying that the true Church would at least follow the prayer that the Lord taught her to pray and say, "Forgive us our trespasses," something that the Donatists believed they had no need of doing.[201]

Like the Donatists, Augustine believed that the Holy Spirit, with His gifts, was given to the believer at baptism. But the validity of baptism is dependent neither upon the moral and doctrinal purity of the baptizer nor that of the baptizand, according to Augustine.[202] The Spirit is free and blows where it will. The validity of baptism depends finally upon the Spirit alone; it is dependent upon God's election. And, indeed, some are elect who never undergo baptism, though the command of Jesus to baptize does not allow the Spirit's freedom to be an excuse for not baptizing. Nor, for that matter, does the fact that the validity of baptism is not dependent upon the moral purity of the baptizand allow for moral carelessness, according to Augustine.[203]

---

201. *Ep.,* 185.39 (ad Bonifacium).

202. *Contra litteras Petiliani* (Against the Letters of Petilian) iii.15.18.

203. E.g., *De baptismo contra Donatistas* (On Baptism Against the Donatists)

The same fact of predestination touches the efficacy of the other sacraments as well. They are efficacious only when and through whom and to whom the Spirit wills. There is absolutely no precondition to their efficacy except the Spirit's will.[204] So, the sacraments do not bring the Spirit and holiness in and of themselves. It is the Spirit who brings the sacraments. He inhabits them as He chooses. To believe that the sacraments could be used to induce the Spirit's presence or to induce holiness would be to seek to control the Spirit, to fall again into the heinous crime of seeking to usurp the sovereignty of God. So it is that grace brings holiness, that sanctification (that is, the active presence of the Spirit) begets purity; and only where the true Church is, will there be spiritual perfection.[205]

The holiness of the Church, then, for Augustine, is objective. It is a gift of grace to the Church and does not depend upon the moral character of the priest nor of the members. But it is mediated through the sacraments (though not solely through them, since the Spirit is free to blow where He wills). So, in an ordinary sense, the sacraments and the priesthood that administers them are necessary to holiness. They are vehicles of holiness even though their celebrants and recipients may not be morally holy.

Do the sacraments in any way sanctify the recipient? Do they actually make the believer holy or at least move the believer in that direction?

Here, Augustine seems to make two very different responses. The more optimistic one he made in the years before 410, even while doing battle with the Donatists. But after about that year, he

---

iii.2.3; v.24.35. Augustine admits that the doctrine of election creates deep difficulties for reason. Earlier in his career as a Christian, he had been confident that many of them could be resolved by better exercise of the intellect. But he became increasingly skeptical of it as his conviction of the pervasiveness of sin grew. More and more frequently, then, he appeals to the mere fact that Scripture says thus-and-so or that the Church teaches thus-and-so—and, of course, in his mind there could never be contradiction between Church and Scripture. Each authenticated the other.

204. Cf. the discussion and the sources noted by Pelikan, *Christian Tradition,* 1:302-03, 309-10. It is, of course, the will of God that the Church should celebrate the sacraments. So the benefits do accompany that celebration. But all is dependent upon the grace of God, not upon some human activity. Also cf. Harnack, *History of Dogma,* 5:143-68.

205. This is said most pungently in *Sermo* IV.11: "All of those who are perfect *(fuerunt perfecti)* belong to the Church."

became embroiled in the bitterest of debates with Pelagius and his disciples, the bitterness largely being confined to the disciples.

In 410 Pelagius, perhaps Welsh and probably a Christian monk, wrote a book entitled *Defense of the Freedom of the Will.*[206] He seems to have had in view the morality of the despair that had overtaken the western portion of the Roman Empire. To him, it seemed that Christians, no less than pagans, had become almost fatalistic in their attitudes and had decided that whether one did good or evil was of little consequence in the flow of history. He attacked the problem by insisting that Christians accept their call to moral responsibility and bend their wills to the doing of good.

Augustine did not oppose Pelagius' concern, but he did see in Pelagius' basic theological presuppositions and postulates a fundamental flaw. It was a flaw that Pelagius' disciples caricatured and celebrated as if it were not a flaw but a positive contribution to Christian faith and morality.[207]

Pelagius was theoretically committed to the proposition that "the fact that we have the possibility of accomplishing every good thing by action, speech and thought comes from Him who has endowed us with this possibility, and who also assists us."[208] Practically, what he was committed to was a confidence that the human will was created capable of choosing good or evil and that while the Fall had corrupted the functioning of that will and the world in which it functions, it had not corrupted the basic character of the will itself.

So God is the author of our basic freedom, but whatever is made of it from that point on, by the use of that freedom for either good or ill, is of our own doing.[209] Or, to put matters in another way, Pelagius believed that the human being lives in a world that is morally fallen but that the individual's participation in that fallenness is up to the individual.

Augustine held that the individual is as fallen as the world and that the individual is as much the moral problem as the world

---

206. *De libero arbitrio.* This work is now known only by a few fragments and by citations of it in other authors.

207. Unfortunately, the most useful works that treat this matter are not in English: Friedrich Loofs, "Pelagius und der pelagianische Streit," *Realencyklopadie für protestantische Theologie und Kirche,* 15:747-74; S. Prete, *Pelagio e il Pelagianesimo* (Brescia, 1961).

208. Augustine, *De gratia Christi* (On the Grace of Christ), 1.17.

209. Ibid., 1.17-18.

is. The individual does not so much participate or not participate in the fallenness of the world as that the individual is, in the profoundest sense, the very fallenness of the world. Or, as Charles Williams said, for Augustine: "Man is not *in* an evil circumstance; man *is* the evil circumstance."[210]

It seems rather obvious from this distance that Pelagius himself would not push matters that far; but his disciples certainly did, and did so without distorting or skewing the foundation that he had laid. Nor would Pelagius cleanse (to change the figure) those premises that served to breed heresy. So Augustine was probably correct in responding negatively to both Pelagius and Pelagius' disciples.[211]

We do not review the whole of Augustine's response here but aim directly at showing how that larger response shaped Augustine's understanding of sanctification.

Augustine believed that experience shows us that humankind, having rebelled against God, is a mass or heap of sin. It cannot bring itself to goodness, it cannot return to God in its own strength any more than an empty tumbler can refill itself. So, if human beings are to be saved, the process of salvation must begin outside of them, objectively. And since there is nothing good in them, that is, nothing in their own natures that can do any reconstructing in righteousness, the process must also be sustained from outside.

> Human nature lost the former type of immortality [that in which mankind was capable of not dying] through abuse of free will. It receives the latter [in which mankind is incapable of dying] through grace—though had it not sinned it would have received it through merit. However, even then, there could not

---

210. Charles Williams, *The Descent of the Dove* (New York: Meridian Press, 1956), 66. The actual quotation is: "Man precisely was not *in* a situation—not even in a difficult situation. He was, himself, the situation."

211. Augustine responded directly to the positions of Pelagius and the Pelagians in 12 major works: (listed here in chronological order and only by their English titles) *On the Merits and the Remission of Sins and the Baptism of Infants, On the Spirit and the Letter, On Grace in the New Testament* (also known as Epistle 140), *On Nature and Grace, On Man's Perfection in Righteousness, On the Proceedings of Pelagius, On the Grace of Christ and Original Sin, On Marriage and Concupiscence, On the Soul and its Origin, Against Two Epistles of the Pelagians, Against Julian, Incomplete Work Against Julian.* The controversy elicited four other major works from Augustine: (again listed in chronological order and by usual English title) *On Grace and Free Will, On Rebuke and Grace, On the Predestination of the Saints, On the Gift of Perseverance.*

be any merit without grace. For while sin did originate in free will alone, free will would have been insufficient to maintain justice. This maintainance would have been possible only by divine aid, aid given by the gift of participation in the unchanging good. . . . The unaided will is insufficient at the point of maintaining life.

In much the same way, man in Paradise could self-destruct by willfully abandoning righteousness. But, on the other hand, his will alone would not have been sufficient to maintain the life of righteousness. That would be possible only if he who made him had helped him. But, following the Fall, God's mercy is yet more copious, for now the will itself had to be loosed from servitude to the masters, sin and death. In no way can it be loosed by itself. God's grace is the only way. And this is made effective in Christ's faith. So, as it is written, even the will by which "the will itself is made ready by the Lord" (so that we may accept the other gifts of God by means of which we come to the eternal Gift) also comes from God.

So, even eternal life, which is certainly the compensation for good works, is called a gift of God by the Apostle. . . . But a gift is not a gift if it is not gratuitous. So we should understand that even one's deserved goods are gifts from God. And when eternal life is given through them, is this not "grace in return for grace"? (*Enchiridion* 18.106).

This grace comes to the elect through the Person and work of Christ, of course. His death bridged the gulf between mankind and God so that grace could work. Its principal work is to annul the state of sin. Viewed from this angle, Christ is himself grace, for it is He who annuls the work of Adam (ibid., 108).

Here we begin to touch on the doctrine of predestination in Augustine. And the reader must now do two things: (1) Understand that we cannot present here a full explication of Augustine's position, but only suggest further bibliography in a footnote and go on to mention the doctrine only as it relates to the matter at hand; and (2) not allow an emotional (or even rational) dislike of the doctrine to obscure reflection on the remainder of the system.[212]

---

212. Perhaps the most thorough study of Augustine's doctrine of predestination is Gotthard Nygren, *Das Praedestinations-problem in der Theologie Augustins* (Lund, 1956). In the same class is J. Chêne, *Théologie de Saint Augustine: Grâce et prédestination* (Le Puy, 1962). Very useful is M. Rist, "Augustine on Free Will and Predestination," *Journal of Theological Studies* (1969), 420-47. Also valuable in helping the reader to think about predestination theologically, instead of philosophically, are N. P. Williams, *The Grace of God* (New York: Longmans, Green, 1930), and Oscar Hardman, *The Christian Doctrine of Grace* (New York: Macmillan, 1937). See also F. J. Thonnard, "La prédestination augustinienne et l'interprétation de O. Rott-

All humankind deserves damnation for all humankind has rebelled against God. Such is Augustine's observation of the world and his understanding of the Incarnation. Further, while none will love the infernal destiny awaiting them, none of the non-elect really want to be among the elect on God's terms, though they may wish it on their own. And none of the elect wish to be other than elect. The genuine surprise in the universe (for there is no reason for it whatsoever and no reason to expect it) is that God has chosen to save anyone at all. But this He has done in His own love and freedom, and He has chosen to do it through Christ. Such is grace.

This grace is both prevenient and cooperative. Prevenient in that it first creates in the elect a good will or faith;[213] cooperative in that it results in and sustains growth in righteousness.[214] It is this latter mode that involves sanctification.

Grace, as it applies cooperatively, evolves by stages toward the complete regeneration or remaking of the believer. When the regeneration is complete, the believer will be truly Christlike. This regeneration enables the believer actually to do good works. It involves a growing faith, which moves from an initial stage of unquestioning acceptance of the word of Scripture and the teachings of the Church, on through stages of obedience and trust to believing God himself, then to belief about God, next to belief on God, and finally to love of God—pure love and the faith that works in love.[215] Aiding in this development, and actually giving grace, are the sacraments of the Church.

It is really only when the believer reaches perfect Christlikeness that he is truly "justified by faith."[216] It is complete in essence at the beginning of the process but is not complete in fact until death enables us to pass beyond the limitations that fleshly existence imposes.[217] Experience had taught Augustine that justification, insofar as it may be equated with love of God (love of the

---

manner," *Revue des études augustiniennes* IX (1963), 259-87 and "La prédestination augustinienne. Sa place en philosophie augustinienne," ibid. X (1964), 97-123.

213. *De spiritu et littera* (On the Spirit and the Letter), 34.

214. *Enchiridion,* 32; *De gratia et libero arbitrio* (On Grace and Free Will), 33.

215. *Enchiridion,* 31.117; *De gratia et libero arbitrio,* 20. Augustine is not completely consistent in his presentations of the order of stages except for the first and the last. Also cf. *Enchiridion,* 31.118, where the stages are "before the law," "under the law," "under grace," and "full and perfect peace."

216. *De spiritu et littera,* 45; *Contra Julianum* (Against Julian) ii.23.

217. *Enchiridion,* 30.115; 31.118-19.

Good) or with coveting the Good, simply cannot be completed in this life, though it may be ever more closely approximated.[218]

In using the term *justification* to refer to the process of regeneration or sanctification, Augustine enters some confusion into the Christian vocabulary, which has had its effect ever since. Used in this way, justification becomes the *goal* of Christian faith rather than its starting block and a formula is developed in which regeneration = justification = sanctification. All of this leads to and is completed by the perfect union with God that is achieved at the close of this life. Entire sanctification, in this light, is entire justification or completed regeneration. None of the three is possible until there is release from any and all effects of the Fall, including release from the flesh, which, while created good and even yet not evil in itself, is corrupted—a point made earlier.

From this direction, then, we seek in vain for any doctrine of sanctification that would indicate completion of the process in this life except insofar as sanctification is completed in essence, but not in fact, at the time of baptism. Here "in essence" means that the holiness of Christ is applied to, or imputed to, the believer from the beginning of his Christian walk. One can never be more holy than one is in that moment since all of Christ's righteousness is put to the believer's account.

This imputation or application, through the sacraments of the Church and the deepening faith of the believer, does become more and more "actual." It does make the believer more and more righteous; the Spirit does fill the believer with divine (and thus perfect) love to the limit of the believer's capacity at a given moment. But as Augustine sees it, this is not an *entire* sanctification because it cannot be an *entire* regeneration. It is not perfection. It is not entire sanctification nor perfection because the final measure or standard for both of these, according to Augustine, lies beyond anything we can be in this life. It lies in utter Christlikeness, in being "new creatures in Christ Jesus," in fulfilling the gracious role of being not just human beings but being absolutely good beings.

Augustine uses such verses of Scripture as 1 John 3:2, which puts the accomplishment of Christlikeness into that moment after the end of this life in which we shall actually see Christ—"we shall be like him; for we shall see him as he is." He thus places the

---

218. *De spiritu et littera,* 6; *Enchiridion,* 64.

completion of regeneration, of re-creation, and thus of sanctification, beyond the boundaries of fleshly or earthly existence.[219]

> We are then truly free when God directs our lives; that is, when he shapes and makes us not as men (something he has already done), but as good men. He is doing that now by his grace, so that we may truly be new creatures in Christ Jesus. That is why the prayer, "Create in me a clean heart, O God." God has already created the natural human heart—so the reference must be to another sort of heart (*Enchiridion* 9.31).

The fact is that Augustine, as we have already said, can be read in two ways with respect to the possibilities of grace in this life. And he has been.[220] He can be read with the emphasis upon what is already given in essence, and he can be read with the emphasis upon what will be given in fact. If the emphasis be upon essence, then the possibilities of grace in this life are severely limited, for it is a bit beside the point to think about actually becoming righteous. In fact it is a bit presumptuous to think about it when our best righteousness is nothing compared to that of Christ, which is already imputed to us. Most of the ethical thinking with this emphasis will focus upon forgiveness, on adjusting to the necessity of evil, on the struggle or warfare of the Christian with his own sinful nature. This approach was generally taken by the Church in western Europe, and from thence it has come to dominate theology.

If, on the other hand, the emphasis be laid upon what is given in fact in baptism (the Spirit and His gifts), and upon what will be given in fact after death (perfect Christlikeness), then the possibilities of grace, for Augustine, are limited only by the limitations of being human, being a son or daughter of Adam, and being in a sinful world. Ethical thinking will focus on the process of becoming truly righteous and on the disciplinary and devotional practices that will reflect not only the grace that has already begun making us righteous but also those that will express what we are.

---

219. Cf. *Decem tractatus in epistolam Joannis I* (Exposition of the First Epistle of John), 3.2.

220. For the more positive view, see, e.g., Cuthbert Butler, *Western Mysticism: The Teaching of Augustine, Gregory and Bernard on Contemplation and the Contemplative Life* (3rd ed.; New York: Barnes and Noble, 1967). For the more negative, a useful example is Peter Brown, *Augustine of Hippo: A Biography* (Berkeley and Los Angeles: University of California Press, 1967), 233-43. Brown (correctly, it would seem) makes much of a shift in Augustine's position from a more optimistic to a more pessimistic point of view.

Such practices will help us to fulfill in fact what we already are in essence.

Here, monasticism tuned in to Augustine. But it did so only to distort this way of reading him at times. Becoming legalistic about those practices, they fell into the error of believing that such practices would bring grace, rather than understanding that grace was their seedbed. It was precisely this distortion of this side of Augustine that caused the reformers of the 16th century to see only the other, more pessimistic side of his thought.

So it is that Augustine both contributes to the doctrine of entire sanctification and militates against it. He contributes to it by insisting that God's perfect love is indeed made present in us by the Spirit as a gift of grace and that we possess it fully—that is, insofar as our personalities and circumstances allow at any given time. We are, says Augustine, genuinely dead to sin and we are new creatures in Christ Jesus, insofar as we can be, at any given moment on earth. This sanctification is a cleansing (symbolized by baptism); it is an authentic regeneration; it is done by the Holy Spirit, not by us; and it is always complete for the stage it is in. There are, of course, ever new and advanced stages to be occupied.

Augustine militates against any doctrine of entire sanctification by confusing sanctification with justification. He makes sanctification, like justification, a divine declaration and an imputation of Christ's righteousness rather than an authentic regeneration. (This is a contradiction in Augustine's own system since, on other grounds, he had made it a very real regeneration.) And he further militates against any doctrine of entire sanctification by so identifying life in the flesh with sinfulness itself as to eliminate the possibility of entire regeneration in this life.

Lastly, Augustine militates against any doctrine of entire sanctification by associating sanctification so closely with doing good works. It was but a short step from his ideas to those insisting that Christianity is principally a religion of doing or feeling good. The conclusion could be drawn that we must be sanctified before we may be justified. None of these above-stated views would please Augustine if they were left to stand alone. Over against each he would place another of his own views and call upon us to hold both in proper tension. And above all, he would insist that any sanctification must begin and end in faith; sanctification is no less by faith than is justification.

History has not taken into account the fact that most of Augustine's doctrinal development came in the white heat of controversy. It was shaped in an atmosphere of the most serious kind of debate. The case against the opponent was put in its worst possible light and one's own case was stated with a sharpness and lack of qualification that calmer deliberation would rectify. Nor has history reckoned with the fact that the good bishop was given to understanding the faith in terms of grand paradoxes—both practical and more reflective.

Because these facts were ignored, Augustine became the father of both sides of many an argument and of both sides of many a doctrinal development in which the opposing viewpoints came to be irreconcilable. So it has been in the case of the doctrine of entire sanctification.

We have taken considerable space to present the position(s) of Augustine because his view(s) came to be the root of what Western Christianity was to cultivate in the way of ideas of holiness. In the 18th century will be seen the unique fusion of a genuinely Augustinian perspective with the perspective of Eastern Christianity in the unique context of the thought and worship of the Church of England. Out of this will come the doctrine of entire sanctification taught by John Wesley and his circle.

In Eastern Christianity, the elements of that perspective were already present and as fully developed as they would ever be in the theology of Gregory of Nyssa. In the West, Augustine's contribution was to undergo considerable development, some of it positive and some of it negative, on the way to the 18th century. It is to that development that we now turn.[221]

---

221. This is not to say that Augustine's is the only influence on the development of the doctrine of entire sanctification in the West, but it is to say that it is certainly the fundamental one.

3

The Doctrine of Entire Sanctification in the Medieval West

Before we proceed to study the development of the doctrine of entire sanctification in the Middle Ages, it may be well to remind ourselves that it is precisely that doctrine that we are investigating and not the broader, and by now somewhat separated, doctrine of Christian perfection. Everywhere the student turns in the literature of the medieval church, a concern for Christian perfection will be apparent. But that interest is not the same as an interest in the doctrine of sanctification, especially entire sanctification.

The medieval theologians generally followed the lead of Augustine and the even clearer direction of Gregory the Great (whose position we shall examine shortly) and kept the two doctrines distinct. Further, since many of them were monastics, their interest focused upon perfection. The doctrine of sanctification was not usually among their sustained concerns. Sanctification was seen to be given in baptism or in confirmation and was seen as the door to perfection. But that was that. The pathway, not the gateway (we are thinking as they would think), held their attention.

Nonetheless, there were several medieval thinkers who did give some thought to sanctification and they ordinarily sought to reunite it, theologically, with the doctrine of Christian perfection.

In this section, we shall consider three whose influence was great at the time and has endured: Gregory the Great, Bernard of Clairvaux, and Thomas Aquinas.

A. Gregory the Great: The Sundering of Sanctification and Perfection

Gregory the Great,[1] more mundanely titled Pope Gregory I (590-604) has received very divergent evaluations from the historians of Christian thought. The greatest of them all, Adolph von Harnack, blamed Gregory for much that went astray, theologically, in the medieval church:

> A more motley farrago of Augustinian formulas and crude work-religion *(ergismus)* could hardly be conceived. Gregory has nowhere uttered an original thought; he has rather at all points preserved, while emasculating, the traditional system of doctrine, reduced the spiritual to the level of a coarsely material intelligence, changed dogmatic, so far as it suited, into technical directions for the clergy, and associated it with popular religion of the second rank. . . . Gregory created the vulgar type of mediaeval Catholicism by the way he accented the various traditional doctrines and Church usages.[2]

Harnack is quite correct in saying that Gregory is the father of Western medieval Christianity, which makes him the source of

---

1. Bibliography on Gregory is rich. There are two very good modern biographies in English: P. Battifol, trans. by T. Stoddard, *Saint Gregory the Great* (London: Burns, Oates and Washbourne, 1929), and F. Homes Dudden, *Gregory the Great: His Place in History and Thought,* 2 vols. (London: Longmans, Green, 1905). Battifol is the better biography, Dudden gives the better account of Gregory's thought. C. Dagans, *Saint Gregoire le Grand. Culture et experience chretienne* (Paris, 1977) is also a very useful and valuable study, though not strictly speaking a biography. Also useful as general works on Gregory's papal reign are E. Caspar, *Geschichte des Papsttums von den Anfangen bis zür Höhe der Weltherrschaft,* vol. II: *Das Papsttum unter byzantinischer Herrschaft* (Tübingen, 1933), 306-514, and E. M. Marian, *San Gregorio I, papa della carita* (Rome, 1951).

The best complete edition of Gregory's literary work is in MPL LXXV-LXXIX. Critical editions of various of his works have been issued, but none of the entire collection. English translations of Gregory's major works are scattered in several collections. NPNF, Series II, vols. XII-XIII contain many letters and the *Liber regulae pastoralis (Pastoral Rule);* FC, vol. 39, is a translation of *Dialogi de vita et miraculis patrum Italicorum (Dialogues); Moralia in Job* has been Englished in *A Library of Fathers of the Holy Catholic Church* (Oxford: John Henry Parker, 1850), vols. XVIII, XXI, XXIII, XXXI. F. L. Battles, *A Translation and Critical Study of the First Book of the Homilies on Ezekiel* (unpublished Ph.D. dissertation: New Haven: Hartford Theological Seminary Foundation, 1950) is the sole English translation of any major portion of Gregory's homiletical works.

2. *History of Dogma,* trans. by Neil Buchanan, 5:262.

much modern Roman Catholicism as well. For better than 500 years, no one was read more frequently nor more avidly by the church's scholars. But Harnack probably judges Gregory's theological work too negatively. And he credits the good pope with more direct theological influence than he really had.

For the most part, Gregory's theology only reflected what was already commonly held, as Harnack himself notes. So Gregory was more conduit than source. What he did do was to administer the church exceptionally well (something for which Harnack does give him due credit), administer it as an authentically saintly leader, and thus give an indelible official sanction to much popular belief. His pontificate came to be remembered as a sort of golden age—a memory that sanctified much pious practice that perhaps would otherwise have been forgotten. He revived a dispirited Christian populace, one that had become Christian more by habit and name than by conviction. And he struck again the dying chord of evangelism, sending missionaries even to faraway Britain and to the imperfectly Christianized Germanic tribes along the Rhine and elsewhere.

As we have noted, Gregory's theology was popular theology. That is to say, his concern was that the grass roots should understand the faith at least well enough to live morally. To that end, he worked from two directions: *(a)* his preaching and writing sought to show the practical import of the rich intellectual heritage of the Church, particularly the heritage from Augustine, whom Gregory reckoned to be the greatest of all the Fathers since the apostles themselves;[3] and *(b)* his preaching and writing gave official sanc-

3. In the process of bringing the heritage to bear on his own circumstances, Gregory popularized almost to the point of caricature the thought of earlier thinkers, especially Augustine. Perhaps the following example can stand for the entire process. Augustine said that evil has no ultimate reality. Only God is totally existent and God alone gives being, giving it where He will. Evil cannot grant being. It can only give death. So evil is precisely opposite to God and can have no being. Augustine is here thinking metaphysically, not morally. He is keenly aware of the moral reality of evil. Gregory, seeking to retain Augustine's position actually reverses it. Like Augustine, Gregory says that evil has no ultimate reality. But Gregory is thinking in terms of morality, not metaphysically. Evil has no status with God, and while he may permit it for our own good, he overrules it according to his purpose. And so should we overrule it in our lives. In that way, it has no ultimate reality. But from a metaphysical perspective, Gregory gives separate and authentic (if not ultimate) reality to evil by his understanding of Satan and demons. These are very real and exist quite apart from God and divine purpose. Their doom is sealed, their destruction is assurred, but for now they are as real as God is real. They generate a kind of being, just as God is the source of being. Cf. *Moralia* XIV.17-18.

tion to widespread customary beliefs and practices either by accepting as appropriate the theology already implicit in them or by supplying them with theological underpinnings. These are the aspects of Gregory's work at which Harnack takes aim.

Jean Leclercq, a Benedictine scholar-monk, is among those giving us a much more favorable view of Gregory.[4] He refers to Gregory as the "Doctor (that is, Teacher) of Desire." In our present essay, we will align ourselves with this more positive perspective than with that of Harnack and take our lead from the title suggested by Leclercq.

Like Augustine, Gregory is very much aware of the misery of the human condition—not simply as it may be separated from the operations of grace but also as a consequence of being on this earth. And in this, he recasts Augustine's awareness. For Augustine, the essence of that misery lay in separation from God, from the source of authentic being and the true Good. For Gregory, the essence of that misery is our self-centeredness.[5] For Augustine, our mortal misery is a sort of ongoing numbness of spirit, an endemic condition. For Gregory, it is an aggressive misery, a lively antagonist. It makes us aware of itself at every turn. "We must understand that human life is not said merely to have trials. It is described as being a trial."[6]

Where does this misery come from? Gregory says that it comes from our parents. We inherit it as a warp in our character and we augment it by imitating our ancestors' behavior.[7] (Here Gregory walks the paths of both Augustine and Pelagius.) Of course, its roots are in Adam and Eve: "The enfeeblement of the originating guilt is inherited by the offspring, and because the human branch was made rotten in the root, it does not continue in the verdure of its original creation."[8] Both in this rather "natural" way and by

---

4. *L'Amour des lettres et le désir de Dieu* (Paris, 1956). Under the title *The Love of Learning and the Desire for God,* trans. by Catharine Misrahi (New York: New American Library, 1961) the New American Library has published an English translation that is occasionally problematic. Nonetheless, it is sufficiently accurate to be of use to the student and is, in fact, of an indispensible character in one edition or the other to any who would really know medieval spirituality.

5. E.g., *Moralia* VIII.21-25 (on Job 7:5).

6. *Moralia* VIII.8 (on Job 7:1). Also cf. *Moralia* VIII.53-54 (on Job 7:20).

7. *Moralia* XV.57 (on Job 21:19).

8. *Moralia* XVII.21 (on Job 25:4).

imitative behavior Adam's fall is passed on. And it is passed on both as an act and as a state.[9]

The tragedy of this state of affairs lies in the continuing concern of the human race to hide it, both from itself and from God. Time and again in the *Moralia,* his commentary on the Book of Job, Gregory returns to Adam's refusal to meet God openly and to confess his fault. The divine question, "Adam, where art thou?" is met by the twin follies of silence at first, then an attempt to escape moral responsibility by shifting it to others. The entire episode, whether in its original occurrence or in its historical replication in each and all of Adam's children is testimony to the freedom of the human will. But, of course, it is sad testimony to its abuse.[10]

The sinfulness of the human race, then, results from Adam's abuse of his volitional freedom, from the kinship of the race to Adam, and from the imitation of Adam. This sinfulness, an expression of selfish pride, begets the misery of this world in a continuing stream, and the human body is its principal vehicle of manifestation.

In a passage meant as a formal disclaimer to any special expositional talent that his hearers and readers might believe him to have, Gregory states clearly his understanding of the role of the body in helping to produce the wretchedness of earthly life.

> What is the role of the body if it is not to be the instrument of the mind? Now, even if the musician be ever so skilful, he cannot exercise that skill to best effect unless he has a fit instrument for it. We all know that the bidden melody will not be produced if the instrument be out of order.[11]

And even worse, the body "weighs down the soul" (*Wisdom* 9:15). In its devolution, its march to death and corruption, the body still demands much of the soul and drags it down.[12] Even the righteous or just suffer the downward pull of the body.

---

9. *Moralia* XXII.30-32 (on Job 31:32).

10. "The devil himself, conquering us in the conquest of our first parent, rightly held (if that be the correct term) mankind in servitude to himself. And mankind, even as he was created with a free will, gave consent to the devil when the devil prompted what was unrighteous. So, though created to life in the freedom of his own will, mankind made himself the debtor to death of his own accord" (*Moralia* XVII.46 [on Job 26:12]).

11. *Moralia,* "Epistle to Leander", sec. v. The *Moralia* is dedicated to Leander, bishop of Hispalis (now Seville) and primate of Hispania. Gregory and Leander had been together in Constantinople in the early 580s.

12. *Moralia* VIII.50 (on Job 7:19). The quotation is Gregory's own and is from *Wisdom* 9:15.

> For even though the righteous are not in the grip of the tumult of carnal passions, yet the fetters of corruption tie them down in this life, and onerous chains they are. . . . So it is that being yet mortal they are burdened down by their own corrupt condition. They are chained and trussed by its shackles because they are not yet resurrected to the liberty of an incorruptible life.[13]

Life in the flesh is an awful struggle for the believer, for not only does the body drag the soul downward and away from its loftier ideals, but its demands also press the more urgently as the yearning for authentic freedom increases. Such a struggle would be inconceivable in the unbeliever, for it arises from the acknowledged disparity of spiritual vision and spiritual reality. The unbeliever, mired in self-centeredness, has no authentic vision.

Has the believer any hope of release from the struggling of this life? Like Augustine, Gregory responds both yes and no. And in doing this, he drives even deeper the wedge between the doctrines of sanctification and perfection.

For Gregory, sanctification is a gift of God's grace, bestowed upon the believer by the sending of the Holy Spirit. It is understood to be given in baptism, as a rule. Its principal negative characteristic is cleansing, a cleansing "from whatever might be offensive in the hearts of his disciples."[14] Its principal positive characteristic is holiness, which Gregory describes as proven "not in the performance of miracles [a proof commonly appealed to in the case of ascetics—ed.] but in loving every man as one's self; thinking what is true about God and thinking better of one's fellows than of one's self."[15]

All of this is related to perfection, but perfection and sanctification are not to be equated. While sanctification is a divine gift, usually given in baptism, and is, in a very technical sense, complete or entire at that moment, perfection is not entirely a gift of God and is not complete until this life be passed. Perfection is a goal, not a gift. It is to be striven for,[16] and progress toward it is made in disciplined steps or grades. This disciplined walk may lead us very close indeed to perfection here, but as long as we be in the flesh,

---

13. *Moralia* IV.68 (on Job 3:18). Here, too, Gregory draws upon *Wisdom* 9:15. Also see *Moralia* VIII.33.56. (on Job 7:21).

14. *Moralia* I.22.30 (on Job 1:5).

15. *Moralia* XX.7.17 (on Job 30:2).

16. *Moralia* VI.37, esp. 59 (on Job 5:26).

we really may only approximate it.[17] "However elevated may be the state of a person through holy living, there yet springs up in him from his old state something burdensome."[18]

Is this "burdensome thing" sin? Responding to this question, or at least to one with the same intent, Gregory seems to be taking into account several factors that foreclose upon any unequivocal answer. First, he must account for the fact that believers do suffer evil circumstances in this life. On this point, Gregory adopts the growing consensus that all misfortune that comes upon believers is somehow chastisement for their sin. He does not see the suffering of good people as a mystery—and, ironically, thus misses the point of the very book he is exegeting. He says that we suffer, no matter how saintly we are, because we are not entirely saintly. Second, the standard for perfection is utter conformity to the jots and tittles of divine law. Third, God's judgment brooks nothing short of that meticulous conformity and thus every failure to meet utter conformity must be both punished and remedied.

All of this casts a shadow over even that perfection that we do attain (so Gregory) by rigorous discipline. The scales of the "severe Judge" would show that our very perfection itself is infected by sinfulness and would be dealt with accordingly did He not temper His reading of those scales with mercy.[19]

Put baldly, entire sanctification is possible in this life; perfection is not. But entire sanctification is twofold, for it deals both with the demand that the Law be perfectly fulfilled and the incapacity of human character, stuck in this miserable world in a morally feeble body, to fulfill it. Sanctification is both the actual making righteous of the believer, usually at baptism, insofar as that believer is capable of righteousness; and it is a divine forensic or legal declaration that the righteousness of Christ is accounted to the believer as the believer's own.[20] (Perfection lies beyond all of this.)

In both the "actual" and forensic senses, sanctification is complete in this life. In fact, in being part of the act of baptism, sancti-

---

17. *Moralia* XXII.20.46-51 (on Job 31:36).

18. *Moralia* V.33.59 (on Job 3:15).

19. *Moralia* V.11.21 (on Job 3:26).

20. *Moralia* XXIV.708.13-21 (on Job 33:26-27). For a statement on the imputation of Christ's righteousness to the believer, cf. *Moralia* IX.38-40.60-63 (on Job 9:32-35).

fication is complete at the very outset of the Christian's walk. But, as we have just noted, it is complete only in a relative sense. It is complete only insofar as the believer's own human character can receive it.[21] So, it is both complete and incomplete. In fact, it may be said that the believer's recognition of its incompleteness is one indication of its completeness in that believer, for sanctification is a matter of both purity of heart (of intention) and of maturity. And maturity includes both real growth in grace and an increasing recognition of the distance yet to be closed.

Gregory gives no place to any sense of achievement that would nourish spiritual pride. He plays the theme continually: Our righteousness, even that righteousness granted by grace itself, must always be compared only with absolute divine righteousness, and in that comparison it is as filthy rags.[22] Our sense of achievement is born of our sense of need, our yearning for Christlikeness in obedience to the will of God. Such a yearning is forever self-critical, is forever finding previously hidden faults in ourselves or hidden depths of righteousness in God. So it is that desire and compunction jointly fuel growth in sanctification.[23]

Our advance in purity infuriates the hosts of evil and they, being inordinately clever and adept at using the flesh to work our downfall, set about to undo that advance. And, while never fully successful in the life of the constant believer, they win some minor successes.[24]

Here it is that Gregory would have us understand that at the base of our righteousness, so susceptible to adulteration, is the unadulterated and invincible righteousness of Christ. It is both imputed to us and infused in us.[25] Being Christ's, it is perfect in itself, and being Christ's gift to us, it is imputed and infused in its perfection. And again, we see that *sanctification is entire, that it is for this life, and that it is both an act and a condition in which maturation is expected.*

But here we see how liturgical expression affects doctrine.

---

21. E.g., *Moralia* IX.35-36.55-58 (on Job 9:30-31). Also see *Moralia* V.36-38.65-69 (on Job 4:16-19).

22. E.g., *Moralia* V.38.68-69 (on Job 4:18-19).

23. E.g., *Moralia* XXIV.6.10-12 (on Job 33:26); *Moralia* XXXI.46.93 (on Job 39:26).

24. E.g., *Moralia* I.36.50-54 (on Job 1:40).

25. E.g., *Moralia* IX.38-40.60-63 (on Job 9:32-35).

Gregory understood the means of that imputation and impartation to be the sacraments of the church. What was given initially in baptism was readministered in the Eucharist. The Eucharist sanctified the believer again and again, just as baptism or confirmation did it for the first time. To be sure, the theology was not yet clearly worked out in Gregory's time. But it was universally held that the Mass (as it had come to be called) was a repetition of the sacrifice of Christ and a reapplication of its benefits to His people. And it was believed that apart from it, there could be no spiritual life.

Such a perspective made it quite impossible to think in terms of God's having done anything once-and-for-all in the life of the believer. And, in fact, medieval theology developed an enormous ambiguity concerning the assurance of salvation, which had its roots in a stout confidence in the power of the sacraments on the one hand and the continuing need for them on the other. This ambiguity beclouded the doctrine of sanctification and tended to cast the doctrine of perfection in terms of what the believer must *do* to attain salvation. In Gregory, we see Christian thought having taken a long stride in that direction.

For Gregory, sanctification, while related to perfection, is not perfection. Sanctification is the cleansing gift of the Holy Spirit; perfection is the final step in the process of coming to absolute conformity to all of the divine commandments and requirements. Perfection, in its strictest sense, belongs to the life that is to come. Sanctification is a cleansing of the affective side of life; perfection is an aligning of the life with the p's and q's of the divine will.

There certainly is sanctification without perfection, but there can be no perfection without sanctification. Sanctification is, in a sense, repeated by the applications of the benefits of Christ's sacrifice in the Mass—the very prayers of the Mass make for this. Perfection is once-for-all and irrevocable. Gregory is primarily concerned with perfection, not with sanctification.

Here, then, was a very serious step in the history of both doctrines. Thanks to Gregory, and in some measure to others before him, the monk became the ideal Christian and monasticism the ideal form of the Christian walk for the next 900 years. And the term *perfection* came to be tied more and more closely to that ideal. (In fact, the monks were called "the perfect.") So, the idea of perfection and the doctrine of perfection were generally thought of in the context of the disciplined life-style of the monastics.

"Perfection" had to do with practice and therefore with the "doing" of Christian life—and obviously there were but few who were flawless practitioners of everything thought to be Christian. So, where Gregory had equivocated the term and had sometimes spoken of the "perfect man" and his ways, while generally limiting the word in the strictest sense to the believer's life after death, the Middle Ages became even more precise. The monks were "the perfect" because of the aim of their lives, but perfection was understood to be nearly nonexistent among those this side of eternal life.

As for the term *sanctification,* it fell into almost a millennium of disuse as a term applicable to the daily life of the Christian. Of course it was more or less clearly held that it was granted either in baptism (in the case of adult converts) or in confirmation (in the case of baptized children), and, in a vague way, it was held to be repeated at varying levels, so to speak, in other sacraments—particularly in the Mass. But serious study of it as an aspect of Christian experience was generally muted.

Perfection, understood as the believer's responsibility, became the principal concern of the medieval Christian. Not that any believed that they could achieve it; but nearly all believed that it was the path to justification. Only when one reached perfection could one be justified, and for that, one needed to rely upon the Church with her sacraments, her priesthood, and her magnificent treasury of merit collected over the centuries. The term *sanctify* and its cognates were more usually applied to consecrated objects, to relics and buildings, to days and seasons, even to fields and weapons, than to individuals. For such a legacy, Gregory the Great must take considerable responsibility.

For all that we have said of the influence of Gregory's thought on later intellectual patterns, however, it would give a false picture of medieval thought were we to leave the impression that Gregory alone shaped the thought of the period. Especially is this so at the point of our concern in this section, the doctrine of entire sanctification. There was indeed quite another perspective. It was not unappreciative of Gregory. In fact, it very often lauded his spirituality. But rather than commencing from the standpoint of the misery of the human condition, it seems to have taken its departure from an optimism about what grace can do, and that gave it a very different outlook on the doctrine with which we are concerning ourselves.

B. Bernard of Clairvaux: Reuniting Sanctification and Perfection in the Contemplative Mode

Few figures in the history of Christianity have retained such universal respect and admiration as Bernard (d. 1153), founder and abbot of the monastery of the Cistercian order at Clairvaux in what is now France.[26] Not that he was always right: His treatment of Abelard was too harsh and narrow-minded, his rousing of Europe to the Second Crusade was wrongheaded, and his personal austerities were practically suicidal. But, though not always right, he was always authentically Christian. Where he was wrong, the motives still ring true with purity of intention. He also shows a remarkable spirit of self-criticism. We would analyze him these days as a very secure person.

In looking at Bernard's doctrinal stance, in particular at his understanding of sanctification, we must be careful to shift intellectual gears, as it were, so that we may empathize with both his cultural setting and his own way of reflecting theologically. We have had to do this from time to time throughout this section, but it may be well to remind us to do it again.

Monastic theology and theologizing were, and still are, different from the theology and the theologizing that transpires elsewhere—sometimes radically different. To be sure, the aim of monastic theology usually has differed little from the other common sorts: investigation of the faith and reflection upon it for apologetic, systematic, polemic, and devotional purposes. The degree of intensity of each purpose and its proportioning in any given thinker varied greatly, however. Monastic investigation and reflection arose out of the daily round of disciplined prayer, Bible study,

---

26. Strange as it may seem, there is no really definitive biography of Bernard in English and very few that move away from the hagiographic aim. However, certainly fundamental and containing first-rate research and reflection is W. W. Williams, *Saint Bernard of Clairvaux* (Westminster, Md.: Newman Press, 1952). Also very useful is Bruno S. James, *St. Bernard of Clairvaux* (New York: Harper, 1957). S. J. Eales, *The Life and Works of St. Bernard of Clairvaux,* 4 vols. (London: SPCK, 1889-96), is now valuable primarily for its translations of complete works. The best single biography remains E. Vacanard, *Vie de Saint Bernard,* 2 vols. (Paris, 1895). *Bernard de Clairvaux, Commission d'histoire de l'ordre de Citeaux,* III (Paris, 1953), is exceptionally valuable for bibliography and critical summaries covering both the life and the works of Bernard. The most readily available collection of Bernard's own writings is MPL 182-85. There is no complete English translation of his works, but Eales, *Life and Works of St. Bernard,* presents a useful selection. See also W. W. Williams (ed.), *Select Treatises of S. Bernard of Clairvaux* (London: Cambridge University, 1926); and Priest of Mount Melleray, *Sermons on the Canticle of Canticles,* 2 vols. (Dublin, 1920).

reading of the Fathers, and other aspects of community life. And such investigation and reflection were supposed to be reinvested in the life of the spiritual community.

So it is that medieval monastic theology is both intensely devotional and intensely practical. It is thoroughly biblical, as a rule, and thoroughly traditional, being rooted in continual exposure to the Bible and the Fathers, even hearing them read at mealtimes. And, it is profoundly Christocentric, for it takes its form under the influence of the frequent celebration of the Mass.[27]

This being true, we expect from Saint Bernard no systematic exposition of sanctification, nor of any other doctrine. What we may expect, and do indeed find, is an analysis, in a devotional-practical mode, of Christian experience from which we more mundane sorts may extrapolate more systematic expression. Always to be kept in mind, too, is the fact that Bernard addresses his works to those who are already believers.

Bernard's most striking and typical way of expressing the believer's relationship to God is to put it in terms of a marriage. The marriage and wedded relationship are between the believer and the Spouse, who is Christ, the Word. And, of course, fundamental to this marriage is love.

Bernard consistently and vigorously presses the point that this greatest of all love affairs is initiated by God himself, is moved along by the grace of God at work in the believer, and is issued in the believer's love for God in His own divine self. "He kindles thy desire himself, who is himself its Goal."[28]

> At the outset, I said that the reason we love God is God. And this is true because he is both the instigator and the end of our love. He occasions our human love. He gives power to love. He draws yearning to its consummation. In his very essence he is the Lovable One, and he gives himself over, as the object of our love. He wants our love for him to result in our happiness, not in emptiness and vanity. His love clears the path for ours and it is the reward for ours.
>
> So kind-heartedly does he direct us in the way of love! Such generosity is there in the love he returns to us for our

---

27. Cf. Leclercq, *Love of Learning,* for an excellent introduction to monastic theology.

28. *De diligendo Deo* (On the Love of God), 7. Here, the translation of "A Religious of C.S.M.V." has been utilized. It appears in Williams (ed.), *Select Treatises,* 40. Also cf. Ray C. Petry (ed.), *Late Medieval Mysticism,* vol. XIII of the *Library of Christian Classics* (Philadelphia: Westminster, 1957), 59.

> own. How delightful he is to those waiting for him. To all who call upon him he is extravagant, for he is able to give nothing more valuable than himself. He gave himself in order to be our righteousness; he is retaining himself in order to be our great reward. With the refreshing of our souls he busies himself; to liberate the captives he spends himself.
>
> To the soul seeking you, how good you are, O Lord! And to the soul that finds? The wonder is that no one can seek you who has not already found you. It is your will that we find in order to seek, to seek in order to find. So, we are able both to seek and to find you, but we cannot ever precede you in these things. Even though we say, "My prayer shall come before thee early," that prayer would be cold and without love were it not warmed by your own breath and generated by your own spirit.[29]

This insistence by Bernard that God is the initiator, sustainer, and goal of Christian love is in no way new, of course. But what is new in Bernard (new insofar as it had been missing or mute since Augustine) is the expectation that through the action of divine love, our love can be perfect in this life. Augustine had begun to shift the context of the word *perfection* away from the biblical concept of love and spiritual aim or purpose to a more legalistic perspective. His emphasis was upon the question of explicit obedience to the commandments of God, understood rather literally. Gregory and later Westerners had taken the term even farther upon that path. Motive or intention was read in terms of deed or activity, rather than deed or activity being read in terms of motive or intention.

In fact, the very term *love* had undergone something of a metamorphosis in the translation from the Greek *agape* to the Latin *caritas.* The latter had about it a calculating quality that *agape* did not have. The question "How much?" could hardly be asked of *agape;* it was perfectly legitimate to ask it of *caritas,* which could mean "high cost of living" as well as "love."

Of course, Augustine and others were well aware of the possibility of equivocation and meant by *caritas* to speak of love. But the connotation hung on, and there was no small tendency to try to keep *caritas* and perfection separate because of it. That is to say, perfection had to do with meeting a standard in behavior; *caritas*

29. Ibid.

or "love" had to do with the affective condition, the motive or intention, behind meeting it.[30]

Bernard reunites the two—love and perfection. Signal of this is the change of terms used for "love." Bernard generally prefers *diligendo,* the gerund or verbal noun form of *diligo:* "to single out," "to love," "to esteem," "to be content with," "to appreciate." In itself, *diligendo* is not that much freer of the calculative connotations of *caritas.* And, while it does not carry the sensual baggage that the word *amor* had come to bear by Bernard's time, it did denote a certain sensuality in place of the commercial tones of *caritas.* Latin both arose from a culture and shaped cultures that could not carry the precise weight of *agape.*

By using the verbal noun, Bernard places his understanding of Christian love in the realm of doing, of activity. And *diligo* includes the element of the affective to which *amor* is almost totally given and the element of the intellective to which *caritas* is more closely tied. Then, by uniting love, as activity, with perfection, he moves perfection away from the strictly legal and abstract connotations it had always borne in Latin thought. This moves it away from the legal and abstract toward a more relative and practical definition.[31]

This is not to say that in Bernard's thought love and perfection are solely described by activity—by doing. By insisting that we love only because we are loved by love divine, Bernard roots love and perfection in the very character of God. But now, rather than making unadulterated love and perfection primarily goals to be achieved, Bernard makes them initiatory gifts of God to the believer. The believer lives out their implications; that is, he manifests them. In that way, the believer does indeed become more loving and "more perfect." But in another sense, the increase lies in the expression of what the believer has been given from the beginning. It lies in increased *expression,* not, strictly speaking, in an increasing *possession* of love and perfection.[32]

As we have seen, this notion is presented by Augustine, but in a very tentative way, for his emphasis is upon perfection as a su-

---

30. For a thorough though somewhat overdrawn discussion of the theological implication of the use of *caritas* for *agape,* cf. Anders Nygren, *Agape and Eros,* trans. by Philip S. Watson (rev. ed.; Philadelphia: Westminster Press, 1953), 452-58, 476-558.

31. Cf., ibid., 645-51.

32. There is increased or intensified expression, not increased possession of love.

pernatural goal wrought by manifesting the gift of sanctification. And Augustine is the mentor of most of the medieval thinkers on this matter. But Bernard is more optimistic about the possibilities of grace in this life and seems not to make Augustine's equation of perfect love, perfection and glorification. On the other hand, Bernard is quite clear in saying that there is a degree of love reserved only to those who die in the Lord—and yet, even this degree is sometimes tasted in this life.

The highest degree of love, the fourth by Bernard's reckoning, is one in which one loves oneself, only for God's sake.

> My own opinion is that the command to love the Lord our God with all our heart and soul and strength will not be perfectly fulfilled until the mind no longer has to consider the flesh, and the soul has to sustain the life and powers of the body no more. Only when it is relieved of these impeding concerns will it be completely buttressed by the power of God. It cannot focus its faculties on God nor set its eyes upon his countenance while these are being preoccupied and spent with caring for this feeble, fractious frame.
>
> But in the spiritual and immortal body—the body made whole, harmonious and at one; the body in everything subject to the spirit—the soul may hope to attain the fourth degree of love. Or, better said, may hope to be taken up into it, for it is not reached by human striving. It is given by the power of God to whomever he wills to give it. At this point, this perfect love will easily be attained; no blandishment of flesh delays, no vexation of body can distract, the willing, eager transition to the joy of Christ the Lord.[33]

And yet, while Bernard seems to hold this fourth degree to be a blessing of the life that is to come, he is unwilling to curb his enthusiasm for the possibilities of grace here in this life, and he makes it quite clear that the hindrance to reaching this highest degree of love here is not the evil or frailty of being human as such. He does not accept the widely held view that to be in the body is necessarily to be in sin.

First, as we have noted, the fourth degree may be savored even in this life: "Happy is he, and holy as well, who has been granted a tasting of this kind of love right here in this mortal life, even if rarely or but once, even if for but a brief moment."[34]

---

33. *De diligendo Deo,* 10.

34. Ibid.

Second, Bernard deliberately avoids the two alternatives usually taken in describing just how the soul will be enabled in eternity to enjoy blessings not open to it in this life. These were either to denigrate the value of the human self and to make of eternal life a sort of swallowing up or absorption into divinity of whatever was worth preserving of human nature, or to see the soul alone as worth preservation and as the real essence of human being so that eternal life involved discarding of anything that might be called "the body."

In popular thought, the idea of the resurrection of the body was stoutly retained, often in very crude terms. But the philosophers and theologians had been profoundly affected by the idea of the immortality of the soul—an idea much more philosophically manageable than that of the resurrection of the body. Bernard rejects both of the philosophical alternatives and the crude popular idea as well. He will hold to the resurrection of the body, without crudity.

> We read in the Scriptures that God made all things for himself. So it is that his creatures must aim at conforming themselves perfectly to their creator and at living according to his will. And thus we must set our love on him, little by little conforming our will to his who made everything for himself, making only his will and not our own satisfaction the object of our desire, not wanting anything, neither ourselves nor anything else, to be or to have been other than as would satisfy him. . . . O chaste and holy love, delightsome and charming! O pure and spotless intention of will—purer because now at last rid of self-will, the more delightsome and charming because at last its whole outlook is divine.
>
> To become like this is to be deified. As a tiny water droplet when mingled with much wine assumes so completely the taste and color of the wine as to appear no longer to have separate existence; as molten, white-hot iron, so much like the fire when it appears to have renounced its natural state; as air when inundated by the pure light of the sun is changed so much as to seem not to be lit but to be light itself; so it is in the case of the saints. Their human love will then be melted out of them and poured over into the very will of God, as it were (for this is really indescribable). It must be this way. Otherwise, how could God be "all in all" if anything merely human remained in man? And yet, our human substance will remain. We shall still be ourselves, though in another form, another glory, a different capacity.[35]

35. Ibid.

So, death, according to Bernard, is not an escape from humanness but a perfecting of it—or, better, what lies the other side of death is a perfecting of humanness. And spiritually, it is not so much an end of the impossibility of perfectly loving God as it is the opportunity to take yet another step in a path of love already well-traversed in this life. In fact, the third degree of love, a degree to be fulfilled in this earthly life, is itself described in terms of joyous commitment to God and to neighbor in "pure love, without self-interest." Even "our natural self, our fleshly desires" are transformed to the loving service of God and others.

> We tell our natural self, our fleshly appetites, "It is not because of your importunings that we now love God. It is because we have tasted for ourselves and know how gracious the Lord is." So it is that our fleshly needs come to be a language of sorts which joyfully declares the benefits of which those needs have taught us the value. And, this having been learned, we find no problem in fulfilling the commandment to love our neighbor.
>
> The person who loves like this truly loves; and in loving like this he loves the things of God. He loves purely and disinterestedly, and, as Peter says, for this reason that person will quickly obey the chaste command of God, purifying his heart in the obedience of love. He loves righteously, and takes to heart this righteous commandment. He does not make this love, so true and just and pure, to hang on contingencies, and for this reason it is acceptable to God.
>
> It is pure love, for it is demonstrated in deed and in truth, not merely in hollow words. It is righteous love, for the one who has received freely gives freely. This love has the quality of God's own love, for it seeks not its own but those things which are Christ's, just as he sought ours. Or, better, just as he sought us, and never sought his own. . . . This is love of God for God's sake, not merely for oneself.[36]

We have let Bernard speak at length for himself in this section and his message is quite clear. There is, for this life, an experience of perfect love, of purity of heart, that is to be sought after, attained, and nourished. And what Bernard has said in these passages from *De diligendo Deo* he says in other of his works as well.

We must not make of Bernard a John Wesley before John Wesley, but it is quite clear that he breaks out of the Augustinian impasse, not by some optimistic estimate of human nature, especially not by a reversion to the path of the Pelagians nor even semi-

---

36. *De diligendo Deo,* 9.

Pelagians, but by a very different estimate of what God's grace can do. "Indeed, just what is man unless you take notice of him?"[37]

The divine agent in this "taking notice" is the Holy Spirit, of whom Bernard speaks in a way not generally heard for half a millennium in the West. For Bernard, the Spirit is both the Spirit in the Church and the Spirit in the believer. Of course, the sacramental theology of the Church had always said both and said it clearly. At baptism-confirmation, the Spirit came to dwell in the believer. But Bernard is the first writer in five centuries to elaborate upon the spiritual possibilities and privileges that the divine presence opens to the believer.

In his consideration of the three ways in which we love God, for instance, Bernard notes the special role of the Spirit in especially the second and third ways—the rational and the spiritual. In preaching concerning the rational or intellectual love of God, he speaks of those whose faith is fixed on the historical person of Christ, "the flesh of Christ," and says that their devotion "is a gift of the Holy Spirit, and a great gift."[38] But as he had earlier urged believers to move from "carnal," or, better, "mundane" love of God to rational, now he invites them to move to perfect rational love and thence to "spiritual" love of God. This "spiritual" love of God is a love "distinguished by the fulness of the Spirit."[39]

Mundane love is loving God with all the heart. Rational love is loving God with all the soul. Spiritual love is the perfection of loving—loving with the whole heart, whole mind, and all the strength.

> If [loving God with all the soul] be augmented by an energy so great and an aide so powerful as that of the Holy Spirit, so that neither vexations nor sufferings (no matter their raging), nor even the fear of death, can ever bring about defection from righteousness, then is God loved with all the strength. And that is spiritual love. Further, it seems to me that this label is especially suitable to such love because what so particularly distinguishes it is the fulness of the Spirit.[40]

---

37. *Cantica canticorum, serm.* XX.1. The English title of this work is *Sermons on the Song of Songs.* Again, we use the Latin form because it will be the one most encountered by the reader in the literature.

38. *Cantica canticorum, serm.* XX.8.

39. *Cantica canticorum, serm.* XX.9.

40. Ibid.

The agent is the Spirit, the norm is Christlikeness. But the norm is not slavish imitation, nor an attempt at it. Rather it is the likeness of mind and will that characterizes spouses deeply in love with one another. Marriage is, as we have already noted, Bernard's typical metaphor for the relationship between Christ and the believer.

> When you see a soul which, having left behind all, adheres to the Word with each thought and yearning, lives for the Word alone, disciplines itself according to the Word and even becomes fruitful, as it were, by the Word—a soul which can say, "To me to live is Christ, to die is gain"—then you may be very certain that this soul is a Bride, married to the Word.[41]

Obviously, Bernard is here describing both aspiration and spiritual reality in this life. True to the tradition going back to Augustine, he reserves the ultimate perfection for life beyond the grave. But his reading and experience, including the daily liturgical exercise, bring him to speak of a very high degree of perfection in love, of identity with Christ, of loving obedience to God, and of service to neighbor here in this life. Again, unlike many others whose outlook on the possibilities for Christlikeness in this life were equally as optimistic, Bernard continually insists that this is an optimism of grace, not of sheer human moral capability. But it is a matter of authentic righteousness developing in the believer. Mere imputed righteousness is far from Bernard's mind, it seems.

It is all the Spirit's work and is therefore sanctification, a sanctification that is complete or entire but also admits of stages or degrees, and a sanctification that is perfection, for the essence of both sanctification and perfection is love. So, as we have stated earlier, and as we may now see more clearly, the genius of Bernard's understanding of sanctification is that he reunites it with the doctrine of perfection under the rubric of love.

While this theological step, taken again after a 500-year stall, was almost forgotten again for another half-millennium. Still, it was made. And, as far into the recesses of the forgetfulness of the majority as it fell, when it did surface again, from time to time, its orthodoxy, its spiritual legitimacy, and its practical sanity were fully recognized. Medieval thought was neither surprised nor threatened by it.

The mystics stated the case most clearly. And, of course, Ber-

---

41. *Cantica canticorum, serm.* LXXXV.12.

nard is found in the first rank among them. But there were other styles of expression as well, so we turn to one of those "other styles," the scholastic mode, as it is represented by the greatest scholastic of them all, Thomas Aquinas.

C. Thomas Aquinas: Reuniting Sanctification and Perfection in the Intellectual Mode

The Christian Church has been blessed beyond measure along the course of her history with great thinkers—and even more, great thinkers who were great saints, examples to believers. Of these, there are a score or more whose ideas have shaped Western civilization, but among this score a handful stand so tall as to merit special notice as formative, creative personalities whose contributions to how we understand God, ourselves, and our world stand as foundation blocks. Here we see the apostle Paul, Augustine, Thomas Aquinas, John Calvin, and Isaac Newton.

In this section, we consider the thought of one of these, Thomas Aquinas.[42] We cannot, of course, review his entire theology, nor need we. Instead, we will look at it as it comes to bear on the broad issue of Christian perfection and the narrower one within it, entire sanctification. But we must first say a few words about the man and then a few about the theological system within which he talks about Christian perfection.

Thomas, often called Aquinas (he was from the Italian town of Aquino), was born in 1225, in one of the most fruitful periods of intellectual cultivation that Western civilization has known. The son of an aristocrat, he was afforded the privilege of studying under the most noted scholar of his time, Albert, a German academic

---

42. Literature on Thomas and editions of his work abound. The best critical collection of his works is the so-called Leonine text, *S. Thomae Aquinatis Doctoris Angelici Opera Omnia, Iussu impensaque Leonis xiii* (Rome, 1882-1948), which has undergone a number of editings. There is no English translation of his collected works though all of his works have been Englished in one collection or another. The most useful translation of his major work, the *Summa Theologica* (hereinafter abbreviated ST) has been done by the Fathers of the English Dominican Province, *The Summa Theologica of St. Thomas Aquinas* (2nd rev. ed.; London: Eyre and Spottiswoode, 1912-1936). For his very important *Summa Contra Gentiles,* see the translation by Anton C. Pegis, *St. Thomas Aquinas: On the Truth of the Christian Faith, Summa Contra Gentiles* (Garden City, N.Y.: Image Books, 1955). Among studies of Thomas's thought, the student should not overlook Etienne Gilson, *The Philosophy of St. Thomas Aquinas,* trans. by E. Bullough (3rd rev. ed.; St. Louis and London: B. Herder, 1937); or Jacques Maritain, *The Angelic Doctor, The Life and Thought of St. Thomas Aquinas,* trans. by J. F. Scanlan (Toronto: Longmans, Green, 1931).

who belonged to the new order of mendicant monks called the Dominicans or Order of Preachers. So much appreciated was this teacher's skill that he was called Albert the Great (in Latin, Albertus Magnus). But Albert was eclipsed, even in his lifetime, by his student, Thomas. Thomas, who also became a Dominican, taught at Paris, Naples, and Rome and died at the age of 49 in 1274, on the way to the church council at Lyons, France. He left the Church an enormous literary legacy and a theological system, called Thomism, which even today is fundamental to Roman Catholicism, though it is no longer the norm.

Basic to understanding Thomas is his opposition to any thinking that sets God and His world in opposition to each other or in contrast and discontinuity with each other. Thomas firmly believes that sin has separated God and man and God and man's world. But that separation is a consequence of sin, not a consequence of nature. The separation was not originally there. The opposition, contrast, and discontinuity are results of sin, not characteristics of creation. Furthermore, even in the face of these doleful consequences of evil, Thomas sees remaining in the mire a "demand" on nature's part that it be supernaturally completed and a grace-moved striving on the part of human nature to find its ultimate good. "Man's inclination to virtue cannot be totally destroyed."[43]

On the other hand, no one can capitalize on such virtue as remains and thereby save himself. "If one is to know any truth at all, he needs divine help."[44] "In the state of pure nature one needs a power added by grace to his natural power, for this reason: to do and to will supernatural good. And in the state of corrupt nature, he needs grace for two reasons: in order to be brought to health and in order to achieve the meritorious good of supernatural virtue."[45] "A man cannot, by his natural powers, do the meritorious works that are worthy of eternal life."[46] "One cannot prepare himself for the light of grace unless God gives him gracious help, mov-

---

43. ST II. i. Q. 85, art. 2. Re: the abbreviation II. i: II refers to the second part (secundae) usually noted 2ae or ii, i to the first part of the 2nd. Older works frequently reverse these so that II, i means 2nd part of the first part. Our abbreviation means Part II, first part (section).

44. ST II. i. Q. 109, art. 1.

45. ST II. i. Q. 109, art. 2.

46. ST II. i. Q. 109, art. 5.

ing him inwardly."[47] "One cannot in any way rise from sin by himself, without the help of grace."[48]

We have strung together this series of quotations to show how firmly Thomas declares both the presence of some virtue even in corrupt humankind, and the utter necessity of divine grace for salvation at every step of the way. It is important for us to remember this because when Thomas writes of sanctification the Protestant reader is likely to accuse Thomas of works-righteousness. It might appear that he is teaching that somehow we do indeed save ourselves by capitalizing on the virtue still in us, and that we sanctify ourselves by joining to our virtue deeds of goodness.

The accusation is not altogether unjust, since Thomas does indeed believe that our works play a positive role in our salvation. Grace, for Thomas, is an enabler and an aid to salvation; it is not the sole ground and cause of salvation that it is for Protestants who really are true to their Protestantism. On the other hand, salvation does begin in grace and cannot proceed without it, according to Thomas.[49] He will not allow a sharp disjuncture between the human being who is being saved and the one who is not being saved, insofar as their being human is concerned.[50] The human being not being saved can still have true knowledge, even knowledge of God, through natural means. In fact, by use of his senses, such an individual can gain knowledge even of that which transcends sense.[51]

All of this means that when Thomas talks of perfection and of sanctification, he will sound rather different from, say, Augustine or Luther or Calvin—or Wesley. He will differ from Augustine, Luther, and Calvin in his understanding that the definition of perfection is relative, depending on the thing perfected. Behind this, of course, lies an understanding of human nature and of sin, that

---

47. ST II. i. Q. 109, art. 6.

48. ST II. i. Q. 109, art. 7.

49. ST II. i. Q. 109.

50. E.g., ST II. i. Q. 109, arts. 2, 8.

51. Cf. ST II. i. Q. 109, art. 1: "We must say, then, that if one is to know any truth whatsoever, he needs divine aid so that his intellect may be moved to its action by God. But one does not need new light added to the natural in order to know the truth in everything—only in those things that transcend one's natural knowledge. Still, God sometimes teaches human beings miraculously, by grace, in what could be known anyway through natural reason."

must also differ from those of Augustine or the others named. It bears investigation.

Thomas's understanding of human sinfulness and sin is not substantially different from that of his scholastic predecessors. And they, in turn, depended heavily upon Augustine for the particulars of their doctrine, though they seem to have missed or rejected his utter pessimism about human nature apart from grace.

Thomas wants to insist that original sin is both negative and positive, both defect and affect or source of action (whether physical or attitudinal). So, citing Anselm, who had followed Augustine in the matter, Thomas agrees that original sin "is the absence of original justice," Adam having been created perfect in righteousness and able not to sin.[52] At the same time, he defines original sin as a habit *(habitus)*. It is the *habitus* of concupiscence, the disposition toward lack of moral order or the lack of moral order itself brought about as the powers of the soul turn inordinately toward the impermanent and changeable instead of toward God.[53] So original sin is both the absence of something (original righteousness) and the presence of something (concupiscence).

But original sin does not entirely destroy nor obliterate "the good nature." If that were so, the human being would be incapable of sin or sinning.

> The good of nature that is diminished by sin is the natural inclination to virtue, which is appropriate to man by the very fact that he is a rational being. It is because of this that he acts according to reason, which is to act virtuously. Now then sin cannot entirely remove from man his rationality, for then he would be no longer capable of sin. Therefore, it is impossible that the good of nature should be completely destroyed.[54]

We must hasten to note, however, that Thomas is not about to propound a view of the "good of nature" that would dispense with the need of grace for salvation.[55] Original righteousness (or original justice, as he calls it), an inborn *habitus*; a natural ethical state from which concupiscence was absent, characterized Adam. And it was a gift of grace. But that *habitus* would not have saved him. Salvation depended, and yet depends, upon the "superadded gift" or "superadded grace."

---

52. ST II. i. Q. 83, art. 1. Cf. Anselm, *De conceptu virginal*, 27.
53. ST II. i. Q. 83, art. 3.
54. ST II. i. Q. 85, art. 2.
55. ST II. i. Q. 109, art. 7.

Even before the Fall, grace was needed, for while original righteousness enabled Adam to "love God naturally above all things," he needed grace to move him to that love.[56] The reason for this is that "eternal life is an end exceeding the proportions of human nature." That is to say, human nature as human nature was not created to reach eternal life. Eternal life is beyond the range given it naturally. "Man, in his own strength, cannot produce meritorious works proportionate to eternal life." So, "without grace man cannot merit eternal life."[57]

What was true before the Fall is surely true in the wake of it. Original righteousness has been forfeited. That *habitus* or disposition to "love God naturally above all things" has been lost. And what remains is a *languor naturae,* original sin, an enfeebled nature, the *fomes peccati.*[58]

Sin, as such, that is, sin as act, whether physical or otherwise, arises from this languor of nature. Original sin is a *habitus,* actual sin is not. "Actual sin is lack of order in an act," not a disposition.[59] But in both cases, there is but a single remedy. That is, the grace of God. And this is begun in baptism, which both makes the soul able to do good and forgives sin and cancels penalty.[60] But does this cleansing then make the recipient unable to sin? Thomas is clear. It does not, for although an "infused disposition" is granted in baptism,[61] the hold of concupiscence is only weakened. It is not broken. But why not? And, is there any reason to hope that it might be in this life? To answer these, we must turn first to Thomas's doctrine of sin itself.

Thomas understands sin to reside ultimately in the will.[62] Here, he follows Augustine.[63] "Since an act must be voluntary in order to be moral (as has been said), it follows that the will, which

---

56. ST II. i. Q. 109, art. 3.

57. ST II. i. Q. 109, art. 5.

58. ST II. i. Q. 85, arts. 1-4. Also cf. ST II. i. Q. 82, art. 1. The phrase *langour naturae* is from Peter Lombard, *Sentences* II. xxx. 8.

59. ST II. i. Q. 82, art. 1.

60. ST III. Q. 69, arts. 2, 3, 6.

61. ST III. Q. 69, arts. 4-5.

62. ST II. i. Q. 74, arts. 1-5.

63. Thomas cites Augustine, *Retractationes* i.9; *De duabus animabus* (On two souls against the Manichaeans) 10; *De vera religione* (On true religion) 14; and *De Trinitate* (On the Trinity) xii. 12.

is the source of all voluntary activity—good or bad, is the source of sin."[64]

Having said, "There is no sin unless the act is ultimately controlled by the will,"[65] Thomas must respond to the criticism that if sin be strictly a matter of voluntary transgression, he has exempted too much of what a human being is and does from moral responsibility.

What of the emotional side of life, the side that has to do with feeling—the affective side?[66] What are its moral ramifications? "Sin can be found in the affective side of life," says Thomas. In fact, even though the stain of original sin is taken away in baptism, there remain the effects of that state, which include "the perpetual corruption of the affective aspects of life." There always remains the *fomes peccati,* the tinder for sin. In fact, so effective is its presence that while avoiding one form of sinfulness (temptation to which has come through the affective character of life), one often falls into another. For instance, avoiding impure thoughts, he falls into vanity over his intellectual and spiritual prowess in substituting science (let us say) for sex. For this, one is culpable. And, such culpability is inescapable. The *fomes* is always with us. But insofar as such "falling" is in consequence of the *fomes* without deliberation on the victim's part, it is not really a human act "in the perfect sense." It can be neither perfectly virtuous nor perfectly sinful. It is venial sin and therefore needs the benefits of the atonement but it does not, in itself, separate the perpetrator from God.[67]

Sin, then, can be found in the affective side of life, but only as "imperfect sin." That is to say, the affective side of life *in itself* is not capable of sin that separates from God. Where there is mortal sin in the affective side of life, it is signal of the working of the will in the affective. The affective may *dispose* the will to mortal sin, but

---

64. ST II. i. Q. 74, art. 1. Cf. ST II. i. Q. 1, art. 1, and Q. 18, arts. 6 and 9. Thomas has made it clear in another portion of the article quoted that "sin is an action," and by action he means either some physical activity or some attitude or "motive" (as we would say).

65. ST II. i. Q. 74, art. 2.

66. Thomas uses the word *sensualitas,* which is too easily translated "sensuality" and taken to have voluptuous connotations. Better to think of it as meaning "feeling" or "emotion," the affective aspects of life, which is much nearer the Latin *sensus—sensualis—sensualitas.*

67. Unfortunately, the great Blackfriars' edition/translation of ST translates *fomes* as "spark," which changes Thomas's meaning. Cf. ST II. i. Q. 74, art. 3. *Fomes* is "tinder," that upon which the spark falls.

the culpability lies with the will. Virtue lies, then, not in mere control of the affective, but in the disposition of the will. And behind the will lies reason, which orders life, which aims life toward God.

Can the reason, then, be sinful? Or has Thomas, by making sin a matter of the will, exempted reason from fundamental culpability as he has the affective side of life? Thomas responds that sin "can be found in the reason." It is there either "as a defect which is voluntary or as an act which is the source of something voluntary." Reason can err or be in ignorance about what it should know (and know correctly), and it can initiate or fail to inhibit disorder in the affective life. In these cases, reason is sinful.[68] And where is the will in this malfeasance of reason?

The will is the rational appetite. That is, the will is the means by which reason seeks to actualize itself; and reason actualizes itself as it comes to know God perfectly. So, reason proposes the will's object (that is, to know God) and the will moves the reason to keep before the will that object. Or, at least that is how the human *psyche* would work if sin did not interfere.[69]

Sin enters on the one hand by reason's proposal or approval of some object other than authentic knowledge of God himself; and on the other hand by the will's failure to move reason to be true to itself, either by sloth or by deliberation.

So it is that while Thomas is convinced that the affective side of life is corrupted, it is never guilty of mortal sin out of its own resources. If mortal sin be found in the affective, it is because the affective is moved by the will. Such sin as does exist in the affective aspect of character needs the atonement of Christ, but it is not sin in the specifically moral sense. Sin, properly so-called, is a matter of volition, not affective appetite.

And sin, properly so called, cannot be a matter of faulty reason as such. But here, Thomas reasons very subtly. If the fault in reason arises from reason itself (for example, ignorance or insanity), then there is no moral culpability. But if the fault in reason arises from the failure of the will to move reason to seek its true end (that is, the knowledge of God), as for instance in the case of intellectual laziness or in the case of deliberately fostering a known prejudice when contradictory evidence is plainly at hand, the rea-

---

68. ST II. i. Q. 74, art. 5.

69. Cf. ST II. i. Q. 17, art. 1.

son is fully culpable. Reason should, in both cases, press the will back to its proper object. So it may be said that sin, properly so-called, remains a matter of volition, not of rational failure, but, reason must keep will on target.

While Thomas draws explicitly from Augustine for the details of his doctrine of sin, he finally rejects Augustine at the most fundamental level. Thomas will not say that the human being *is* the sinful situation. His positive regard for creation, including human nature, and for the possibilities of grace is too high for that. On the other hand, Thomas refuses to go the way of the Pelagians and claim for humanity the ability to save itself. Salvation is not merely the grace of God cooperating with a debilitated and poorly taught, but not fundamentally ruined, human nature. His sensitivity to the Pauline interpretation of the Atonement and to the aggressiveness and deceitfulness of sin will not allow even that first step toward Pelagius.

So what we have in Thomas is a sense of the sinfulness of sin that is as bleak as Augustine's, but much more confidence in the regenerative character of grace than the Bishop of Hippo would allow.

Let's look at this more positive side, then. We discover it in Thomas's concern with perfection and sanctification.

Thomas states his doctrine of perfection with his typical clarity and thoroughness. His best-focused discussion of it is in his *Summa Theologica,* part two, section two, question 184, articles 1 through 8 (ST, II.ii. Q. 184, arts. 1-8). Here, having agreed in the previous question that Gregory the Great was correct in asserting that there are three conditions among converts, "the beginning, the middle, and perfection,"[70] Thomas goes on to discuss that third condition. And although he follows the opinion of his era in thinking that its reality is known chiefly among monastics, he begins broadly, writing of perfection in general, then moving to perfection among various classes of cleric and monastic.

Our interest lies particularly in the first four articles of question 184: (1) "Whether the perfection of the Christian life consists principally in charity"; (2) "Whether anyone can be perfect in this life"; (3) "Whether perfection in this life consists in observing precepts or counsels" (that is, whether perfection consists in observing

70. ST II. ii. Q. 183, art. 4. He cites Gregory, *Moralia* XXIV.2.

law or recommendations)[71]; (4) "Whether everyone who is perfect is in the state of perfection." It may help the reader to think of the articles in the following way: (1) The nature of perfection; (2) the possibility of perfection in this life; (3) the way of perfection; (4) the difference between doing perfectly and being perfect.

Just as sin is believed by Thomas to reside chiefly in the will, so he also locates love or charity there.[72,73] The nature of perfection, then, is intimately related to volition, since perfection is precisely perfection in charity.

> Anything is said to be perfect insofar as it attains its own appropriate end, for this is its perfection. Now, it is charity that unites us to God, who is the ultimate end of the human soul, since, as it is said in I John, "He that abideth in charity abideth in God and God in him." So, the perfection of the Christian life consists principally in charity.[74]

This view of perfection counters two other perspectives afloat in Thomas's time: (1) that perfection cannot consist principally in charity since there are biblical passages calling for us to be perfect in other ways, and (2) that "the perfection of the Christian life consists not only in charity but also in other virtues." Thomas responds to these, taking his lead from Paul: "Above all these things have charity, which is the bond of perfection" (Col. 3:14).

To the assertion that since the Bible calls for perfection of various characteristics other than charity, charity cannot be the heart of perfection, Thomas responds that without charity the other virtues have no root. To the assertion that the perfection of the Christian life consists in other virtues in addition to charity, Thomas responds that charity is in an absolute sense the perfection of the Christian life. It is charity by which the soul is united to God. More abstractly, charity brings us to lack nothing essential to Christian life; with it, we lack nothing. Other virtues constitute the Christian life only in a relative sense—that is, their perfection is

---

71. The Latin title reads "utrum perfectio viae consistat in praeceptis, an in consiliis." Thomas's example of a precept would be any one of the Ten Commandments. A counsel would be Matt. 19:21, "If you would be perfect, go sell what you have and give to the poor, and come, follow me." At ST II. i. Q. 108, art. 4: "Here is the difference between counsel and precept: precept carries with it necessity while counsel depends upon the option of the one to whom it is given."

72. Thomas's word for love is *caritas* this time.

73. ST II. ii. Q. 184, art. 1.

74. Ibid., Thomas's biblical quotations are generally from the Vulgate, although on occasion he quotes in free form.

relative, for all must relate to the absolute, the principal, the maximum, to charity.[75]

For Thomas, then, charity is the main content of Christian perfection. But can anyone be perfect in this life?[76] Thomas faces the question squarely. Presenting first the negative response to the question, he first cites the apostle Paul (1 Cor. 13:10), who implies that as long as hope and faith remain, then "that which is perfect" has not come. So, since hope and faith do remain in this life, perfection is not possible. Then he cites Aristotle, who defines perfection as a matter of lacking nothing, and goes on to note James 3:2 and Ps. 139:15, both of which affirm human imperfection—"therefore no one is perfect in this life." Finally, arguing from his own assertion that "the perfection of the Christian life consists in charity," he cites Gregory the Great to the effect that we'll certainly have more love when we see Christ than we now have (implying lack of perfection). Noting that we do not *actually* love all of our neighbors but are only *disposed* to do so in this life, he again concludes that perfection eludes us in this life. But then, presenting the positive argument, he quotes Matt. 5:48 and concludes, "Therefore, it would seem that one can be perfect in this life."

In typical fashion, then, Thomas sets about to synthesize all of this into his own response. Again, he lays the foundation by reiterating that when we speak of perfection in relation to the Christian life, we are speaking of love. But he wants, too, to take seriously Aristotle's observation that perfection implies a certain universality: "That is perfect to which nothing is lacking." So, he notes that we can consider perfection in three ways.

First, there is absolute perfection, a perfection in which one's loving would reach as far as the lovableness of the object of that love. Specifically, it would be to love God to the extent that He is lovable. Obviously, only God can have or be this sort of love. *Second,* there is that perfection in which one loves at one's own full capacity. This would not be simply a matter of a disposition to love fully, but a matter of actively, actually loving fully. Such love, says Thomas, is impossible to attain here, but will be possible in heaven. *Third,* there is a perfection that does not demand such totality as the first and second but does demand a total exclusion of

75. Ibid. See the *"responsio"* or "reply to objections."

76. ST II. ii. Q. 184, art. 3.

everything "contrary to the motive or movement *(motus)* of love for God."[77] This third sort of perfection "is possible in this life in two modes": in the exclusion from the will of anything "contradictory to love, that is, mortal sin" and in the will's rejection of anything that prevents the disposition of the soul *(mentis)* toward God from being total.

Here, in discussing this third sort of perfection, this attainable perfection, Thomas makes another distinction that we only mention now but with which we will work in more detail shortly. Love, says Thomas, cannot exist without the exclusion from the will of anything contradictory to it. So, this level of perfection is absolutely necessary to salvation. Love *can* exist where the will has not yet perfectly rejected those things that prevent a total disposition toward love of God. It is this second condition that is the subject, or object, of sanctifying grace.

Thomas's replies to the objections to the proposition that we can be perfect in this life are instructive. In the case of the quotation from 1 Cor. 13:10, Thomas looks at the larger context and says that Paul is, of course, correct, but he is not speaking of the second nor the third sort of perfection. In response to Aristotle's definition and the assertions from James and the Psalms, Thomas does not deny the imperfection of even the perfect in this life. But he does insist on the relative character of perfection—it is when compared to heavenly perfection that there is no perfection on earth. This he goes on to explicate in responding to the observation that "habitual" love, that is, a disposition to love as against an actually practiced love, may be continual in us. But it is imperfect and therefore perfection in this life is impossible. Thomas says,

> To the third objection, one responds by saying that since our present (i.e., earthly) mode of life does not permit us to continually move toward God "actu," in all our performance, neither can we continually move toward each person in particular in all our performance. But it is enough that one tend toward all in general and to each in disposition (to love) and by readiness of spirit.[78]

---

77. The Latin term *motus* may take either an attitudinal meaning (impulse, inspiration; emotion, passion) or one denoting activity (movement, motion; gesture; rebellion). A *motus animi,* a *motus* of the spirit, was an emotion; a *motus terrae,* a *motus* of earth, an earthquake.

78. ST II. ii. Q. 184, art. 3.

On this ground, there *is* perfection in this life. One can live without holding affections contrary to love of neighbor. Without this, there is no charity at all. And one can live in a spirit that preserves charity by loving strangers and even enemies as well as friends and acquaintances, by sacrificing even to the point of death for one's neighbor, and by giving materially, spiritually, and even of oneself to one's neighbor.

In Article 3, to which we have been referring, Thomas builds his concept of the nature of Christian perfection upon the finding that perfection is possible in this life. He does this by raising the question as to "whether perfection in [this] life consists in [keeping] precepts or counsels." By this question he means to determine two things: (1) Whether the command to be perfect is fundamental in itself or whether it is based upon an even more universal or basic principle; and (2) precisely what the role of the counsels is; that is, the function of those advices in Scripture that do not seem to be given to everyone but which seem to imply a higher level of Christian living than is ordinarily required of the majority. At issue here is the question of whether perfection (in love) is necessary to the salvation of every Christian or whether it is an "option" as it were.

Again, in his usual fashion, he sets forth the position opposite his own and presents those arguments that conclude that the perfection obtainable in this life consists in observing the counsels; that it does not consist in obedience to precepts. He begins by citing Matt. 19:21, a favorite verse of monasticism in its concern for perfection. Here our Lord says, "If you would be perfect, go, sell what you have, and give to the poor, and come, follow me." This word of Jesus, says Thomas, agreeing with the entire history of Christian exegesis, is not a commandment in the strict sense. It is not stated imperatively but subjunctively. It is not binding upon all. So, it is a "counsel." Thus, "perfection consists in counsels, not commandments." (Remember, Thomas is *not* stating his own position here, but one with which he disagrees.)

The second argument concluding that perfection consists in accepting advice and not in obeying commandments is based on observation. If perfection were commanded, then it would be necessary to be perfect in order to be saved, for none can be saved who do not keep the Lord's commands. But obviously not all Christians are perfect, though they are obviously Christian. So perfection must not be a "precept" or commandment, but an advice.

The third argument concluding that Christian perfection is a matter of following counsels rather than obeying commandments is more complex. Perfection of the Christian life is perfection in love. But there is a beginning to this love and an increase in it until perfection is attained, says Augustine. And his words, plus the words of Jesus in John 14:23 ("If anyone loves Me, he will keep My word" [NASB]), which indicate that loving cannot even begin without the keeping of commandments, would say that though perfection *begins* in obeying precepts, it is really attained in following counsels. So "perfection of life is not a matter of being directed by commandments, but by counsels."

Then Thomas turns to meet these arguments. He notes first the commandments to love God (Deut. 6:5) and neighbor (Lev. 19:18), and the fact that our Lord cited these as basic to "the whole Law and the Prophets" (Matt. 22:40, NASB). "But the perfection of love, which constitutes the perfection of the Christian life, is directed by our loving God with our whole heart and our neighbor as ourselves," that is, precisely according to divine *commandment,* not just counsel. So how to reconcile the authorities?

There are two ways in which perfection can consist in something, says Thomas. First, it can be of the very essence of that "something." Or, second, it can be a property or characteristic of something. It is of the very essence of Christian life as perfection in love, love of God and neighbor. And this perfection is commanded, not just advised. But there is no statement of limitations here in the commandments to love, nothing about how little love is necessary nor how much love is possible. The essential issue is simply that we love God and neighbor totally—that is, perfectly.

On the other hand, it is a fact of Christian experience, Thomas points out, that there are in this life impediments to perfect love and there are proven means, borne out of love itself, to remove them.[79] Though these impediments are *not* incompatible with love, they are impediments nonetheless. Not being incompatible with love, they are not contrary to the commandment to be perfect, to love perfectly. But they do impede our obedience, so there are bib-

79. The impediments Thomas notes are not such as we might list—marriage and secular occupations—but the point is well-taken. And the means of overcoming or removing them are not generally those that seem satisfactory to most Protestants—fastings, vigils, penury—but again the point is understood and well-taken.

lical advices (counsels) concerning their removal or destruction—or at least the mitigation of their usual effects. Here, then, is where perfection does consist of counsels.

Since the *commandment* to be perfect is without limit, there must be absolute removal of those things contrary to love, but there is also opened a vast range of possibility for the exercise of that perfection. The counsels are accepted because one is already living out the commandments. In a sense, we could say that Thomas is talking about the increase in perfection that follows upon one's having been perfected.[80]

This is the nature of the Christian life, then. It begins in its own level of perfection as the believer submits to the *commandment* to love God with a whole heart, mind, and strength, and to love neighbor as self. All that is contrary to love is removed. But in the development of such a life, it is clear that some matters not contrary to love are nonetheless incompatible with it. These are countered by the counsels. And as the counsels are followed, one becomes even more loving, even more perfect.

Thomas's responses to the specific objections to the proposition that perfection consists in obedience to precept (commandment), not simply adherence to counsels, are instructive and clarify his point of view for us. To the objection that Matt. 19:21 is a counsel, Thomas responds by making a distinction. The clauses, "Go and sell what you have and give to the poor," are stated as a way to perfection. But they certainly cannot constitute perfection, for one could obey the command for unworthy motives or follow up on that action with some act or attitude far from perfect charity. The selling and giving must be followed by coming to Christ and following Him. It is the coming to and the following of Christ that constitute perfection.

To the objection that perfection must be a counsel, and not a commandment because it is obvious that all Christians are not perfect, Thomas answers: "A person does not become a transgressor of the commandment simply by failing to fulfil it in the best way possible. It is sufficient if he fulfil it in *some* way. . . .

---

80. Language is much more problematic than experience at this point. To talk of "increase in perfection" or of becoming "more perfect" is, of course, logically improper, since, in Western society, "perfect" means "complete, full." The word usually has a static connotation. It is possible, however, to talk of "perfect" in dynamic terms, in which case it means "thoroughly," "perfectly for its kind."

Whoever attains the perfection of divine love in any degree avoids transgressing the commandment."[81]

Responding to the position that while perfection begins in obeying precepts or commandments it is really attained by following counsels, which makes perfection essentially a matter of the latter, not of the former, Thomas notes the various levels of perfection, especially of perfection in charity. By insisting that these are levels of the same perfection, he would indicate that they must begin and continue as *all* Christian perfection does—in response to precept or commandment, not in simple adherence to counsel.

The fundamental concern of this entire article is to show that perfection in love is not an option for the believer, but a divine commandment. And it is not merely a commandment but a gift of which the believer is in possession at one level or another from the very beginning of the Christian life.

At the same time, Thomas is opposing any view of perfection in which it is seen as a "state," especially any view that limits the meaning and practice of perfection to the rights and responsibilities of those in the various ranks of ecclesiastical vows. So, he raises the question as to "whether anyone who is perfect is in a state of perfection."[82]

Here, Thomas is working with the very practical problem of the relationship between acts of charity, or their absence, and the disposition to love, or its absence. The Thomistic way to say it is to inquire of the relationship between affective love and effective love and of the relationship between those acts of love that come from the affective faculties and those that "elicit" the activity of other virtues.

The first position contrary to Thomas's own says that the analogue for spiritual growth is physical growth. Just as the body can come to full maturity, so can the spiritual life. And when the believer has reached that maturity, "he is in a state of perfection."

---

81. ST II. ii. Q. 184, art. 3, resp. 2. Thomas goes on to say here: "The lowest grade of divine love consists in not loving anything more than God, or contrary to God, or as much as God. The person who does not have this degree of perfection in no way fulfils the commandment. However, as we stated earlier, there is a level of perfect love not attainable in this life. If one falls short of this level, he is not transgressing the commandment. In the same way, one does not transgress the commandment by failing to attain intermediate levels of perfection so long as he attains the lowest level."

82. ST II. ii. Q. 184, art. 4.

The second position contrary to Thomas's says that there is an analogy between passing from a state of sin to the state of grace and passing from less to more grace until the state of perfection be attained. That is, just as one can pass to a state from which sin is absent and only grace is present, so one may pass from less to more grace to the point that grace is present in fullness and perfection. This would be a state of perfection.

The third position contrary to Thomas's says that since the believer is in a state of love, in place of being in a state of slavery to sin, and since the believer is made perfect by love, being in a state of love is the same as being in a state of perfection.

But then, says Thomas, there are some who are perfect insofar as the Church is concerned (that is, those who have taken certain ecclesiastical vows or received consecration, such as monks and bishops) who "are totally lacking in love and grace." Isn't theirs a "state" of perfection?

Thomas is here having to work with his own assertion (in II.ii. Q. 183, art. 2) that the various ranks of clergy are perfect insofar as they exercise functions and divine gifts within a Church that is perfected by the Holy Spirit. Objectors to his position concerning the life of the perfected believer, that the believer is not in a *state* of perfection, are saying that bishops and various "religious" are indeed (as Thomas himself says) perfected, and since their perfection comes about in duly prescribed rituals and since they serve the Church in perpetuity, they can be said to be in a "state" of perfection.

Thomas responds with a careful definition of "state." Originally, it had referred basically to one's obligations or one's exemption from obligations. The clearest illustration was the case of the "states" of slavery or freedom. In the former "state," it was the nature of the case that one discharged obligations. In the latter "state," it was the nature of the case that one was exempt from those obligations. But, says Thomas, true perfection in love cannot involve this sort of obligation or exemption from it. If perfection in love be defined as a "state," it must have a far subtler denotation.

For Thomas, a "state" is a distinct condition of freedom or servitude. It is not simply any condition, but is clearly a rather fixed and permanent position affected by one's disposition, which, in turn, is dependent upon one's personal characteristics.[83] So, a

83. ST II. ii. Q. 183, art. 4.

"state" of perfection may mean either of two things: a position or condition in which one has certain obligations to exercise external acts of love, or an internal "bent" to loving. The Church can judge whether the external acts be fulfilled, but only divine judgment knows of the internal "bent."

To go one step deeper, the Church may lay persons under obligation with respect to external acts of charity by means of various vows and rites, such as ordination. In a sense, this is a matter of placing such persons in a "state," for now they are under obligation, they are disposed to discharge such obligation by their vows, and the gifts and graces of the Spirit provide the requisite personal characteristics. And their condition is permanent. But only divine grace can create the internal disposition of love, and acts of charity done from this disposition are not reflected upon from the perspective of obligation or exemption from obligation. So, if perfection in love be a "state" of perfection, it is a "state" in a way very different from that usually connoted by the term.

Thomas follows through on this discussion and comes to conclude that

> one is in what may rightly be called a state of perfection not because his act of charity is perfect but because he perpetually binds himself with some solemn rite to those things that pertain to perfection. But in fact, some oblige themselves in this way but do not observe those things while others observe them without making solemn obligation. . . . So it is that there is nothing that keeps some from being perfect who are not in a state of perfection and others from being in the state of perfection who are not perfect.[84]

Responding to those positions contrary to his own, Thomas insists in each case that there is no question as to whether the believer can attain an internal "state" of perfection so long as "state" in this sense is not confused with its usual meaning, which is essentially structural, external, and legal. "Perfection" may be thought of as a "state" when it refers to a perpetual disposition to love. With this, Thomas is opposing any attempt to make of any ecclesiastical status some sort of spiritual sinecure.

At first glance, Thomas's efforts may seem to relate only to some peculiarly medieval problem, and a rather picayune one at that. But in fact, he has touched upon a perennial problem in Christian faith: the temptation to assign to certain roles or offices a

---

84. ST II. ii. Q. 184, art 4.

sanctity in and of themselves and thus to deny fullest sanctity to any role or office not so well placed in the structure of the Church. Thomas's principle is that while "perfection" may be used to describe the character of some ecclesiastical roles (and thus ecclesiastical persons), its more fundamental meaning is personal, internal, and dispositional, rather than structural, external, and legal. Perfection in love is incumbent upon all believers.

And both the sign of this universality and its affective agent is the sacrament of confirmation. This is also the point in Thomas at which sanctification and perfection are inextricably bound together.

Let us begin to consider this matter at the point of the relationship between sanctification and confirmation. And let us allow Thomas to speak for himself.[85]

> Article 7. *Does Confirmation confer sanctifying grace?*
>
> Objection 1. It would seem that sanctifying grace is not conferred by this sacrament because that kind of grace is a remedy for sin. And we have already said that confirmation is given only to the baptized—those who have been cleansed from sin. Therefore, confirmation does not confer sanctifying grace.
>
> Objection 2. Furthermore, it is sinners who need sanctifying grace, since it is only by such grace that they can be justified. But if sanctifying grace be given by confirmation, it is not given to those in a sinful state, those to whom it ought to be given. But, of course, this is not the case.
>
> Objection 3. Then, too, sanctifying grace is not divided into different types because it is ordained to one result. Now, two forms of the same species cannot be in the same subject. Thus, since sanctifying grace is bestowed in baptism, it would seem that it is not the same grace that is conferred by confirmation—confirmation being given only to those already baptized.
>
> On the other hand, Pope Melchiades says, "The Holy Spirit grants the fullness of innocence at the baptismal font. In Confirmation, he gives an increase in grace."[86]
>
> I reply: As has been said, this sacrament gives the Holy Spirit to the baptized for strengthening them, just as he was given to the Apostles on the day of Pentecost and to those baptized then through the laying on of the hands of the Apostles. It was shown in the First Part [of the *Summa Theologica*]

85. ST III. Q. 72, art. 7.

86. ST I. i. Q. 43, art. 3. It should be noted here that "Pope Melchiades" never existed. But Thomas and his age were convinced he did.

> that the sending or the giving of the Holy Spirit is always accompanied by sanctifying grace. So it is clear that sanctifying grace is conferred in this sacrament.
>
> To the first objection, one would say that the first effect of sanctifying grace is the remission of sin. However, it also has other effects, for it suffices to move one ahead through each step of perfection, to eternal life itself. This is why St. Paul was told, "My grace is sufficient for you," and it is why he could say of himself, "It is by the grace of God that I am what I am." Thus, sanctifying grace is given not only for the remission of sin but also for growth and for making us firm in righteousness. This is the way it is conferred in this sacrament (i.e., Confirmation).
>
> To the second objection, one would say that this sacrament is given to confirm what is already acquired. That is why it should not be given to those not in the state of grace. And, just as it is not given to the non-baptized, neither should it be given to adult sinners who have not been renewed through penance. So it is that the Council of Orleans declared, "Before Confirmation they should fast and they should be admonished to confess their sins first of all so that in being cleansed they might be able to receive the gift of the Holy Spirit."[87] Confirmation perfects the effect of penance as well as that of baptism, for through the grace granted in this sacrament the penitent person acquires a more complete remission of his sins. And if an adult who is in the state of sin is unaware of it or is even imperfectly contrite should present himself for this sacrament, he obtains remission of sins through the grace that is bestowed.
>
> To the third objection, one might respond that, as has already been said, considered in its more general sense, sacramental grace adds to sanctifying grace the power to effect that special effect to which the sacrament is ordained. So, if we consider the grace conferred in this sacrament in a general way, it does not differ from baptismal grace but merely augments what is already there. On the other hand, if we consider it from the perspective of its added special effectiveness, it is not of the same species as baptismal grace.

This article is generally quite clear as to the relationship between confirmation and sanctifying grace and for this reason we have let Thomas speak for himself. But it may be that a note or two might help us to see more deeply into what he is saying.

One thing that should be noted throughout this section on confirmation is his frequent reference to the fact that confirmation is the sacrament that brings the Spirit in fullness. He affirms that the Spirit is both the gift given in confirmation and the agent of the

87. This council was held in 511. The reference is to Gratian, *Decretum* III. 5, canon 6.

sacrament. At the same time, it must be noted that Thomas is careful to assure us that the Spirit is the agent of sanctification but not its end, not its purpose, and not its ultimate source. The ultimate source of sanctification is Christ.[88] And the end of the Spirit's work is that we might be like Christ in perfected love. The tangible symbol for this is the sign of the Cross made upon the confirmand by the bishop in the ritual itself. "Confirmation is not ordained solely to the inward sanctification of a person but also to external spiritual combat, (and for this reason) it outwardly signs one with the standard of the cross, for the external spiritual battle."[89]

The aim of the Spirit, then, is to bring us to maturity in love, a maturity that is granted immediately in confirmation insofar as one is initially capable of maturity and able to be completely and unreservedly open to maturing in this life. In this way, the "character" granted to the Christian in confirmation by the Spirit is quite different from the "character" granted by the same Spirit in baptism. Baptism is a spiritual generation, a birth.[90] "In baptism, power is received for doing those things which pertain to one's own salvation insofar as one lives for oneself."[91] The power granted in confirmation is for combat.

Thomas is thus quite insistent upon the difference between what is received in baptism and what in confirmation. And he is equally insistent upon the fact that the character of confirmation necessarily presupposes the character of baptism. Confirmation is both in continuity with baptism and spiritually different from it.

At least one other matter should be broached here regarding Thomas's view of sanctification and its relationship to confirmation—that is, his understanding that baptism, not confirmation, is the sacrament of cleansing. In a sense, this removes from sanctification the aspect of cleansing and places the emphasis upon empowerment as the principal characteristic of sanctifying grace.

Here was a note that was to remain clear and usually strong in Western theologies until the present day. In Protestant theologies, however, the empowerment of sanctification has to do with making it possible to make manifest that which has already been done for us in Christ's justifying work in us. In Catholic theology, the

---

88. ST III. Q. 72, art. 7.

89. ST III. Q. 64, art. 3; III. Q. 72, art. 3.

90. ST III. Q. 72, art. 4.

91. ST III. Q. 65, art. 1; III. Q. 72, art. 5.

empowerment of sanctification is aimed at enabling us to accomplish those good works that bring us at last to justification.[92] (In fairness it must be said, however, that Roman Catholic theology has been diligent in the last several decades to reassert that older theological tradition that places justification at the beginning of the process of salvation and not at the end as a goal.)

At any rate, we do have in Thomas an attempt to reunite the concepts of sanctification and perfection. And this he does primarily by way of his development of sacramental theology. But his understanding is threatened by inconsistency so long as justification lies at the end of salvation's road and not at its beginning. It is precisely this inconsistency that Luther was to encounter—not in an intellectual but in a deeply spiritual sense. And thereby hangs the tale of the Protestant Reformation and the near loss of the doctrine of sanctification.

It is to those developments that we now turn.[93]

---

92. This is admittedly a caricature of careful Roman Catholic theology, but it is a caricature that squares quite well with popular Catholic thought and piety. Only recently, with the publication of such works as Hans Küng, *Rechtfertigung. Die Lehre Karl Barths und eine katholische Besinnung* (Einsiedeln, 1957), which appeared in English translation as *Justification* (trans. from the 4th ed., 1964; New York and London, 1964), have Protestants begun to recognize the grace-centeredness of at least some Roman Catholic understandings of justification. Indeed, here was a doctrinal tradition that even many Catholics had not known, such was the nature of Catholic-Protestant polemic against each other.

93. The author closes off his discussion of the medieval period here with great reluctance, though with an understanding of space limitations. While we have, we believe, fairly presented the primary positions with respect to the question at hand, it would have been quite helpful to have presented the nuances presented in such medieval thinkers as Walter Hilton, Meister Eckhart, and the authors of *Imitatio Christi* and the *German Theology*.

4

The Doctrine of Entire Sanctification in Early Protestantism

A religious revolution swept through Christianity in the 16th century, a revolution that permanently divided the Church, at least at the level of organization. It also created ever narrower categories of doctrine and behavior by means of which believers would assess the quality of the faith of other believers. Not that the Church was united before that time. It had the appearance of unity in its stated loyalty to the bishop of Rome.

But that unity was a chimera. On the one hand there were the various Christian bodies of the East who recognized the bishop of Rome only as being first among equals. Even that recognition was given grudgingly—and sometimes not at all. On the other hand, there were those occasions when Christians in the West had two and even three persons each claiming to be the genuine bishop of Rome.

Then, too, many a time in the Middle Ages the bishop of Rome hardly dared express his primacy in any concrete or practical fashion because kings and princes and even other bishops and abbots, all of whom adhered to the theoretical unity of the Church by way of a commonly recognized single head, took matters of organization and even doctrine into their own hands. The Church became both the victim and the perpetrator in a vast game of politics, which might even be described as theologized politics. Such conditions made its unity, or its claims to unity, impossible to believe.

But as bad as the situation was in the period before 1517, division and mutual recrimination became even more serious and less tractable with the coming of the Protestant Reformation. Not that the breach was all bad. Spiritual vitality swept both the Roman Catholic camp and the Protestant side. The question of what constitutes genuinely Christian spirituality became important again and serious responses were proposed—theologically consistent responses and responses with wide-ranging practical consequences.

True, the emotional tide was frighteningly high and there were fakes, quacks, pious frauds, fanatics, one-issue cranks, and well-intentioned but careless-thinking folk all about Europe practicing varying degrees of organizational skill. And this led, in turn, to dreadful atrocity in the name of Christ. Atrocity must not be overlooked nor explained away. It was evil—a sometimes-attempted remedy that testified to a sin-infection at least as serious as the disease it proposed to remedy. Nonetheless, there was a healthy, if not entirely wholesome, revival of concern that the Church be church and that a Christian be more and better than merely a person baptized as an infant who for the rest of his days more or less entrusts to the Church the care of his spiritual life.

This concern itself encouraged careful consideration of the doctrines of sin, of salvation, of the nature of the Christian life. Such careful consideration was enhanced by the fact that in this era published materials were becoming ever cheaper and easy to produce in great numbers. Correspondingly, it was an era in which the literacy rate was rising rapidly. It was also an era in which one side of the religious struggle was insisting on the individual's own access to God and his responsibility for that access, under grace. It is no wonder that there was such a variety in viewpoints. And each proponent of a position felt obliged to show not only the logical and biblical weakness of other points of view but also their detrimental effect upon the believer's spiritual life.

Under such conditions any talk of Christian perfection was practically dangerous. One's opponents could easily pillory any claims to perfection—one of the most typical methods being that of accusing any "perfectionists" of spiritual pride. Such a charge needed no evidence other than the claim to perfection itself.

Talk of sanctification was likewise unwise. The Protestants had thoroughly undermined the credibility of the Roman Catholic view that sanctification is principally our working out of our salvation. (At least this was the popular understanding of it, though many a Roman Catholic theologian knew better.) Protestants had also so emphasized the doctrine of justification by grace alone that it was difficult for many of them to think of salvation in any terms beyond the forensic—those of imputed righteousness. They could believe that the believer could be *accounted* pure, but it was difficult, if not impossible, to believe that the believer could actually be *made* pure in this life. For them, the difference between the nonbeliever and the believer had very much to do with the believer's confession that he is a sinner. The nonbeliever is a sinner who will not confess that such he is.

It is easy to see where this would put anyone claiming to be free from sin. They would be among the very worst of sinners, for they would be claiming freedom from sin in the name of Christ. But this is a spiritual impossibility since (said they) if we have no sin we do not need Christ. But all need Christ, always (the implication being that we *cannot* be free from sin), they said. So we cannot claim freedom from sin in the name of Christ. That would be using His name in vain—blaspheming.

With many variations upon the theme, such was the prevailing view; perfection in righteousness is impossible and claims to it are blasphemous. Sanctification is principally a matter of works and is therefore at the foundation of Christian life only insofar as Christ's work does impute holiness to us.

But in many respects this prevailing view was only a caricature of what the great thinkers of the Reformation believed. Caricatures bear truth, but not the *whole* truth. It was very easy to hear and to read the great Reformers in precisely the ways we have described. But it must also be remembered that caricatures falsify, most often by oversimplification. And this is precisely what happened to the views of Luther, Calvin, and others, in the heat of the battle for true faith in the 16th century. And the results are still with us.

Luther's doctrine of justification by grace alone (a doctrine heartily endorsed by Calvin) and Calvin's own doctrine of election so emphasized the forensic aspects of salvation as almost to exclude any actual sanctification of the believer. Least of all did they allow for the believer's perfection in righteousness in this life. But both thinkers did go much farther along the theological paths of perfection and entire sanctification than many have thought. And they did not do it unawares.

Let's concern ourselves, then, with their points of view.

I. Entire Sanctification Among the Protestant Reformers

A. Martin Luther: Entire Sanctification as "Alien Holiness"

The apostle Paul spoke of salvation as salvation from sin and as salvation from sinfulness. He wrote movingly of the Christian's great hope, of the resurrection of the body, of the joy of being forever with the Lord. But this was the *Christian's* hope, the hope of one already saved from sin and from sinfulness. The old walk in sin and sinfulness was really death—a death march. The new walk is new life. It is life itself in Jesus Christ. And in passing from death to life, the convert underwent moral transformation. For Paul, this transformation took place in this earthly life and was instantaneous. Only in the perception of just how it touched the various facets of life and in the practical application of those perceptions was it a matter of process. So, Paul continually reminds his readers, "Become what you already are in Christ."

Little by little, however, Paul's emphasis upon the here and now character of the Christian's moral transformation was pushed into the background of Christian thinking. This was especially true in the Christian West, where people were more inclined to think in concrete, practical, and legal terms than were those in the East. The constant whirring and buzzing of political and social problems in the secular state and of heresy and attendant issues in the Church made people much more aware of the pervasiveness of sin and of the inability of the Church to destroy it. So, any hope that one could attain perfection in righteousness in this life was put farther and farther into the future. Salvation came to be viewed as a very gradual process with completion attained only at the very end of this life or postponed into the next.

Paul's note of moral transformation was retained, but full salvation was no longer believed to be instantaneously received, nor was it usually believed to be attained in this life. In the minds of many, Christian faith had come to be an enterprise in preparing oneself for salvation. Many thought the Christian life to be a matter of seeking to make oneself worthy of salvation rather than a matter of responding to and receiving the gift of salvation already given. If course, grace was needed for the entire enterprise, but it was grace to do good works so that at last one could be justified. There was no diminishing of the demand for moral transformation as the sign and seal of conversion or salvation, but now that transformation was seen to come little by little and to be completed in the earthly lives of few.

Martin Luther (1483-1546),[1] seeking peace for his own soul by faithful adherence to this understanding of Christian faith, came to utter despair over it, perhaps as early as 1509. His conviction was that while he was doing all of the good works suggested by the church, and then some, he was moving ever farther from genuine moral transformation. Pride and self-will, concupiscence (which is what he called the craving to satisfy one's own desires, sexual and otherwise) and distrust of God all seemed to deepen right along with his increasing acts of piety. The religious enterprise that his mentors had said would lead finally to salvation seemed to Luther to be carrying him away from it. He even wondered whether God in His freedom might not have changed the rules of the game—and might not change them again as it suited Him.

---

1. Biographies of Luther abound. One of the very best is Roland Bainton, *Here I Stand: A Life of Martin Luther* (New York and Nashville: Abingdon, 1950). Probably the best single-volume study of Luther's thought in English is Paul Althaus (trans. by Robert C. Shultz), *The Theology of Martin Luther* (Philadelphia: Fortress, 1966). A good guide to those being introduced to Luther's thought is John R. Loeschen, *Wrestling with Luther: An Introduction to the Study of His Thought* (St. Louis: Concordia, 1976). The most comprehensive study of Luther's thought is Theodosius Harnack, *Luthers Theologie, mit besonderer Beziehung auf seine Versöhnungs und Erlöhsungslehre* (Erlangen: Blaesing, 1862-86; new ed., Munich: Kaiser, 1927).

The definitive edition of Luther's work is J. Knaake, P. Pietsch, and K. Drescher (eds.), *D. Martin Luthers Werke* (Weimar, 1883—). This edition is organized in four sections: the major works, *Tischreden* (Table Talk), *Briefe* (Letters), and *Deutsche Bibel* (German Bible). The standard abbreviation for this edition is WA (for *Weimar Ausgabe*), and may be followed by TR (for *Tischreden*), BR (for *Briefe*), or DB (for *Deutsche Bibel*). WA without additional abbreviation refers to the major works. The best and most complete of English translations is Helmut T. Lehmann and Jaroslav Pelikan (eds.), *Luther's Works* (55 vols.; Philadelphia and St. Louis: Fortress and Concordia, 1955—). The standard abbreviation for this edition is LW.

Luther, even the very young adult Luther, was not simply one more Saxon monk. He was a doctor in theology, educated at Erfurt, one of the very best of Europe's universities, and at Wittenberg, a new and ambitious university with a good faculty even in its infancy. He was a priest (ordained in 1507) and a monk. As a monk, he was entrusted with very important administrative tasks, especially that of representing his order in a ticklish situation before the papal curia itself, in Rome. This was in 1510, when he was 27 years old. By age 30 he was professor of theology in Wittenberg and began lecturing on the Scriptures, a post reserved only for those with the very best available education in liberal arts and technical studies. So, when Luther despaired, it was the despair of one who had tested every possible means of escape and found them all blocked. All but one, and that single one changed the Christian world.

We do not know just when Luther experienced his evangelical discovery—he speaks excitedly of it, but leaves the date uncertain—except that it was sometime between 1509 and 1517.[2] In later years, he refers to it in terms of the interpretation of Rom. 1:17.

> I had indeed been captivated with an extraordinary ardor for understanding Paul in the Epistle to the Romans. But up till then it was not the cold blood about the heart, but a single word in chapter 1, "in it the righteousness of God is revealed," that had stood in my way. For I hated that word "righteousness of God," which, according to the use and custom of all the teachers, I had been taught to understand philosophically regarding the formal or active righteousness, as they called it, with which God is righteous and punishes the unrighteous sinner. . . .
>
> At last, by the mercy of God, meditating day and night, I gave heed to the context of the words, namely "in it the righteousness of God is revealed, as it is written, he who through faith is righteous shall live." There I began to understand that the righteousness of God is that by which the righteous lives by a gift of God, namely by faith. And this is the meaning: the righteousness of God is revealed by the Gospel, namely the passive righteousness with which a merciful God justifies us by

---

2. One very important issue tied to the date of Luther's "evangelical discovery" is the degree to which Lutheran theologians of the second and third generations really interpreted him correctly. For a thorough discussion of the problem of date and of the more fundamental issues, cf. Uuras Saarnivaara, *Luther Discovers the Gospel: New Light upon Luther's Way from Medieval Catholicism to Evangelical Faith* (St. Louis: Concordia, 1951).

faith as it is written, "He who through faith is righteous shall live." Here I felt that I was altogether born again and had entered paradise itself through open gates.[3]

The "righteousness of God," then, is that by which God saves us. It is not a standard by which we must measure our works, facing condemnation for our failure. Rather, "the just shall live by faith"—shall live by trusting that God does save him. No more striving by works to achieve righteousness that will satisfy God, but living in the faith that God's own righteousness is given to us in salvation.[4] This was Luther's "evangelical discovery," and it changed the face of Christendom.

The idea had never been lost in Christianity, not even in the Church's worst moments. But by Luther's time it had been obscured sufficiently that it sounded like a new idea, especially as it stood over against the vast system of salvation-by-works, which was supported even by many who should have known better. The Church had established herself as the guardian of the gospel and as the guide to salvation rather than as the steward of the grace of God and as the company of the redeemed. She had gotten to where she needed the works righteousness system to preserve herself.[5]

What Luther retained from medieval notions of piety was the deep sense of sinfulness; the recognition that piety itself can create spiritual stumbling blocks—especially out of pride. Consequently, authentic piety will seek to retain a sharp sense of unworthiness, of not having arrived, of absolute dependence upon the grace of God and the God of grace. On the other side of Luther's faith was God's forgiveness in Christ. Always there must be forgiveness. This is the great practical expression of the righteousness of God. It is a foun-

---

3. WA, 54:185-86. (Cf. LW, 34:336-37).

4. For more comprehensive analyses of Luther's own theological development with respect to this point, cf. Heinrich Boehmer, *Road to Reformation* (Philadelphia: Augsburg, 1946) and Gordon Rupp, *Luther's Progress to the Diet of Worms, 1521* (London: SPCK, 1951).

5. On the issue of the state of the Church, theologically perceived, at the time of the Protestant Reformation, cf. Willy Andreas, *Deutschland vor der Reformation* (5th ed.; Stuttgart and Berlin, 1948); Yves Congar, *Vraie et Fausse Reforme dans l'Église* (Paris, 1950); Lucien Febvre, *Au Coeur Religieux du XVIe Siècle* (Paris, 1957); Joseph Lortz, "Die Reformation und Luther in Katholischer Sicht," *Una Sancta X* (1955); Norman Sykes, *The Crisis of the Reformation* (London: J. Heritage, 1938); Steven Ozment, *The Age of Reform: 1250-1550* (New Haven, Conn.: Yale University Press, 1980).

dation stone of salvation itself. It lies at the heart of Christ's redeeming work, and it is an effect of faith in Christ. Forgiveness serves as a guarantee that we are saved by grace alone, through faith, not by works.[6]

So we see here a return to Paul's understanding that salvation is a gift of God and that it is, in a sense, granted in complete form even in this life, and is granted instantaneously.[7]

But Luther and Paul part company at the point of the inner character of the Christian life. For Paul, it begins in a moral transformation made manifest as life itself passes. But that transformation is complete, or should be, from the beginning. Paul has no such thing as a sinful Christian in mind when he writes of the Christian ideal for this life. Luther sees the Christian life beginning in forgiveness and justification (that is, God's decision to account his righteousness in Christ to the individual). There should be moral transformation as life passes, but the new life does not begin there as it does for Paul.[8]

In understanding that Luther sees the Christian life beginning in forgiveness and justification, we must take into account two doctrines of critical importance to Luther's thought. These two doctrines are predestination and imputation.[9] As a young monk,

---

6. Eg., WA, 25:331; 40, II:421; 40, III:358; 52:273. For English trans. of these examples, cf. LW, 6:625; 5:573; 4:2058; 13a:549, respectively.

7. E.g., WA, 47:662-63, where Luther talks of the benefit of forgiveness in the context of the sacrament of baptism. Also cf. WA, 10, I:113: "Our salvation is not gotten through works but is given to us in an instant. For birth produces an entire life, and a complete human, not just a single member—a hand or a foot. And this human being is not active in order to be born, but is born to be active. So it is that works do not make us clean and pious, nor do they save us. Rather, we are first made clean and pious—saved. Then we do works freely to the glory of God and to the benefit of our neighbor."

8. E.g., WA, 52:264-65: "A Christian is at the same time sinner and saint. Simultaneously he is wicked and pious." For a clear passage on the progressive nature of sanctification, cf. WA, 32:522-23. Also cf. WA, 15:727: "Pardoning sin and removing sin are different matters. When one believes and is baptized, all his sins are forgiven. But after that sin has to be cleansed away by way of many sorts of crosses and austerities throughout one's lifetime. Sin stays in us as long as our mortal body endures, though it is not charged against us by the wrath of God—for Christ's sake. Yet it is purged and cleansed with paternal chastening."

9. Regarding Luther's understanding of predestination, which he prefers to call election, cf. e.g., WA-DB, 7:23-24 (English trans., LW, 35:378-379). Also cf. Althaus, *Theology of Martin Luther,* 274-86. For Luther's understanding of imputation, which he sometimes calls "alien righteousness," cf. e.g., WA, 39, I:83 (English trans., LW, 34:153). Also cf. Althaus, *Theology of Martin Luther,* 227-34.

Luther had been profoundly shaken by the doctrine of predestination. This was because of his concern, in his despair, that perhaps God had changed the rules of salvation. He wished, throughout his lifetime, to allow to God absolute and utter sovereignty. Now, having discovered that justification comes by grace through faith, he insisted that God is the sovereign God of grace. That is to say that grace is totally within the power and will of God to distribute as He wills.

Luther had found a gracious God. Therefore, Luther believed that he was among the elect.[10] So it is that Luther's doctrine of predestination is not an abstract concept. Rather, it is an expression of his faith in the constancy and consistency of God. It is also an expression of his confidence that salvation is of God alone, and not of any of our works. Beyond these simple declarations of faith, Luther will not discuss the doctrine of predestination.[11] It is in no way, for Luther, an academic or a philosophical doctrine. It is an expression of spiritual confidence in the faithfulness of God.

What about imputation? For Luther, faith in no way makes for forgiveness. In fact forgiveness has long since been offered and granted to all in the Cross of Jesus Christ. Faith, for Luther, is a matter of receiving that which God has already declared in Jesus Christ. Faith, then, is a matter of receiving or taking the forgiveness granted to us in Christ Jesus. This is to say that forgiveness is an objective reality.[12] God's justification of us is an objective declaration. This reality and this declaration are not dependent upon our works, not even our acceptance. Of course, for them to be applied to me, I must take them. In fact, the tragedy of sinfulness lies in large part in our refusal to recognize that we need either forgiveness or justification.[13]

What God does when we accept or take the forgiveness and justification offered to us is to declare us, personally, righteous. It is

---

10. E.g., WA, 28:121-22.

11. E.g., WA-BR, 11:166.

12. E.g., WA, 40 II:401; WA, 46:692; WA, 30, I:391. In the latter passage, the reader can see why Luther insisted on the "objective" presence of Christ in the Lord's Supper. Without that kind of presence, the would-be believer would be thrown back on his own resources to induce the divine attendance. These resources are, of course, totally inadequate, even detrimental. Without the divine presence, there is no forgiveness.

13. E.g., WA, 28:14-19 (English trans. LW, 10:1202-09); WA, 52:799 (English trans. LW, 13, I:441).

not that we have any righteousness of our own. Rather, Christ's righteousness is granted to us, imputed to us. We are declared righteous in Him.[14] In this way nothing but faith is needed. As Luther says, "Nothing more is required for justification than to hear of Jesus Christ and to believe on him as our savior."[15] This is not a good work—this matter of believing on Him. We believe on Him because we have been predestined to do so. But predestination, or election, we recall, is not to be seen as some metaphysical necessity. We are not elect as a result of faith. We believe because we are elect. Our faith is an expression of our confidence that we have come to God because He wanted us to come to Him, from the foundation of the world.[16]

Plaguing our justified relationship to Him is original sin. Listen to Luther describe original sin.

> The original sin in a man is like his beard, which, though shaved off today so that a man is very smooth around his mouth, yet grows again by tomorrow morning. As long as a man lives, such growth of hair and beard does not stop. But when the shovel slaps the ground on his grave, it stops. In just this way original sin remains in us and exercises itself as long as we live, but we must resist it and always be cutting off its hair.[17]

This quotation is from Luther's *Table Talk,* and we must not draw any profound doctrinal conclusions from the *Table Talk.* Nonetheless this is a very representative picture of Luther's understanding of original sin. He believed that the struggle with original sin ends only at the grave.

This raised several serious questions. For one, what is the meaning, then, of baptism? Luther faces this question, meeting it head on.

> Since original sin has been taken away in baptism, why do we say that it still remains and that one must constantly battle with it? Augustine answers the question this way: Original sin is certainly forgiven in baptism; but not in such a manner that it no longer exists. Rather in such a manner that God no longer imputes it to us. When the Samaritan (Luke 10:34-45) poured oil and wine into the wounds of the injured man, he did not immediately heal him but took him to the inn and let the host

---

14. E.g., WA, 39, I:83, 97 (English trans. LW, 34:153, 166). This is a constant note throughout Luther's works.

15. WA, 10, 1:328. This citation is one example from among a multitude.

16. E.g., WA, 28:121-22 (English trans. LW, 8:785). Also see WA, 43:461.

17. WA-TR, I: No. 138.

> care for him until he should return. So it is that all sins are indeed removed through baptism, but in such a way that God does not impute them to us. Nonetheless, they are gone. One must continue to heal them constantly as one has begun to do. When we die, we will all be completely healed.[18]

What we see here is Luther's insistence that new spiritual life does not begin in moral transformation. Rather, it begins in a new standing before God, granted by God himself through the forgiveness and justification offered in the sacrifice of Christ. But what about moral transformation? And, can one ever become fully Christian, in the sense that he is totally free of sinfulness, in this life? Luther's basic discovery had been that salvation is by grace alone through faith, not of works. This put him in conflict with a long tradition of confidence in man's ability, even if guided by grace, to sanctify himself to the point that God would account him worthy of salvation and justify him. Luther had come to believe that Catholic thought had reversed the order of salvation. Catholic thought, as Luther saw it, insisted on sanctification before justification. Luther wished to declare that sanctification followed justification. In his struggle with the problem of works-righteousness, Luther also struggled valiantly with the relationship of the idea of salvation by faith alone, which gives certainty of salvation, and the commandments to love and good works found in the New Testament.

Luther had been brought up on the idea that faith is formed by love.[19] He had been taught that by acts of love and piety faith is developed to the point that one finally believes sufficiently that God may then grant salvation. Luther concluded that this is false, for it is not love that forms faith, rather it is faith that forms love. Love is the testimony of faith, making faith certain of its genuineness and of its truth. So it is that Luther says, for instance, "Good works do not make a good man, but a good man does good works."[20] This remark helps us to understand that, for Luther, good works, which he accounted as the practical expression of sanctification, are an expression of our having been justified. They are a response to our justification rather than a means of earning justifi-

---

18. WA, 17, II:285.

19. E.g., WA, 40, I:229, 239-40; WA, 40 III:368; WA, 45:691.

20. This is a continuing theme in Luther's work. It is most fully expressed and explicated in his *Treatise on Good Works* (WA, 6), written in 1520 and reprinted many times, even in Luther's lifetime.

cation or of earning righteousness in any way even after we have been declared just.

Theologically, then, how does Luther move from justification to sanctification? What does he understand the relationship to be between Christ's declaring us to be justified and imputing His righteousness to us and whatever it is within us that makes us respond to that grace with good works? Here Luther struggles and often states himself paradoxically.[21] But his thought is probably clearer than most non-Lutherans have allowed it to be. When he speaks of the relationship between justification and sanctification, he begins with the proposition that justification always sanctifies.

> In a world apart from Christ all are damned and lost; in Christ all are good and blessed. Therefore even the sin inherited from Adam and remaining in our flesh and blood cannot harm and condemn us.
>
> However, this should not be taken to mean that permission is thereby given freely to sin and to do evil. For since faith brings forgiveness of sins, and Christ came in order to destroy and take away sin, it is impossible for the person to be a Christian and a believer who openly, impenitently, and securely lives on in sin according to his evil lusts. For where such a sinful life is found there is no repentance; but where there is no repentance there is no forgiveness of sins, and, therefore no faith, which receives the forgiveness of sins. But he who really has faith in this forgiveness resists sin, does not follow its lusts, rather he fights against sin until he finally gets rid of it entirely. Moreover, although we cannot get rid of sin altogether in this life and some of it always remains, even in the most saintly, yet believers have the comfort that these sins are covered for them through the forgiveness of Christ and are not put to their account for condemnation as long as they continue to believe in Christ.[22]

What we see here is that, for Luther, justification and sanctification may be separated in the abstract, but in life they are never separated. There is no such thing as justification without sanctification for Luther. One of his favorite ways of distinguishing be-

---

21. In fact, so paradoxical was Luther's position that his disciples broke into opposing camps, both of them quoting their master. The best English review of the issues as Luther generated them and as his successors debated them is in R. D. Preus, *The Theology of Post-Reformation Lutheranism: A Study of Theological Prolegomena* (St. Louis: Concordia, 1970).

22. WA, 46:39. The trans. is from Ewald M. Plass (ed.), *What Luther Says: An Anthology* (3 vols.; St. Louis: Concordia, 1959), II.723 (No. 2256).

tween justification and sanctification is to discuss the difference between saying "I live in Christ" and "Christ lives in me."

> This is the first chief article: that a man go out of himself and rise above himself into Christ. Thereafter the descent from above begins like this: as I am in Christ, so Christ, in turn, is in me. I have assumed him and have entered into him, have stepped out of sin, death, and the power of the devil. So he now manifests himself in me and says: Go your way, preach, comfort, baptize, serve your neighbor, be obedient, patient, and so forth. I will be in you and will do everything: what you do I want to have done. Only be confident, courageous, and undismayed in me and see to it that you remain in me; then I will certainly also be in you.[23]

It is in the context of this understanding of the relationship between justification and sanctification, then, that Luther can speak of the moral necessity laid upon Christians. He was forced, perhaps by his times, to be wary of speaking of moral transformation. Yet, he was not at all reluctant to speak of the Christian's moral necessity.[24] This moral necessity is not laid upon the Christian as some means of salvation. Rather it is a necessity almost after the manner of a natural necessity. Listen to Luther speak of the motivation for our good works.

> It is as absurd and stupid to say: the righteous ought to do good works, as to say: God ought to do good, the sun ought to shine, the pear tree ought to bear pears, three and seven ought to be ten. For all of this follows of necessity by reason of the cause and the consequence. . . . It all follows without commandment or bidding of any law, naturally and willingly, uncompelled and unconstrained. . . . The sun shines by nature, unbidden; the pear tree bears pears of itself, uncompelled; three and seven ought not to be ten, they are ten already. There is no need to say to our Lord God that he ought to do good, for he does it without ceasing, of himself, willingly and with pleasure. Just so, we do not have to tell the righteous that he ought to do good works, for he does so without that, without any commandment or compulsion, because he is a new creature and a good tree.[25]

What is the source of this doing of good? Luther insists that salvation does not begin in love, from the manward side, but in faith. Faith first, then love. In fact, says Luther, love will be the

---

23. WA, 45:591. English trans., Plass, 722 (No. 2253).

24. E.g., WA, 46:39; WA 49:472.

25. WA-TR, II:355. English trans. is from W. Hazlitt, *The Table Talk of Martin Luther* (London, 1848).

inevitable consequence of faith. "This is what Christ meant when he finally gave no commandment except that of love (John 15:12), by which men were to recognize those who are his disciples and true believers. For where works and love do not appear, faith is not genuine, the gospel has not taken hold, and Christ is not recognized aright."[26] Luther goes on to say that where love is lacking, there is no faith. There may be no such thing as a loveless Christian. In fact, while Luther insists that God forces no one to serve Him, we will serve Him as we love Him.

> God often causes Scripture to testify that he desires no forced service and no one is to become his own unless he does so out of love and delight. God help us! Will we not listen? Have we no reason or ears? I say again: God does not desire any forced service. I say for the third time, I say a hundred thousand times: God desires no forced service.[27]

Nonetheless, Luther insists that in this life we shall never love God perfectly. At this point he recognizes certain difficulties posed by Scripture. And in 1527 and 1532 he turned his attention to 1 John 4:13-21 in both lectures and sermons.[28] He recognized that perfect love was the demand of this particular passage, especially verse 17. How does he treat this clear call to Christian perfection?

In his 1527 lectures on First John, Luther understood the love of God mentioned in 4:17 to be God's love toward us. So verse 17 would read, "In this is God's love toward us perfected in us, that we may have confidence on the day of judgment because as He is so are we in this world." He indicates that this verse declares that God's love is given to us in full measure. That is, insofar as we are capable of receiving God's love, it is perfect in us. God's love is perfect by nature; it cannot be any less than perfect. The problem lies with our capacity to receive it and to express it. But Luther recognized that verse 18 demanded that perfect love be looked at in terms of human love: "There is no fear in love, but perfect love casts out fear." This verse, Luther recognized, could not be inter-

---

26. WA-DB, VI:10. English trans., Plass, 823 (No. 2554). The passage is from Luther's introduction to his translation of the NT.

27. WA, 15:87. English trans., Plass, ibid. (No. 2558).

28. The 1527 lectures are titled *Exposition of the First Epistle of St. John* and are in WA, 20. The sermons of 1532 are in WA, 36.

preted totally in terms of God's love in us. Rather, the perfect love of verse 18 does have an anthropological reference.[29]

In 1532, preaching a series of sermons on this passage, Luther recognized that perfect love must include the love that Christians express. This led him to speak of love at two levels in this particular passage. Whenever he asks what makes a man righteous before God, Luther holds faith and love apart, insisting that faith, that is to say, confidence in the promises of God, makes a man righteous before God. Love is always an expression of faith. Love is not a means of gaining salvation. On the other hand, Luther joins faith and love together when he asks whether the faith with which we receive justification is genuine. We know that we are justified because we love God. We cannot be justified without loving God. But if God's love to us, expressed in his justifying of us, is perfect, it does not mean that our expression of receiving justification is, in turn, perfect. God's perfect love in us casts out fear. Even fear of judgment. But perfect love on our part comes to us only as a gift of life in eternity.[30]

> You will not produce anyone on earth who loves God and his neighbor as the law requires. But in the future life, where we shall be entirely cleansed from all faults and sins and shall be as pure as the son, we shall love to perfection and shall be just by perfect love. But in this life such purity is hindered by our flesh, to which sin still clings as long as we live. Therefore our sinful self-love is so strong that it greatly exceeds our love of God and our neighbor. Nevertheless, in order to be just also in this life, we meanwhile have a propitiation and a throne of grace, Christ; if we believe in him, our sins are not imputed to us. Faith then is our righteousness in this life. However, in the future life, where we shall be thoroughly purged and entirely freed from all sin and evil desires, he shall no longer have need of faith and hope but shall love to perfection.[31]

What we must understand here is that Luther has separated, theologically, perfect love and sanctification. Martin Luther believed in entire sanctification. However, that sanctification was understood to be imputed by Christ. It was not the impartation of

---

29. Cf. Althaus, *The Theology of Martin Luther* (Philadelphia: Fortress, 1966), 446-58, for an illuminating and helpful source-based treatise on Luther's treatment of 1 John 4:17.

30. E.g., WA, 36:462, 635. See also WA, 32:543.

31. WA, 7:337. Also see, e.g., WA, 39 I: 204, 251, 432.

perfect love. For, as we have seen, perfect love is available only in the future life.

It remains, then, simply to cite some passages from Luther concerning the imputation of entire sanctification or holiness.

> He has purified everything through his body, so that because of him everything which belongs to our natural birth and this life does not damage us; but it is considered to be as pure as what belongs to him, because through baptism and faith I have been clothed with his birth and life. Therefore everything I do is pleasing to God and is properly called a holy walking, standing, eating, drinking, sleeping, and waking, etc. In every Christian this becomes a pure and holy thing, even though he still lives in the flesh and is definitely impure in himself; through faith, everything about him is pure. Thus it is an alien holiness, however, and yet our own, because God wills to see nothing which we do in this life as impure in itself; but everything becomes holy, precious and acceptable to him through this child who makes the whole world holy through his life.[32]

Luther is quite clear that God imputes to the believer entire sanctification, Christian holiness. However, it is, as he says, "an alien holiness." It is the holiness of God, not a moral transformation. So it is that Luther, as we have said, separates perfection in love and entire sanctification. It remains for Wesley to bring them together.

B. John Calvin: Entire Sanctification as Imputed Holiness

Seldom in the history of Christian thought has any theological system evoked a greater depth of response than that of John Calvin.[33] Whether of praise or of condemnation, words have seldom failed those who have given it careful study. Nor have they failed

---

32. WA, 37:57. This entire passage, WA, 37:53-62, is an exposition of this point. Also see Althaus, *Theology of Martin Luther,* 227-34, for a discussion of the important concept of "alien righteousness."

33. As in the case of Luther, Calvin does not lack biographers or commentators on his thought, though the latter are far more numerous than the former. The best biographies include Q. Breen, *John Calvin: A Study in French Humanism* (Grand Rapids: Wm. B. Eerdmans, 1931); E. Doumerque, *Jean Calvin—Les hommes et les choses de son temps* (7 vols.; Lausanne: G. Bridel, 1927); G. Harkness, *The Man and His Ethics* (New York: Henry Holt, 1931). Good studies of Calvin's thought include James Mackinnon, *Calvin and the Reformation* (London: Longmans, Green, 1936); John T. McNeill, *The History and Character of Calvinism* (New York: Oxford University Press, 1954); Wilhelm Niesel (trans. by Harold Knight), *The Theology of Calvin* (Philadelphia: Westminster, 1956), and Albert-Marie Schmidt (trans. by Ronald Wallace) *John Calvin and the Calvinistic Tradition* (New York: Harper, 1960).

all too many who did not give it study but felt compelled to pass an opinion upon it.

In 1521, Philipp Melanchthon, Luther's friend and disciple, published the *Loci communes rerum theologicarum (Cardinal Theological Themes)*, the first Protestant system of theology. This earliest edition very clearly speaks the mind of Luther, but subsequent editions bear more and more deeply the imprint of Melanchthon himself. While some major points of difference did evolve between the two men, it took very sharp theological eyes and a rather contentious set of mind to discover all of the variations that were discovered. They were to become the foci of much debate, even before Luther went to his rest in 1546. Melanchthon had not meant to write a full systematic theology, but only to present thoughts on some principal concerns. Consequently, even the final edition of the *Loci,* though a hefty volume, leaves many points undiscussed.

It remained for John Calvin, then in his mid-20s and a representative of the second generation of the Reformation, to present Protestantism with its first authentic systematic theology. The first edition appeared in 1536, the last Latin edition in 1559. While the final edition is much longer than the first, with editions of increasing size between them, Calvin maintained striking consistency in his thought across these years. So it is that the *Institutes of the Christian Religion* allow us the luxury of more firmly stated conclusions in summarizing and evaluating Calvin's thought than we have in working with Luther's.

Luther's literary work was very largely produced in response to this or that particular situation and for that reason may at times appear even to be self-contradictory. Calvin, too, wrote to specific occasions, but he also left the *Institutes,* a work of a sort that Luther seems never to have contemplated writing.

Of course, Luther's task was quite different from Calvin's, to say little of their differences in education and temperament. Luther's theology developed in the white heat of upheaval and controversy. It confronted people with a call to radical decision—a decision that could be physically lethal. And while Roman Catholic response was relatively slow, due in part to a complex political situation, alert Catholics answered first with emotion and later with reason. They answered as men cut to the quick. So Luther's thought has an energy to it, a sense of deep calling unto deep.

If Luther, with his pioneer spirit, be a sort of Abraham, Calvin is Isaac. Quiet, reflective, domesticated. Calvin's task is to bring order to ardor. The evangelicals knew, for the most part, why they had broken with Rome, but they were less sure about the positive ground upon which they could unite and close ranks. They tended to be much more sure of what they were fighting against than of what they were fighting for. Here Calvin was of immense aid. He reduced the Protestant "program," at least its theological dimension, to print. Not everyone agreed with it, but no Protestant leader disagreed entirely and only a few offered major criticism at more than a point or two.

It is true that Lutherans came to despise Calvinists, and vice versa. But that had more to do with the scholastic development of the two points of view than it did their original forms.

But for all of this, there were indeed genuine and significant differences between the theologies of Luther and Calvin that ran deeper than the differences in task or temperament. And these differences make for variations in their understandings of the doctrine we are studying, the doctrine of entire sanctification.

1. *Law and Gospel: Luther and Calvin Compared*

In large measure, the differences between Luther and Calvin on the doctrine of sanctification may be traced to the differences in their understanding of what "law" is, in the biblical sense, and its relation to the gospel.

Luther contrasted law and gospel. The theological or spiritual role of the law is to show us how great is our sinfulness. The law expresses the will of God, but when we compare its demands to the way we live, it shows us how far from God we are. It pronounces awful judgment upon us. At the same time, in order to escape judgment, we try to keep it. But this leads only to despair, for we cannot do so. So it condemns us farther. We see all human effort at salvation condemned.

However, if we allow the law to lead us only to despair, we are allowing only the devil to use it. It is also God's instrument to drive us to rely only on the promises of grace in Christ Jesus—only on the gospel. Once we have done that (which means to be converted), the law remains as a prod to our continued trusting only in Christ. It continues to remind us of how far we are from authentic righteousness and to drive us into the arms of Christ. Now that we are converted, we see that Christ has fulfilled it for us and has applied the benefits of that fulfillment to us. Therefore we need never despair, for we are "justified," we are accepted by God, we are accounted by Him as righteous.

Calvin did not contrast law and gospel. He agrees with Luther that the law is meant both to show us the awfulness of our sinfulness and to restrain the wicked. But he adds to these a purpose of the law that Luther only dimly perceived, if at all. For Calvin, the law also reveals the will of God to those who believe concerning the way they are to live righteous lives.

So it is that Calvin would agree with all that Luther had said about the law's terrible work of judgment, but he would place it in continuity with the gospel, not in contrast to it. It drives us either to despair or to the gospel, but having driven us to the gospel, it then forms the basis for what we are to do thereafter. Basically, of course, what we are to do is to imitate Christ, through the presence of the Spirit in us. It is the law that gives specific direction to that imitation—both positively and negatively. The Spirit guides our imitation so that it is authentic both outwardly and inwardly, for the law itself has to do both with actions and their sources in our spirits.

2. *Holiness, the Goal of Life*

Listen to Calvin as he expresses the goal of the Christian's life and the motivations for pursuing that goal.

> Ever since God revealed himself father to us, we must prove our ungratefulness to him if we did not in turn show ourselves his sons (Malachi 1:6; Ephesians 5:1; 1 John 3:1). Ever since Christ cleansed us with the washing of his blood, and imparted this cleansing through baptism, it would be unfitting to befoul ourselves with new pollutions (Ephesians 5:26; Hebrews 10:10; 1 Corinthians 6:11; 1 Peter 1:15, 19). Ever since he engrafted us into his body, we must take especial care not to disfigure ourselves, who are his members, without any spot or blemish (Ephesians 5:23-33; 1 Corinthians 6:15; John 15:3-6).
>
> Ever since Christ himself, who is our head, ascended into heaven, it behooves us, having laid aside love of earthly things, wholeheartedly to aspire heavenward (Colossians 3:1 ff.). Ever since the Holy Spirit dedicated us as temples to God, we must take care that God's glory shine through us, and must not permit anything to defile ourselves with the filthiness of sin (1 Corinthians 3:16, 6:19; 2 Corinthians 6:16). Ever since both our souls and bodies were destined for heavenly incorruption and an unfading crown (1 Peter 5:4), we ought to strive manfully to

keep them pure and uncorrupted until the day of the Lord (1 Thessalonians 5:23; cf. Philippians 1:10).

These, I say, are the most auspicious foundations upon which to establish one's life. One would look in vain for the like of these among the philosophers who in their commendation of virtue, never rise above the natural dignity of man.[34]

But what relationship has this statement of the goal of the holy life to Calvin's doctrine of predestination, or, as he preferred to call it, election? Calvin meets this question head on. He recognizes that among his opponents there are those who say that if spiritual life or death has been appointed by God's eternal and unchangeable decree, then it makes no difference how one lives since God's predestination can neither be halted nor helped by human effort. Calvin responds by saying that those who understand predestination in this way understand neither Scripture nor the ways of God.

For Scripture does not speak of predestination with intent to rouse us to boldness that we may try with impious rashness to search out God's unattainable secrets. Rather, its intent is that, humbled and cast down, we may learn to tremble at his judgment and esteem his mercy. It is at this mark that believers aim. But the foul grunting of these swine is duly silenced by Paul. They say they go on unconcerned in their vices; for if they are of the number of elect, vices will not hinder them from being at last brought into life. Yet Paul teaches that we have been chosen to this end: that we may lead a holy and blameless life (Ephesians 1:4).

If election has as its goal holiness of life, it ought rather to arouse and goad us eagerly to set our mind upon it than to serve as a pretext for doing nothing. What a great difference there is between these two things: to cease well-doing because election is sufficient for salvation, and to devote ourselves to the pursuit of good as the appointed goal of election! Away, then, with such sacrileges, for they wickedly invert the whole order of election.[35]

We see plainly, then, that Calvin's doctrine of election, or predestination, is not a metaphysical doctrine. Rather, it is, as Luther's doctrine of predestination is, an expression of God's faithfulness in keeping His promises. Predestination is a "package." That package

---

34. John Calvin, *Institutes of the Christian Religion,* John T. McNeill (ed.), trans. by Ford Lewis Battles as vols. XX and XXI, "Library of Christian Classics" (Philadelphia: Westminster, 1960) III.6.3. Hereinafter, translations from the *Institutes* will come from this edition. The abbreviation will be Calvin, *Inst.* III.6.3, etc.

35. Calvin, *Inst.* III.23.12.

includes good works on the part of one who is among the elect. From this perspective, Calvin could agree with Luther when Luther says, "Good works do not make a good man, but a good man does good works." This is to say that while good works do not necessarily indicate one's election, where they are lacking, we may be sure that there is no election to salvation.

The other side of the coin is that we need not expect the elect to live lives of perfect holiness. Calvin is well aware that many of the promises of Scripture are conditional, depending upon perfect obedience. Again, he meets the problems head on:

> Even if the promises of the law, insofar as they are conditional, depend upon perfect obedience to the law—which can nowhere be found—they have not been given in vain. For when we have learned that they will be fruitless and ineffectual for us unless God, out of his free goodness, shall receive us without looking at our works, and we in faith embrace that same goodness held forth to us by the gospel, the promises do not lack effectiveness even with the condition attached.[36]

This is another of Calvin's ways of insisting that salvation is by grace through faith and not by works. He makes it clear that salvation begins in the gracious election of God, not in our fulfillment of the law. So it is that even though the law may not be fulfilled by us, it stands over against us to remind us, who are the elect, that salvation has come to us in spite of our failure to fulfill the law. He says very bluntly, "The observance of the law is impossible."[37] However, he does not claim this impossibility so much upon the grounds of abstract theology as upon the grounds of experience. But, of course, he also moves to the Scriptures to ratify his point.

> For this point there are enough manifest testimonies of Scripture. "There is no righteous man upon the earth who . . . does not sin," said Solomon (Ecclesiastes 7:21, Vulgate; cf. 1 Kings 8:46). Moreover, David says: "Every man living will be unrighteous before thee" (Psalm 143:2). Job affirms the same idea in many passages (cf. Job 9:2; 25:4). Paul expresses it most clearly of all: "The flesh lusts against the Spirit, and the Spirit lusts against the flesh" (Galatians 5:17). That all those under the law are accursed he proves by no other reason, except that "it is written, 'cursed be everyone who will not abide by all things written in the book of the law'" (Galatians 3:10; Deuter-

---

36. Calvin, *Inst.* II.7.4.

37. Calvin, *Inst.* II.7.5.

> onomy 27:26). Here he is obviously intimating, in fact assuming, that no one can so abide. But whatever has been declared in Scripture it is fitting to take as perpetual, even as necessary.[38]

Calvin lays the blame for the impossibility of complete fulfillment of the law at the feet of imperfection in our love to God. Here he draws on Augustine and says, quoting Augustine: "Love so follows knowledge that no one can love God perfectly who does not first fully know his goodness. While we wander upon the earth, 'we see in a mirror dimly' (1 Corinthians 13:12). Therefore, it follows that our love is imperfect." Calvin himself then goes on to say, "Let us be quite agreed, then, that the law cannot be fulfilled in this life of flesh if we observe the weakness of our own nature; as will, moreover, be shown from another passage of Paul (Romans 8:3)."[39]

It must be reiterated, however, that from Calvin's point of view, this impossibility in fulfilling the law is not altogether bad. Again, it reminds us that we are saved by grace and not by our own fulfilling of the law. By accusing us it moves us continually to seek grace and not to rely upon our own resources.

3. *Sanctification*

For all Calvin's insistence that we cannot in this life completely fulfill the demands of God's law, he will not let go of the idea that we must live holy lives. How, then, does he reconcile the impossibility of such a life and the commands to follow after it? Here is how he sets out what he calls the "plan."

> Here then is the beginning of this plan: the duty of believers is to "present their bodies to God as a living sacrifice, holy and acceptable to him" and in this consists the lawful worship of him (Romans 12:1). From this is derived the basis of the exhortation that "they be not conformed to the fashion of this world, but be transformed by the renewal of their minds, so that they may prove what is the will of God" (Romans 12:2). Now the great thing is this: we are consecrated and dedicated to God in order that we may thereafter think, speak, meditate, and do, nothing except to his glory. For a sacred thing may not be applied to profane uses without marked injury to him.
>
> If we, then, are not our own (cf. 1 Corinthians 6:19) but the

38. Calvin, *Inst.* II.7.5.

39. Ibid.

> Lord's, it is clear what error we must flee, and whither we must direct all the acts of our lives.[40]

For Calvin, the demand remains an imperative in spite of the impossibility of completely fulfilling it. For Calvin, there is no excuse for holding back from the way, from moving in the direction of fulfillment.

> Let each one of us, then, proceed according to the measure of his puny capacity and set out upon the journey we have begun. No one shall set out so inauspiciously as not daily to make some headway though it be slight. Therefore, let us not cease so to act that we may make some unceasing progress in the way of the Lord.[41]

We are, then, to aspire to our goal, in no way excusing our evil deeds, but continuously striving toward that goal "that we may surpass ourselves in goodness until we attain to goodness itself."[42] What we are to know, of course, is that we shall attain goodness itself only "when we have cast off the weakness of the body, and are received into full fellowship with him."[43]

Why is it that we may not attain to perfect goodness, entire sanctification, or perfect love, this side of death? There have been those who have argued that Calvin has a platonic view of the body. That is to say, he views the body as essentially evil and therefore because it is fleshly or material it is incapable of being perfected. To be sure, there are passages in Calvin's writing that sound as if this is precisely what he believes. For instance, he says, "As long as we inhabit the prison of our body we shall have to maintain an incessant conflict with the vices of our corrupt nature."[44]

There are at least three ideas, however, that keep Calvin back from commitment to a platonic view of the body. In the first place, we find his commitment to *the Christian doctrine of creation.* Man is not an accident, nor is he the product of material forces only. Rather he is a special creature direct from the hand of God himself.[45] Calvin directly criticizes the position of the Manichaeans, which insisted that the soul was an emanation of God and that, since God breathes the breath of life upon man's face, the soul is

---

40. Calvin, *Inst.* III.7.1.
41. Calvin, *Inst.* III.6.5.
42. Ibid.
43. Ibid.
44. Cf. Calvin, *Inst.* IV.15.11-12.
45. Calvin, *Inst.* I.14.2; I.15.3.

therefore a derivative of God's substance.[46] Calvin cannot accept the moral consequences of this position. For, says he, "If man's soul be from the essence of God through derivation it will follow that God's nature is subject not only to change and passions, but also to ignorance, wicked desires, infirmity, and all manner of vices. Nothing is more inconstant than man."[47] Obviously, Calvin will not insult God with such declarations concerning His character.

Also included in the idea of the body as a creation of God himself is the consciousness of the seriousness of sin—a consciousness that would not be pressing were man simply an emanation from God. Calvin insists that the tragedy of the Fall lies in the fact that Adam himself chose to fall.[48] Adam fell as a morally responsible creature. Calvin here recognizes the problems raised by the doctrine of election. But he insists that whatever the doctrine of election may entail, it does not curtail the moral responsibility of Adam for his own fall.

A second Christian notion that holds Calvin back from commitment to a platonic understanding of the body is his belief in *the doctrine of the resurrection of the body.* Calvin argues that the body that will be resurrected is that body in which we have been clothed in this life. "Nor does Scripture define anything more clearly than the resurrection of the flesh that we now bear, 'for this perishable nature,' says Paul, 'must put on the imperishable, and this mortal nature must put on immortality' (1 Corinthians 15:53). If God made new bodies, where would this change of quality appear?"[49] He rests his case for the resurrection of the body as resurrection of this body in which we now live on the resurrection of Christ himself. He says, "Christ arose: was it by fashioning a new body for himself? No, as he had foretold 'destroy this temple and in three days I will raise it up' (John 2:10). He received again the mortal body which he had previously borne."[50] Such respect for the body can have no place in the platonic understanding that the body is evil.

The third Christian idea that keeps Calvin from committing himself to a platonic understanding of the body is *the incarnation*

46. Calvin, *Inst.* I.15.5.

47. Ibid.

48. Calvin, *Inst.* I.15.8.

49. Calvin, *Inst.* III.25.7.

50. Ibid.

and with it the insistence that *the life of the Christian is to be Christlike.* Calvin sees no life-style for the Christian as finally valid except the Christlike life. This life is a life of doing good to others, not solely to their souls but to their bodies, to human societies, and to other earthly entities, including the creatures and nature itself.

If it is not because the body is sinful, why, then, do we continue in sin even after our justification? Why *must* we continue in sin after our justification? As we have said above, it is not because Calvin has committed himself to a platonic view of the body that he insists that we remain in sin as long as we remain alive. However, he does insist that it is because we are in the body that sin continues to dwell in us. He says, for instance, "So long as we live cooped up in this prison of our body, traces of sin will dwell in us."[51] The body is not the source of sin in the sense of being the foundation of sinfulness, but it certainly is the occasion for sinfulness. It is the context, as it were, in which we sin. Calvin senses that he is at the edge of mystery here and pulls back from saying that the body is evil and is sinfulness itself by pointing to the opportunity that life in the body presents for glorifying God.

> Let no one deceive himself, let no one cajole himself in his sinfulness, when he hears that sin always dwells in us. When we speak thus it is not that those who otherwise are all too prone to sin should slumber untroubled in their sins, but only that those who are disturbed and pricked by their own flesh should not faint and be discouraged. Let them rather think that they are still on the way, and believe that they have made good progress when they feel that a bit is being taken away from their lust each day, until they reach their destination, that is, the final death of their flesh, which shall be accomplished in the close of this mortal life.
>
> Meanwhile, let them not cease to struggle manfully, to have courage for the onward way, and to spur on the full victory. For the fact that, after long striving, they see no little difficulty still remaining ought to sharpen their efforts all the more. This we must believe: we are baptized into the mortification of our flesh, which begins with our baptism and which we pursue day by day and which will, moreover, be accomplished when we pass from this life to the Lord.[52]

What hope is there, then? Here Calvin points to baptism. Precisely in the midst of this talk about the perversity that never

51. Cf. Calvin, *Inst.* IV.15.11.

52. Calvin, *Inst.* IV.15.11.

ceases in us, about the continuing presence of sin with us, about the prison of our body, he speaks of the great promises of this sacrament. "Baptism indeed promises to us the drowning of our Pharaoh (Exodus 14:28) and the mortification of our sin . . . but if we faithfully hold fast to the promise given us by God in baptism, they [the traces of sin] shall not dominate or rule."[53] Here, and in the quotation to which we are coming, we see again that tension in which Calvin believes the saints live. As long as we are in the flesh there resides as he says, "that depravity of inordinate desiring which contends against righteousness."[54] The following rather long quotation contains the tension almost to the point of bursting.

> God is said to purge his church of all sin, in that through baptism he promises that grace of deliverance, and fulfills it in his elect (Ephesians 5:26-27). This statement refers to the guilt of sin rather than to the very substance of sin. God truly carries this out by regenerating his own people, so that the sway of sin is abolished in them. For the Spirit dispenses a power whereby they may gain the upper hand and become victors in the struggle.
>
> But sin ceases only to reign; it does not also cease to dwell in them. Accordingly we say that the old man was so crucified (Romans 6:6), and the law of sin (cf. Romans 8:2) so abolished in the children of God, that some vestiges remain; not to rule over them, but to humble them by the consciousness of their own weakness. And we, indeed, admit that these traces are not imputed as if they did not exist; but at the same time we contend that this comes to pass through the mercy of God, so that the saints—otherwise deservedly sinners and guilty before God—are freed from this guilt. And it will not be difficult for us to confirm this opinion, since there are clear testimonies to the fact in Scripture.
>
> What clearer testimony do we wish than what Paul exclaimed in the seventh chapter of Romans? First, Paul speaks there as a man reborn (Romans 7:6). This we have shown in another place, and Augustine proves it with unassailable reasoning. I have nothing to say about the fact that he uses the words "evil" and "sin," so that they who wish to cry out against us can cavil at those words; yet who will deny that hindrance to righteousness is sin? Who, in short, will not grant that guilt is involved wherever there is spiritual misery, but Paul proclaims all these facts concerning this disease.
>
> Then we have a reliable indication from the law by which

53. Ibid.

54. Calvin, *Inst.* III.3.10.

> we can briefly deal with this whole question. For we are bidden to "love God with all our heart, with all our soul, and with all our faculties" (Deuteronomy 6:5; Matthew 22:37). Since all the capacities of our soul ought to be so filled with the love of God, it is certain that this precept is not fulfilled by those who can either retain in the heart a slight inclination or admit to the mind any thought at all that would lead them away from the love of God into vanity.
>
> What then? To be stirred by sudden emotions, to grasp in sense perception, to conceive in the mind—are not these powers of the soul? Therefore, when these lay themselves open to vain and depraved thoughts, do they not show themselves to be in such degree empty of the love of God? For this reason, he who does not admit that all desires of the flesh are sin, but that the disease of inordinantly desiring which they call "tinder" is a wellspring of sin, must of necessity deny that the transgression of the law is sin.[55]

Several points in this long quotation are worth noting with respect to Calvin's doctrine of sanctification. *First,* Christ's deliverance is said to be a deliverance from guilt—from *all* guilt. It is not a deliverance from sin. *Second,* the traces of sin in us are not imputed to us, according to Calvin. From the Godward side, with respect to our moral account as it were, they do not exist. In fact, Calvin says in another place (II. 2. 27) that they are really not ours now anyway. That is to say they are not ours in that they do not arise from our regenerate nature. Calvin uses Romans 7 as proof of this. *Third,* our awareness of our sinfulness, our continuing sinfulness, is itself a sign of our being elect. Were we not aware of our sin, it would be indicative of our complicity in it.

On the other hand, refusal to admit our sinfulness, even as regenerate believers, is refusal to accept the grace of God in forgiveness. Refusal to accept the broadest possible definition of sin—that is, sin as any hindrance to righteousness—is also a sign of reprobation. For Calvin, recognition of sinfulness is a necessary step and a continuing necessity in our sanctification. Where there is no recognition of continuing sinfulness, there is no sanctification. Failure to recognize our continuing sinfulness is failure to love God with all our heart, with all our soul, and with all our faculties.

So it is that Calvin very clearly insists upon the sanctification of life. He insists, in fact, upon entire sanctification. But, for him, entire sanctification includes a recognition that we are not all that

---

55. Calvin, *Inst.* III.3.11.

God would have us to be. It entails recognition that we continue in our sinfulness, but that we are striving by the grace of God to be more and more Christlike as our lives pass. And, Calvin is very careful to insist, as we have said, that at least entire sanctification is imputed to us.

We have already indicated one passage in which Calvin speaks of this imputation. We cite now another, which makes the case even clearer.

> In this sense we shall concede not only a partial righteousness in works, as our adversaries themselves hold, but also that it is approved by God as if it were whole and perfect. But if we recall the foundation that supports it, every difficulty will be solved. A work begins to be acceptable only when it is undertaken with pardon. Now whence does this pardon arise, save that God contemplates us and our all in Christ? Therefore, as we ourselves, when we have been engrafted in Christ, are righteous in God's sight because our iniquities are covered by Christ's sinlessness, so our works are righteous and are thus regarded because whatever fault is otherwise in them is buried in Christ's purity and is not charged to our account. Accordingly, we can deservedly say that by faith alone not only we ourselves but our works as well are justified.[56]

Again, we see Calvin insisting upon entire sanctification—demanding holiness. However, he insists that this holiness begins with the imputation of Christ's righteousness to our account. We are righteous because we have been engrafted into Christ. Good works will flow in abundant measure from this imputed righteousness. These will in turn make us righteous in fact, although they in no way redeem us.

We see in Calvin a view of entire sanctification quite different from that which we saw in the thought of Martin Luther. Both men felt compelled to struggle against the Roman Catholic view that declared one must be sanctified, that is to say one must make himself holy by means of his works, before he may be justified. Luther insisted that God imputes to the believer entire sanctification or Christian holiness following his justification. However, Luther insisted that this sanctification is "an alien holiness."[57] Luther could not see that the holiness of God is both imputed and imparted to the believer and works a genuine moral transformation in

---

56. Calvin, *Inst.* III.17.10.

57. Cf. Luther, WA, 40, I:70. This reference is to his 1531 *Commentary on Galatians* (1:2).

him. He separates perfection in love and entire sanctification. To be sure, in his sermons Luther takes a more optimistic path and calls for moral transformation, or at least something like it. But in his theological treatises he disallows or at least depreciates the possibilities of moral transformation.

Calvin, on the other hand, while he believes that God imputes to the believer entire sanctification or Christian holiness, does not believe that this sanctification, this holiness, is an alien holiness. Rather, while it is the holiness of God, it also becomes the source of our holiness. And our holiness brings about a genuine moral transformation. This transformation is not complete in this life. And we must understand, according to Calvin, that it is not moral transformation that brings holiness; rather it is holiness that brings moral transformation. Calvin, then, keeps perfection in love and entire sanctification bound together as motive to consequence. In Calvin, then, we have taken a long step forward toward the position that will be developed 200 years later by John Wesley.

II. Entire Sanctification in Dutch Pietism

A. Dirck Coornhert, Catholic Pietist

Dirck Volkertsz Coornhert (1522-90) was a convinced and able humanist who never formally renounced his Roman Catholic faith. By pen and by deed, however, he excoriated both Catholics and evangelicals whose lethal intolerance seemed to him to make a mockery of true Christianity. He witnessed firsthand the pious cruelties of the Inquisition in Spain, and he read with profound sympathy Sebastian Castellio's *De haereticis an sint persequendi,* a noteworthy defense of Servetus, whom Calvin had burnt in Geneva.[58] Convinced that love had been set aside and that dogma, hierocracy, and sacrament had taken its place as the fundamental characteristic of the faith, he called for a "Christianity superior to confessional diversity." Such a faith would practice tolerance and be faithful to Scripture, Scripture untrammeled by gloss or commentaries.[59]

---

58. This work, written in 1554, under the pen name Martinus Bellius, has been put into English by Roland Bainton in vol. XXII of the *Columbia University Records of Civilization, Sources and Studies* (New York: Columbia University Press, 1935).

59. Cf. Coornhert's *Van de aangheheven dwangh in der conscientien* (Leiden, 1579). Also important here is the exchange of tracts between Calvin and Coornhert.

Even more important for our work, however, is Coornhert's understanding of the nature of the Christian life. Catholic Spiritualist that he was, he insisted that authentic Christianity depends upon inner and inward experience, not upon external and visible forms and practices. Its verification is the development of Christlikeness in character.[60]

This inner and inward experience comes about because God himself seeks us and unites himself with us. This unity gives us a new birth, "the true mortification of the evil in man and an enlivening of the godly life in the genuinely repentant."[61] With the new birth comes enablement to believe and to trust God. And in believing and trusting Him, we receive good gifts from Him that empower us to live righteous lives. "All of our life is made up of acting or not acting, and action or inaction involves what is good or what is evil."[62] Basic to life itself is moral involvement.

This latter being granted, moral neutrality or ethical indifference is impossible. We are either saints or we are sinners, and that not merely on the basis of a forensic divine declaration. Coornhert will not have righteousness relegated to imputation alone. Christ's righteousness and the presence of His Spirit in us regenerate us. We are made righteous in fact. The true Christian presses ever closer to perfect conformity to the will of God, to Christlikeness. "God is good and so is his will. So it is that he wants all who understand and do his will continually to become good."[63]

Coornhert's ethical concern and his emphasis upon regeneration sounded to many Reformed thinkers in his day like a call

---

In 1543, Calvin had written his *Petit traité montrant que c'est que doit faire un homme fidèle . . . quond il est entre les papistes* (What the Faithful Man Ought to Do When Among Papists). Belatedly (1562), Coornhert responded in his *Verschooninghe van de Roomsche Afgoderye,* arguing that Calvin's demands that his followers always and everywhere testify to their evangelical commitment was encouraging unnecessary martyrdoms. Calvin answered the charge quickly in a letter: *Réponse à un certain Hollandais lequel sous ombre de faire les Chrétiens tout Spirituels, leur permet de polluer leur corps en toutes idolatries* (Reply to a certain Hollander who under pretext of making Christians entirely spiritual would permit them to completely defile their bodies in idolatries).

60. Coornhert's *Hertspiegel godlijker Schrifturen vertoonende een klare, korte ende sekere wegh . . . (Dieryck Volkertszoon Coornherts Werken* [Amsterdam, 1630], vol. I).

61. Cf. *Vande Wedergeboorte, Hoe die gheschiet, ende waar by de Mensch mach sekerlijk weten of die in hem is ghescheit of niet* (in *Werken* [Amsterdam, 1630], vol. I, folio, p. 178).

62. Cf. *Hertspiegel . . .* (*Werken,* vol. I, folio, p. 8).

63. Cf. *Hertspiegel . . .* (*Werken,* vol. I, folio, p. 20).

for works-righteousness. And, indeed, Coornhert's insistence upon putting his point in language that pointed up his differences with orthodox theologians and his taste for the pagan classics—especially the Stoics and moralists—beclouded the essential orthodoxy of his understanding of the way of salvation. Especially critical in this regard is his carefulness to declare consistently that salvation is totally dependent upon the divine initiative and the continuous operations of divine grace. Also of fundamental significance is the Christocentricity of his "system."

Salvation is offered only in Christ. Spiritual life is possible only as it is in Him, and only He can empower us to live righteous lives. But the other side of this coin is our willing complicity. We seek to know and to fulfill Christ's will for us, and this brings genuine regeneration.

> Christ wants us first to purify ourselves internally so that externally we shall also be clean. Internally, one purifies himself when, acknowledging his want of understanding, he abandons his own faulty judgment, no longer insists on his power of choice, and dies to his will. Then, calling upon God day and night, he looks for, yearns for and wills only that by forsaking himself thus, by patiently bearing his cross, and by walking in Christ's footsteps, he will become ever more obedient to God.[64]

Here, then, is a doctrine of sanctification that includes authentic personal regeneration. And this regeneration is progressive. The most elementary form of Christian life is that of the repentant sinner—as distinguished from the unrepentant sinner. The repentant sinner has been converted "somewhat." His motivation is either that of fear or of the hireling. The most advanced form of Christian life is that of the saint. Here the motivation is love and the means to expressing that love is the true understanding of the Bible. There are three classes of saint: children in the faith, adults, and parents. Children in the faith understand Scripture and do the will of God, but with wavering and weakness of resolution and in poverty of resources in knowledge and experience. Adults in the faith understand Scripture and do the will of God with confidence; richer resources in knowledge and experience make them more trusting. They do God's will readily and vigorously. Parents in the

---

64. Cf. H. L. J. Heppe, *Geschichte des Pietismus und der Mystik in der Reformirten Kirche, namentlich der Niederlande* (Leiden: E. J. Brill, 1879), 83.

faith actually induce others to come to Christ and to grow in grace.[65]

Coornhert intends by this classification to declare his confidence that an evangelical perfection is possible in this life, and he deliberately parts company with the older Roman Catholic view of perfection by placing it in the context of evangelizing (that is, being parents in the faith) instead of in the context of monastic insulation.[66] Even more significantly, Coornhert draws rather sharp lines of distinction between the classes of Christian, and these lines are especially important in the comparison of Christians of the first and second stages. A profound inner change has taken place between the two. The child in faith struggles with worldly yens. The will of God appears as a duty to be fulfilled, often against the child-Christian's natural inclinations. In the adult in the faith, the struggle with worldliness continues but on an entirely different basis. Now worldliness is entirely an external foe, not an internal subverter. And the will of God is gladly sought and fulfilled in love, not as duty but as privilege; not against the adult-Christian's inclinations but precisely as an expression of them.

While Coornhert's theology is miles from John Wesley's in many ways, especially in Coornhert's rather more optimistic view of human nature apart from grace, at this point of describing the character of sanctification they are remarkably similar. The basic difference yet remaining lies in the fact that Wesley investigates carefully just how the stage of adult-Christian is entered upon.

Coornhert, as we have indicated, never really became a Protestant, and in that way is a bridge from late medieval Dutch Catholic piety to Reformed Pietism. We should, then, consider a person or persons more representative of the latter in order to maintain some sense of historical and ideational continuity in our survey.

The act of selecting is neither so arbitrary nor so difficult as it may at first appear to be; for standing obviously in the foreground of Reformed Pietism are the Teellincks, the brothers Willem and Eewout, and Willem's son Jan. We will consider here Willem Tee-

---

65. *Hertspiegel . . .* (*Werken,* vol. I, folio, p. 8).

66. To be sure, monasticism (i.e., the religious life of those called "the perfect") had once been intensely missionary in orientation, but by the 16th century that orientation had largely disappeared, except among the mendicants and the Jesuits—a large exception, certainly.

llinck only.[67] And for lack of space, we shall treat him but briefly. He should be studied very extensively by the serious student of either Pietism or the history of the doctrine of sanctification.

B. Willem Teellinck, Reformed Pietist

Teellinck (1579-1629), a pastor in the Dutch towns of Haamstede (1606-12) and Middleburg (1612-29), considered himself to be nothing other than an orthodox Reformed minister in the controversies that surrounded him. This he did with the skill and knowledge of a highly educated scholar (he had a Dr. Theology from the University of Poitiers) and in the face of some authentic threats to "mainline" Reformed orthodoxy from within the tradition itself (such as Arminianism). On the other hand, he knew very well that his emphasis on practical holiness cut cross-grain of the usual orthodox caricature of the doctrine of justification by grace alone. Reformation of life, not simply of doctrine or of polity, was Teellinck's aim. And his ceaseless and well-aimed efforts in that direction had a very telling effect in the Netherlands, even in his lifetime.

With his emphasis on piety and the life of holiness, Teellinck avoided the acrimony of the debate over predestination. While generally in accord with something like the position taken at the Synod of Dort (1618), he saw clearly the ethical indifference often created by the rigid predestinarian positions. For him, the test of true doctrine was true holiness of life.

Unlike the Lutheran Pietists, whose thought we shall consider shortly, Teellinck and the rest of the Reformed tradition were not

---

67. For an extended biographical sketch of Willem Teellinck, see H. Heppe, *Geschichte des Pietismus und der Mystik in der Reformirten Kirche, namentlich der Niederlande* (Leiden: E. J. Brill, 1879), 106-40. For a collection of Teellinck's works, cf. *Alle de Wercken van Mr. Willem Teellinck,* 3 vols. (Amsterdam, 1659-64). Actually, "alle" is incorrect. For a comprehensive bibliography of the elder Teellinck's works, cf. Heppe, *Geschichte des Pietismus,* 115-28 and W. J. M. Engleberts, *Willem Teellinck* (1898), 211-23.

On Pietism generally, the most thorough work is in Dutch and German. In addition to Heppe's work, already cited, see Wilhelm Goeters, *Die Vorbereitung des Pietismus in der reformirten Kirche der Niederlande bis zur labadistischen Krisis 1670* (Leipzig, 1911); Manfred W. Kohl, *Studies in Pietism. A Bibliographical Survey of Research Since 1958/59* (unpub. Ph.D. dissertation, Harvard University, 1969); and F. Ernest Stoeffler, *The Rise of Evangelical Pietism* (2nd ed.; Leiden: E. J. Brill, 1971) and *German Pietism During the Eighteenth Century* (Leiden: E. J. Brill, 1973). The most thorough study, though the reader must understand the author's purposes, is Albrecht Ritschl, *Geschichte des Pietismus* (3 vols.; Bonn: Marcus, 1880-86).

saddled with a view of baptism that made almost any talk of real regeneration or sanctification following baptism appear to take away from the efficacy of that rite.

In typical Reformed fashion, Teellinck guards his baptismal theology from the "errors" of either the Roman Catholics, the Lutherans, or the Anabaptists. Baptism, says he, is a pledge or an initiation into the heavenly kingdom, so the Roman Catholics are in error in viewing it as a washing away of sin, freeing the conscience from condemnation.

Lutherans, too, understood baptism as a washing away of sin and a freeing of the conscience, but they threw the emphasis upon the element of justification. Now baptized, the individual was all right and righteous in the sight of God. Catholicism saw baptism as the beginning of the process of becoming Christian: Lutheranism saw it as a decisive act making one as Christian as he would ever be. Teellinck argued that the Lutheran position stood too near to Catholicism in that it held that baptism actually did something fundamental to the person baptized.

Reformed Pietist that he was, Teellinck would say that baptism does not make any fundamental changes in the person baptized, but is, rather, a testimony to fundamental changes having been made, or at least begun—a confession before others. But more importantly, it is an aid to faith. It is a symbol of the remission of sins, of the death and resurrection with Christ of the person baptized, and of spiritual union with Christ.[68] It does not justify; it does not bestow grace. But it is the divinely ordained symbol for justification and certainly justification bestows grace.

The Anabaptists, while believing that baptism was for believers only, held to no single view of the character of baptism itself since the New Testament presents no theology of baptism, except that they saw the rite as a witness to conversion and the washing away of sin. They used the word *symbol,* but only in its abstract meaning—"sign" or "indication." Teellinck's objection to this is that it makes the sacrament useless, and our Lord commanded nothing useless.

We have written at length here of the varying views of baptism because they came to play increasingly significant roles in the

---

68. Here, the Reformed tradition understood "symbol" in its classical sense; i.e., not as an abstraction from reality but as a window into reality that participates in the reality itself. The distinction is a critical one, often overlooked.

doctrine of entire sanctification. This is especially true as the old, traditional language is more and more subjected to theological refinement and qualification, from about 1550 onward. This increasing theological nicety, in turn, led to hardening of the differences between groups, but that story is beyond our purpose.

The Reformed understanding of baptism, which Teellinck accepted as his own,[69] did not prove to be the barrier to advocating the holy life that the Lutheran view then current in the Netherlands did. Deep within the Reformed tradition was the confidence that sanctification is the very evidence of justification. In Lutheranism, sanctification was complete at baptism. Any good works or Christlike attitudes taken were seen as superfluous. Of course, Teellinck was not about to argue that all who lived what appeared to be sanctified lives were indeed justified. But the justified would seek holiness of life. That yearning was seen as a simple and clear witness to one's justification. And, in fact, the yearning was also seen as a signal of sanctification already begun.

If a given baptism symbolizes accurately the state of the person being baptized, new life is begun, new life in Christ. This new life, according to Teellinck, is not simply a new intellectual outlook, nor a commitment to certain doctrines, nor even sheer trust in the atoning merits of Christ. Rather, with the Christocentrism typical of the Reformed tradition at its best, Teellinck insists that the new birth and its subsequent newness of life are essentially matters of personal commitment to the living Christ, whom he calls the New-Maker.[70] And at the heart of this commitment is love, love that sets itself "against [the] corrupt flesh."[71]

In this experience, one is to deny oneself so that the Spirit, who entered when one was originally justified, might have absolute mastery of the life.[72] But what is the purpose of the Spirit's mastery? To what end do we delight in the establishment of the new life in us and seek the deepening of our loving commitment to the New-Maker in a life of holiness? Again, maintaining the Chris-

---

69. Cf. *Anmerkingen over Lucas 22:19 . . .* (Amsterdam, 1621).

70. Cf. *Den Nieuw-maecker ende sijn nieuw werck uyt Apoc.* 21:5 (Middleburg, 1624).

71. *Paul, His Complaint About His Natural Corruption: With the Means How to Be Delivered . . .* (London: printed by John Dawson, 1621). Teellinck wrote this in English. The title has been conformed to modern spelling.

72. This is a recurring theme in Teellinck, e.g., ibid., 14.

tocentric understanding of salvation, Teellinck says that our goal (the goal of the Spirit in us) is union with Christ.[73] Here, Teellinck speaks with the language of the mystics, which is sometimes highly metaphysical, but maintains the Reformed position, which is not metaphysical but religious.[74] The mystics sometimes spoke of union in terms of absorption, of loss of personal identity in a complete personal identification with God. Teellinck spoke of the identification of our will with the divine will, of a love so profound that all other loves, lusts, and desires will be replaced by the fullness of the presence of Christ.[75]

Is such an experience, such a state of self-denial (grace-granted, of course), such a condition of perfect love, possible in this life? Teellinck's response is equivocal. We at least receive a foretaste of it here, and it may be a continuing experience. But only after death will it be known in its fullness.

At what point is the experience, the foretaste, entered here in this life? And is the entry gradual or instantaneous? It certainly is arrived at gradually, but Teellinck's resort to mystical language would lead us to believe he was conceiving it as an experience quite different, qualitatively, from that which preceded it and one into which one comes very much aware of having crossed a spiritual boundary at a definite time. Further (to respond to our first question), while we may only extrapolate from Teellinck's descriptions, it would seem that this experience is entered upon as one reaches the point of complete self-denial. Teellinck saw faith as active, not passive. So while any spiritual experience is dependent upon grace alone, through faith, faith does precipitate the experience by fulfilling its covenantal obligations. And at the base of these obligations is that of self-denial.

We leave the study of Teellinck (as representative of early Reformed Pietism in the matter of entire sanctification) with a hunch that he was intuitively on to what Wesley was to articulate almost

---

73. E.g., *Sleutel der Devotie Ons openende de deure des hemels* (Amsterdam, 1624), in *Wercken* III. pt. 1., p. 19.

74. While the language of the mystics was often metaphysical or ontological, they were themselves frequently concerned to admonish their hearers and readers that what they sought (or knew) was union beyond even metaphysical or ontological union. They simply utilized the most elevated language at hand to describe the indescribable, which was at any rate even more elevated. Cf., for instance, Teellinck's *The New Jerusalem.*

75. *Sleutel der Devotie Ons openende de deure des hemels, Wercken* III. pt. 1, p. 14.

150 years later. There certainly is in Teellinck an awareness of a qualitatively different life beyond justification for the Christian, and basic to this life is loving self-denial in response to the presence of Christ in the individual. The goal is both attainable and not attainable in this life. Perfection, for Teellinck, is perfection in love, in self-denial, and in Christlikeness. Entire sanctification would be perfection in self-denial, a perfection possible only as the Holy Spirit in fullness displaces our egoism.

It would seem, then, that with Teellinck, we move a long way toward Wesley.

III. Entire Sanctification in Lutheran Pietism

The theology of any person is bound to be destorted by its later advocates, and this is precisely what happened in the 17th century to the theology of Martin Luther. The great Saxon reformer had emphasized the objective side of our salvation—the imputational, as distinguished from the impartational. So, he puts great weight on the forensic side of justification—our being *declared* righteous. Baptism brings us perfect cleansing from original sin and we are *imputed* perfect righteousness. Originally, Luther had developed this side of his understanding as a check against any form of justification by works. But he most assuredly had not given up the grand Christian themes of regeneration (actually being made righteous) and the call to a holy life.

His careful insistence upon the Christian's lifelong struggle with sin—the inward impulse to disobey God, which, he says, is taken from the believer only at death—is in tension with another insistence of his. It was later Lutheranism and some of Luther's detractors who helped make it appear that Luther neglected the theme of sanctification and that he also practically ignored the so-called subjective side of religion. But this view is incorrect. Early, midstream, and late in his career Luther called his followers to allow regeneration and sanctification to be made manifest in their lives. In 1518 or 1519 he said, "He who trusts in Christ exists in Christ; he is one with Christ, having the same righteousness as he. It is therefore impossible that sin should remain in him."[76] In

---

76. *Works* (Philadelphia ed.), 31:298.

1545, the year before his death, in a sermon on 1 John 4:16 ff., he said much the same thing.

> Christ has not died so that you can remain such a sinner; rather, he died so that sin might be put to death and destroyed and that you might now begin to love God and your neighbor. Faith takes sins away and puts them to death so that you should not live in them but in righteousness. Therefore demonstrate by your words and by your fruits that you have faith.[77]

In the 17th century, representatives of these two positions, held in creative tension by Luther but now resolved into contending principles, took their respective sides and each claimed to be the truly Lutheran party.[78] It is the thinking of those who held to his insistence on regeneration and the impartation of righteousness that we shall investigate briefly.

Most of those who picked up Luther's interest in genuine regeneration or sanctification came to be called Pietists; some were not so closely identified with Pietism as others. There was no Pietist denominationalizing in Lutheranism as there was in both the Reformed and Anglican branches of the Reformation. But there was bad blood between the two positions. Suspicion oozed from more orthodox Lutherans. They were certain that the Pietists were allowing for salvation by works. On the Pietists' side, suspicions arose that the Church, *their* church after all, was spiritually effete and worldly.

Pietism did not arise out of nowhere. We have already seen its seeds in the thought of Luther himself.[79] And we can trace its ancestry in the two or three generations after Luther before it becomes a clearly identifiable spiritual perspective.[80] For our pur-

---

77. WA, 49:783.

78. Perhaps it would appear foolish on their part even to be so concerned with being "truly Lutheran." Why not simply move on without deference to Luther? The answer is twofold: the immense authority of Luther on both sides of the argument and the fact that independence of the state established church was extremely difficult to obtain, let alone sustain. The Diet of Augsburg's "Peace" (1555) and the Treaty of Westphalia at the end of the Thirty Years War fixed religious boundaries in continental Europe and did so in terms of but two (1555) or three (1648) theological confessions—Catholic, Lutheran, and Reformed. No more divisions were recognized as licit. So, it was important for those who wished to exercise their religion under duly established "constitutional" rights to claim their inheritance in the appropriate one of the two or three confessions.

79. Cf. Heinrich Bornkamm, *Mystik, Spiritualismus und die Anfänge des Pietismus* (Giessen, 1926).

80. Sources to investigate would include the works of Stephan Praetorius

poses, however, we will begin with Johann Arndt and then consider Philipp Jakob Spener.

A. Johann Arndt (1555-1621)

With Lutheran Pietism in general, any study of the doctrine of sanctification, especially as it relates to the Wesleyan doctrine of entire sanctification, throws us into a terminological swamp. The Lutheran Pietists stoutly maintain Luther's doctrine of *simul iustus et peccator*—the belief that the Christian is (always, in this life) simultaneously justified and a sinner.[81] Their definition of sin in this case is based upon a standard of absolute holiness, a perfect rightness in thought, word, and deed. No one ever measures up to such a standard in this life. Such a definition of sin and of righteousness rules out any possibility of a flawless keeping of the law of love as long as we are in the flesh, living in a sinful world. This does not allow us any right to relax our vigilance or our warfare against sin in our lives and in our world. The commandment of Christ to perfection still stands and must be approximated ever more closely. But only as "this mortality puts on immortality" will it be fulfilled.

It is precisely at this point of approximating the ideal that Lutheran Pietism differed most from Lutheran Orthodoxy. Orthodoxy had come at first simply to emphasize the objective, the forensic, aspect of sanctification. "We are holy," said the Orthodox. "We are perfectly holy. But not at all in ourselves. Christ's perfection has been accredited to us." By about 1600, the emphasis had become the sole point and that fact occasioned the Pietist's protest. "Your doctrine," said they to the Orthodox, "leads to ethical

---

(1536-1603), Philipp Nicolai (1556-1608), and Valentin Weigel (1533-88). Cf. Stoeffler, *Rise of Evangelical Pietism,* 180-227, for a helpful overview of the positions of each of these, and of the relationship between Luther and Pietism. The best outline of the latter is in an article by Martin Schmidt, "Spener und Luther," *Luther Jahrbuch* 24 (1957), 102-29. For an older interpretation that was standard for many years, cf. A. Ritschl, *Geschichte des Pietismus.*

81. E.g., Johann Arndt, *Vier Bücher von Wahre Christentum* (first printed in 1610), Book I, chapter 16. Hereinafter, abbreviated as WC, I.16, etc. Abbreviating thus, the author hopes to accommodate both the reading of the various German editions and those of the various English translations and editions. The translations are this author's based on the German edition of 1866, titled *Sechs Bücher von Wahre Christentum,* which includes as books V and VI tracts not included in the 1610 edition; and a potpourri of apologetic materials, letters, and prefaces to the *Theologia Germanica.*

indifference, to spiritual carelessness. The presence of Christ in the believer actually changes the believer. And this change is evidenced in behavior."

But how is this change in behavior not a matter of salvation by works? What keeps the discipline of the Christian life from being an attempt at self-sanctification? To be sure, one can attribute the doing of righteousness to the presence of Christ within. But how, then, does one avoid either totally negating one's own participation in sanctification, or (on the other extreme) claiming that Christ and His grace are only aids and encouragements to holy living and nothing more?

Johann Arndt seemed to his orthodox Lutheran contemporaries to have all of the wrong answers to these questions, though he himself said that he wished only to be truly Lutheran, in harmony at every point with the Augsburg Confession and the Formula of Concord, the Lutheran doctrinal standards.[82]

In fact, Arndt began where Luther began and they walked along together most of the way, theologically. Both define justification as God's free and gracious act, a declaration that can in no way be induced by our strivings. Further, both insist that the Christian life is maintained only by the grace of God, not by works. Such good works as may characterize the Christian's life are in consequence of his being Christian, not in hope of thereby becoming more Christian. So Arndt begins his immensely influential book *True Christianity (Vier Bücher von Wahre Christentum)* by stating it as his aim to show "what constitutes authentic Christianity, namely the demonstration of authentic, vital, active faith through genuine godliness."[83] If this is not pure Lutheranism, the reason is that Arndt is only moving beyond the great Saxon Reformer, not contradicting him. Where Luther had struck sparks, Arndt would build beacon fires.

For Arndt, as for Luther, regeneration, the process that produces sanctification, begins with baptism.[84] But Arndt has little to say about baptism itself. Instead he gives his attention to regen-

---

82. E.g., WC, IV. praef. The most complete study of Arndt's life and thought is Wilhelm Koepp, *Johann Arndt: Eine Untersuchung über die Mystik in Luthertum* (Berlin, 1912). Unfortunately, there is no full-length work on Arndt in English.

83. WC, vorwort.

84. E.g., *Paradiesgärtlein, voller christlichen Tugenden* (first pub. in 1610), 1866 ed. (bound with *Sechs Bücher von Wahre Christentum*), 67. Also cf. WC, V.2.11.

eration, which he also refers to as the new birth[85] and as conversion.[86] In this way, Arndt redressed Lutheran orthodoxy's concentration on the objective character of baptism, its once-and-for-all cleansing of original sin and its enrolling of the baptizand in the Body of Christ. He corrected only the preoccupation. So he prays, "Grant that I may remember every day that I am baptized into a new life."[87]

In typical Lutheran fashion, Arndt understands baptism to bestow a certain perfection—a perfect cleansing from original sin. "With your blood you have so perfectly cleansed us that there remains not a fleck of sin."[88] This understanding of baptism had led most Lutherans of Arndt's day to set aside the idea of living a holy life. After all, why live a holy life if we have already been made perfect through baptism? Luther would have been appalled with such logic, of course. But whether he would have applauded Arndt is another matter. He maintained that while "good works do not make a good man, a good man does good works."[89] Arndt shifted Luther's concept from the category of ethics to the category of regeneration. Being made perfect in baptism, we seek to lead a holy life.[90] And the source of this seeking is the presence of Christ within us.[91] Baptism not only united us with Christ's Body, the Church. It unites us to Christ personally, which means that the divine nature is at work in us, and that not only as a separated, objective nature but as our own. United to Christ, like Him we have both a divine and human nature. Of course, the divine nature is given us as a gift. It was natural to Him but not to us.[92]

At first glance, this may appear to be mysticism. And, in fact, his opponents accused Arndt of being a mystic. But when Arndt speaks of the union of the believer with Christ, he does so re-

---

85. WC, I. 3.

86. E.g., WC, I.37.

87. *Paradiesgärtlein . . . ,* 1866 ed., 90.

88. E.g., *Paradiesgärtlein . . . ,* 1866 ed., 67.

89. *Sämmtliche Werke,* 58:355. (The *Sämmtliche Werke* is usually known as the Erlangen edition from its place of publication in 1826-57. It is abbreviated E.A., for Erlangen Ausgabe. The other major collection of his works, still technically unfinished, is the W.A., for Weimar Ausgabe, 1883 —).

90. This is the principal theme of WC, V.2.11. Also see WC, I.21.

91. WC, II.1-3.

92. This is the principal theme of WC, II, esp. 3, 7, 11, 12.

taining the separate and distinct identities of both.[93] The union of which Arndt speaks is ethical and religious, not metaphysical. The believer imitates Christ by the power of the Spirit rather than by being swallowed up in Christ (as the mystics would have it) or by being only the passive vehicle used by Christ (as the majority of Lutheran orthodoxy believed).[94] The believer is indeed clothed in the righteousness of Christ, but this imputation does not make us holy. Rather, our purification occurs as we weep over our imperfection and impurity, thus allowing the Spirit to open the way for Christ's blood actually to cleanse us perfectly, through faith. And it is out of this cleansing brought on by weeping over our impurity that we live a holy life.[95]

It is obvious that the life of holiness is entered upon at some time subsequent to justification and is dependent upon baptism, in which original sin is said to be washed away.[96] Equally obvious is the fact that the life of holiness, though dependent upon baptism, is not a necessary consequence of baptism. The perfection granted in baptism by the agency of the Holy Spirit is not simply an imputed perfection; it is that and more. "What is baptism? It is nothing else than being baptized in the name of God the Father, Son, and Holy Spirit, being taken up as children and heirs of God—receiving this status and being adorned and beautified, being made holy, being prepared as a dwelling for the Trinity, which is lauded indeed."[97]

But Arndt still beckons the believer to a perfection beyond this perfection. In the same way that weeping over our impurity is an expression of both our having been made pure in Christ in baptism and our becoming pure in fact, the perfection beyond the perfection of baptism is expressed by our recognition of a struggle between the "inner man" and the "outer man," the "old man" and the "new man." Only in this struggle, says Arndt, is the merit of Christ imputed and only in this struggle is true righteousness attained. The struggle is not an enemy, it is integral to victory. It is not a sign of the rule of sin. It is a sign of precisely the opposite—that while sin is there, it is *not* in charge. "Indwelling sin does not damn

---

93. WC, II.1-11.
94. E.g., WC, II.16-18.
95. WC, I.22.
96. WC, V.2.11.
97. Ibid.

but reigning sin does."[98] Further, what we seek is not perfection in itself. It is but a by-product. What we seek is the greatest of all gifts, Christ, the all in all.[99] And the thoroughness with which Christ is allowed to rule is the measure of perfection, not some external measure. Sanctification, no less than justification, is by faith, not by works. So, we are to judge our Christianity according to the heart. Here again, consciousness of our imperfection is precisely a mark of our perfection. Were Christ not reigning within, we would be oblivious to our own weakness and distance from Him.[100]

In this sense, we are never perfect in this life, never entirely sanctified, for we are never without weakness. On the other hand, "all that one does in faith and love will be, once again, good, holy, godly."[101] And Arndt has no doubt that love may be perfected in us in this life.[102] It would seem fair to Arndt's position to say, then, that in baptism Christ's presence in us is made perfect. He could not be any more present than He becomes at that moment. That constitutes one sort of Christian perfection and generates another, which is qualitatively very different from the first.[103] This is the perfection that comes as we understand that we ourselves have the presence of Christ but have it in such weakness and sinfulness. In this sort of perfection, we live penitent lives seeking to allow the Holy Spirit to let Christlikeness and His presence be completely expressed in our lives. In a sense, our penitent spirit is precisely a sign that His presence *is* being expressed, a sign of the perfection of His presence.

Is there ever a moment in this life when we get free of sin? When the presence of Christ perfectly given in baptism is expressed unhindered in the daily round? When as far as the fundamental problem of inner sinfulness is concerned, renewal is complete in this life? Arndt certainly goes a long way in that direction in several sections of *True Christianity.*[104]

---

98. WC, I.16.

99. WC, II.1-3.

100. E.g., WC, II.4-6.

101. WC, I.24 (pt. III).

102. E.g. WC, I.24 (pts. I and II).

103. WC, VI, "Second Essay to All Lovers of True Godliness." In this essay, Arndt counterbalances the idea that "Christ and faith are so joined together that Christ's all is ours through faith" with the more cautious "Insofar as a person dies to himself, Christ lives in him."

104. E.g., WC, I.3; I.5; V.2.7, chap. 7. In this last passage cited, Arndt expresses

But, finally, he seems each time to fall back on the language and understanding of Lutheran orthodoxy: sanctification is by definition a never-completed process and the reason for its lack of completion is the simple fact that to be human is to be sinful. Nonetheless, this language and this understanding clearly collide with Arndt's insistence that we have been made perfect in Christ and are therefore to live like it, a consequence he does not see as an option that can be ignored or an ideal to be met in part. He has in mind nothing less than perfect love and obedience.

B. Philipp Jakob Spener (1635-1705)

It would be impossible to write the history of the doctrine of entire sanctification without giving an important place to the thought of Philipp Jakob Spener, the most prominent pastor in the Evangelical (Lutheran) Church in the German territories in the last half of the 17th century.[105] Mere mention of some of his friends and close acquaintances helps us to see his importance then: Johann Konrad Dannhauer (1603-66), probably the most influential orthodox Lutheran theologian of the time; Gottfried Wilhelm Liebnitz (1646-1716), one of the greatest of all philosophers; Georg Calixtus (1586-1656), an early ecumenist; Abraham Calovius (1612-1686), Calixtus' opponent, a fussy, orthodox theologian; and Nikolaus von Zinzendorf (1700-60), to whom he was godfather, so much was he admired by the elder Zinzendorfs.

Born not far from Strasbourg, a city in which both the Lutheran and the Reformed traditions were strong, Spener came early under Pietist influences from within both traditions. Even as an adolescent, he was greatly taken by Johann Arndt's *True Christianity.* After an eight-year period of study, including the theological course at the University of Strasbourg, and two years of travel, chiefly in Switzerland, he returned to Strasbourg and earned a doctorate in theology, which was granted just hours after his marriage. In 1666, he was called to Frankfurt am Main as principal

---

himself in the language of the mystics but not in a manner inconsistent with what he says elsewhere.

105. As yet, there is no adequate biography of Spener in English. The best biography available to date is Paul Grünberg, *Philipp Jakob Spener,* 3 vols. (Gottingen: Vandenhoeck und Ruprecht, 1893-1906). Less exhaustive but also less precise and useful for serious study is Hans Bruns, *Ein Reformator nach der Reformation: Leben und Werken P. J. Speners* (Marburg: Spener-Verlag, 1937). For a comprehensive listing of Spener's writings, see Grünberg, *Spener,* 3:213-64.

pastor. There he was quickly recognized as a forceful leader among the Pietists—a position that guaranteed him both steadfast friends and ferocious enemies.

While in Frankfurt, Spener developed several of the ideas and practices that were to become the hallmarks of Lutheran Pietism by way of the encouragement of thoughtful lay participation in exercises designed to ripen the spiritual life.[106] The vehicle for this process was small groups that met regularly for biblical-devotional study. They were called *collegia pietatis*—"devotional guilds." It was also while in Frankfurt that Spener published his *Pia Desideria* (1675), a work originally written as a simple preface to a new edition of Johann Arndt's sermons on the gospel pericopes.[107]

Pia Desideria first rehearses the moral and ethical failings of Lutheranism at that time. Then, after a section meant to encourage the reader to believe actively in the possibility of reform of the Church, it sets forward Spener's plan for reform. Spener clearly has no radical notions to peddle. *Pia Desideria* is in no way a revolutionary book. It contains no really new ideas.[108] But its cumu-

---

106. Nineteenth and early 20th-century interpretations of Spener, drawing principally upon Albrecht Ritschl's *Geschichte des Pietismus* (Bonn: Marcus, 1880-86), have read Spener, and often the Pietists in general, as mystics, or, at least, as having mystical presuppositions and leanings. This viewpoint has then been passed over into the interpretation of the Pietists' understanding of perfection, especially via R. Newton Flew, *The Idea of Perfection* (London: Oxford University Press, 1934). To be sure, later Pietism often did move in the direction of mysticism. But such Pietists as Arndt, Spener, and Francke, while appreciative of the piety and spiritual insights of the mystics, cannot be said to have joined them. The proof of this lies in the varying definitions of the goal of the Christian life held by the mystics and the Pietists named. For the mystics, the goal is absorption in God or in Christ—a metaphysical or ontological (at any rate, "spiritual") union with Him. For Arndt, Spener, and Francke, who do indeed speak of union with God or with Christ, "union" invariably is spoken of in ethical terms or in terms of the will. Their typically Augustinian pessimism about human nature, even when grace dominates it, keeps them at a considerable distance from the mystics.

107. For a critical text, which is an important matter given the history of the editions of the work, see Kurt Aland (ed.), *Philipp Jakob Speners Pia Desideria* (Berlin: Walter de Gruyter, 1940 and 1952). A fine English translation, in fact the only English translation of the complete work, with a helpful introduction has been published by Theodore Tappert under the title, *Philipp Jacob Spener, Pia Desideria* (Philadelphia: Fortress, 1964). The longer title of the original (1675) edition is *Pia desideria oder hertzliches Verlangen nach gottgefälliger Besserung.* References to the work in these pages will be to page numbers in Tappert's translation.

108. Following the publication of *Pia Desideria* in 1675, Spener published five major works for which we list only the short titles: *Der Klagen über das verdorbene Christentum Missbrauch und rechter Gebrauch* (The Use and Abuse of Laments over Corrupted Christianity) (1685); *Gründliche Beantwortung* (A Thorough Reply)

lative effect, along with that of his printed sermons and devotional addresses, brought either keen opposition or enthusiastic support.[109]

The opposition leaders, primarily orthodox Lutheran theologians with a rationalistic perspective, heard in Spener's call for a renewal of true piety an echo of the old "salvation by works" theology that had been so stoutly turned back by Luther. Others saw a new legalism in the wings.[110] Spener's supporters spoke of him as completing the Reformation begun by Luther. Giving Luther due credit for slaying the leviathan of works-righteousness, they praised Spener for adding to that essentially negative beat the positive insistence upon living a holy life. Luther himself had set off in that direction, so they thought, but his preoccupation with justification by faith (a preoccupation produced by the circumstances, they agreed) had unfortunately left sanctification a neglected theme. Now Pastor Spener was rounding out the account.[111]

A major difficulty in developing both a sound doctrine of sanctification and the practice of holiness, so Spener thought, was the Lutheran understanding of just how the Word and the sacraments are affective and what their effects are. This matter was especially pressing in theological considerations of baptism and the implications for the Christian life.

On the one hand, like Arndt, Spener was committed to the view that the Word and the sacraments are both affective and effective apart from human merit. The Word both convicts and

---

(1693); *Auffrichtige Übereinstimmung mit der Augsburgischen Confession* (A Candid Statement of Agreement with the Augsburg Confession) (1695); *Gründliche Verteidigung* (A Thorough Defense) (1696); *Theologische Bedencken und andere briefliche Antworten* (Theological Consideration and Other Written Replies) (4 vols.; 1700-1702). Grünberg, *Spener*, 3:213-64 lists at least 250 works by Spener.

109. At first, the response was overwhelmingly positive. Cf. Grünberg, ibid., 3:265-388 for an examination of Spener's bibliography, which includes an investigation of works about him and his theological position.

110. E.g., Conrad Dilfeld, *Theosophia Horbio Speneriana* (1679). While Dilfeld's work is indeed aimed at Spener himself, much of the criticism that arose against Spener was misdirected. He was blamed for the excesses of his followers.

111. Spener himself believed that the Lutheran reformation was not complete and that Luther had recognized that as fact. As Spener saw it, Luther had deeply yearned for a reformation of life to issue from the reformation of doctrine that he had brought about but could only trust to the future for it. At the heart of Spener's complaint, therefore, is a conviction that it is the Lutheranism of his own day that is posing the obstacles to the fulfillment of Luther's desire by refusing to concern itself seriously with the question of sanctification. He is calling Lutheranism back to the vision of its founder, not away from it. E.g., *Pia Desideria*, 64-65.

promises because the Holy Spirit accompanies it, not because we read it. "It is the divine hand which offers and presents grace to the believer, whom the Word itself awakens through the Holy Spirit." Writing of baptism, Spener says, "Nor do I know how to praise Baptism and its power highly enough. I believe that it is the real 'washing of regeneration and renewal in the Holy Spirit' (Titus 3:5)." "Nor less gladly," he says, "do I acknowledge the glorious power in the sacramental, oral, and not merely spiritual eating and drinking of the body and blood of the Lord in the Holy Supper."[112] Here, he differed not a whit from accepted Lutheran doctrine.

On the other hand, Spener objected to any view of the Word or the sacraments that held that they "worked" (that they were "efficacious," to use the proper term) apart from the believer's keeping his covenant of faith and a good conscience. "Accordingly, if your Baptism is to benefit you, it must remain in constant use throughout your life."[113] To "remain in constant use" means that the believer allows it to bear fruit in a life of holiness. Confidence in justification by grace alone through faith alone was no substitute at all for a holy life, according to Spener. And it was blasphemous to use that confidence as an excuse for an unholy life. God's call is a call to perfection, a perfection that is not understood solely in forensic or imputational terms but which is marked by genuine change in the life of both the believer and the church.

Of course, "the farther a godly Christian advances, the more he will see what he lacks, and so he will never be farther removed from the illusion of perfection than when he tries hardest to reach it." Yet, "even if we shall never in this life achieve such a degree of perfection that nothing could or should be added, we are never the less under obligation to achieve some degree of perfection."[114]

But what is this "some degree of perfection"? Spener at first defines it in terms of the perfection of the Church, then offers an exposition of it in terms of the individual believer, with illustration, as it were, from the Early Church. Extrapolation may thus be made from the Church to the individual in the passage we cite.

> We may say, then, that the [biblical] injunctions to become more and more perfect apply to the whole church, and what Paul says in another place should become true in each and

---

112. All of the quotations in this paragraph are from *Pia Desideria,* 63.

113. Ibid., 66-67.

114. Ibid., 80.

> every individual: "Till we all come in the unity of the faith and of the knowledge of the Son of God, unto a perfect man, unto the measure of the stature of the fulness of Christ." (Eph. 4:13)
>
> We do not understand the perfection which we demand of the church in such a way that not a single hypocrite is any longer to be found in it, for we know that there is no field of grain in which there are no weeds. What we mean is that the church should be free of manifest offenses, that nobody who is afflicted with such failings should be allowed to remain in the church without fitting reproof and ultimately exclusion, and that the true members of the church should be richly filled with many fruits of their faith.[115]

The perfection of which Spener speaks is a perfection in love. Love is both the source of and the motivation toward perfection. "If we can therefore awaken a fervent love among our Christians . . . and put this love into practice, practically all that we desire will be accomplished."[116] The principal characteristic of this love is that its intention is always to do the will of God.

But is this intention to love, an intention born of love itself, granted in a moment and in perfect measure or is it gradually developed to a point of perfect measure? Certainly at baptism, according to Spener, we are granted God's full love in Christ. Never will He love us more than He loves us then. And this love of His for us is "shed abroad in our hearts." That perfection is ours. Its benefits bless us all our days so long as we do not renounce our baptism and its benefits.

Here Spener emphasized much more than most Lutherans of his day the rite of confirmation. Baptism was God's act of commitment to the new Christian. Confirmation was an act of commitment on the part of the believer, commitment to the grace bestowed at baptism by way of a commitment to live a holy life in response to that grace.

At confirmation, the believer is thought to receive the presence of the Spirit in at least a heightened way, if not a new way, and also to receive the gifts of the Spirit. Symbolically, at least, this is the moment in which the perfect love of God given at baptism is transformed and becomes both His perfect love toward the believer and the believer's perfect love toward Him and the neighbor. This transformation is accomplished by the Spirit and is in no way dependent upon human work or merit.

---

115. Ibid., 80-81.

116. Ibid., 96. Cf. the larger section, pp. 95-102.

But, of course, Spener was forced by his observations to admit that even confirmation was insufficient in this regard. The only "proof" of perfection is a life of holiness. And too many confirmed persons lived far beneath their privileges in grace. However, if there is a moment in which the believer is perfected in love, it is the moment of confirmation.

Theologically, Spener's position is inconsistent. It holds to two contradictory types of regeneration: a regeneration that occurs in baptism, which is essentially imputational (that is, we are declared holy by being placed under Christ's holiness; God reckons us to be holy), and a regeneration that begins in baptism but which continues only as we conform, in faith and by grace, to the will of God. Later Pietism was to retain the language of baptismal regeneration in its ritual, but it placed by far the greater weight on regeneration as conformity to the will of God. The process of manifesting and cultivating regeneration was called sanctification.

Notice that sanctification, for Spener, is a process, a process beginning in baptism. In this sense, Spener could not have talked about entire sanctification, at least he could not talk about it as a possibility for this life. But he could, and did, speak of perfection in this life—of our being perfected in an objective sense at our baptism (that is, Christ's atoning benefits apply perfectly to us), of our being perfected in commitment at our confirmation, and of our being perfected in all righteousness at our death. Sanctification, then, is a process of moving, by grace, from one perfection to another. Entire sanctification and ultimate perfection meet at the moment of death. To be entirely sanctified, for Spener, would be to be perfected in all righteousness, to have no more possibility for growth in grace in this life. But, we repeat, it is appropriate to speak of at least two types of perfection that are available even earlier in the Christian life, and both are absolutely necessary to the last.

What Spener contributes to the doctrine of entire sanctification, then, is twofold. First, he restores the idea of the relative character of Christian perfection—that in the Christian life, perfection has to do primarily with intention and direction, not with flawlessness in performance. Further, this relative character of perfection does not diminish its force. It remains perfection, nothing less.

Second, he reunites the doctrines of sanctification and perfection on evangelical terms. In the medieval West, sanctification itself was understood as Spirit-aided good works and spiritual disciplines. Perfection was understood as perfect love on our part, manifest in perfect practice and attitudes. Luther had restored the notion of sanctification as a gift of grace, and a completed work at that, at least insofar as Christ is our sanctification and his holiness is imputed to us. But he had separated sanctification from perfection by accepting the medieval definition of the latter, then (usually) rejecting it as a possiblity in this life.

Spener accepts Luther's definition of sanctification and extends it by insisting that God's gift of holiness imputed to us is also imparted to us. Insofar as it is both imputed and imparted from the hand of God by the Spirit, it is imputed and imparted perfectly. Perfection in sanctification is a gift of grace. There remains the necessity for our acceptance of this baptism-granted sanctification/perfection. This we do in confirmation, which brings us to yet another stage of perfection, no less grace-given than the first. Now we are perfected in love by the gift of the Spirit. Our will is to do only the will of God. Perfectly loving, we will it. Imperfectly do we practice it, and it is as an aspect of our perfection that we are increasingly aware of our imperfection. Our love grows stronger; our awareness of imperfection keeps pace. But rather than give up and fall back on the sanctification imputed to us or on the perfection of intention granted us at confirmation, we press, by grace alone, toward that perfection of act and attitude that we see in Christ. Only at death do we find that perfection granted to us, a gift that makes our sanctification complete.

Spener, like Arndt, was limited by the language of Lutheran theology. Arndt drew then upon the language of the mystics, but not always was this in the interests of clarity. Spener drew heavily on Arndt himself, lightly on the mystics, and thus tied himself more closely to Lutheran orthodoxy for expression than Arndt had done.

Later, by a complex process that included a distaste for theological reflection in favor of practical considerations, Pietism was to become strictly experience-oriented, ignoring orthodox theological expression. It had, after all, failed them. But Spener saw the need for remaining at least respecting of formal theology, whatever the anomalies it presented. This respectfulness left us with a bit of a muddle terminologically, but with a clear sense of a profoundly revised *ordo salutis* in his commitment to a life of holiness here and now.

It is now that the *theological* groundwork for Wesley's doctrine of entire sanctification is completed.

SECTION II

From Wesley to the American Holiness Movement

by William M. Greathouse

5

The Wesleyan Concept of Perfection and Sanctification

"The Wesleyan reconstruction of the Christian ethic of life," claims George Croft Cell, "is an original and unique synthesis of the Protestant ethic of grace with the Catholic ethic of holiness." In Wesley's thought the distinctively religious emphasis of the early Protestant doctrine of justification by faith is reunited, as in the New Testament, with the special interest of Catholic thought and piety in the ideal of holiness and evangelical perfection.[1]

Cell argues convincingly that the "homesickness for holiness," the yearning for Christlikeness that caught the imagination of St. Francis of Assisi, constitutes "the innermost kernel of Christianity." It was precisely this "lost accent of Christianity" that fell into the background of interest in early Protestantism. Cell approvingly quotes Harnack's observation that Lutheranism, in its purely religious understanding of the gospel, neglected too much the moral problem, the *Be ye holy; for I am holy* (1 Pet. 1:16). "Right here," Cell continues, "Wesley rises to mountain heights. He restored the ne-

1. George Croft Cell, *The Rediscovery of John Wesley* (New York: Henry Holt and Co., 1935), 347.

glected doctrine of holiness to its merited position in the Protestant understanding of Christianity."[2]

From the perspective of historic Christianity, therefore, the Wesleyan doctrine of Christian perfection is no theological provincialism. In fusing justification and sanctification, original sin and Christian perfection, it restored the New Testament message to its original wholeness. Wesley "had glimpsed the underlying unity of Christian truth in both the Catholic and Protestant traditions."[3]

Wesley understood his message in this way. In his sermon "On God's Vineyard," he says:

> It has been frequently observed, that very few were clear in their judgment both with regard to justification and sanctification. . . . Who has wrote *[sic]* more ably than Martin Luther on justification by faith alone? And who was more ignorant of the doctrine of sanctification, or more confused in his conceptions of it? . . . On the other hand, how many writers of the Romish Church (as Francis Sales and Juan Castiniza, in particular) have wrote strongly and scripturally on sanctification, who, nevertheless, were entirely unacquainted with the nature of justification; inasmuch as the whole body of their Divines at the Council of Trent . . . totally confound sanctification and justification together. But it has pleased God to give the Methodists a full and clear knowledge of each, and the wide difference between them.
>
> They know, indeed, that at the same time a man is justified, sanctification properly begins. For when he is justified he is "born again," "born from above," "born of the Spirit"; which, although it is not (as some suppose) the whole process of sanctification, is doubtless the gate to it. Of this likewise, God has given [the Methodists] a full view. . . .
>
> They maintain, with equal zeal and diligence, the doctrine of free, full, present justification, on the one hand, and of entire sanctification both of heart and life on the other; being as tenacious of inward holiness as any Mystic, and of outward, as any Pharisee.[4]

The genius of the Wesleyan teaching, says Dr. Cell, is that it neither confounds nor divorces justification and sanctification but places "equal stress upon the one and the other."

---

2. Ibid., 359.

3. Albert Outler, *John Wesley* (New York: Oxford University Press, 1964), viii.

4. John Wesley, *The Works of John Wesley* (reprint of Third edition; Kansas City: Beacon Hill Press of Kansas City, 1978), 7:204-05.

A. The Wesleyan Formulation

Wesley's fully developed doctrine is set forth in his *A Plain Account of Christian Perfection,* which first appeared in 1766. Its fourth edition, in 1777, remained Wesley's definitive statement of his position. The *Plain Account* contains in full quotation the heart of what Wesley had written on the subject before its publication. Here is the doctrine of perfection as he proclaimed and defended it. In reading the *Plain Account,* one must remember that Wesley is delineating in it the *progress* of his thought, and quotations from its earlier sections do not necessarily represent his final position. It is in the latter part of the work that we discover the mature Wesleyan insights into Christian perfection.

Wesley's own 11-point summary, found in the closing pages of the *Plain Account,* is a succinct presentation of the doctrine:

> 1. There is such a thing as perfection; for it is again and again mentioned in Scripture.
>
> 2. It is not so early as justification; for justified persons are to "go on to perfection" (Heb. vi. 1).
>
> 3. It is not so late as death; for St. Paul speaks of living men that were perfect (Phil. iii. 15).
>
> 4. It is not absolute. Absolute perfection belongs not to man, nor to angels, but to God alone.
>
> 5. It does not make a man infallible: None is infallible, while he remains in the body.
>
> 6. Is it sinless? It is not worthwhile to contend for a term. It is "salvation from sin."
>
> 7. It is "perfect love" (1 John iv. 18). This is the essence of it; its properties, or inseparable fruits, are rejoicing evermore, praying without ceasing, and in everything giving thanks (1 Thess. v. 16 & c).
>
> 8. It is improvable. It is so far from lying in an indivisible point, from being incapable of increase, that one perfected in love may grow in grace far swifter than he did before.
>
> 9. It is amissible, capable of being lost; of which we have numerous instances. . . .
>
> 10. It is constantly both preceded and followed by a gradual work.
>
> 11. But is it in itself instantaneous or not? . . . It is often difficult to perceive the instant when a man dies: yet there is an instant when life ceases. And if ever sin ceases, there must be a last moment of its existence, and a first moment of our deliverance from it.[5]

---

5. Ibid., 11:441-42.

Such are the salient features of the Wesleyan teaching. But the doctrine has too ancient and continuing a history, as we have seen, to be classified merely as Wesleyan. John Wesley would be the first to repudiate such a suggestion. As Cell observed, he found the truth of perfection "in the warp and woof" of Holy Scripture. His immediate quest was stimulated by reading Thomas à Kempis' *Imitation of Christ,* Bishop Jeremy Taylor's *Rules and Exercises of Holy Living and Holy Dying,* and William Law's *Christian Perfection* and *A Serious Call to a Devout and Holy Life.*[6] But long before Wesley and these devotional writers who sparked his desire for holiness, the Greek and Latin Fathers had presented the doctrine in extended exposition, as it has been the purpose of this book to show. In formulating his doctrine of perfection, John Wesley drew from the richest and deepest stream of Christian tradition. The conclusion of Dr. Flew is surely just:

> The doctrine of Christian perfection—understood not as an assertion that a final attainment of the goal of the Christian life is possible in this world, but as a declaration that a supernatural destiny, a relative attainment of the goal which does not exclude growth, is the will of God for us in this world and is attainable—lies not merely upon the bypaths of Christian theology, but upon the high road.[7]

Nevertheless, John Wesley gave the doctrine an entirely new cast. His originality is seen chiefly in the way he put the truth of perfection in the very center of a Protestant understanding of Christian faith. He freed the idea from any notion of merit and presented it as wholly the gift of God's grace. Perfect love or entire sanctification is attainable now, by simple faith.

It is because Wesley saw this giftedness of heart holiness so clearly that Colin W. Williams questions Cell's claim that Wesley's theology is a "synthesis of the Protestant ethic of grace with the Catholic *ethic* of holiness."[8] In the Catholic ethic, merit attaches to holiness, but Wesley completely removed the doctrine from the order of merit to the order of grace. His view of sanctification is by faith alone. This, says Gordon Rupp, is what gave the Wesleyan gospel its shape and coherence.[9]

---

6. Ibid., 366-67.

7. R. Newton Flew, *The Idea of Perfection in Christian Theology* (London: Oxford University Press, 1934), 397.

8. Colin W. Williams, *John Wesley's Theology Today* (London: Epworth Press, 1960), 174 (italics added).

9. Cited by Williams, ibid., 176.

In Wesley's view the very center of perfection is *agape*—God's love for man. Its "burning focus" is the Atonement. "Pardoning love is at the root of it all."[10] One of Wesley's most oft-quoted verses is the sentence in First John, "We love him, because he first loved us" (4:19). Love for God is not the natural love of *eros,* but man's answering response to God's prior love. Sanctification for Wesley, like justification, is from first to last the work of God. Justification is what God does *for* us through Christ; sanctification, what He does *in* us by the Holy Spirit. "All things are of God, who has reconciled us to himself by Jesus Christ." This thoroughgoing theocentricity frees his doctrine of perfection from its mystical and humanistic tendencies, which are found in most of the Roman formulations.

Moreover, Wesley has overcome the objectionable features of the Augustinian doctrine of original sin. In the *Plain Account* he says, "Adam fell; and his incorruptible body became corruptible; and ever since, it is a clog to the soul, and hinders its operations."[11] But missing is the idea of a *sinful* body and Augustine's emphasis on concupiscence, with its attendant tendency to equate human nature with sin. For Wesley, the meaning of the flesh in Romans 7 is "the whole man *as he is by nature*"[12] (that is, apart from Christ), embracing both "an inward constraining power of evil inclinations and bodily appetites."[13] The essence of original sin is not concupiscence but "pride, whereby we rob God of his inalienable right, and idolatrously usurp his glory."[14] William Cannon says of Wesley's doctrine: "The sins of the flesh are the children, not the parents, of pride; and self-love is the root, not the branch, of all evil."[15]

This Hebraic understanding of sin is Wesley's controlling view as he develops his teaching of sanctification. *If the quintessence of sin is a perverted relationship to God, the quintessence of holiness is a grace-restored right relationship.* For Wesley, therefore, all holiness or perfection is in Christ, and in Christ alone; for only through Him

10. Cell, *Rediscovery of Wesley,* 297-310.

11. *Works,* 11:415.

12. *Explanatory Notes upon the New Testament* (London: Epworth Press, n.d.), 545 (italics added).

13. Ibid. (italics added).

14. *Works,* 6:60.

15. William R. Cannon, *The Theology of John Wesley* (Nashville: Abingdon-Cokesbury Press, 1946), 193.

are we restored to fellowship with God. The sin that has spread like leprosy through the soul of fallen man is healed by the grace that comes through Christ.

> We have this grace, not only from Christ, but in him. For our perfection is not like that of a tree, which flourishes by the sap derived from its own root, but . . . like that of a branch which, united to the vine, bears fruit; but, severed from it, is dried up and withered.[16]

Williams correctly says: "The 'holiness without which no man shall see the Lord,' of which Wesley speaks, is not a holiness that is judged by objective moral standards, but a holiness in terms of unbroken relationship to Christ the Holy One. The Christian is holy, not because he has risen to a required moral standard, but because he lives in this state of unbroken fellowship with Christ."[17]

This is a Protestant doctrine of perfection. Faith *is* perfection. But perfection is not merely imputed, it is also imparted. Through sanctifying faith the believer experiences the infilling of God's love by the gift of the Holy Spirit (cf. Rom. 5:5) and is thereby purified in heart (cf. Acts 15:8-9). "What is perfection?" Wesley asks. "It is love excluding sin; love filling the heart, taking up the whole capacity of the soul."[18] In his insistence on this truth Wesley broke with Zinzendorf. *Faith perfected in love through the fullness of the Spirit and purifying the heart from sin is the essence of the Wesleyan doctrine of Christian perfection.*

B. Sanctification and the Order of Salvation

To grasp Wesley's idea of Christian perfection, we must see it in relation to his entire program of salvation. The new birth and entire sanctification are popularly understood as two isolated crises having no organic relationship to each other or to salvation as a whole. Actually the idea of gradual development is a fundamental feature of Wesley's thought. He merges these two elements, the instantaneous and the gradual, in an order of salvation in which one passes through a series of successive stages, each representing a different and higher level of Christian experience.[19]

---

16. *Works,* 11:417.

17. Williams, *Wesley's Theology Today,* 175.

18. *Works,* 6:46.

19. Harald Lindström, *Wesley and Sanctification* (London: Epworth Press, 1950), 105.

In his sermon "Working Out Our Own Salvation," Wesley gives his order of salvation:

> Salvation begins with what is usually termed (and very properly) *preventing grace;* including the first wish to please God, the first dawn of light concerning his will, and the first slight transient conviction of having sinned against him. All these imply some tendency toward life; some degree of salvation; the beginning of a deliverance from a blind, unfeeling heart, quite insensible of God and the things of God.
>
> Salvation is carried on by *convincing grace,* usually in Scripture termed *repentance;* which brings a larger measure of self-knowledge, and a farther deliverance from the heart of stone.
>
> Afterwards we experience the *proper Christian salvation;* whereby, "through grace," we "are saved by faith"; consisting of those two grand branches, justification and sanctification. By *justification* we are saved from the guilt of sin, and restored to the favour of God; by *sanctification* we are saved from the power [in the new birth] and the root of sin [in entire sanctification] and restored to the image of God.
>
> All experience, as well as Scripture, show this salvation to be *both instantaneous and gradual.* It begins the moment we are justified, in the holy, humble, gentle, patient love of God and man. It gradually increases from that moment, . . . *till, in another instant, the heart is cleansed from all sin, and filled with pure love to God and man.* But even then that love increases more and more, till we "grow up in all things in him that is our Head," till we attain "the measure of the stature of the fulness of Christ."[20]

In a sermon titled "The Spirit of Bondage and Adoption," Wesley gives a slightly different description of the three states of man: the natural, the legal, and the evangelical state.[21] Harald Lindström summarizes these states as follows:

The Natural State	*The Legal State*	*The Evangelical State*
Man sleeps in death	Is awakened	Is a child of God
Neither fears nor loves God	Fears God	Loves God
Has no light in the things of God	Sees the painful light of hell	Sees the joyous light of heaven
Has false peace	Has no peace	Enjoys true peace
Has fancied liberty	Is in bondage	Enjoys true liberty
Sins willingly	Sins unwillingly	Does not sin

20. *Works,* 6:509 (paragraphing and some italics added).

21. *Works,* 5:98-108.

Concluding:		
Neither conquers nor fights	Fights but does not conquer	Fights and conquers; is more than conqueror[22]

These states, however, are not mutually exclusive but may merge into one another. "These several states of soul are often mingled together," Wesley explains, "and in some measure meet in one and the same person. Thus experience shows that the legal state, or state of fear, is frequently mixed with the natural. . . . In like manner, the evangelical state, or state of love, is frequently mixed with the legal."[23]

Wesley's journal account of his spiritual pilgrimage reveals he saw himself as being in the legal state from 1725, when he first devoted himself to God and the Anglican priesthood, to his Aldersgate experience in 1738, at which time he became an evangelical Christian. He viewed this as a transition from the bondage of Romans 7 to the liberty of Romans 8.[24]

Strictly speaking, the natural state is a logical abstraction, "Seeing there is no man that is in a state of mere nature; there is no man, unless he has quenched the Spirit, that is wholly void of the grace of God. No man living is entirely destitute of what is vulgarly called *natural conscience.* But this is not natural: It is more properly termed *preventing grace.* Every man has a greater or less measure of this, which waiteth not for the call of man."[25]

The evangelical state of love, furthermore, is divided into stages. For Wesley, "There are several stages in Christian life, as in natural; some of the children of God being but new-born babes; others having attained to more maturity," corresponding to the "little children," "young men," and "fathers" of 1 John 2:12-14.[26]

The awakened man under law who turns to God in repentance and sincere obedience may be said to have a degree of faith, but it is "the faith of a servant." To trust in Christ and be born of the Spirit is to receive "the faith of a son" and become an evangelical Christian.[27] But the man who has entered the evangelical state

---

22. Lindström, *Wesley and Sanctification,* 109-10.
23. *Works,* 5:110.
24. See footnotes, *Works,* 1:76-7.
25. *Works,* 6:512.
26. *Explanatory Notes,* 907.
27. *Works,* 1:76-77 (footnotes); cf. footnotes on 86, 97.

must undergo a "second change" in order to reach Christian perfection, the stage of "pure love to God and man." By the new birth one becomes a "babe in Christ," or a "little child." Following this he develops into a "young man," during which period he becomes aware of remaining sin. By faith he may then "in another instant" experience full sanctification and become an "adult son" or "spiritual father."

Commenting on the Johannine declaration that "there is no fear in love" (1 John 4:18), Wesley says, "No slavish fear can be where love reigns. *But perfect,* adult, *love casteth out* slavish *fear: because* such *fear hath torment*—and so is inconsistent with the happiness of love. A natural man has neither fear nor love; one that is awakened, fear without love; a babe in Christ, love and fear; a father in Christ, love without fear."[28]

C. The Path to Perfection

In the broadest sense, as has been shown, sanctification may be said to begin with prevenient grace. This grace comprises "all the drawings of the Father—the desires after God, which, if we yield to them, increase more and more."[29] These workings of grace all "imply some tendency toward life; some degree of salvation; the beginning of a deliverance from a blind, unfeeling heart, quite insensible of God and things of God."[30]

As man responds to prevenient grace it becomes "convincing grace," or repentance, which is the first real step on the path of salvation. In repentance the awakened sinner acknowledges himself guilty and unclean before God, deserving nothing but wrath and hell. Such conviction of sin becomes "evangelical repentance" when it produces "real desires and sincere resolutions of amendment."[31] Other fruits include the forgiveness of one's brother, ceasing to do evil and instead doing what is good, employing the means of grace ordained by God, and generally obeying after the measure of grace one has received. The fruits of repentance can also be described as an outward change in the whole form of life, springing from a penitent state of mind.[32]

---

28. *Explanatory Notes,* 915.

29. *Works,* 6:44.

30. Ibid., 509.

31. *Works,* 8:47; *Explanatory Notes* (on Matt. 3:8), 23.

32. Ibid., 203.

At this point saving faith issues in "proper Christian salvation." Saving faith is faith that acknowledges Christ's death and resurrection as "the only sufficient means of redeeming man from death eternal" and restoring him to life and immortality—"inasmuch as he 'was delivered for our sins, and rose again for our justification.'" It is trust in Christ, *and Christ alone,* for salvation.

> Christian faith is then, not only an assent to the whole gospel of Christ, but also a full reliance on the blood of Christ; a trust in the merits of his life, death and resurrection; a recumbency upon him as our atonement and our life, as *given for us,* and *living in us;* and in consequence hereof, a closing with him, and cleaving to him, as our "wisdom, righteousness, sanctification, and redemption," or, in one word, our salvation.[33]

At the moment of saving faith, justification and the new birth are given. These are bestowed together but are of widely different nature, as Wesley explains. Justification is what God does *for* us, through Christ; the new birth is what He does *in* us, by the Spirit.

> The former changes our outward relation to God, so that of enemies we become children; but by the latter our inmost souls are changed, so that of sinners we become saints. The one restores us to the favour, the other to the image, of God. The one is taking away the guilt, the other the taking away the power, of sin; so that, although they are joined together in point of time, yet they are wholly distinct natures.[34]

By the new birth, therefore, we are truly sanctified in an initial sense. While it is not the whole, it is "a part of sanctification, . . . the gate to it, the entrance into it. When we are born of God, then our sanctification, our inward and outward holiness begins."[35]

> From the time of our being born again, the gradual work of sanctification takes place. We are enabled "by the Spirit" to "mortify the deeds of the body" . . . and as we are more and more dead to sin, we are more and more alive to God. We go on from grace to grace, while we are careful to "abstain from all appearance of evil," and are "zealous of good works," as we have opportunity, doing good to all men.[36]

"It is thus that we wait for entire sanctification," Wesley continues; "for a full salvation from all our sins—from pride, self-will,

33. *Works,* 5:9.
34. Ibid., 224.
35. *Works,* 6:74.
36. Ibid., 46.

anger, unbelief; or, as the Apostle expresses it, 'go on to perfection.'"[37] Thus, while he insists on the reality of the gradual work of sanctification, Wesley at the same time preserves the integrity of his doctrine of entire sanctification as an instantaneous gift of God.

Accompanying justification and the new birth is the witness of the Spirit, which for Wesley is twofold. First it is the direct testimony of the Spirit of God, assuring the believer of God's love, forgiveness, and acceptance. Answering to this is the testimony of our spirit that we have passed from death to life, that we now "love, delight, and rejoice in God" and enjoy the fruit of the Spirit.[38] This awareness that God has wrought a great change within us is thus a confirmatory witness, assuring us that we were not deceived by the prior divine Witness.[39] The testimony of the Spirit of God must, in the very nature of things, precede the witness of our own spirit: "We love him, because he first loved us." It is the witness of the Spirit of God that assures us of His love, which is the root of all holiness.[40]

Sanctification therefore properly begins with justification and the new birth, as faith working by love through the gift of the Spirit. But just as there is a repentance and a faith that precede the intervention of God's saving grace, so there is another repentance and another faith that are necessary to the second change of entire sanctification. The Christian who comes to know himself becomes painfully aware of remaining inward sin. This conviction Wesley speaks of as "the repentance of believers." While believers feel the witness of the Spirit within them, they also "feel a will not wholly resigned to the will of God."

> The conviction we feel of inbred sin is deeper and deeper every day. The more we grow in grace, the more do we see the desperate wickedness of our heart. The more we advance in the knowledge and love of God, through our Lord Jesus Christ . . . the more do we discern of our alienation from God, of the enmity that is in our carnal mind, and the necessity of our being entirely renewed in righteousness and true holiness.[41]

Wesley is careful to point out that the repentance consequent

---

37. Ibid.
38. *Works,* 5:111-44.
39. Ibid., 125.
40. Ibid., 115, 127.
41. Ibid., 257-58.

upon justification is widely different from that which is antecedent. The repentance of the believer

> implies no guilt, no sense of condemnation. . . . It does not suppose any doubt of the favour of God, or any "fear that hath torment." It is properly a conviction, wrought by the Holy Ghost, of the *sin* which still *remains* in our heart, of the *phronēma sarkos,* the carnal mind, which "does still *remain*" . . . although it does no longer *reign* . . . the tendency of our heart to self-will, to Atheism, or idolatry; and, above all, to unbelief.[42]

It is also the conviction of our own utter inability to do good on the basis of our own resources or to deliver ourselves by our own strength from inward corruption.[43]

Furthermore, as the first repentance was evidenced by its fruits, so is the second. As believers seeking entire sanctification, we are to await the fulfillment of God's promise,

> not in careless indifference, or indolent inactivity; but in vigorous, universal obedience, in the zealous keeping of all the commandments, in watchfulness and painfulness, in denying ourselves, and taking up our cross daily; as well as in earnest prayer and fasting, and a close attendance on all the ordinances of God. And if any man dream of attaining it any other way (yea, or of keeping it when it is attained, when he has received it even in the largest measure,) he deceiveth his own soul. It is true, we receive it by simple faith: *But God does not, will not, give that faith, unless we seek it with all diligence, in the way he hath ordained.*[44]

The distinctiveness of Wesley's doctrine is his conviction that the work of full sanctification is a gift, a divine work wrought by God to be received by faith. Colin Williams says: "This expectation of the fulfillment of the promises of Christ in our lives is the essence of the doctrine of holiness. The faith that leads to sanctification is essentially a conviction 'that what God hath promised He is able to perform' and that 'He is able and willing to do it now.'"[45] To this there needs to be added only the conviction that He *does* it.[46] In that instant, "He cometh unto them with His Son and blessed Spirit, and fixing His abode in their souls, bringeth them into the 'rest which remaineth for the people of God.'"[47]

---

42. *Works,* 6:50.

43. Ibid., 51.

44. *Works,* 11:402-03 (italics added).

45. Williams, *Wesley's Theology Today,* 187.

46. Lindström, *Wesley and Sanctification,* 117.

47. *Works,* 11:381.

By the new birth we are saved from the power or dominion of sin; by entire sanctification, from the *root* of sin. Wesley explained this in terms of "expulsion." "Entire sanctification," he said, "is neither more nor less than pure love—love excluding sin; love filling the heart, taking up the whole capacity of the soul. . . . For as long as love takes up the whole heart, what room is there for sin therein?"[48]

Just as a person can be assured of his initial salvation, he can also enjoy the assurance of full salvation. "But how do you know that you are sanctified, saved from your inbred corruption?" Wesley asks. "I can know it no otherwise than I know that I am justified. 'Hereby know we that we are of God,' in either sense, 'by the Spirit that he hath given us.' We know it by the witness and by the fruit of the Spirit."

> As when we were justified, the Spirit bore witness with our spirit, that our sins were forgiven; so, when we were sanctified, he bore witness, that they were taken away. Indeed, the witness of sanctification is not always clear at first; (as neither is that of justification;) neither is it afterward always the same, but, like that of justification, sometimes stronger and sometimes fainter. Yea, and sometimes it is withdrawn. Yet, in general, the latter testimony of the Spirit is both as clear and as steady as the former.[49]

Lycurgus Starkey explains: "Inwardly to *know* the temple has been cleansed by God, who remains in the fullness of his Spirit as its consecration, is the significance and content of this full assurance. There is no doubt in Wesley's mind that both the cleansing and the testimony of the event is by the power of the Holy Spirit."[50] Answering to this divine testimony within the heart is the consciousness of the abiding fruit of the Spirit, without the admixture of self-will or any temper contrary to love.[51]

While the blessing of entire sanctification brings an end to the condition of corrupt self-idolatry and fills the heart with pure love for God and man, it is not the end of spiritual development. There is no perfection, he says, "which does not admit of a continual increase." However far a believer may advance in sanctification "he

---

48. *Works,* 6:46, 52.

49. *Works,* 11:420.

50. Lycurgus Starkey, *The Work of the Holy Spirit* (Nashville and New York: Abingdon Press, 1962), 67.

51. *Works,* 11:422-23; "one undivided fruit of the Spirit," *Works,* 6:413.

hath still need to 'grow in grace,' and daily to advance in the knowledge and love of God his Saviour."[52] It is impossible for the fully sanctified Christian to stand still.

> Yea, and when ye have attained a measure of perfect love, when God has circumcised your hearts, and enabled you to love him with all your heart and with all your soul, think not of resting there. That is impossible. You cannot stand still; you must either rise or fall; rise higher or fall lower. Therefore the voice of God to the children of Israel, to the children of God, is, "Go forward!" "Forgetting the things that are behind, and reaching forward unto those that are before, press on to the mark for the prize of your high calling of God in Christ Jesus"![53]

The end of the Christian life is final justification and glorification. For Wesley, final salvation is conditional upon the believer's continuing to heed the warnings of Scripture and walk in the light of God. "If there were any state wherein [it would be impossible to sin at all] it would be of these who are sanctified, who are 'fathers in Christ, who rejoice evermore, pray without ceasing, and in everything give thanks'; but it is not impossible for these to draw back. They who are sanctified, yet may fall and perish (Heb. x. 29)."[54] In his *Farther Appeal* he therefore says, "With regard to the condition of salvation, it may be remembered that I allow, not only faith, but likewise holiness or universal obedience, to be the ordinary condition of final salvation."[55]

In his doctrine of final justification, Wesley comes close to the Roman Catholic dogma of "double justification."[56] In the *Minutes*

---

52. Ibid., 6:6.

53. *Works,* 7:202.

54. *Works,* 11:422.

55. *Works,* 8:68.

56. The Council of Trent declares "that man is justified by faith and freely," i.e., without meritorious works on his part: ". . . none of those things that precede justification. For, *if by grace, it is not by works;* otherwise, as the Apostle says, *grace is no more grace"* (Canons and Decrees of the Council of Trent, A.D. 1563, Chapter VIII). But while this first justification is by faith and not works, final justification is by faith and meritorious works. "To those who work well *unto the end* and trust in God, eternal life is offered, both as grace mercifully promised to the sons of God through Christ Jesus, and as a reward promised by God himself, to be faithfully given to their good works and merits." Those who thus persevere to the end "truly merited eternal life . . . provided they depart in grace" (Chapter XVI). Canon 32 states: "If anyone says . . . that the one justified by the good works he performs by the grace of God and merit of Jesus Christ . . . does not truly merit an increase of grace, eternal life, and in case he dies in grace, the attainment of eternal life itself, . . . let him be accursed."

of 1770 he made certain unguarded statements that caused some to accuse him of denying justification by faith and turning Papist. Commenting on our Lord's admonition, "Labour (literally, work) for the meat that endureth to everlasting life," he declared. "And in fact, every believer, till he comes to glory, works *for* as well as *from* life. . . . Is not this salvation by works? Not by the merit of works, but by works as a condition. . . . We are every moment pleasing or displeasing to God, according to our works; according to the whole of our present inward tempers and outward behavior."[57] But the next year Wesley made a declaration that clarified his position:

> Whereas the Doctrinal points in the Minutes of a Conference in London, August the 7th, 1770, have been understood to favour Justification by Works: Now the Revd. John Wesley and others assembled in Conference, do declare, "That we had no such meaning; and that we abhor the Doctrine of Justification by Works as a most perilous and abominable Doctrine. And as the said Minutes are not sufficiently guarded in the way they are expressed, we hereby solemnly declare, in the sight of God, that we have no trust or confidence but in the alone merits of our Lord and Saviour Jesus Christ, for Justification or Salvation, either in Life, Death, or the Day of Judgment. And though no one is a real Christian Believer (and consequently cannot be saved) who doth not good works, where there is time and opportunity, yet our Works have no part in meriting or purchasing our Justification from first to last, either in whole or in part."[58]

Final justification is closely joined to glorification. At the moment of our glorification our mortal bodies shall *"be fashioned like unto his glorious body* . . . which He wears in His heavenly kingdom, and on His triumphant throne."[59] *"We know . . . that when he,* the Son of God, *shall appear, we shall be like him*—the glory of God penetrating our inmost substance. *For we shall see him as he is* . . . and that sight will transform us into the same likeness."[60] Final perfection will be perfected Christlikeness.

The sanctification that begins in prevenient grace is consummated in glorification. And in this process it is Christ himself

---

57. *Works,* 8:337-38.

58. L. Tyerman, *Life and Times of John Wesley* (London: Hodder and Stoughton, 1876), 3:100.

59. *Explanatory Notes,* 836.

60. Ibid., 910.

who is "the author and finisher of our faith—who begins it in us, carries it on, and perfects it."[61]

D. The Development of Wesley's Doctrine

On January 1, 1733, Wesley preached his first University sermon on the subject "The Circumcision of the Heart," in which he described Christian perfection in these words:

> It is that habitual disposition of soul which, in the sacred writings, is termed holiness; and which directly implies the being cleansed from sin, "from all filthiness both of flesh and spirit"; and, by consequence, the being endued with those virtues which were in Christ Jesus; the being so "renewed in the image of our mind," as to be "perfect, as our Father in heaven is perfect."[62]

Of this sermon, the first of his published writings, Wesley says in the *Plain Account,* "This was the view of religion I then had, which even then I scrupled not to term *perfection.* This is the view I have of it now, without any material addition or diminution."[63] The year before his death he wrote of it: "This doctrine is the grand depositum which God has lodged with the people called Methodists."[64]

Wesley's definitive term for this teaching is "Christian perfection."[65] At times he spoke of it as "the great salvation," promised by the prophets and given to the apostles at Pentecost.[66] Since it was subsequent to justification, he sometimes used the terms *second blessing*[67] or *second change.*[68] Referring to its character as com-

---

61. Ibid., 847.

62. *Works,* 11:367. This statement appears in the final edition of "A Plain Account of Christian Perfection, as believed and taught by The Reverend John Wesley, from the year 1725, to the year 1777" (cf., ibid., 5:203).

63. Ibid., 369.

64. *Letters of the Reverend John Wesley,* John Telford (ed.) (London: Epworth Press, 1931), 8:238. Reprint of 1790 edition.

65. His main reason for holding to this term, despite the misunderstanding it creates, was that it was scriptural: "We may not, therefore, lay these expressions aside, seeing they are the words of God and not of man" (Sermon, "Christian Perfection," *Works,* 6:1).

66. See *Works,* 11:375; 6:10-11, 395, 419.

67. *Letters,* 3:212 (24 March 1757); 5:315 (3 April 1772); 6:116 (8 October 1774).

68. Sermon, "The Repentance of Believers," *Works,* 5:165; *Letters,* 5:215 (28 December 1770).

plete freedom from sin he spoke of it as *full salvation*[69] or *entire sanctification.*[70] In the *Minutes* of 1747 Wesley points out the distinction between sanctification and entire sanctification. Since St. Paul referred to all justified believers as "sanctified," the term should not be used of those who are saved from all sin without the addition of *wholly* or *entirely.*[71] Although he generally observed this distinction, Wesley tended in his later years to use *sanctification* alone as equivalent to Christian perfection.[72] In defining its ethical meaning, he called it *perfect love* or *pure love.*[73]

"Wesley was struggling with a vital doctrine that had held a strong place in the earliest Christian tradition," says Williams, "but had proved very difficult to define and had led to considerable confusion."[74] His first serious interest in perfection was aroused just prior to his graduation from Oxford in 1725, by his reading of Bishop Jeremy Taylor's *Rules and Exercises of Holy Living and Holy Dying.* "Instantly I resolved to dedicate all my life to God, all my thoughts, and words, and actions," Wesley tells us.[75] His reading of à Kempis and Law further informed his understanding and intensified his quest. In 1729 he joined the Holy Club (of which his brother Charles was leader) and began the study of ancient Christian literature, with the assistance of John Clayton, a member of the club who was a competent patristics scholar. Says Albert Outler:

> In the thought and piety of the Early Church he discovered what he thereafter regarded as the normative pattern of catholic Christianity. He was particularly interested in "Macarius the Egyptian" and Ephraem Syrus. What fascinated him in these men was their description of "perfection" *(teleiōsis)* as the goal *(skopos)* of the Christian in this life. Their concept of perfection

---

69. Sermon, "The Scripture Way of Salvation," *Works,* 6:51; *Letters,* 7:90 (7 November 1781); p. 102 (entire salvation) (19 January 1782); p. 314 (full and present salvation) (3 February 1786), p. 322 (4 March 1786).

70. Minutes, 1747 (*Works,* 8:293); sermon, "The Scripture Way of Salvation," *Works,* 6:51 (full sanctification); *Letters,* 5:210 (full sanctification) (27 November 1770).

71. *Works,* 8:294.

72. *Works,* 11:420; 6:51-52; *Letters,* 4:71 (19 August 1759); p. 188 (15 September 1762); ibid., 5:255 (31 May 1771); p. 325 (1 July 1772).

73. *Letters,* 3:221 (6 September 1757); 4:10 (5 April 1758); p. 71-2 (22 August 1759).

74. Williams, *John Wesley's Theology Today,* 172.

75. *Works,* 11:366.

> as a process rather than a state gave Wesley a spiritual vision quite different from the static perfectionism envisaged in Roman spiritual theology of the period and the equally static quietism of those Protestants and Catholics whom he deplored as "the mystic writers." The "Christian Gnostic" of Clement of Alexandria became Wesley's model of the ideal Christian. Thus it was that the ancient and Eastern tradition of holiness as *disciplined* love became fused in Wesley's mind with his own Anglican tradition of holiness as *aspiring* love, and thereafter was developed in what he regarded to the end as his most distinctive doctrinal contribution.[76]

Wesley regarded the fathers of the Early Church as being "the most authentic commentators on Scripture, as being both nearest the fountain and eminently endued with that Spirit by whom 'all Scripture was given.'"[77] We should understand, furthermore, that at this time Wesley became "a man of one Book." "In the year 1729, I began not only to read, but to study, the Bible, as the one, the only standard of truth, and the only model of pure religion. Hence I saw, in clearer and clearer light, the indispensable necessity of having 'the mind which was in Christ,' and of 'walking as Christ also walked'; even of having, not some part only, but all the mind which was in him."[78]

During this stage of his thought, which found expression in his 1733 Oxford sermon, Wesley crystallized what he came to term later the "substance" of his teaching on perfection—viz., "salvation from all sin, by the love of God and man filling the heart."[79]

In 1737-38, however, a new theological influence came to bear upon Wesley, eventually effecting what Cell calls a "Copernican revolution" in his thought. Through contact with Moravian missionaries in Georgia, but especially through his long conversations with Peter Böhler, Wesley came to understand and embrace the Reformation teaching of justification by faith. He was now free to develop a *Protestant* doctrine of perfection.

---

76. Outler, *John Wesley*, 9-10.

77. *Works*, 11:484 (cited by Outler, loc. cit.).

78. Ibid., 367. In a letter to Dr. Dodd (1756) Wesley says, "I therein [i.e., in the sermon on perfection] build on no authority ancient or modern, but the Scripture. If this supports any doctrine, it will stand; if not, the sooner it falls the better. . . . My father gave me thirty years ago, to reverence the ancient Church, and our own. But I try every church and every doctrine by the Bible. This is the word by which we are to be judged in that day"—cited by Harold William Perkins, *The Doctrine of Christian or Evangelical Perfection* (London: Epworth Press, 1927), 208.

79. *Works*, 8:328.

Q. 4. What was the rise of Methodism, so called?

A. In 1729, two young men, reading the Bible, saw they could not be saved without holiness, followed after it, and incited others so to do. In 1737 they saw holiness comes by faith. They saw likewise, that men are justified before they are sanctified; but still holiness was their point. God then thrust them out, utterly against their will, to raise a holy people.[80]

During the earlier stage of his thought, Wesley conceived of perfection as "an inherent ethical change in man," preparatory to glorification, and the Christian life as a progressive development toward it. "Such perfection was the purpose of religion," Lindström observes. "In this general position just as in the teleological alignment of his theology, Wesley, after as well as before 1738, agrees with practical mysticism."[81]

The resemblance, however, is still more pronounced. For Wesley, perfection means (1) "purity of intention," (2) "having all the mind which was in Christ, enabling us to walk as He walked," and (3) loving God and neighbour with "a whole and undivided heart."[82] Lindström shows that these three points of view, which determined Wesley's description of Christian perfection, are reflections of the view that appears in à Kempis, Taylor, and Law. His thesis seems sustained by Wesley's own summary of his idea of perfection near the conclusion of the *Plain Account:*

> In one view, it is purity of intention, dedicating all the life to God. It is the giving God all our heart; it is one desire and design ruling all our tempers. It is the devoting, not a part, but all our soul, body, and substance to God.
>
> In another view, it is all the mind which was in Christ, enabling us to walk as Christ walked. It is the circumcision of the heart from all filthiness, all inward as well as outward pollution. It is a renewal of the heart in the whole image of God, the full likeness of Him that created it.
>
> In yet another, it is loving God with all our heart, and our neighbour as ourselves. Now, take it in which of these views you please, (for there is no material difference,) and this is the whole and sole perfection, as a train of writings prove to a demonstration, which I have believed and taught for these forty years, from the year 1725 to the year 1765.[83]

---

80. Ibid., 300.

81. Lindström, *Wesley and Sanctification,* 129.

82. *Works,* 11:367.

83. Ibid., 444.

We see, therefore, how deeply Wesley imbibed the Catholic tradition of practical mysticism.[84] With respect to the "substance" of perfection, he himself saw 1738 as effecting no material change. His mature doctrine of Christian perfection, however, is far from identical with the Catholic teaching. As Colin Williams says, "Wesley put his doctrine within the Protestant framework of justification by faith, not within the Roman framework of justification by faith and works. He put it within the order of personal relationship to Christ, not within the order of a legal relationship to a moral standard."[85] Wesley's adoption of Reformation principles did in fact reshape his doctrine.

First and foremost, Wesley's new understanding of justification by faith gave his doctrine of Christian perfection the character of a gift of God wrought by the Holy Spirit, to be received by faith alone. Just as we are justified by faith, so we are entirely sanctified by faith.[86]

Furthermore, since full sanctification is by faith, it is to be regarded as an instantaneous work of God. This instantaneity is a correlative of Wesley's new understanding of grace. In "The Scripture Way of Salvation," he asks: "But what is that faith whereby we are sanctified—saved from all sin, and perfected in love?"

> It is a divine evidence and conviction, first, that God hath promised it in the holy Scripture. . . . It is a divine evidence and conviction, secondly, that what God hath promised He is able to perform. . . . It is, thirdly, a divine evidence and conviction that He is able and willing to do it now. And why not? Is not a moment to Him the same as a thousand years? He cannot want more time to accomplish whatever is His will. And He cannot want or stay for any more *worthiness* or *fitness* in the persons He is pleased to honour. . . . To this confidence, that God is both able and willing to sanctify us now, there needs to be added one thing more—a divine evidence and conviction that He doeth it.
>
> If you seek it by faith, you may expect it *as you are;* and if as you are, then expect it *now.* . . . Expect it *by faith;* expect it *as you are;* and expect it *now.* To deny one of them, is to deny them all; to allow one, is to allow them all.[87]

---

84. For a rather extensive demonstration of Wesley's excursion into mysticism, see Robert G. Tuttle, Jr., *John Wesley, His Life and Theology* (Grand Rapids: Zondervan Publishing House, 1978), 113-59.

85. Williams, *Wesley's Theology Today,* 175.

86. *Works,* 8:341-47; *Letters,* 5:7 (1 April 1766).

87. *Works,* 6:52-53.

This modification of the idea of perfection, obviously the result of the influence of his conception of grace, does not mean, however, that perfection ceased to be a requirement. But just as the law of God was regarded by Wesley as simultaneously a gospel too, so perfection was seen simultaneously both as a requirement and as a promise.[88] Preaching from our Lord's Sermon on the Mount, Wesley makes this point clear:

> From all this we may learn that there is no contrariety at all between the law and the gospel; that there is no need for the law to pass away, in order to the establishing of the gospel. Indeed neither of them supersedes the other, but they agree perfectly well together. Yea, the very same words, considered in different respects, are parts both of the law and of the gospel: if they are considered as commandments, they are parts of the law; if as promises, of the gospel. *Thus, "Thou shalt love the Lord thy God with all thy heart," when considered as a commandment is a branch of the law; when regarded as a promise, is an essential part of the gospel—the gospel being no other than the commands of the law, proposed by way of promise.* Accordingly, poverty of spirit, purity of heart, and whatever else is enjoined in the holy law of God, are no other, when viewed in a gospel light, than so many great and precious promises.[89]

This is true because the Holy Spirit is now given in His sanctifying graces, in a way unknown under the old covenant. "The fulness of time is now come; the Holy Ghost is now given; the great salvation of God is brought unto men, by the revelation of Jesus Christ. The kingdom of heaven is now set upon earth."[90]

Although he was convinced that Christian perfection is scriptural, he was willing to submit the teaching to the crucible of experience.

> Q. But what does it signify, whether any have attained it or no, seeing so many scriptures are for it?
>
> A. If I were convinced that none in England had attained what has been so clearly and strongly preached by such a number of Preachers, in so many places, and for so long a time, I should be clearly convinced that we had all mistaken the meaning of those scriptures.[91]

But witnesses were never wanting. From near the beginning of his evangelical ministry he found in London, Bristol, and Kings-

---

88. Lindström, *Wesley and Sanctification,* 135.

89. *Works,* 5:313 (italics added).

90. *Works,* 6:10-11; 11:375.

91. Ibid., 11:406.

wood clear witnesses to full salvation. A few years later Wesley called together all in London who made a profession of heart holiness, to meet with him and "that man of God, Thomas Walsh," to give account of their experience. "We asked them the most searching questions we could devise," says Wesley. "They answered every one without hesitation, and with the utmost simplicity, so that we were fully persuaded they did not deceive themselves."[92]

But it was in 1760 that witnesses began to multiply, not only in London and Bristol, but throughout England and in various parts of Ireland. In London alone Wesley found 652 of his society "who were exceedingly clear in their experience."[93] As Wesley wrote in his 1781 *Concise Ecclesiastical History,*

> Here began that glorious work of sanctification, which had been at a stand for twenty years. But from time to time it spread, first through various parts of Yorkshire, afterwards in London, then through most parts of England; next through Dublin, Limerick, and all the south and West of Ireland. And wherever the work of sanctification increased the whole work of God increased in all its branches. Many were convinced of sin, many justified, many backsliders healed.[94]

The witnesses invariably testified to full sanctification as a gift distinct from justification. Wesley never found reason to retract an observation he made in the *Plain Account,* "We do not know a single instance, in any place, of a person's receiving, in one and the same moment, remission of sins, the abiding witness of the Spirit, and a new, a clean heart."[95]

---

92. *Works,* 6:490-91.

93. Ibid.

94. Quoted by Williams, *Wesley's Theology Today* (from John S. Simon, *John Wesley, the Master Builder* [London: Epworth Press, 1927], 70).

95. *Works,* 11:380. By "constant experience" he also found that the more earnestly seekers expect the instantaneous blessing of heart holiness "the more swiftly does the gradual work of God go on in their souls; the more watchful they are against all sin, the more careful to grow in grace, the more zealous of good works, and the more punctual in their attendance on all the ordinances of God. Whereas, just the contrary effects are observed whenever this expectation ceases. They are 'saved by hope,' by this hope of a total change, with a gradually increasing salvation. Deny this hope, and that salvation stands still, or rather, decreases daily. Therefore whoever would advance the gradual work in believers should strongly insist on the instantaneous" (ibid., 8:329).

E. Christian Perfection

In both his standard sermon on the subject[96] and the *Plain Account,* Wesley takes care to explain what perfection is not, before he proceeds to set forth his positive teaching. Williams writes:

> In his doctrine Wesley desired to express the promise of the great transformation of life that opens up before the believer in the living relationship with Christ. But he knew that he must guard against the *theologia gloria,* which would so define the miracle of grace our creaturely limitations would be destroyed or the disorders of our nature due to the effects of original sin would be forgotten.[97]

1. *What Perfection Is Not*

Perfection is not glorification. While the grace of God may destroy sin in our hearts and enable us to live a life pleasing in the sight of God, we still inhabit a body that bears the effects of the Fall and is often a "clog to the soul."[98] Moreoever, our very finitude subjects us to creaturely limitations we must never forget.

> The Son of God does not destroy the whole work of the devil in man, so long as he remains in this life. He does not yet destroy bodily weakness, sickness, pain, and a thousand infirmities incident to flesh and blood. He does not destroy all the weakness of understanding, which is the natural consequence of the soul's dwelling in a corruptible body; so that still,
>
> *Humanum est errare et nescire:*
>
> "Both ignorance and error belong to humanity." He enlists us with only an exceeding small share of knowledge, in our present state; lest our knowledge should interfere with our humility, and we should again affect to be as gods. It is to remove from us all temptation to pride, and all thought of independency, (which is the very thing that men in general so earnestly covet under the name of liberty,) that he leaves us encompassed with all these infirmities, particularly weakness of understanding; till the sentence takes place, "Dust thou art, and unto dust thou shalt return!"[99]

A distinctive feature of Wesley's theology of perfection is this frank recognition of its relative nature. He reminded his brother Charles that to set the mark too high is "effectively to renounce

---

96. "Christian Perfection," *Works,* 6:1-22.

97. Williams, *Wesley's Theology Today,* 168.

98. *Works,* 11:415.

99. *Works,* 6:275-76.

it."[100] He rebuked Thomas Maxfield for denying its relativity: "I dislike your supposing man may be as perfect as an angel; that he can be absolutely perfect; that he can be infallible, or above being tempted, or that the moment he is pure in heart he cannot fall from it."[101]

Christian perfection is evangelical, not legal. Wesley removes his doctrine completely from the order of law and merit and places it squarely within the order of grace and faith.

> Christ is the end of the Adamic, as well as the Mosaic, law.[102] By his death, he hath put an end to both; he hath abolished both the one and the other, with regard to man; and the obligation to observe either one or the other is vanished away. Nor is any man living bound to observe the Adamic more than the Mosaic law.
>
> In the room of this, Christ hath established another, namely, the law of faith. Not every one that *doeth,* but every one that *believeth,* now receiveth righteousness, in the full sense of the word; that is, he is justified, sanctified, and glorified. . . .
>
> Is love the fulfilling of this law?
>
> Unquestionably it is. The whole law under which we now are, is fulfilled by love. (Rom. xiii. 9, 10.) Faith working or animated by love is all that God now requires of man. He has substituted (not sincerity, but) love, in the room of angelic perfection.
>
> How is "love the end of the commandment"? (1 Tim. i. 5.)
>
> It is the end of every commandment of God. It is the point aimed at by the whole and every part of the Christian institution. The foundation is faith, purifying the heart; the end love, preserving a good conscience.
>
> What love is this?
>
> The loving the Lord our God with all our heart, mind, soul, and strength; and the loving our neighbour, every man, as ourselves, as our own souls.[103]

Sangster thinks that "perfect love" is the true name for Wesley's doctrine.[104] This name underscores the positive, social nature

---

100. *Letters,* 5:20 (9 July 1776).

101. *Letters,* 4:192 (2 November 1762).

102. The "Adamic law," according to Puritan theology, was the law under which Adam lived before the Fall, requiring perfect performance of the divine commandments.

103. *Works,* 11:415-16.

104. W. E. Sangster, *The Path to Perfection* (New York: Abingdon Press, 1944), 142-49.

of holiness. Wesley himself shrank from using the term *sinless perfection,* since the saintliest of Christians "come short of the law of love" as it is set forth in the 13th chapter of First Corinthians.[105] Because of their finiteness and imperfect understanding, those who have been filled with God's love are guilty of "involuntary transgressions"[106] of His law. "It follows that the most perfect have continual need of the merits of Christ, even for their actual transgressions, and may say of themselves, as well as for their brethren, 'Forgive us our trespasses.'"[107]

> These very persons feel more than ever their own ignorance, littleness of grace, coming short of the full mind that was in Christ, and walking less accurately than they might have done after their Divine Pattern; and are more convinced of the insufficiency of all they are, have, or do to bear the eye of God without a Mediator; and are more penetrated with the sense of the want of Him than ever they were before. . . . "Are they not sinners?" Explain the term one way, and I say, "Yes"; another, and I say, "No."[108]

Therefore, "None feel their need of Christ like these; none so entirely depend upon him. For Christ does not give life to the soul separate from, but in and with, himself." He then quotes the words of Jesus, "Without (or separate from) me ye can do nothing."[109]

Wesley thus makes two qualifying points. First, Christian perfection is not absolute but relative to our understanding of God's will. Hence the truly sanctified feel deeply their imperfections and lapses from the perfect law of love and maintain a penitent and open spirit, which saves them from Pharisaism. They never forget they are justified, not by works but by grace, and thus lean wholly upon the Lord. Second, they know that the perfect love, which is God's gift through the Spirit, is a "moment by moment" impartation of Christ to their souls.

> The holiest of men still need Christ, as their Prophet, as "the light of the world." For he does not give them light, but from moment to moment: The instant he withdraws, all is darkness. They still need Christ as their King; for God does not give them a stock of holiness. But unless they receive a supply every moment, nothing but unholiness would remain. They

---

105. *Works,* 11:417-18.

106. Ibid., 396.

107. Ibid., 394-95.

108. *Letters,* 4:189-90 (15 September 1762).

109. *Works,* 11:395.

still need Christ as their Priest, to make atonement for their holy things. Even perfect holiness is acceptable to God only through Jesus Christ.[110]

Wesley found the scriptural basis for this so-called imperfect perfection in Phil. 3:11-15. Answering those who would set aside the term *perfection* because of its ambiguity, he insists that we are obligated to declare "*all* the counsel of God."

> We may not, therefore, lay these expressions aside, seeing they are the words of God and not of man. But we may and ought to explain the meaning of them; that those who are sincere in heart may not err to the right hand or left, from the mark of the prize of our high calling. And this is the more needful to be done, because, in the verse already repeated [Phil. 3:12], the Apostle speaks of himself as not perfect: "Not," saith he, "as though I am already perfect." And yet immediately after, in the fifteenth verse, he speaks of himself, yea, and many others, as perfect: "Let us," saith he, "as many as be perfect, be thus minded."[111]

Wesley would agree with E. Stanley Jones' observation that we are, in one sense, only "Christians in the making." We have not yet attained to the mark of final Christlikeness for which we were claimed by the gospel. The full truth of perfection is gained, not by removing the tension between the two poles ("not already perfected"[112]—"perfect"), but by holding these two scriptural truths with equal emphasis. Only thus does the Christian life flower into Christlikeness.

2. *What Perfection Is*

Wesley's view of perfection, as we have already seen,[113] derives not from static perfectionism envisaged by one strand of Roman thought *(perfectus est)* but from early Eastern thought in which perfection is a process *(teleiōsis)* rather than a state. This latter understanding, Wesley felt, flowed directly from the fountain of Holy Scripture. "Being persuaded of this very thing, that he who

---

110. Ibid., 417.

111. *Works,* 6:1-2.

112. Wesley's translation of Phil. 3:11 (*Explanatory Notes,* 735). He comments here: "There is a difference between one that is perfect and one that is *perfected.* The one is fitted for the race (verse 15); the other, ready to receive the prize."

113. See footnote 76.

hath begun a good work in you will *perfect* it until the day of Jesus Christ" (Phil. 1:6, Wesley's translation).[114]

This perfecting process begins at the moment of justification, "in the holy, humble, gentle, patient love of God and man."[115] At this stage of spiritual infancy the believer is in a low degree perfect: "Even babes in Christ are so far perfect as not to commit sin."[116] By the birth of the Spirit, which accompanies justification, we experience "a general change from inward sinfulness, to inward holiness," and receive "the mind that was in Christ Jesus."[117]

Christian perfection in the proper sense, however, is the consequence of the deeper, subsequent work of entire sanctification, when "the heart is cleansed from all sin." In that instant one's heart is "filled with pure love to God and man,"[118] so that Wesley can say, "Pure love reigning alone in the heart and life—this is the whole of Scriptural perfection."[119]

"But even this love increases more and more," Wesley insists, "till we 'grow up in all things into Him that is our Head'; till we attain 'the measure of the stature of the fulness of Christ.'"[120]

Wesley's position may be defined as a theology of holy love. Says Mildred Wynkoop:

> The principle by which to understand Wesley's doctrine is love to God and man, in the biblical sense of the word. Love is the dynamic of theology and experience. Love, structured by holiness, links all that we know of man. Love is the end of the law. It is the goal of every step in grace and the norm of the Christian life in this world.[121]

"Renewal to the lost image of God, meaning 'love to God and man,' expressed as Christlikeness, sums up Wesley's definition of Christian perfection."[122] Lindström writes in the same vein: "The essence of perfection and the goal of faith are . . . love. Seen in this way,

---

114. Wesley comments: "He who, having justified, hath begun to sanctify you, will carry on this work, till it issue in glory."

115. *Works,* 6:509.

116. *Works,* 11:375-76.

117. *Works,* 6:488.

118. Ibid., 509.

119. *Works,* 11:401.

120. *Works,* 6:509.

121. Mildred Bangs Wynkoop, *A Theology of Love* (Kansas City: Beacon Hill Press of Kansas City, 1972), 269.

122. Ibid., 271.

therefore, the Christian life is a development in love. Perfection comes to mean perfection in love."[123]

Entire sanctification is the critical aspect of the process of perfection. The distinctive feature of the doctrine, says Paul Bassett, is "John Wesley's conviction that there is an experience of grace subsequent to regeneration, instantaneously receivable, which renders the believer capable of acting and being in complete conformity to the Great Commandment."[124] But this "does not imply any new *kind* of holiness," says Wesley.

> From the moment we are justified, till we give up our spirits to God, love is the fulfilling of the law; of the whole evangelical law, which took the place of the Adamic law. . . . Love is the sum of Christian sanctification; it is the one *kind* of holiness, which is found, only in various *degrees*, in the believers who are distinguished by St. John into "little children, young men, and fathers." The difference between the one and the other properly lies in the degree of love.[125]

The "babe in Christ" has the love of God and neighbor in his heart, along with the Christian graces. "But all of these are then in a low degree, in proportion to the degree of his faith. The faith of a babe in Christ is weak, generally mingled with doubts or fears." But—

> In the same proportion as he grows in faith, he grows in holiness; he increases in love, lowliness, meekness, in every part of the image of God; till it pleases God, after he is thoroughly convinced of inbred sin, of the total corruption of his nature, to take it all away; to purify his heart and cleanse him from all unrighteousness; till he fulfil that promise which he made first to his ancient people, and in them to the Israel of God in all ages: "I will circumcise thy heart, and the heart of thy seed, to love the Lord thy God with all thy heart, and with all thy soul."[126]

When this deeper work of heart cleansing has occurred, the believer's "whole soul is consistent with itself."[127] Then he can testify with St. Paul, "I am crucified with Christ; nevertheless I live; yet

123. Lindström, *Wesley and Sanctification,* 141.

124. Paul Bassett, "Conservative Wesleyan Theology and the Challenge of Secular Humanism," *Wesleyan Theological Journal* (Spring 1973), 8:74.

125. Sermon "On Patience," *Works,* 6:488 (italics Wesley's).

126. Ibid., 489.

127. Ibid.

not I, but Christ liveth in me."[128] And then he bears "the one *undivided* fruit of the Spirit."[129]

Love is the source, love is the essence, love is the norm, love is the goal of the Christian life.

> There is nothing higher in religion; there is, in effect, nothing else; if you look for anything but more love, you are looking wide of the mark, you are getting out of the royal way. And when you are asking others, "Have you received this or that blessing?" if you mean anything but more love, you mean wrong; you are leading them out of the way, and putting them upon a false scent.
>
> Settle it then in your heart, that from the moment God has saved you from all sin, you are to aim at nothing more, but more of that love described in the thirteenth of the Corinthians. You can go no higher than this till you are carried into Abraham's bosom.[130]

F. The Sanctifying Spirit

Implicit in all that Wesley taught about Christian holiness or perfection is the conviction that it is from first to last the work of the sanctifying Spirit.

> The title "holy," applied to the Spirit of God, does not only denote that he is holy in his own nature, but that he makes us so; that he is the great fountain of holiness to his church; the Spirit from whence flows all the grace and virtue, by which the stains of guilt are cleansed, and we are renewed in all holy dispositions, and again bear the image of the Creator.[131]

If pure love to God and man is the essence of Christian perfection, the sanctifying Spirit is its agency. "Entire sanctification is neither more nor less than pure love; love expelling sin, and governing both the heart and life of a child of God. The Refiner's fire purges out all that is contrary to love."[132]

Although Wesley recognized that certain persons in the Old Testament anticipated by faith the New Testament promise of heart purity, he saw clearly that Christian perfection as a common privi-

---

128. *Works,* 11:377.

129. *Works,* 6:413 (italics added).

130. *Works,* 11:430.

131. Sermon, "On Grieving the Holy Spirit," *Works,* 7:486.

132. *Letters,* 5:223 (21 February 1771). See *Explanatory Notes* (on Matt. 3:11-12), 24.

lege for God's people was the distinctive promise of the Messianic age of the Spirit.[133]

John N. Oswalt has pointed out that two Old Testament prophecies were of special significance for Wesley: Joel 2:28-29 and Ezek. 36:25-27. The coming of the Spirit promised in Joel refers to the inauguration of the Christian faith: the gift of the Spirit for all who believe in Christ. Ezekiel 36:25-27, however, promises heart cleansing by the deeper working of the Spirit within the being of one who is already a believer. At the conclusion of his sermon on Christian perfection he can therefore quote with approval his brother Charles' hymn on Ezekiel 36, which says in part:

Thy sanctifying Spirit pour,
To quench my thirst and wash me clean;
Now, Father, let the gracious shower
Descend, and make me pure from sin.
Within me Thy good Spirit place,
Spirit of health, and love, and power;
Plant in me Thy victorious grace,
And sin shall enter nevermore.[134]

---

133. Early in the *Plain Account* he says, "The privileges of Christians are in nowise to be measured by what the Old Testament records concerning those who were under the Jewish dispensation; seeing the fulness of time is now come, the Holy Ghost is now given, the great salvation of God is now brought to men by the revelation of Jesus Christ" (*Works,* 11:375). Also, in his early sermon on Christian perfection he makes the same point in commenting on John 7:39. The verse cannot mean the miracle-working power of the Holy Spirit for He was not yet given. The Lord had bestowed this power on the apostles as He sent them forth to preach. "But the Holy Ghost was not yet given in his sanctifying graces, as he was after Jesus was glorified. . . . And when the day of Pentecost was fully come, then first it was that they who 'waited for the promise of the Father' were made more than conquerors over sin by the Holy Ghost given unto them" (*Works,* 6:10).

134. John N. Oswalt, "Old Testament Concept of the Holy Spirit," *Religion in Life,* Vol. XLVIII, No. 3 (Autumn 1979), 283-92. In Wesley's *Explanatory Notes upon the Old Testament* he applies Ezekiel 36:25-27 expressly to the New Testament gift of heart holiness. The expression "sprinkle" in v. 25 "signifies both the blood of Christ sprinkled upon the conscience, to take away their guilt . . . and the grace of the Spirit sprinkle(d) in the whole soul, to purify it from all corrupt inclinations and dispositions." The "new heart" promised in v. 26 is "a new frame of soul, a mind changed, from sinful to holy, from carnal to spiritual. A heart in which the law of God is written, Jer. xxxi. 33. A sanctified heart, in which the almighty grace of God is victorious, and turns it from all sin to God." The "spirit" promised in v. 27 is "the holy spirit of God, which is given to, and dwelleth in all true believers" which causes them to keep God's judgments "sweetly, powerfully, yet without compulsion; for our spirits, framed by God's Spirit to a disposition to his holiness, readily concurs" (3:2385).

Wesley insisted that the sanctifying Spirit comes to the heart of the believer at the moment of saving faith. Objecting to some who spoke of entire sanctification as "receiving the Holy Ghost," he wrote:

> If they like to call this "receiving the Holy Ghost," they may; only the phrase in that sense is not scriptural and not quite proper; for they all "received the Holy Ghost" when they were justified. God then "sent forth the Spirit of His Son into their hearts, crying, Abba, Father."[135]

And commenting on Rom. 8:9, he said, "If any man have not the Spirit of Christ . . . he is not a member of Christ; not a Christian, not in a state of salvation."[136]

But as early as 1740 Wesley distinguished a deeper offer within the promise of the Spirit, the offer of heart holiness. In an obvious reference to Jesus' promise of Pentecost in Luke 24:49, he said in a sermon at the Foundery directed to those "who have known and felt your sins forgiven":

> Your finding sin remaining in you still is no proof that you are not a believer. Sin does remain in one that is justified, though it has not dominion over him. For he has not a clean heart at first, neither are "all things" as yet "new." But fear not, though you have an evil heart. Yet a little while, and you shall be endued with power from on high, whereby you may "purify yourselves, even as He is pure"; and be "holy, as He which has called you is holy."[137]

Writing to Joseph Benson in 1771 Wesley is even more explicit at this point. Making his familiar distinction between babes, young men, and fathers in Christ, he explains:

> A *babe* in Christ (of whom I know thousands) has the witness *sometimes.* A young man (in St. John's sense) has it continually. I believe one that is *perfected in love,* or *filled with the Holy Ghost,* may be properly termed a *father.* Thus we must press both babes and young men to aspire after—yea, to expect. And why not now? I wish you would give another reading to the *Plain Account of Christian Perfection.*[138]

On the next day he urges upon Mary Stokes "the mighty blessing" of full salvation, referring, quite atypically, to "receiving" the Spirit in sanctifying power:

---

135. *Letters,* 5:215 (to Joseph Benson, 28 December 1770).

136. *Explanatory Notes,* 547.

137. *Journal of the Rev. John Wesley,* A. M. Nehemiah Curnock (ed.) (London: Charles H. Kelly, 1919), 2:359.

138. *Letters,* 5:229 (16 March 1771).

> Now stand fast in that beginning of liberty wherewith Christ has made you free. Yet do not stand still. This is only the dawn of the day: the Sun of Righteousness will rise upon you in quite another manner than you have hitherto experienced. And who knows how soon? Is He not near? Are not all things now ready? What hinders you from receiving Him now? . . . Only unbelief keeps out the mighty blessing.[139]

Faith perfected in love through the fullness of the Spirit is thus the essence of the Wesleyan doctrine of Christian perfection. The gift of the Spirit received in justification is but the harbinger of heart purity. In the 1739 "Hymn for Whitsunday," gratitude is expressed for the coming of the Comforter as the pledge of inward holiness for all believers:

Never will He them depart,
Inmate of a humble heart,
Carrying on His work within
Striving 'til He cast out sin.[140]

But if it is the Spirit's work to cast out sin and fill us with pure love to God and man, it is ours to pray the prayer of faith, which brings the blessing of perfect love.

Jesus, Thine all-victorious love
Shed in my heart abroad;
Then shall my feet no longer rove,
Rooted and fixed in God.

Oh, that in me the sacred fire
Might now begin to glow,
Burn up the dross of base desire,
And make the mountains flow!

Oh, that it now from heav'n might fall,
And all my sins consume!
Come, Holy Ghost, for Thee I call;
Spirit of Burning, come!

Refining Fire, go thro' my heart;
Illuminate my soul;
Scatter Thy life thro' ev'ry part,
And sanctify the whole.

---

139. Ibid., 231 (17 March 1771).

140. John and Charles Wesley, *Hymns and Sacred Poems* (London, 1739), reprinted in *The Poetical Works of John and Charles Wesley*, collected and arranged by G. Osborn; 13 volumes (London: Wesley Conference Office, 1869), i, 188-39.

My steadfast soul, from falling free,
Shall then no longer move,
While Christ is all the world to me,
And all my heart is love.[141]

141. Ibid., 328-29.

6

Perfection in English Methodism

For the most part, English Methodism during its first century held rather closely to the main lines of John Wesley's teaching. Differences of viewpoint, emphasis, and spirit were present from the outset, but these were only minor divergences within a broader framework of general agreement.

The most lively discussion arose between Wesley himself and his contemporary, John Fletcher (1728-85), concerning the relation of the "baptism of the Holy Ghost" to Christian perfection. While Wesley taught entire sanctification through the Holy Spirit given to us, and at times spoke of a "coming"[1] or "infilling"[2] of the Spirit as accomplishing the purification of the heart, he was restrained in his treatment of the Acts passages that refer to the dispensational coming of the Spirit and only rarely mentioned the baptism with the Holy Spirit. On the other hand, Fletcher made much of this dispensational baptism and distinguished sharply between those who had received it and those who, like the disciples before Pentecost, were still in the dispensation of the Son. Both men, however, implied *degrees* of Spirit baptism so that the remaining difference was more one of emphasis than of substance.

---

1. See chap. 5.
2. Cf. Wesley's *Works,* 11:404.

Following Wesley, the leading exponents were Adam Clarke (1762-1832) and Richard Watson (1781-1833). Clarke's most influential work was his six-volume commentary on the Bible (1810-26), but his most extended treatment of perfection is found in his *Christian Theology*, published posthumously in 1840.[3] Robert E. Chiles calls Richard Watson "the single most determinative of the early Methodist theologians."[4] His *Theological Institutes* devotes a section to the topic, and scattered references are found in his sermons. E. Dale Dunlap says of Clarke and Watson:

> The difference between John Wesley and his early successors was not so much one of clear-cut distinction as it was a subtle shift of spirit. As a result of this subtle shift of spirit, the theological enterprise of Clarke and Watson was more "scholastic" and less dynamic than the theology of Wesley. However, . . . it must be acknowledged that in general both Adam Clarke and Richard Watson were faithful to the essential emphases of John Wesley's theology.[5]

The final theologian of this period was William Burt Pope (1822-1903) whose three-volume *Compendium of Christian Theology* was published in 1880. Of him Chiles says, "Pope stands out as one of the towering figures in all of Methodist theology who with remarkable fidelity recaptured the essence of Wesley's theology."[6]

A. John Fletcher

Fletcher came to the fore of the Methodist movement during the Calvinistic controversy of the 1770s. His *Checks to Antinomianism*, written in defense of the 1770 *Minutes*,[7] reveal his true theological talent.

1. *The Doctrine of Dispensations*

The key to Fletcher's system is the doctrine of dispensations. Taking a salvation-history approach to the Bible, he traces the divine self-revelation through the dispensations of the Father, Son,

---

3. *Christian Theology: By Adam Clarke, LLD., F.A.S., Selected from His Published and Unpublished Writings, and Systematically Arranged: With a Life of the Author,* by Samuel Dunn (New York: T. Mason and G. Lane, 1840).

4. Robert E. Chiles, *Theological Transition in American Methodism, 1790-1935* (New York: Abingdon Press, 1965), 42.

5. E. Dale Dunlap, "Methodist Theology in Great Britain in the Nineteenth Century," unpublished Ph.D. dissertation, Yale University, 1956, 218 (quoted by Chiles, ibid., 39).

6. Chiles, *Theological Transition,* 34 (fn.).

7. See chap. 5.

and Holy Spirit. The dispensation of the Father was that of the Gentiles under general revelation and prevenient grace and of the Jews under special revelation. The promise of this dispensation was the coming of Christ as Redeemer, in fulfillment of both Gentile and Jewish expectations. The dispensation of the Son was that of John the Baptist and the apostles before Pentecost. The promise of this dispensation was the coming of the Holy Spirit. The dispensation of the Holy Spirit was that of Pentecost and "the perfect gospel of Christ." The promise of this dispensation is the second coming of Christ.[8]

Since these dispensations not only refer to the progressive revelation of God in history but also depict "facets of knowledge which characterize all men in general," every one of us ordinarily goes through successive stages analogous to the ages of the Father, Son, and Holy Spirit.[9] In every congregation there are "converted sinners, or believers" who are living in these several dispensations, "according to the different progress they have made in spiritual things." The faithful pastor is acquainted with the various levels of spiritual attainment in his congregation as a teacher is acquainted with the differing aptitudes of his several students.[10]

Believers under the dispensation of the Father are ordinarily under a cloud of doubt and uncertainty, although they are visited at times with scattered rays of hope.[11] These persons are heard frequently to exclaim, "O wretched man that I am, who shall deliver me from the body of this death?" (Rom. 7:24).[12] Their expectation is for Christ the Redeemer.[13]

Believers under the dispensation of the Son are like the two disciples who journeyed to Emmaus, who were given a clearer understanding of the gospel.[14] While still troubled with weakness and doubt,[15] they learn to address the Heavenly Father "with a

---

8. "The Portrait of St. Paul," *The Works of the Reverend John Fletcher* (Salem, Ohio: Schmul Publishers, 1974), 3:166-69.

9. John A. Knight, *The Holiness Pilgrimage* (Kansas City: Beacon Hill Press of Kansas City, 1973), 66. For an overview of Fletcher's theology see this work.

10. Fletcher's *Works,* 3:170.

11. Ibid.

12. Ibid., 171.

13. Ibid., 179.

14. Ibid., 170.

15. Ibid.

degree of humble confidence" although they do not enjoy the Spirit of adoption.[16] They are strangers to "the spiritual baptism so frequently mentioned in the New Testament."[17] However, they do apprehend Christ as "a Saviour manifested in the flesh, to accomplish the external act of redemption." Justified before God through Christ, the Spirit is *with,* not truly *in* them.[18]

Believers under the dispensation of the Holy Spirit have received the baptism of the Holy Ghost, promised by Joel and reaffirmed by John the Baptist (Matt. 3:11-12) and our Lord (John 7:37-39; 14-16; Acts 1:5).[19] "They cry out, in transports of gratitude, 'God, according to his mercy, hath saved us, by the washing of regeneration and renewing of the Holy Ghost, which he hath shed on us abundantly, through Jesus Christ, our Saviour' (Titus 3:5-6)."[20] They are now enabled to say with one voice, "We have not received the spirit of bondage again to fear; but we have received the Spirit of adoption, whereby we cry, Abba, Father! The Spirit itself beareth witness with our spirit, that we are the children of God, and joint heirs with Christ" (Rom. 8:15-17).[21] "Henceforth, he is a Comforter, not only with, but in us; where he spiritually exercises his acknowledged offices, instructing, purifying, and finally subduing all things to himself."[22]

It is difficult to assess with real certainty all the fine distinctions Fletcher makes between the dispensations of the Son and Spirit. In one place he seems to equate the baptism of the Spirit with the birth of the Spirit. "Now all those Christians, who have not yet received the spiritual baptism so frequently mentioned in the New Testament, are shut up in this state of weakness and doubt. But as soon as they are born of the Spirit, they cry out no longer with trembling fear, 'Save us; we perish!'"[23] But a few pages later in discussing the "peculiar language" to be employed under the dispensation of the Spirit he says, "If at any time it is to be apprehended that believers are still carnal, and unrenewed by the

---

16. Ibid., 195.
17. Ibid., 170.
18. Ibid., 179.
19. Ibid., 166-68.
20. Ibid., 171.
21. Ibid., 171, 195.
22. Ibid., 179.
23. Ibid., 170-71.

Spirit of God, the pastor who is conversant with these different economies of grace, inquires with St. Paul, 'Have ye received the Holy Ghost since ye believed?' (Acts 19:2)."[24]

Whatever Fletcher's meaning, Wesley seemed to understand him to teach that the believer "receives the Holy Ghost" in order to be sanctified wholly. Joseph Benson, who was associated with Fletcher at Trevecca College in Wales, apparently so understood Fletcher. After urging Benson to confirm his hearers at Trevecca "in expecting a second change, whereby they shall be saved from all sin and perfected in love," Wesley continued:

> If they like to call this "receiving the Holy Ghost," they may: only the phrase in that sense is not scriptural and not quite proper; for they all "received the Holy Ghost" when they were justified. God then "sent forth the Spirit of His Son into their hearts, crying, Abba, Father."

Wesley then added this fatherly advice: "O Joseph, keep close to the Bible, both as to sentiment and expression!"[25]

Three months later Benson had left Trevecca, but Wesley felt it necessary to caution him again:

> You seem to be providentially thrust out into the harvest. But consider what you do. Read the *Minutes* of the Conference, and see whether you conform thereto. Likewise think whether you can abstain from speaking of Universal Salvation and Fletcher's late discovery.[26]

John Telford, editor of the *Letters,* prefaces this entry by explaining, "Fletcher's discovery was his doctrine of 'Receiving the Holy Ghost,' which Wesley thought unscriptural and prejudicial to the spread of the truth. Wesley had said that it was improper to separate the work of sanctification from justification, and that all who were justified had received the Holy Spirit. Benson had expressed Fletcher's view, though not altogether approving it."[27]

2. *Christian Perfection*

Two references may be cited to summarize Fletcher's view of Christian perfection. The first is from his *Fourth Check:*

> Christian perfection . . . which Christ purchased for us by his Blood . . . is the internal *kingdom of God ruling over all;* . . . it is *Christ* fully *formed in our hearts, the* full *hope of glory;* it is the

---

24. Ibid., 173.
25. *Letters,* 5:215 (28 December 1770).
26. Ibid., 5:228 (9 March 1771).
27. Ibid.

> *promise of the* Father; i.e. *the Holy Ghost given unto us,* to make us abound in righteousness, *peace, and joy in believing;* and in a word . . . it is the *Shekinah, filling* the *Lord's* human *temples with glory.* . . . All who are *filled with the Spirit* experience it.[28]

The second quotation is from a letter to Miss Bosanquet, dated March 7, 1778. Pointing out the difference between his and Wesley's emphasis, he writes, "I lay the stress of the doctrine on the great 'promise of the Father' and 'the Christian fulness of the Spirit.' . . . I do not rest the doctrine of Christian perfection on 'the absence of sin' . . . nor on 'loving God with all one's power.'" This perfection, he says, was possible even under the first dispensation, among both Gentiles and Jews. The Christian "fulness," on the other hand, is "that superior, nobler, warmer, and more powerful love which the apostle calls 'the love of the Spirit,' or 'the love of God shed abroad by the Holy Ghost,' given to Christian believers, who, since the day of Pentecost, go on to the perfection of the Christian dispensation." He then adds:

> You will find my view of this matter in Mr. Wesley's sermons on Christian Perfection and on Spiritual Christianity; with this difference, that I would distinguish more exactly between believers baptized with the Pentecostal power of the Holy Ghost, and the believer who, like the Apostles after our Lord's ascension, is not yet filled with that power.[29]

After reading the preliminary version of Fletcher's four closing addresses in the *Last Check* Wesley wrote his friend:

> It seems our views of Christian perfection are a little different, though not opposite. It is certain every babe in Christ has received the Holy Ghost, and the Spirit witnesses with his spirit that he is a child of God. But he has not obtained Christian perfection. Perhaps you have not considered St. John's threefold distinction of Christian believers: little children, young men, and fathers. All of these had received the Holy Ghost, but only the fathers were perfected in love.[30]

During the following weeks, Fletcher rewrote sections of the *Last Check* in the light of Wesley's criticism. The published version allowed the 3,000 converted on the Day of Pentecost to stand as those who had received the Holy Spirit in regenerating power, as

---

28. John Fletcher, *Fourth Check to Antinomianism* (Bristol: W. Pine, 1772), 125.

29. L. Tyerman, *Wesley's Designated Successor* (London: Hodder and Stoughton, 1882), 411.

30. *Letters,* 6:146 (22 March, 1775).

Wesley had always taught;[31] they had received the Spirit, but were not yet perfect in love.[32]

3. *Baptism with the Holy Spirit*

It is in his "address to unbelievers, who cordially embrace the doctrine of Christian perfection," that Fletcher explains his view of the baptism with the Holy Spirit as the agency of heart holiness.

The Promise of the Father, of which our Lord speaks in Luke 24:49 and Acts 1:5, "when it is received in its fulness, is undoubtedly the greatest of all the 'exceeding great and precious promises, which are given to us, that by them you might be partakers of the Divine nature' [that is, of pure love and unmixed holiness], 2 Peter 1:4."[33]

In emphasizing this promise, Fletcher quotes John 14:15-18, 23, and cites Wesley's note on the last verse: "Which implies such a large manifestation of the Divine presence and love, that the former, in justification, is as nothing in comparison of it."[34] He then quotes John 17. Christ's promises and prayer were not in vain. At Pentecost the Spirit came, and the world was given "a *specimen* of the power which introduces believers into the state of Christian perfection,"

> and therefore we read that on the day of pentecost the kingdom of Satan was powerfully shaken, and the kingdom of God, "righteousness, peace, and joy in the Holy Ghost," began to come with new power: then were thousands wonderfully converted, and clearly justified: then was the kingdom of God taken by force; and the love of Christ and of the brethren began to burn up the chaff of selfishness and sin with a force which the world had never seen before.[35]

Some time after, "another glorious baptism, or capital outpouring of the Spirit," carried these new converts "farther into the kingdom of grace which perfects believers in one. And therefore we find that the account which Luke gives of them after this second, capital manifestation of the Holy Spirit in a great degree answered to our Lord's prayer for their perfection." Fletcher added, however, that "the multitude of them that believed" were not *all*

---

31. See Wesley's *Works*, 6:11.

32. As Fletcher's 1778 letter to Miss Bosanquet shows, however, differences remained between Wesley's and Fletcher's terminology and emphasis.

33. Fletcher's *Works*, 2:630.

34. Ibid.

35. Ibid., 631.

perfected in love, witness "the *guile* of Ananias and his wife, and the *partiality* or selfish *murmuring* of some believers." This is because God "does not usually remove the plague of indwelling sin" until individuals have "discovered and lamented" it. But "those chiefly, who before were strong in the grace of their dispensation, arose *then* into sinless fathers."[36]

The first four chapters of Acts teach clearly, Fletcher concludes, that "a peculiar power of the Spirit is bestowed upon believers under the Gospel of Christ"; and that "when our faith shall fully embrace the promise of full sanctification, or of a complete 'circumcision of the heart in the Spirit,' the Holy Ghost . . . will not fail to help us to love one another without sinful self-seeking; and as soon as we do so, 'God dwelleth in us, and his love is perfected in us.'"[37] The outpouring, and in that sense baptism, with the Spirit was here a corporate experience; the particular work God wrought in each person's heart was according to his faith and readiness for it.

Using the term *baptism of the Spirit* in this sense, Fletcher continues: "Should you ask, how many baptisms, or effusions of the sanctifying Spirit are necessary to cleanse a believer from all sin, and to kindle his soul into perfect love; I reply, . . . if one powerful baptism of the Spirit 'seal you unto the day of redemption, and cleanse you from all [moral] filthiness,' so much the better. If two or more are necessary, the Lord can repeat them." "Before we can rank among perfect Christians," Fletcher adds, with a true Wesleyan touch,

> we must receive so much of the truth and Spirit of Christ by faith, as to have the pure love of God and man shed abroad in our hearts by the Holy Ghost given unto us, and to be filled with the meek and lowly mind which was in Christ. And if one outpouring of the Spirit, one bright manifestation of the sanctifying truth, so empties us of self, as to fill us with the mind of Christ, and with pure love, we are undoubtedly Christians in the full sense of the word.[38]

Although Fletcher departs from Wesley here, the difference is not as great as is sometimes supposed. For the latter, the apostles on the Day of Pentecost received "that baptism of the Holy Ghost

36. Ibid.

37. Ibid., 632.

38. Ibid., 633.

. . . which, in a lower sense, is given to all believers."[39] For Wesley as for Fletcher, the baptism with the Holy Spirit embraces the total work of the Spirit in the heart. The justified apostles, who received the baptism in the highest sense on the Day of Pentecost, were truly sanctified the moment their Christian faith was perfected.[40] The 3,000 who received the gospel that day were justified and received the Spirit in the power of the new birth and initial sanctification. "All true believers to the end of the world" are baptized with the Spirit in this lower sense; but they must not rest until they have experienced the higher purpose of this baptism, until they have been purified in heart and made perfect in love. They must "press on" to perfection, so Wesley taught.[41]

Fletcher differs from Wesley in speaking of further effusions or baptisms of the Spirit. Frequently, however, he implies that there are *degrees* of Spirit baptism, more in harmony with Wesley's position. He speaks of being "completely baptized"[42] or "fully baptized"[43] by the Spirit. "O for a deeper baptism of the Spirit!" he writes John Walton. "I want that promise *more fully* accomplished, 'I and my Father will come, and will make our abode with you.'"[44] "Fletcher would ask not whether a believer had received his baptism," David Cubie thinks, "but whether he or she had 'received the Comforter in his fulness.'"[45]

B. Adam Clarke

John L. Peters quotes approvingly the estimate of Adam Clarke as "the greatest name in Methodism in the generation which succeeded Wesley. . . . He was not only the greatest scholar in Methodism, . . . to his own people he was a father in God and a

39. Sermon, "Of the Church," Wesley's *Works*, 6:395.

40. See Wesley's definition of Christian faith, see Wesley's *Works*, 5:9. See also 6:10-11 and 419, *re* "the great salvation."

41. John Wesley, *Explanatory Notes upon the New Testament* (New York: Eaton and Mains, n.d.), 393.

42. John Fletcher, *Checks to Antinomianism* (New York: Phillips and Hunt, n.d.), 1:160.

43. Fletcher's *Works*, 2:636.

44. Tyerman, *Wesley's Designated Successor*, 517.

45. David Cubie, "Perfection in Wesley," *Wesleyan Theological Journal* (Spring 1976), 25.

brother beloved."[46] His *Commentary on the Old and New Testaments* reveals the breadth of both his biblical and classical knowledge, and from its publication in 1826 it enjoyed immense popularity in both Britain and America.

In recognition of his scholarship, the University of Aberdeen in 1806 conferred upon him the degree of master of arts and the following year awarded him the degree of doctor of civil and canon law.[47] Converted at the age of 18 through the ministry of Methodist preachers in his parish, he received instruction concerning holiness of heart six years later from another local preacher who "was partaker of this precious privilege." Having "received powerful convictions of the need for entire sanctification of his heart," he reports,

> While earnestly wrestling with the Lord in prayer, and endeavoring, self-desperately, to believe, I found a change wrought in my soul, which I endeavored through grace to maintain amid grievous temptations. My indulgent Saviour continued to support me, and enabled me with all my power to preach the glad tidings to others.[48]

Clarke's clear experience of entire sanctification gave him an abounding confidence in the attainability of heart purity. Holiness of heart is the precious privilege of all believers. "The very Spirit which is given them, on their believing in Christ Jesus, is the Spirit of holiness." Preeminently He is "the Spirit of judgment, the Spirit of burning" who "condemns to utter destruction the whole of the carnal mind, and purifies the very thoughts of the heart by his inspiration, enabling the true believer perfectly to love God and worthily to magnify his holy name."[49]

1. *Christian Perfection*

As for the name of the doctrine, Clarke admits that the term *perfection* has its inadequacies—not that it is too strong but that it is not vigorous enough to convey the full meaning of God's sanctifying grace.[50]

---

46. John L. Peters, *Christian Perfection and American Methodism* (Nashville: Abingdon Press, 1956), 103 (quoted from M. L. Edwards, *Adam Clarke* [London, Epworth Press, n.d.], 32).

47. Ibid.

48. Ibid.

49. *Christian Theology,* 162-63.

50. Ibid., 184-85. "Had I a better name, one more energetic, one with a greater plenitude of meaning, . . . I would gladly adopt and use it. Even the word 'per-

Recognizing the various suggestions of the term, Clarke fastens on its central meaning: fitness for purpose. A thing is perfect that answers the end for which it was made. "And as God requires every man to love him with all his heart, soul, mind, and strength, and his neighbour as himself; then he is a perfect man that does so; he answers the end for which God made him."[51]

> The whole design of God was to restore man to his image, and raise him from the ruins of his fall; in a word, to make him perfect; to blot out all his sins, purify his soul, and fill him with holiness; so that no unholy temper, evil desire, or impure affection or passion shall either lodge, or have any being within him; this and this only is true religion, or Christian perfection.[52]

While Clarke recognizes the gradual aspect of sanctification, his emphasis is upon the divine act of purification. "The life of a Christian is a growth: he is at first born of God, and is a little child: becomes a young man and a father in Christ. Every father was once an infant; and, had he not grown, he would never have been a man." He goes on to warn against the danger of "a continual state of infancy," and of spiritual death, if we do not continue to grow."[53] Citing Heb. 6:1, he exhorts: "Let us never rest till we are *adult Christians*—till we are saved from all sin, and are filled with the Spirit and power of Christ."[54]

Growth in holiness, however, is a minor note in Clarke; as Peters says, purification from sin is "the dominant feature" of his view.[55] It is "the blessing of a clean heart, and the happiness consequent on it" he everywhere stresses. And the blessing of heart holiness is always instantaneous:

> In no part of the Scriptures are we directed to seek holiness *gradatim*. We are to come to God as well for instantaneous and complete purification from all sin, as for instantaneous pardon.

---

fection' has in some relations, so many qualifications and abatements that cannot comport with that full and glorious salvation recommended in the gospel, . . . that I would gladly lay it by, and employ a word more positive and unequivocal, and more worthy of the merit of the infinite atonement of Christ, and the energy of his almighty Spirit; but there is none in our language; which I deplore as an inconvenience and a loss."

51. Ibid., 183.
52. Ibid., 184.
53. Ibid., 203-04.
54. *Commentary*, 6:723.
55. Peters, *Christian Perfection*, 106.

> Neither the *seriatim* pardon, nor the *gradatim* purification, exists in the Bible.[56]

2. *Baptism with the Holy Spirit*

Clarke's view of the baptism with the Holy Spirit agrees essentially with that of Wesley and Fletcher. It encompasses the total work of the Spirit within the heart, but its goal is always the destruction of remaining sin. Commenting on Acts 1:5 he writes: "Christ baptizes with the Holy Ghost, for the destruction of sin, the illumination of the mind, and the consolation of the heart." Noting Christ's word indicates "the communication of the Holy Spirit on the following pentecost," he says the emphasis must be laid, not on the mode of Spirit baptism, but on "receiving the *thing* signified—the Holy Ghost, to *illuminate, regenerate, refine,* and *purify* the heart."[57]

Clarke's comments on John 7:39, like his later observations on the Acts passages, emphasize the central purpose of "that abundant effusion" of the Spirit "which peculiarly characterized Gospel times" and which "was not granted till after the ascension of Christ." The Spirit would come to apply the benefits of the Atonement and "supply the place of Christ to his disciples and all true believers."[58] He interprets Peter's words in Acts 2:38-39 to mean, "Ye shall receive the Holy Ghost, by whose agency alone the blood of the covenant is applied, and by whose refining power the heart is purified."[59]

Typical of his commentary on the several Acts passages is his observation on 19:2:

> To this day the genuine disciples of Christ are distinguished from all false religionists, and from nominal Christians, by being made partakers of this Spirit, which enlightens their minds, and convicts of sin, righteousness, and judgment; quickens their souls, witnesses to their conscience that they are the children of God, and purifies their hearts.[60]

The work of the sanctifying Spirit encompasses our total salvation, but its intended issue is always the purification of the heart. This is Clarke's unvarying point.

At times he employs language suggestive of Fletcher. Coming to the conclusion of his treatment of entire sanctification in his

---

56. *Christian Theology,* 207-08.
57. *Commentary,* 5:683 (italics Clarke's).
58. Ibid., 572.
59. Ibid., 699.
60. Ibid., 841.

Christian Theology, he exhorts, "Arise, then, and be baptized with a greater effusion of the Holy Ghost."[61] And commenting on 1 John 4:18 he says of those who would be cleansed from the enmity of the carnal mind and made perfect in love: "Let such earnestly seek, and fervently believe on the Son of God; and he will soon give them another baptism of his Spirit, will purge out all the old leaven, and fill their whole souls with that love which is the fulfilling of the law."[62]

As strongly as Clarke urges the immediacy of heart cleansing, he reminds those who believe Christ has purged their hearts from all sin:

> Learn this, that as it requires the same power to sustain creation as to produce it; so it requires the same Jesus who cleansed to keep clean. . . . It is only through his continued indwelling that they are kept holy, and happy, and useful. Were he to leave them, the original darkness and kingdom of death would soon be restored.[63]

C. Richard Watson

Richard Watson was the first Methodist to produce a systematic theology. His *Theological Institutes,* published serially and completed in 1829, became a doctrinal standard in both English and American Methodism.

Watson's presentation stands in contrast to that of Clarke in both spirit and emphasis, as Peters points out. For all his erudition, Clarke writes as an evangelist, and his *Theology* tends toward "semidogmatic exhortation." On the other hand, Watson impresses the reader as a scholar concerned chiefly with "noncontroversial elucidation." Furthermore, while Clarke tends to move to the left of Wesley and Fletcher in his concentration on the crisis of entire sanctification, Watson tends to move to the right by his stress on the gradual,[64] particularly in his sermons.

1. *Initial Sanctification*

Watson's first references to holiness in the *Institutes* comes in his section on the "concomitants of justification." Here he views

---

61. *Christian Theology,* 206.
62. *Commentary,* 6:920.
63. *Christian Theology,* 209.
64. Peters, *Christian Perfection,* 107.

initial sanctification as deriving from both justification and the new birth.

Describing holiness as "habits and acts of which *love to God* is the principle," he echoes Wesley in reminding us that "we first 'love God,' and then 'keep his commandments.'" "Holiness then is preceded by love as its root, . . . the love of a pardoned sinner to God as his Father."[65] In its root then, as in its full flower, holiness is love fulfilling the law.

Watson's Wesleyan understanding reflects also in his high view of regeneration, "that mighty change in man, wrought by the Holy Spirit, by which the dominion which sin has over man . . . is broken and abolished."[66]

> The regenerate state is, also, called in Scripture sanctification; though a distinction is made by the Apostle Paul between that and being "sanctified *wholly*." . . . In this regenerate, or sanctified state, the former corruptions of the heart may remain, and strive for mastery; but . . . the sanctifying Spirit is given to us to "abide with us, and in us," and then we walk not after the flesh but after the Spirit.[67]

In a sermon he says even more strongly: "Believing in his Redeemer and Saviour with the heart unto righteousness, he (the newly regenerate) knows for himself the power of his merit, and the strength of his grace to regenerate. Thus he becomes a holy man. 'Old things are passed away, all things are become new.' . . . Cleaving to the Saviour, on whom he has believed . . . his holiness will increase."[68]

When he comes to his exposition of perfected holiness, Watson will argue that the initial holiness, which accompanies justification and regeneration and which is advanced by all dying to sin and growth in grace, is not at all inconsistent with the instantaneous work of entire sanctification, which like the new birth is received by faith.[69] In his sermons, however, Watson is not nearly so clear at this point, as we shall see.

---

65. Richard Watson, *Theological Institutes* (New York: Nelson & Phillips, n.d.), 2:280-81.

66. Ibid., 267.

67. Ibid., 269.

68. *The Works of the Rev. Richard Watson* (London: John Mason, 1836), 3:52-53.

69. *Institutes,* 2:455.

2. *Entire Sanctification*

Watson treats this subject as one of the "farther benefits" of the universal redemption provided by Christ's atonement. After delineating the concomitants of justification by faith,[70] he devotes a section of his *Institutes* to another "leading blessing" that flows from Christ's atoning death, "another as distinctly marked, and as graciously promised in Holy Scriptures: this is the *entire sanctification,* or the perfected *holiness* of believers."[71]

He writes: "The apostles, in addressing the body of believers in the Churches to whom they wrote their epistles, set before them, . . . a still higher degree of deliverance from sin, as well as a higher growth in Christian virtues."[72] Quoting 1 Thess. 5:23 and 2 Cor. 7:1, he believes St. Paul to be praying for and promising "our complete deliverance from all spiritual pollution, all inward depravation of the heart, as well as that which, expressing itself outwardly by the indulgence of the senses, is called 'filthiness of the flesh.'"[73]

The attainability of such a state is not so much a matter of disagreement among Christians, he says, as the *time* we are authorized to expect it.

> For as it is an axiom of Christian doctrine, that "without holiness no man can see the Lord"; and is equally clear that if we would "be found of him in *peace,*" we must be found "without *spot* and *blameless*"; and that the Church will be presented to the Father without "fault"; so it must be concluded, unless, on the one hand, we greatly pervert the sense of these passages, or , on the other, admit the doctrine of purgatory or some intermediate purifying institution, that the entire sanctification of the soul, and its complete renewal in holiness, must take place in this world.[74]

Watson then disputes the position that "the final stroke which destroys our natural corruption is only given at death." His answer to this view is twofold: (1) Such a doctrine is neither taught nor implied in any passage of Holy Scripture; (2) it presupposes the unscriptural doctrine that existence in the body is a necessary obstacle to entire sanctification.

---

70. Ibid., 266 ff.
71. Ibid., 450.
72. Ibid.
73. Ibid.
74. Ibid., 450-51.

He then addresses himself to the argument that the seventh chapter of Romans precludes the possibility of holiness in this life. Whether St. Paul is writing autobiographically or in the first person for a more vivid representation of the case, Watson says, he is clearly speaking of a person who seeks salvation by the works of the law, but who, realizing the demands of God's law for heart holiness and confessing his bondage to inward corruption, acknowledges he can be delivered from this thralldom only by the intervention of another. The strong expressions of being "carnal, sold under sin" and doing always "the things he would not," are utterly inconsistent with the description of the believer in the next chapter as one who walks "*not* after the flesh, but after the Spirit." The person in Romans 7 represents one, not in a state of deliverance by Christ but under the law, who, despairing of self-deliverance and praying for the intervention of a powerful Savior, is "thanking God that the very deliverance for which he groans is appointed to be administered by Jesus Christ."[75]

This interpretation is also confirmed by what the apostle says in the preceding chapter, where he unquestionably describes the moral state of true believers. Watson then quotes Rom. 6:2-7, and concludes: "So clearly does the apostle show that he who is *bound* to the 'body of death,' as mentioned in the seventh chapter, is not in the state of a believer; and that he who has a true faith in Christ, 'is *freed* from sin.'"[76]

Moreover, the doctrine of the necessary indwelling of sin in the soul until death involves other "antiscriptural consequences." It presupposes that the seat of sin is in the flesh and thus harmonizes with the pagan philosophy that attributed all evil to matter. The Bible, on the other hand, teaches that sin has its seat in the soul: "The apostle expressly states, that though the flesh stands victoriously opposed to *legal* sanctification, it is not insuperable by evangelical holiness." He then quotes Rom. 8:2-4 in proof of this claim.

> We conclude, therefore, as to the *time* of our complete sanctification . . . that it can neither be referred to the hour of death, nor placed subsequently to this present life. The attainment of perfect freedom from sin is one to which believers are called during the present life; and is necessary to that com-

75. Ibid., 451-52.

76. Ibid., 452.

> pleteness of "holiness," and of those active and passive graces of Christianity by which they are called to glorify God in this world, and to edify mankind.[77]

Having established that the Scriptures promise entire sanctification in this life, Watson is ready to discuss the *manner* (what Wesley spoke of as the "circumstance") of complete sanctification. This has been the other point of disagreement among theologians, "some contending that all attainable degrees of it are acquired by the process of gradual mortification and the acquisition of holy habits; others alleging it to be instantaneous, and the fruit of an act of faith in the Divine promises." He then states his position.

> That the regeneration which accompanies justification is a large approach to this state of perfected holiness; and that all dying to sin, and all growth in grace, advances us nearer to this point of *entire* sanctity, is so obvious, that on all these points there can be no reasonable dispute. But they are not at all inconsistent with a more instantaneous work, when, the depth of our natural depravity being more painfully felt, we plead in faith the accomplishment of the promises of God.

These promises, Watson continues, are all "objects of *present trust;* and their fulfillment *now* is made conditional *only* upon our faith."[78]

He concludes his treatment of entire sanctification by answering "the only plausible objections" that have been made to this doctrine: (1) It implies future impeccability; (2) it renders the atonement and intercession of Christ superfluous for those who thus profess to be sanctified; and (3) those delivered from all inward and outward sin would no longer need to pray the petition of the Lord's Prayer, "Forgive us our trespasses."

Watson dismisses the first objection by reminding us that the angels and our first parents fell when in a state of immaculate sanctity. The fully sanctified may fall just as these. This also answers the allegation that the truly sanctified are beyond the reach of temptation.

So far from removing a holy person from the need of the atonement or intercession of Christ, the work of sanctification proceeds entirely from the grace of God in Christ, through the Holy Spirit, not only in its incipiency but also in its continuation.

---

77. Ibid., 455.

78. Ibid. (italics Watson's).

> The state into which we are raised is maintained, not by inherent native power, but by the continual presence and sanctifying influences of the Holy Spirit himself, received and retained in answer to ceaseless prayer; which prayer has respect solely to the merits of the death and intercession of Christ.[79]

Watson gives several answers to the final objection. He frankly acknowledges the natural weakness, imperfection, and defects that mark the holiest of persons on earth. Judged in the light of "that absolute obedience and service which the law of God, never bent or lowered to human weakness, demands from all," we must always petition God's forgiveness for these deviations. "These defects, and mistakes, and infirmities, may be quite consistent with the entire sanctification of the soul and that *moral* maturity of a being still *naturally* infirm and imperfect." He then gives his doctrine a formulation that, if we always remember, will save us from being deceived by any imagined self-righteousness.

> Still farther, . . . we are not the ultimate judges of our own case as to our "trespasses," or our exemption from them; and we are not, therefore, to put ourselves into the place of God, "who is greater than our hearts." So, although St. Paul says, "I know nothing by myself," that is, I am conscious of no offence, he adds, "yet am I not hereby justified; but he that judgeth me is the Lord": to whom, therefore, the appeal is every moment to be made through Christ the Mediator, and who, by the renewed testimony of his Spirit, assures every true believer of his acceptance in his sight.[80]

We look in vain for any reference in the *Institutes* to the baptism with the Holy Spirit. A few passing references, however, occur in his sermons. In a much more restrained manner than Clarke, but reflective somewhat of the latter's position, Watson speaks holistically of Spirit baptism. In his sermon "Power from on High," from Luke 24:49, he understands Jesus as promising a power that destroys the love of sin, breaks its power, and so fills the soul with the love of God that "temptation falls blunted and broken." "The baptism of secret fire is invisible to the eye," he says; "but it works powerfully and *constantly*, softening the heart, kindling joy, diffusing purity, carrying you up in devout thoughts of heaven."[81] In another sermon he declares, "When the flames of Pentecost descended, and kindled the spark already there into higher ardour,

79. Ibid., 456.
80. Ibid., 456-57.
81. Watson's *Works*, 3:384-85 (italics added).

they (the primitive disciples) became wholly consecrated to Christ."[82]

3. *Gradual Sanctification*

Peters claims that "Richard Watson's views have in them emphases which tend to merge sanctification with the doctrine of regeneration and thus to lose its significant character."[83] This does not seem to be a fair judgment of the *Institutes,* as the preceding summary shows. When we examine the three volumes of Watson's sermons, however, we cannot but feel the weight of this criticism. At least we sense a distinct shift of emphasis in his expositions, which do not include a single sermon on entire sanctification or Christian perfection.[84] Most references stress the gradual phase of the doctrine.

In his sermon on Rom. 1:16-17 he is clear enough in asserting the power of God to regenerate the sinner and create him anew for good works, but he makes no reference to the further work of sanctification until the very end, where he concludes: "The same 'power of God' which begins the work, shall maintain and perfect it; until salvation from sin in this life shall issue in that full and complete salvation which eternity shall reveal and consummate."[85]

In his exposition on "Promises Obtained Through Faith" (from Heb. 11:33) he enumerates these several promises: (1) justification; (2) a constant supply of spiritual life; (3) deliverance from the worldly spirit; (4) victory over temptation; (5) "promises of growth and progress in all religious habits and acts." He omits any reference to 1 Cor. 7:1 or 1 Thess. 5:23-24. Instead, he says: "All the commands on this subject, to 'grow in grace,' and to 'go on to perfection,' have in them the nature of promises. I am directed to grow; and the command implies an engagement to supply the power." He then quotes Phil. 1:9-11 and Eph. 3:14-19, and asks, "Do I grow in grace, so as to be completely delivered from the corruptions of my nature, and to love God with all my heart, and mind, and soul, and strength?"[86]

Watson's strongest sermonic utterance on holiness is found in

---

82. Ibid., 4:388.

83. *Christian Perfection,* 109.

84. Watson's *Works,* vols. 2 through 4.

85. Ibid., 2:283.

86. Ibid., 2:458-59.

his message "Isaiah's Vision," where he says, "The instrument of purification is fire . . . from the altar where atonement is made. . . . Our altar is the cross; . . . by the merit of his death and the baptizing fire of his Spirit, are the guilty and polluted pardoned and sanctified to God."[87]

D. William Burt Pope

Pope's three-volume *Compendium of Christian Theology,* first published in 1875, is an able treatment of the Wesleyan position. After a creative restatement of Wesley's doctrine, which evidences a deep understanding of biblical theology, he presents a comprehensive historical summation of holiness from the time of the apostles to Wesley. Wesley's thought is almost entirely indicated by rather full quotations from the *Plain Account.* His *Higher Catechism of Theology* simplifies and summarizes the *Compendium.*[88]

What Pope wishes to make most clear about the Wesleyan view is given under the heading "cardinal teaching." And this is

> that perfection is solely the Spirit's work in the believer; but implies his most strenuous co-operation: as to the former, it is received merely by faith, and hence may be given instantaneously, "in a moment"; as to the latter, "there is a gradual work, both preceding and following that instant."

As Peters says, "Here was Wesley in undistorted miniature."[89]

1. *Sanctification in Principle and Process*

As a privilege of the New Covenant, Christian sanctification is twofold: purification from sin and consecration to God. Both purification and consecration are viewed by Pope as the direct and sole work of the Holy Spirit, and their unity is seen as holiness.

a. The negative element is *purification,* viewed in both Testaments as the removal of guilt and cleansing from defilement.

Christians, first of all, are sanctified by being cleansed from the *guilt* of sin. Guilt is more than a forensic term; it is also the consciousness of personal transgression. "It is before the Divine altar the *conscience of sins* which would keep the offerer from ap-

---

87. Ibid., 2:152.

88. William Burt Pope, *Higher Catechism of Theology* (New York: Phillips & Hunt, n.d.).

89. Ibid., 159.

proaching." Accordingly, to be purified is to have "our hearts sprinkled from an evil conscience" (Heb. 10:22).[90]

Christians are sanctified also by the purification of sin viewed as *defilement.* "'But ye are washed, but ye are sanctified, but ye are justified': here the middle term seems to unite the others in itself."[91] The Old Testament illustration of this is the "purifying of the flesh" (Heb. 9:13), the outward symbol of deliverance from both the guilt and defilement of sin. In this broad sense David cried out, "Wash me throughly from mine iniquity" (Ps. 51:2). Pope believes that "purifying their hearts by faith" in Acts 15:9 includes this whole work of the gospel, both "on" and "in" these first Gentile believers.[92]

b. The positive element of Christian sanctification is the Holy Spirit's *consecration* to God of what is dedicated to God by man. This is the love of God shed abroad in our hearts by the Holy Spirit, which awakens the principle of personal dedication.

Consecration is seen as twofold: to God's possession and to God's service. The most important idea is that of *possession.* All belong to God by creation, but redemption makes us His in a special sense. Consecration is the believer's acknowledgment of God's redemptive rights over his life. The believer *dedicates* himself, and the Spirit *sanctifies* him to God. "Consecration is a term in English synonymous with both, common therefore to the believer and the Spirit."[93] But consecration is also to the *service* of God. The believer is to be "a vessel unto honour, sanctified, and meet for the master's use" (2 Tim. 2:21).[94]

The Holy Spirit is the seal and power of this consecration. First, he is the *seal* (Eph. 1:13-14). "The consciousness of the presence of the Holy Ghost within is the testimony to the Christian

---

90. William Burt Pope, *A Compendium of Christian Theology* (2nd edition; New York: Hunt and Eaton, 1899), 3:29.

91. Ibid., 30.

92. He cites as suggesting this twofold cleansing 1 Pet. 1:2; Eph. 5:26; Rev. 1:5; Heb. 10:4, 11; 13:12; 1 Cor. 1:2.

93. Ibid., 32. Supporting passages quoted are Eph. 5:26-27; Rom. 6:13; 12:1; Titus 2:14; John 17:17, 23.

94. "The Divine temple and the Divine service are correlative terms. The whole life of the Christian is spent in a sanctuary. The people are the house of God: ye are the temple of the living God; their life is their worship: to offer up spiritual sacrifices; and He is Himself the temple in which we live, and move, and have our being: for he that dwelleth in love dwelleth in God. Hence the spirit of consecration is that of entire devotion to the Divine service" (ibid.).

that is sanctified to God: as to his pardon and adoption the Spirit as it were speaketh expressly; but his sanctification is silently declared by His very presence and indwelling."[95]

Furthermore, the power of the Holy Spirit is the *energy* of the soul's consecration to the will and service of God. "The faith *which worketh by love* is the faith which is the *fruit of the Spirit*. . . . Entire sanctification—to anticipate—is this, and only this. It is the full, unhindered, unlimited, almighty energy of the power of His presence in the soul."[96]

c. The unity of purification and consecration is *holiness*.

> Those who are purged, or sprinkled from sin, which is separation from God, and who are consecrated to Him, are holy or saints, *hâgioi*. Christ is their *hagiásmos:* the ground or principle or source of their sanctification as in process, in every sense negativing their sin. The state in which they live is that of *hagiosúne*, or holiness.[97]

Objectively, holiness is an imputed sanctity, corresponding to forensic righteousness. Those who by justification are called righteous are by sanctification called holy. "Christians are 'sanctified in Christ Jesus, called to be saints': *to be* is not in the text, but it represents the truth. God makes us what He reputes us to be."[98] Man's holiness is always an imputed sanctity, even before the throne;[99] but no imputation will avail without the reality of internal holiness. "In the attainment of Christian perfection the external and the internal are one."[100]

2. *Sanctification, Progressive and Perfect*

While in one sense sanctification is "a permanent and unchanging principle," as we have seen, it is also a process that reaches its consummation, according to the New Covenant and the testimony of the Spirit, in this present life.[101]

Progressive sanctification is an appropriate phrase, Pope

---

95. "After that ye believed—or on believing, *pisteúsantes*—ye were sealed with that Holy spirit of promise, which is the earnest of our inheritance until the redemption of the purchased possession" (ibid., 33).

96. Ibid.

97. Ibid.

98. *Higher Catechism*, 253.

99. As Wesley wrote in *Plain Account*, "Even perfect holiness is acceptable to God only through Jesus Christ" (*Works*, 11:417).

100. *Compendium*, 34.

101. Ibid., 35.

thinks, since in the administration of this grace the Holy Spirit proceeds by degrees. The goal of entire sanctification is represented in Scripture as the end of a process that requires the cooperation of the believer. It is not the believer's active response, however, that sanctifies; this is the work of divine grace alone.

a. Negatively, this process is *the gradual mortification of sin.* Referring to Rom. 6:6 he says, "Crucifixion is a gradual mortal process, disqualifying the body from serving any (other) master, and as certainly tending to death." In Colossians, St. Paul "bids us 'mortify therefore your members' by killing, or weakening down to extinction every individual tendency or disposition to evil."[102]

> Not only is the old man to be destroyed by the doom of crucifixion, but every specific member of his sin is to be surrendered to atrophy: "Make not provision for the flesh, to fulfill the lusts thereof" (Rom. 13:10). Crucifixion is of the whole body; mortification is of each member. . . . "If we live in the Spirit, let us also walk in the Spirit" (Gal. 5:23): walk in . . . the via dolorosa, that leads to death, the death of sin. "If ye *through the Spirit* do mortify the deeds of the body ye shall live. It is the Holy Ghost who does what we do through Him."[103]

As this work of sanctification proceeds, the believer becomes positively more and more alienated from sin and set upon good. "The vanishing point of perfection in the will is to be entirely merged in the will of God. . . . The gradual and sure depression of the sinful principle down to its zero point or limit of nonentity is progressive sanctification."[104]

b. The positive side of sanctification—that of *consecration by the Spirit of love*—is also a gradual process.

Although the Spirit was not given "by measure" to the Incarnate Son (John 3:34), this is not so of believers. Christians are urged to be "filled with the Spirit," like the Pentecostal Christians (Eph. 5:18; Acts 2:4). Hence the love of God that the Spirit sheds abroad in our hearts admits of increase. "That your love may abound yet more and more," St. Paul prays (Phil. 1:9).

c. The state of holiness is thus progressively realized. The phrase "perfecting holiness" (2 Cor. 7:1) "indicates an end to which effort

---

102. Ibid., 37; see also *Higher Catechism:* "They that are Christ's have crucified the flesh; and crucifixion is unto death" (261).

103. *Compendium,* 37.

104. Ibid., 37-38.

is ever converging."[105] This passage, "the force of which can be felt only in the original Greek," should be carefully studied as

> shedding a rich light upon the whole doctrine of human co-operation with Divine grace. . . . St. James says: "*Katharísate*, cleanse your hands, and *hagnísate*, purify your hearts." And St. Paul uses the strong expression, "mortify therefore your members, *nekrósate*." . . .
>
> No one can understand these passages aright who does not see that they all hang upon one principle, that the Spirit's work is made our own. "Having these promises" governs them all. But, on the other hand, such passages would not be found were it not the intention of the Spirit to impress upon us a high estimate of our own responsibility.[106]

Nothing is more constantly declared than that the effusion of the Spirit of consecration keeps pace with the cooperation of the believer. Citing 1 John 2:5; 4:12-13; and 4:16-17 as illustrating this principle, Pope says: "In all three cases the indwelling of God by the Spirit is the efficient cause, while *obedience, charity* to man, and the *imitation of Christ* are the three-one condition. Love is the channel for imparting the instrument for producing love: *from love to love* answering here to St. Paul's *from faith to faith*."[107]

As to the state of holiness, it is a goal toward which Christians must habitually bend their efforts: "Be ye holy; for I am holy" (1 Pet. 1:16). Is, then, holiness attained simply by human endeavor? Assuredly not. The Holy Spirit finishes the work "in His own time, in His own way, as His own act."[108] Galatians 3:3 "shows that the Spirit, the bestowment of whom begins the reign of grace in us, is the same who perfects it; it is His administration from first to last. He is the earliest seal of every privilege, and, in the name of Jesus, the finisher of our salvation: we may be perfected in the Spirit."[109] "Whenever the seal of perfection is set on the work," Pope concludes, "it must be a critical and instantaneous act. . . . But this leads us from the Sanctuary to the Most Holy Place."[110]

3. *Entire Sanctification*

"Provision is made in the Christian covenant," Pope declares,

---

105. Ibid., 38; *Higher Catechism*, 255.
106. Ibid., 39-40.
107. Ibid., 40-41.
108. Ibid., 42.
109. *Higher Catechism*, 269.
110. *Compendium*, 44.

"for the *completeness* of the Saviour's work as the perfect application of His atonement to the believer." This completed holiness may be viewed as entire sanctification, or the destruction of original sin in the believer; perfect love, or entire consecration to God; and evangelical perfection, or the state of consummated holiness.[111]

a. The design of redemption, according to Scripture, is the entire sanctification of the Christian. This includes the complete destruction of sin, promised the believer as his necessary preparation for the future life. The entire removal of sin is never connected with any other means than the promise of God received in faith and proved in experience.

This removal of sin from man's nature in the present life is the grand aim of the work of Christ. No end is kept more constantly before us in Scripture. "For this purpose the Son of God was manifested, that he might destroy the works of the devil" (1 John 3:8). "He was manifested to take away our sins" (1 John 3:5). As Pope puts it in his *Compendium,* "Sinless Himself, He makes His people sinless" (p. 46). "He appeared to put away sin by the sacrifice of himself" (Heb. 9:26). The Greek for "put away" is *athetésai,* meaning "to abolish." This is a term that goes beyond the sacrificial terminology of the Epistle, like that of John the Baptist in John 1:29. Our Lord "gave himself for us, that he might redeem us from all iniquity, and purify unto himself a peculiar people, zealous of good works" (Titus 2:14).[112]

More particularly, the promise of entire sanctification has to do with original sin, which must be understood in two ways: as the *individual* portion of a common heritage, and as a *generic* condition infecting the fallen race until the final resurrection. Entire sanctification as a present experience of grace removes "the carnal mind, or the inbred sin of our fallen nature."[113] Original sin as a generic condition will not be abolished until it is said, "Behold, I make all things new" (Rev. 21:5).

So, "as something of the penalty remains untaken away, so

---

111. Ibid., 45.

112. Other passages cited are 1 John 1:7 (which promises cleansing "from all that is called sin, whether it be its guilt or its power in man"); Rom. 6:6, 7, 11, and 1 John 2:1. "These several passages in their combination establish generally the whole doctrine of a purification provided for all sin" (ibid., 47).

113. Ibid., 97.

also something of the peculiar concupiscence or liability to temptation or affinity with evil that besets man in this world remains."[114] "As to deliverance from evil: *concupiscence as sin* is removed; but as the possible 'fuel of sin' it is never taken away. The venial sins, or sins of defect, which spring from it, do not affect the state of grace or righteousness." The *natural concupiscence,* which remains in the truly sanctified believer, is "no more sin than it was in Adam."[115] Nevertheless, the saint delivered from personal sin is still connected with sin by his own past. He must therefore regard his forgiveness as being "perpetually renewed until the final act of mercy." Thus there is "no man who must not join in the prayer, 'Forgive us our trespasses.'" Hence it is not usual, says Pope, to speak of original sin, absolutely, as done away in Christ. The race has its natural concupiscence and susceptibility to sin, "and we must cease to belong to the lineage of Adam before our unsinning state becomes sinlessness."[116]

Having cleared the way for the Christian idea of entire sanctification, Pope affirms that *the carnal mind that plagues us is abolished* by the sanctifying Spirit when His work is completed in us.

> Original sin in its quality as the "sin that dwelleth in" the Me of the soul, as the principle in man that has actual affinity with transgression, as the source and "law of sin which is in my members," and, finally, as "the flesh with the affections and lusts," is abolished by the SPIRIT OF HOLINESS indwelling in the Christian, when His purifying grace has its perfect work.[117]

In this perfected work of the Spirit "the very principle of self which is the true defilement of original sin" is extinguished.[118] There remains only one redemption reserved for Christ's second coming: "the redemption of the body" (Rom. 8:23).[119]

Entire sanctification is "in reality the perfection of the regenerate state."[120] Pope strongly insists on this view.

> The Spirit of entire sanctification is only the Spirit of the beginning of grace exerting an ampler power. Never do we read

---

114. Ibid., 47.

115. *Higher Cathechism,* 270.

116. *Compendium,* 47.

117. Ibid.

118. *Higher Catechism,* 261. Pope does not mean here the extinction of the psyche but the destruction of the principle of self-idolatry.

119. *Compendium,* 48.

120. Ibid., 89.

of a *higher life* that is other than the intensification of the lower; never of a *second blessing* that is more than the unrestrained outpouring of the same Spirit who gave the first. "Have ye received the Holy Ghost since ye believed?" means, Did you receive the Holy Ghost on believing? *Elábete pisteúsantes?* and cannot refer to a reception of a higher gift superinduced on a lower gift which was without the Spirit of entire consecration.[121]

b. Perfect love, or entire consecration to God, constitutes the positive meaning of entire sanctification. To this end God imparts the fullness of the sanctifying Spirit. "The combination of these two elements, the negative annihilation of the principle of sin and the positive effusion of perfect love is, it may be said, peculiar to Methodist theology as such."[122]

(1) For Pope, *perfect love is another term for entire devotement to God* "as the one Object and Rest and Centre and Life of the soul" (Deut. 10:12). In this grace God becomes the Supreme End of our existence, with "the neighbour and all other things being objects of love only in Him, 'hid with Christ in God' (Col. 3:3)."[123]

This perfect devotement to God opens the life to agape love, "the substance of all personal religion." "Pure faith leads to a cleansed conscience and purified heart, the abode of perfect love" understood as "charity" (1 Tim. 1:5).

> Love to man is purely ethical as it is the reflection of the Divine love. The neighbour is united with self as a creature; and as self, literally understood, is lost in love, love views all creatures and self included as one before God. Hence all the variety of our duty to our fellows is the expression of charity, aiming supremely at the Supreme, but reflected on all men for His sake.

This charity, negatively, works "no ill to his neighbour," and, positively, loves "his neighbour as himself."[124]

---

121. Ibid., 44. "In other words entire consecration is the stronger energy of a Spirit already in the regenerate, not a Spirit to be sent down from on high. This kingdom of God is already within, if we would let it come to perfection. . . . The teaching (that we receive the Holy Ghost as a superadded Spirit in entire consecration) tends to diminish the value of regeneration, which is itself a life 'hid with Christ in God.' . . . (Those who teach the other view) have the highest and purest aims, and need only to guard their doctrine more carefully" (ibid., 64-65). See also *Higher Catechism,* 262.

122. Ibid., 97.

123. Ibid., 51.

124. Ibid., 176. Pope at this point is more Augustinian than Wesleyan. The Christian's "real and essential obligation" is to God alone, neighbor being loved in

(2) *The Holy Spirit, as the Spirit of perfect consecration, is poured out upon the Church.* "He discharges His sanctifying office as the indwelling Spirit: able perfectly to fill the soul with love, and to awaken a perfect love in return."

Pope's pivotal text is 1 John 4:19, which he translates, "We love [him], because he first loved us." The divine love is revealed *to* the soul for its conversion, and then is shed abroad *in* the regenerate spirit as an expression of its gratitude. "We have known and believed the love that God hath to us" (1 John 4:16). This revelation received by faith is the secret of our return to God.

The perfecting of love is the perfecting both of God's love in us and of our love to God. First, God's love is "perfected in us" (1 John 4:12): "that is, as accomplishing its perfect triumph over the sin and selfishness of our nature, and its separation from God." But John also writes: "Perfect love casteth out fear. . . . He that feareth is not made perfect in love" (1 John 4:18). This speaks of the perfection of our returning love. "It is of course the same thing," he thinks, "whether God's love is perfected or ours made perfect in return." He acknowledges, however, that St. John is the only writer who speaks of the Christian's perfect love. "This solitary text, however, gives its meaning to the multitude."[125]

(3) *The Holy Spirit uses the love of God as His instrument in effecting our entire consecration.* That "unction from the Holy One" of which St. John speaks (1 John 2:20) makes us "partakers of the Saviour's consecration." He who received the Spirit not "by measure" (John 3:34), gives *us* the fullness of the Spirit and thereby reproduces the Christly character in us. This was the lesson of Pentecost.

> On the morning of that day the Spirit's elect symbol was fire. First He appeared as the Shekinah glory, without a veil, diffused over the whole Church, and then resting "upon each." The light which touched every forehead for acceptance entered as fire each heart, "and they were all filled with the Holy Ghost": filled literally for the time being; and, if we suppose that indwelling permanent, we have our doctrine substan-

---

Him. Every act is an act of love, "as love is the return of the soul to its rest." He consistently uses "charity" interchangeably with love (see *Compendium,* 217), clearly reflecting Augustine's doctrine of *caritas,* viewed as a combination of *agape* and *eros.* For Wesley, love to neighbor is distinct from love to God, although flowing from the latter; and perfect love is "pure love to God and man," a concept of perfect love more social and "Christian" than Pope's.

125. Ibid., 52-53.

> tiated. Lastly, as a tongue, the symbol signified the sanctification of the outward life of devotion to God and service to man.[126]

"There is no limit to the Spirit's consecrating grace," Pope says. "I sanctify myself, that they also might be sanctified," Christ prayed (John 17:19). Although God's *method* in sanctifying us by destroying our sin finds no pattern in Him, the *result* of our sanctification is Christlikeness. "Beholding as in a glass the glory of the Lord, [we] are changed into the same image from glory to glory, even as by the Spirit of the Lord" (2 Cor. 3:18).

c. Christian perfection is set before believers as the goal of all evangelical aspiration. It is essentially the law fulfilled in love. This doctrine "boldly declares that the righteousness of the law is fulfilled in believers, that is the righteousness of the new law of faith; . . . *that as faith is reckoned for righteousness, so faith working by love is reckoned for perfection.*"[127]

"Injunctions to seek perfection and corresponding promises are few but very distinct." Were there no others our Redeemer's would be enough: "Be ye therefore perfect, even as your Father which is in heaven is perfect" (Matt. 5:48). The primary meaning of this commandment is that we exemplify the Father's impartial love toward all men, even to those who would be our enemies.[128] While this text has a limited significance, it is capable of much wider application.

First, Christian perfection is *evangelical.* That is, it is to be distinguished from every kind of perfection that is not of pure grace, and it bears "the impress of the condescension and lovingkindness of God."

> It is, however much the thought may be disapproved of men, a perfection accommodated to our fallen condition: not lowered but accommodated; a distinction this which is not without a difference. There is a consummation here as well as hereafter.[129]

The consummation here experienced is that of "love . . . fulfilling the law" (Rom. 13:10), of being progressively "conformed to the image of his Son" (Rom. 8:29), "although many infirmities are in us which could not be in Him," and of being "sanctified *wholly*

126. Ibid., 53.
127. Ibid., 97.
128. Ibid., 234.
129. Ibid., 57.

throughout spirit, and soul, and body, and *preserved blameless,"* though we are still ignorant, weak, and inhabiting a body that is on the way to dissolution.

Since such is the case, those who have received this grace "neither think themselves, nor desire to be thought, sinless in the utmost meaning of the word,"[130] and with respect to themselves employ the word *perfection* as a term more appropriate to their aspiration than their professed attainment.[131]

It is for this reason that the term *perfection* should not be adopted without qualification, but with its "guardian adjectives *Christian* or *Evangelical* it is unimpeachable." Understood in this way "it is the vanishing point of every doctrine, exhortation, promise, and prophecy of the New Testament."[132]

Furthermore, Christian perfection is *relative and probationary.* It is "the estate of a spirit every whit whole, but still in a body the infirmity of which is the main part of its probation." It is also at best the perfection of a probationary estate. There is no reason why it may not be lost, "even after the fruition of the result of long years of heavenly blessing."

> The principle of sin extinct in the soul may be kindled into life as it was kindled in Eve. There is no reason why it should not; but there is every reason why it need not and ought not. Such a second fall would be a fall indeed. It is not probable that it was ever witnessed. It is only our theory that demands the admission of its possibility.[133]

Though personally in Christ in the deepest sense, the perfected believer under probation "is still under the generic doom of original sin, with a concupiscence which is not sin but the fuel of it always ready to be kindled." Furthermore, he is the inheritor of a sinful nature that, cleansed in himself, he transmits to his children uncleansed.

> We never read of an entire severance from the first Adam as the prerogative of those who are found in the Second. The entirely sanctified believer may be, as touching his relation to Christ and in Christ, without spot and blameless; at the same time in relation to Adam and in him he is only a sinful man among sinful men.[134]

---

130. Ibid., 57-58.

131. *Higher Catechism,* 275.

132. Ibid., 58.

133. Ibid., 59.

134. Ibid.

Being probationary, Christian perfection is always under the ethical law. Christianity is the "perfect law of liberty" (James 1:25). The service of this law is "perfect freedom," guarded by watchfulness, subjected to a variety of tests, and maintained through divine grace by continued obedience.

> On the one hand it is a state of rest: "filled with the Spirit" the Christian can say, "I can do all things through Christ which strengtheneth me." On the other it is a state in which the soul is safe only in the highest exercise of the severest virtue.[135]

Hence this perfection needs constantly the mediatorial work of Christ. It demands His constant influence "to preserve as a state what is imparted as a gift." Our Lord's abiding intercession for us is prefigured in His high priestly prayer: "I pray not that thou shouldest take them out of the world, but that thou shouldest keep them from the evil" (John 17:15).

> With all these conditions and limitations the word perfection—*teleiótes,* integrity—extends to all the blessings of the covenant of grace as they are provided for man in probation. [The entirely sanctified] are perfect in their imperfection: imperfect, when viewed in relation to the eternal requirement of the Supreme Lawgiver; perfect, when viewed in relation to the present economy of grace.[136]

(1) They are perfect in relation to God's absolute law of justice: "By one offering he hath perfected for ever them that are sanctified" (Heb. 10:14). "In all respects [the believer] is placed in a perfect relation to God through grace."[137]

(2) As children of God their state lacks nothing. Although waiting for the adoption (Rom. 8:23), now are they the sons of God (1 John 3:2). Being by the Spirit "conformed to the image of his Son" (Rom. 8:29), they are "blameless and harmless, the sons of God, without rebuke" (Phil. 2:15).

(3) "And in the temple of God, of which it is said, 'holiness becometh thy house, O Lord' (Ps. 93:5), the perfection of Christianity requires and reaches such a purity and simplicity as can endure the scrutiny of the Searcher of hearts. 'Thou hast tried me, and shalt find nothing.' . . . 'Blessed are the pure in heart, for they

---

135. Ibid., 68.
136. Ibid., 60.
137. *Higher Catechism,* 264.

shall see God.' The vision of God belongs to the consummate sanctity of the temple, whether on earth or in heaven."[138]

138. *Compendium,* 69.

7

Christian Perfection in American Methodism

Christian perfection was one of the characteristic features of American Methodism from its very beginning in the 1760s. When the Methodist Episcopal church was organized at the 1784 Christmas Conference in Baltimore it adopted as its standards the four volumes of the Wesley *Sermons* and his *Notes upon the New Testament,* together with Wesley's abridgment of the Thirty-nine Anglican articles and the *Large Minutes* of the conference. The type of perfection taught was of an experience of perfect love attainable "now and by simple faith," a concept that at the same time made provision for corporate Christian nurture. "It is reasonable to assume," Peters thinks, "that it was with this connotation that the doctrine was embodied in the first *Discipline* of the Methodist Episcopal Church."[1]

John Wesley was the dominant influence in American Methodism until his death. One of the first resolutions adopted at the founding conference declared, "During the life of the Rev. Mr. Wesley, we acknowledge ourselves his sons in the gospel."[2] Francis Asbury, one of the bishops appointed by Wesley and elected at the

---

1. John L. Peters, *Christian Perfection and American Methodism,* (Nashville: Abingdon Press, 1956), 88-89; Robert E. Chiles, *Theological Transition in American Methodism* (New York: Abingdon Press, 1965), 24.

2. Peters, *Christian Perfection,* 92.

conference in December 1784, had written in his journal: "I find no preaching does good, but that which properly presses the use of the means, and urges holiness of heart; these points I am determined to keep close to in all my sermons." Of entire sanctification an entry said: "It must be sought by faith, and expected as a present salvation." By exhortation and supremely by example, Bishop Asbury used his influence to shape the practices and to a considerable degree the doctrinal emphases of early American Methodism.[3]

Concerning the early years of Methodism in America, John A. Knight says:

> Wesley's writings along with those of Fletcher and the hymns of Charles, supplied the standards for theological judgment and belief. . . . Wesleyan theology in America, introduced by Wesley and Fletcher, was sustained by second-generation theologians and Biblical interpreters such as Richard Watson, Adam Clarke, and Joseph Benson.[4]

Fletcher's influence was particularly strong. His "Treatise on Christian Perfection" in his *Last Check* was second only to Wesley's *Plain Account* among the "textbooks of Methodism."[5] The Conference Course of Study, authorized by the General Conference of 1816, is a significant clue to the most influential Wesleyan theologians and writers in 19th-century America. Because the large majority of Methodist preachers at this time were trained in the Course of Study, its widespread influence is obvious.[6]

Nathan Bangs figured prominently in the formation of the Course of Study. In a series of articles later published as *Letters to Young Ministers of the Gospel, on the Importance and Method of Study,* he recommended on the doctrines of repentance, justification, and sanctification Wesley and Fletcher, of whom he said, "No authors have illustrated those subjects with greater clearness and accuracy." He also included Richard Watson among the recommended theologians, and among Bible commentators, Wesley, Clarke, and Benson. Peters comments, "Just how much Bangs was heeded, it would be difficult to say; but of the latter writers he mentions, it was Adam Clarke and Richard Watson whose influence on the

---

3. Ibid., 85-86.

4. John A. Knight, "John Fletcher's Influence on the Development of Wesleyan Theology in America," *Wesleyan Theological Journal* (vol. 13, Spring 1978), 22.

5. Ibid., 23.

6. Ibid., 22.

doctrine of Christian perfection was most pronounced."[7] The value of Clarke's *Commentary* to the Methodist ministry, says Methodist historian Abel Stevens, was "immeasurably great." And Watson's *Institutes* had a profound influence not only on preachers but also upon later Methodist theologians. Daniel Curry wrote in 1877:

> To no other single agency is the continued doctrinal unity of Methodism so much indebted as to the extensive use of Watson's Theological Institutes. . . . This great work has been the standard of Methodist theology for a full half century.[8]

The evidence is clear that Fletcher's teaching of the baptism with the Holy Spirit had its influence on early American Methodist thought, although it was a subordinate concept. For example, it is not found in the writings of any of the Methodist theologians who followed Wesley and Watson rather than Fletcher at this point. But Fletcher's emphasis was occasionally sounded, both from the pulpit and in Methodist publications.

Captain Thomas Webb, in a sermon on the gift of the Holy Spirit at Pentecost, urged upon his New York City hearers that justification by faith was not enough, even for the apostles: "You must be sanctified. But you are not. You have not received the Holy Ghost. I know it. I can feel your spirits hanging about me like so much dead flesh."[9]

The first edition of Fletcher's *Works,* including the *Last Check,* was published in America in 1791, with the second edition in a six-volume set following in 1809. Many of his works were published separately, including "An Address to Imperfect Believers, who cordially embrace the doctrine of Christian perfection,"[10] and his essay on "Christian Perfection."[11]

The *Memoirs* and *Letters* of Hester Ann Rogers were among

---

7. Peters, *Christian Perfection,* 102-03.

8. Chiles, *Theological Transition,* 47.

9. John Fletcher Hurst, *The History of Methodism* (New York: Eaton and Mains, 1902-04), 3:1252 (cited by Frank Baker, *From Wesley to Asbury* [Durham, N.C.: Duke University Press, 1976], 185).

10. See Baker, ibid., 121-23.

11. Allan Coppedge, "Entire Sanctification in Early American Methodism: 1812-1835," *Wesleyan Theological Journal* (vol. 13, Spring 1978), 42. On the basis of more recent research done by Dr. Frank Baker, Coppedge rejects the idea that there was a "gap" in the American teaching of Christian perfection between 1812 and 1832.

See Baker, *From Wesley to Asbury,* 176-80; *contra* Peters, *Christian Perfection,* 98 ff.

the most widely circulated spiritual autobiographies in Methodist circles. In describing her spiritual pilgrimage, Mrs. Rogers relates in detail her quest for the blessing of entire sanctification. In the midst of her prayer for holiness she recalls:

> I thought, Shall I now ask small blessings only of my God: Lord, cried I, make this the moment of my full salvation! Baptize me now with the Holy Ghost and the fire of pure love: Now "make me a clean heart, and renew a right spirit within me." Now enter thy temple, and cast out sin forever. Now cleanse the thoughts, desires and propensities of my heart, and let me perfectly love thee.[12]

The 1830s witnessed a renewed interest in Christian perfection in American Methodism. Peters credits much of this to the life and labors of Nathan Bangs, whose influence can be seen only if his place in American Methodism is understood. Of him Abel Stevens wrote:

> Nathan Bangs was not only a public but a representative man, in the Methodist Episcopal Church, for more than a half century. He was the founder of its periodical literature, and of its "Conference course" of ministerial study, and one of the founders of its present system of educational institutions. He was the first missionary secretary appointed by its General Conference, the first clerical editor of its General Conference newspaper press, the first editor of its Quarterly Review, and, for many years, the chief editor of its Monthly Magazine and its book publications. He may be pronounced the principal founder of the American literature of Methodism. . . . It has been justly said that he ranks next to Asbury in his historical importance in his Church. Twice did his brethren offer him the Episcopal chair.[13]

And Bangs, who professed and preached entire sanctification, gave the cause of holiness within Methodism his wholehearted support. At his funeral Bishop Janes said:

> The Pauline doctrine of sanctification, as defined by Wesley, became his habitual theme of interest and conversation. He delighted to attend social gatherings for prayer on this subject, and during several late years he presided over one of the most frequented assemblies of that kind in our city.[14]

---

12. Thomas Coke, *The Experience and Spiritual Letters of Mrs. Hester Ann Rogers* (London: Milner and Somerby, n.d.), 41 (cited by Coppedge, "Entire Sanctification," 45).

13. Abel Stevens, *Life and Times of Nathan Bangs, D.D.* (New York: Carlton and Porter, 1863), 13, 14, 15 (quoted by Peters, *Christian Perfection,* 114).

14. Peters, *Christian Perfection.* The "social gatherings for prayer" were the

It was not until 1847, however, that the first American Methodist systematic theology appeared. In that year Thomas N. Ralston (1806-91) published his *Elements of Divinity,* which Chiles calls an American translation of Watson's *Institutes.*[15] This volume became popular, especially in the southern church, where it was still read a century later.[16]

A. Thomas N. Ralston

Ralston saw the significance of Wesley's recovery of the doctrine of Christian perfection for the Christian Church.

> As Luther, two centuries before, had stood forth as a mighty champion for "justification by faith," so Wesley now appeared, not only as the defender of that doctrine, but also as an instrument under God to revive and set clearly before the Church the apostolic doctrine of "Christian perfection."[17]

After saying in Wesleyan fashion what Christian perfection is not, he states his positive position: "[It] is regeneration grown to maturity."

> While one regenerated is a "babe," a sanctified Christian is a "father in Christ." Yet it should not be forgotten that sanctification, in its *initial* state, is synonymous with regeneration; while, in its *perfected* state, is synonymous with Christian perfection.[18]

While insisting that regeneration and entire sanctification are the same in nature and differ only in degree, Ralston emphasizes that Christian perfection involves "entire consecration to God and a complete cleansing of the soul from 'all unrighteousness.'"[19] He then proceeds to demonstrate this doctrine by citing numerous precepts, promises, prayers, and exhortations from Scripture that enforce this grace, concluding with examples of persons in the Bible who have attained Christian perfection.

Tuesday Meetings for the Promotion of Holiness, started by Mrs. Phoebe Palmer. See next chapter for a full survey of Mrs. Palmer's view and Nathan Bangs' relationship to this teaching and movement.

15. Chiles, *Theological Transition,* 54.

16. The final edition was edited by Dr. T. O. Summers, professor of systematic theology at Vanderbilt University School of Theology. Ralston's work was in the Course of Study for Nazarene ministers from 1919 to 1940.

17. Thomas N. Ralston, *Elements of Divinity* (Nashville: Abingdon-Cokesbury Press, 1924), 457.

18. Ibid.

19. Ibid., 461.

As to the *time* of attainment, "the general tenor of Scripture" supports the position that "the highest state of religious experience is within the reach of 'the least of the saints'" and "is attainable in this life, whenever we comply with the conditions prescribed in the gospel."[20]

In enforcing this point Ralston introduces an argument based on man's free moral agency. Man, who is "free, through grace, to repent, believe, and be converted" must surely be free after conversion to seek and obtain entire sanctification.

> If, through grace, we forsake *one* sin, we *may* forsake *all* sin. If we may be cleansed from *one* sin, we may be cleansed from *all* sin. If we may keep *one* commandment, we *may*, through grace, "keep the whole law"—that is, the law of faith and love, under which we are placed by the gospel. . . . If we may advance to one degree of holiness or sanctification, which we attain when we are justified, why may we not, on the same principle, "go on to perfection"?[21]

Furthermore, to deny the attainability of true holiness in this life is "inconsistent with those commands, promises, exhortations, and prayers, connected with the doctrine in question."[22] Christian perfection by its very nature is a grace to be exhibited here and now in this present life. The body of sin is to be destroyed so that we may be free from sin "through all subsequent life, extending from the hour in which this great triumph over sin is gained, to the hour of death" (Rom. 6:6-7). The fruit of the Spirit described in Gal. 5:22-23 are, in their nature, such as can be produced only in this life.

> If Christian perfection be not attainable till death, then it must follow, either that *death*, "the last *enemy* that shall be destroyed," is the efficient agent in the work, or that the blood of Christ, and in the influence of the Holy Spirit, are more efficacious in death than they can be in life—both of which positions are too unscriptural to be entertained. (p. 469).

The "perfected love" of which St. John writes in his First Epistle is applicable to "*living* Christians, including himself in the number, and not of such only that were on the bed of death." The "entire cleansing" from sin promised in 1 John 3:3 and 1:7 is not promised at death "but evidently takes place *now*—while 'we walk in the light.'" The "holiness" spoken of in Heb. 12:14 "can only mean

20. Ibid., 466-67.
21. Ibid., 467 (italics his).
22. Ibid., 468.

'perfected holiness;' and this is to be *followed,* not at death, but *now,* while mingling with the affairs of this life."

> Such, according to God's word, are the glorious privileges of all the children of God, even in this world. They not only "know God" in the remission of "past sins," but following "on to know the Lord," they may "know the love of Christ, which passeth knowledge," and "be filled with all the fullness of God."

Ralston then makes a concession regarding the *manner* of entire sanctification that falls short of the historic Methodist position. Wesley had said that while the approach to entire sanctification is usually gradual and the moment of purification may be almost imperceptible, there is nevertheless an *instant* when the soul is separated from sin and begins to live the full life of perfect love. Watson had taken his stand here with Mr. Wesley also. But Ralston hedges:

> It matters but little whether this eminent state of holiness is gained by a bold, energetic, and determined exercise of faith and prayer, or by a more gradual process—whether it is *instantaneous* or *gradual,* or both the one and the other. The great matter is, with each and all of us, that we lose no time, but arise at once, and "press toward the mark for the prize of the high calling of God in Christ Jesus."[23]

B. Randolph S. Foster

The late 1830s and early 1840s witnessed a resurgence of holiness teaching in sectors of the Methodist church. Along with a revival of the traditional Wesleyan view, new ideas were introduced that tended to deviate from the Wesleyan mean. Among these latter was the teaching of Mrs. Phoebe Palmer that "the altar sanctifies the gift"—that is, when the gift is on the altar, the consecration complete, faith can then affirm sanctification. This "altar theology" was understood by some to mean "only believe you have it and you have got it," even though Mrs. Palmer denied this was actually her position.

The holiness revival of this period was not unanimously welcomed. In 1848, opposition to this new emphasis was brought clearly into the open. One full-length book appeared questioning the Wesleyan position,[24] and in an extended article in the *Quarterly Review,* W. C. Hosner argued that regeneration encompasses salva-

---

23. Ibid., 470.

24. Merritt Caldwell, *The Philosophy of Christian Perfection* (no data).

tion in its totality. "If theologians say there are stages in the process," wrote Hosner, "they must all be passed through in a moment, or they are not all necessary to salvation."[25] For all *real* purposes, sanctification is identical with the new birth.

This is the background against which Randolph S. Foster (1820-1903) wrote an able and noncontroversial exposition of Wesley's views, defending the teaching from both the above departures from its historic formulation. Entitled *The Nature and Blessedness of Christian Purity,* Foster's book was published in 1851 and appeared in a second edition 20 years later. A staunch holiness advocate to the end, Foster was soon to become professor of systematic theology at Garrett Biblical Institute, then at Drew Theological Seminary. Later he was elected bishop.

The burden of Foster's treatment is a defense of the distinctiveness of sanctification as a doctrine and of entire sanctification as a phase of that doctrine.[26] He distinguishes four existing views on the subject. (1) Some believe that though regeneration does not imply sanctification, yet it is the highest attainable state during this life. (2) Others, agreeing that regeneration and sanctification are not identical, do hold that regeneration is sanctification begun, and that sanctification will be completed just before death, in the ripeness and maturity of the graces implanted in the moment of regeneration. (3) Still others, agreeing in principle with the preceding class, believe that this maturity may take place long before death and be enjoyed during this life. "In their estimation, sanctification is distinct only as a point in the progress of regeneration, not as a separate and additional work—*attained by gradual growth,* not by direct agency."

> *Fourth.* But finally: another class, agreeing with the former, that sanctification and regeneration are not identical, and, with the two last named, that regeneration is sanctification begun, differ with them all in that they believe sanctification to be an immediate or instantaneous, and distinct work, to be attained by the agency of the Holy Spirit through faith, at any time when the requisite faith is exercised, and to be enjoyed during life.[27]

---

25. *Methodist Quarterly Review,* 31:484 ff. See Peters, *Christian Perfection,* 112, 121-22.

26. Peters, *Christian Perfection,* 123.

27. Randolph S. Foster, *The Nature and Blessedness of Christian Purity* (New York: Land & Scott, 1851), 44-45.

This latter position Foster defends as the Wesleyan view. Regeneration is not entire sanctification. The regenerate are not entirely freed from sin; they are not perfect in love. Their sins are pardoned; their nature is renewed; they are the children of God; they have been rescued from the dominion of sin and become heirs of the promises. But great and glorious as the work of regeneration is, it is not entire freedom from sin. "The old man of sin is not dead, but subjected—not cast out, but bound."

In enforcing the doctrine of remaining sin, Foster appeals to the universal faith of the Church, the universal experience of those who have been "pardoned" and "born again" by the Spirit, and the teachings of Scripture (citing 1 Cor. 3:1-3).

> Let it be remembered, we are now speaking particularly of inbred sin—sins of the heart—or, if any prefer it, evils of the heart. We are aware that the believer does not indulge in outward sins—sins of the life—that he does not transgress in the sense: "For whosoever is born of God doth not commit sin." . . . Regeneration is sanctification begun, but not completed.[28]

"But it may be asked with earnestness, 'Is not the work of God perfect in regeneration?' And we answer, it is a perfect regeneration. But a perfect regeneration is not a perfect sanctification, no more than perfect penitence is perfect regeneration. The soul is perfectly born anew, but it is not perfectly made holy."[29]

Entire sanctification, therefore, is distinct from and subsequent to regeneration. And how is this completed holiness obtained? "Like every other blessing offered in the Gospel, [it] is obtained by 'faith.'"[30] But Foster is not content to leave the matter there. What *is* sanctifying faith, and *how* may it be exercised? he asks. He gives his general position in these words:

> Faith, in order to its exercise, presupposes a certain state of the mind and affections, and without these it cannot exist—its very existence includes them: namely, . . . it supposes the knowledge of sin and sorrow for it, the knowledge that there is a Saviour, and a readiness to embrace Him.[31]

In developing his treatment of this subject Foster gives a helpful exposition of Mr. Wesley's doctrines of "repentance of believers"

---

28. Ibid., 69-73. Foster also reinforces the scriptural evidence for this doctrine by quoting Richard Watson's *Institutes,* 2:450.

29. See chap. 6.

30. Ibid., 120.

31. Ibid., 121.

and sanctifying faith. In addition to a clear view of the offer of holiness in Scripture, the believer must come to a painful and penitent awareness of his need to be cleansed from inbred sin. This comes through the aid and guidance of the Holy Spirit as he prayerfully searches the Bible and probes the depths of his own soul. As he yields in willingness to permit God "to lay the knife to the heart, to amputate its idols," and gives himself up wholly to God in consecration, he is then at the place where he may exercise sanctifying faith. However,

> consecration is not sanctification, it is a part of it. Consecration is your work, God giving the requisite grace; when it is entire, sanctification, which is the work of the Holy Spirit, follows, always follows, immediately follows.[32]

Faith, and faith alone, is the final condition:

> Faith . . . is the only condition upon which the blessings of the gospel are offered. "Justification" is by faith—"regeneration" is by faith—"sanctification" is by faith—"glorification" is by faith—by faith as the instrument, and by the blood of Jesus as the merit, and by the Spirit as the agent. *Whenever faith is exercised, the work will be done.*[33]

At this point Foster explains what he sees to be the difference between the views of Mrs. Palmer and Mr. Wesley.

> It has been indiscreetly said, "We are to believe the work is done, and it will be done." Persons seeking the blessing have been told they must believe they are sanctified, and they will be sanctified. . . . What a manifest absurdity! Making our sanctification depend upon the belief . . . that it is now wrought, in order that it may be wrought!

This view, he says, is a "great delusion." "It is not, and never was, the doctrine of our Church." Nevertheless, "it has gained considerable currency."[34]

Those who teach this new doctrine tend to substitute "mere belief" for "confiding trust." For Wesley, sanctifying faith, like justifying faith, is more than intellectual assent; it is the "warm trust of the heart." Foster then gives Wesley's full exposition of sanctifying faith.[35]

---

32. Ibid., 128.
33. Ibid., 131 (italics added).
34. Ibid., 132-33.
35. Ibid., 135-37. cf. Wesley's sermon, "The Scripture Way of Salvation," *Works*, 6:52-54.

Wesley's definition, Foster says, is a far cry from, "Profess you are sanctified, and you will be." Profession is nowhere required as a condition of faith; it is required as a duty *after* we are sanctified.

> Let those who are clear in the enjoyment of holiness, declare it, with becoming meekness and humility; if there is any need, let them be advised to make a public confession. But let no man be urged to make a profession, the truth of which he does not know certainly, and which he even doubts, with the hope that profession under the circumstances will benefit. It may fasten delusion upon him, but it cannot bring him sanctifying grace.[36]

Foster believes the means described above—repentance, consecration, and faith—will result in entire sanctification.

> With this belief, both experience and the word of God agree. But . . . means do not sanctify. . . . On the contrary. . . . *The Holy Ghost is the great agent in the regeneration and sanctification of souls.* His power alone effects the change. . . . You employ the means only to bring you in contact with the agency. It is the fire which refines the gold.[37]

Moreover, the Holy Spirit himself is the witness that the work is done, corroborated by the fruit of the Spirit. In explaining this truth, Foster gives extensive quotations from Mr. Wesley's writings.[38]

Foster, however, does not close his work here. He devotes three full chapters of guidance to those who have experienced this grace, explaining how it may be "retained and regained." The concluding chapter is largely a quotation of Mr. Wesley's eight advices to those who profess to have been made perfect in love.[39]

Christian Purity, as the work came to be known, was clearly intended to keep the Methodist Episcopal church on the solid foundation of its original Wesleyan position. In the spirit of John Wesley it is more than a doctrinal statement; it is a clear and urgent call to scriptural holiness as it had been understood within Methodism from its beginnings.

---

36. Ibid., 138.

37. Ibid., 140-41.

38. Ibid., 149-58; quotations cited are from his sermon, "Witness of the Spirit, Discourse II," *Works,* 5:124-29; and from "A Plain Account of Christian Perfection," *Works,* 11:422-26.

39. Ibid., 197-214; "A Plain Account of Christian Perfection," *Works,* 11:427-40.

C. Miner Raymond

During the holiness controversy in American Methodism, Miner Raymond (1811-97), professor of systematic theology at Garrett Biblical Institute, produced his three-volume *Systematic Theology.* Published in 1877, it was placed in the Methodist Episcopal Course of Study in 1880, where it remained until 1908.

Raymond adopts and defends at every point the Wesleyan view of entire sanctification. Regeneration is indeed "salvation from the reigning power of sin," he says, but "the regenerated person is not, at the moment of his regeneration, 'wholly sanctified.'"[40] Entire sanctification is approached ordinarily by a gradual process, "as the subject improves his privileges, grows in grace and knowledge, and comes to the exercise of an intelligent, evangelical, saving faith for this special attainment, this higher Christian life."[41] But in another context he says, in true Wesleyan fashion, "God may . . . cut short his work of grace in given cases." We cannot discount the word of many persons who "testify that in answer to prayer offered in faith, they have been instantly translated from a lower to a higher place of spiritual life" and who thereafter have given "indubitable evidence" of "perfect love."[42]

As a theologian Raymond admits a difficulty, however; for

> sanctification, being a matter of experience, and therefore known only by experience, and being variable, different in different persons and in the same person at different times, is incapable of logical definition; that is, the precise idea can not be revealed to one otherwise ignorant of it by any formula of language.[43]

The propriety of affirming the doctrine of Christian perfection, however, cannot be denied. "The Scriptures recognize a state of grace which they speak of as a state of maturity," and they "call that grace perfect love." They further assure that this is "a state of grace which may be sought, obtained, and enjoyed."[44] "Christian perfection, therefore, despite the difficulty of definition includes at

---

40. Miner Raymond, *Systematic Theology* (New York: Phillips & Hunt, 1880), 2:350, 375.

41. Ibid., 350.

42. Ibid., 394.

43. Ibid., 350.

44. Ibid., 384.

least these two ideas: maturity and perfect love. Explore those concepts and the breadth of the doctrine is evident."[45]

Raymond finds support for this teaching in many Scripture passages. But this grace "designated as a state of maturity in Christian experience is most perfectly delineated in Paul's prayer for the Ephesians" (Eph. 3:16-21). While commentators view this as a prayer for the Ephesian church considered as a corporate body, "it is nevertheless obvious that the terms employed, as well as the nature of the case, compel us to refer the blessings prayed for to the individual experience of the members of that Church." It is essentially a prayer that these persons may know "the full extent of Church privileges." This he understands to be "the knowledge of the fullness of redemption."[46]

"What is the import of this remarkable prayer?" Raymond asks.

First, it is a prayer for the supernatural strengthening of Christian *knowledge.* The apostle prays that by "a direct operation of the Holy Ghost" these Ephesians may be given "whatever mental ability is requisite for such an apprehension of God's love in Christ toward men as will awaken perfect love toward God."

"The second blesing sought (second in order of thought) . . . is not merely that the Ephesians might be *able* to know and comprehend, but that they might *actually* know" Christ's love to them so as to quicken their love toward Christ.

"The third and chief blessing, and that to which all else tends, and is subordinate, is the presence of the Holy Trinity abiding in its fullness in the soul of man." By the *Spirit* the inner man is strengthened; *Christ* dwells in the heart by faith; and the measure of this strengthening and indwelling is the fullness of *God.* Raymond sees a parallel here to the promise of Jesus: "If a man love me, he will keep my words: and my Father will love him, and we will come unto him, and make our abode with him" (John 14:23).

> That a state of grace is here presented, far, very far, above the ordinary attainments of Christian believers, must be manifest to any observer of the conduct, conversation, and spirit of those composing the membership of the Christian Church. It is a state of grace to be sought after and prayed for by regenerated persons. It is the highest which we can conceive of as attainable

---

45. Peters, *Christian Perfection,* 157.

46. Raymond, *Systematic Theology,* 385-86. Miscellaneous quotes in the discussion below are from pp. 387-97.

> in this life. If attained, it may, with great propriety, be called Christian perfection.

The only question for the believer who seeks to know the full measure of Christian privilege is whether such a state is attainable in the present life. This assurance is found in the doxology of the prayer, in which we are reminded that God "is able to do exceeding abundantly above all that we ask or think." This is in harmony with the prayer for the Thessalonians that they may be sanctified wholly and preserved blameless to the coming of Christ, "after which we are reminded that God, who hath called us, is faithful and will also do it" (1 Thess. 5:23-24).

When a Christian has reached the point of spiritual apprehension here prayed for, he has nothing to do but to "appropriate" the blessing he comprehends. In Scripture language this is faith. "To such a one God, the Holy Trinity, will surely come and make him his abode—will fill him with all the fullness of a completed Christian character."

> In this view, it is obvious that the work of complete sanctification is both progressive and instantaneous; progressive as to the acquisition of knowledge and the ability to know, and instantaneous as to the appropriation of the blessing comprehended. . . . The Spirit may take time in preparing the holy temple for the habitation of God, but he enters and takes full possession, fills the temple with his presence in a single instant of time; the work may be long in the doing, but there is an instant when it is done, completed, finished.

For most Christians (as we have already noted) the approach to this grace is by a gradual process of spiritual enlightenment; but others have clearly experienced "a sudden, instantaneous transition from a low state of religious enjoyment to a consciousness of completed salvation." Yet "no man's experience should be the basis of another man's faith." Sanctifying faith "must be founded upon the Word of God and the workings of the Spirit in my own mind."

May the believer know that he has received this grace? From what he has said, Raymond answers, it is "manifest" that one who has attained "must have obtained his knowledge by an immediate and special revelation," which Wesley understands as the highest phase of the witness of the Spirit. This "supernatural" witness is then evidenced by a character and conduct in harmony with a profession of perfect love. When this dual witness is present in a person's life "there is no good reason why anyone should doubt his testimony."

D. John Miley

John Miley (1813-95), professor of systematic theology at Drew Theological Seminary, in 1894 published his influential *Systematic Theology,* a two-volume work that "doctrinally, as well as chronologically, stood at the dividing line between two centuries."[47] While Miley tried faithfully to present "the second-blessing view" of entire sanctification, he "object[ed] to any insistence that such is the only possible mode."[48] Despite his efforts to be fair to the historic Wesleyan position, the effect of his treatment was to undermine the doctrine.

1. *Incompleteness of Regeneration*

The incompleteness of the work of regeneration, Miley says, "underlies the doctrine of entire sanctification, particularly in its Wesleyan form." The fact of remaining depravity in the regenerate is a "widely accepted doctrine." "Indeed, exceptions are so few that the doctrine must be regarded as truly catholic."[49]

The depravity that remains, Miley rightly observes, is "a moral state of the soul, not a substance within it." He regards as obscure the exact nature of this remaining sin. However, the truth of a "remnant of depravity" after regeneration is not conditioned on our capacity fully to understand it. Although the Scriptures do not furnish us "any explicit or formal utterance of the incompleteness of regeneration," the truth is certainly *implicit* in them. Furthermore, "There is widely in the consciousness of the regenerate a sense of incompleteness, . . . a sense of the lack of that fullness which is the happy experience of some Christians, and which must be the common privilege of believers. . . . The doctrine thus grounded in the Scriptures and affirmed by the common Christian consciousness may easily command the common Christian faith, and be accepted as a doctrine of the weightiest practical concern."[50]

2. *Sin in Believers*

Miley does not regard the scriptural evidence for remaining depravity as absolutely conclusive. Texts often cited as supporting

---

47. Chiles, *Theological Transition,* 61. This work was immediately placed in the Methodist Episcopal Course of Study, where it remained until 1904. It was also the approved systematic theology text in the Nazarene Course of Study, from 1911 to 1932.

48. John Miley, *Systematic Theology* (New York: Hunt and Eaton, 1894), 2:371.

49. Ibid., 357.

50. Ibid., 361.

the view of a defective Christian life, particularly 1 Cor. 3:1-3 and Gal. 5:17, are seen as instances of very serious degeneration "without an utter forfeiture of the regenerate state." The normal regenerate state is not a life "half carnal." The traditional view of sin in the regenerate, confessed in the Ninth Anglican Article and the Westminster Confession,[51] he thinks reflects the low view of baptismal regeneration. And it is Wesley's sermon on "The Marks of the New Birth" rather than "On Sin in Believers" to which we must turn to find the normative description of the regenerate life.[52]

3. *Entire Sanctification*

It is not Miley's intention, however, to overthrow the teaching of entire sanctification. He is rather opposing a low view of regeneration advocated to make possible a doctrine of complete sanctification.

> If somewhat of depravity remains in the regenerate, or there be any lack of thoroughness in the invigoration of the moral and religious powers, there is need of a deeper work, that both the cleansing and invigoration may be complete. . . . As in a very large measure the work is wrought in regeneration, so is it completed in entire sanctification. . . . There are many examples of such a complete work, many witnesses to its attainment.[53]

---

51. Ibid.

52. Ibid., 366-68. The Anglican article reads: "And this infection of nature doth remain, yea in them that are regenerated; whereby the lust of the flesh, called in Greek phrónēma sarkòs, . . . is not subject to the law of God. And although there is no condemnation for them that believe and are baptized; yet the apostle doth confess that concupiscence or lust hath of itself the nature of sin." This article confuses natural concupiscence with sin, thus expressing the Augustinian view of original sin.

The Westminster statement exhibits the same confusion: "This corruption of nature, during this life,.doth remain in them that are regenerated; and although it be through Christ pardoned and mortified, yet both itself, and all the motions thereof, are truly and properly sin." While Miley correctly rejected these statements, he did not understand original sin biblically, as Wesley most certainly did, namely, as "unbelief, atheism, pride," or self-idolatry.

Miley's position that Gal. 5:17 reflects a degenerate state among the Galatian Christians rather than the typical state of regeneration is well taken. He refers his readers to Gal. 1:6, 3:1-3, and 4:7 as supportive of his objection. Gal. 5:17 (like Rom. 8:5-8) means that there are two opposite modes of moral and spiritual existence: life "according to the flesh" and life "according to the Spirit." Those who are living according to the flesh cannot do the things of the Spirit, and vice versa. That these states are intermingled in actual experience is undeniable, as Wesley said, but the Galatians and Romans passages cannot be quoted to "prove" remaining sin. The case against 1 Cor. 3:1-3, however, is not as strong.

53. Ibid., 363.

Miley, however, is charitable toward those who believe that regeneration effects true sanctification. The doctrine of entire sanctification is "under no necessity of assuming" that regeneration cannot "immediately produce a fullness of the inner spiritual life."[54] "Mr. Wesley himself never denied the possibility, nor even the actuality, of such instances, though he thought them rare, even if ever actual. The common fact is that of incompleteness."[55] Nevertheless, if some teach the completeness of regeneration, while acknowledging the possibility of a degeneration in the Christian life and the need of renewal in such cases, they should be regarded as friends of the doctrine of entire sanctification, provided they insist on "the common privilege and duty of a wholly sanctified and consecrated life."[56]

4. *The Second-Blessing View*

After delineating the "second-blessing view" understood by Wesley as the ordinary mode of experiencing entire sanctification, Miley avers:

> That a subjective purification may be attained according to the definite second-blessing view does not limit the possibility of this single mode. . . . While [the Scriptures] are full of the idea of entire sanctification, they are quite empty of any such teaching respecting the mode of attainment. Hence any insistence upon such a mode as the only possible mode of sanctification must be without definite warrant of Scripture.[57]

The privilege of entire sanctification is "at once so thoroughly Scriptural and Wesleyan," said Miley, he knew of only "rarest dissent" at this point among his contemporaries.

> Yet not a few hesitate respecting the sharply defined second-blessing view. We do not share this hesitation, so far as that view represents a possible mode of entire sanctification; though we object to any insistence that such is the only possible mode.

He calls for a spirit of mutual forbearance: Those who "hold rigidly the second blessing view" may preach sanctification in their own way, but they should be tolerant of those who preach it "in a manner somewhat different."

---

54. Ibid., 356.
55. Ibid., 357.
56. Ibid., 362.
57. Ibid., 370.

> The doctrine itself, and not any rigid form into which we may cast it, is the real interest; the privilege itself, the great privilege; the actual attainment, the highest aim. And if with one consent, even if without regard to definite modes, we should earnestly preach a full salvation . . . as a common privilege and duty, . . . as the true aim of Christian life, surely there would be large gain in a wider spiritual edification, while many would enter "the fullness of the blessing of the Gospel of Christ."[58]

While Miley's presentation of the historic Methodist view was, on the whole, acceptable to those who cherished Wesley's teaching, his sympathies were obviously with those who had begun to advocate the "single mode" of sanctification. This latter school of thought ultimately prevailed in American Methodism, so much so that when Albert Knudson came to consider Wesley's doctrine of the second blessing he could dismiss it as simply a "theological provincialism."[59]

E. Olin Alfred Curtis

Olin A. Curtis (1850-1918) was the last major Methodist champion of Wesley's doctrine of Christian perfection. Tagged by Chiles as an "evangelical liberal," he studied at Boston, Erlanger, Marburg, and Edinburgh universities. His first teaching assignment was at Boston, but in 1896 he moved to Drew Theological Seminary where he enjoyed his greatest productivity. *The Christian Faith,* published in 1905, won for him a deserved reputation as a leading Methodist theologian.[60]

Curtis treats the doctrine in a section titled "personal holiness." "Psychologically this doctrine belongs to the general subject of conversion," he says, "but there are practical reasons for a separate discussion and formal emphasis."

> Our wisest course is to avoid the many controversies, and go back to Wesley himself. We could not deal with the controversies without making use of certain books which, while very penetrating and suggestive, manifest a spirit so narrow and

58. Ibid., 370-71.

59. Albert Knudson, *Doctrine of Redemption* (New York: Abingdon Press, 1933), 411-12.

60. Chiles, *Theological Transition,* 67. Curtis' work was on the Methodist Episcopal Course of Study in 1908 and 1912.

ungenerous as to create an atmosphere unworthy of the theme.[61]

He gives three positive reasons why he feels it of larger importance to return to Wesley for instruction in the doctrine. First, Wesley had almost the same epochal relation to the doctrine of holiness that Luther had to the doctrine of justification by faith. Second, unlike many of the disputants in contemporary discussions of Christian perfection, Wesley as the leader of an epochal spiritual movement had in hand a quantity of data on the "genuine Christian experience" of holiness. Third, John Wesley was a man of "such extraordinary spiritual insight, and such sanity of judgment, that often his most casual statement, especially in his Journal, is more illuminating than many a profound monograph in theology."[62]

Wesley got his "prophetic start" with his reading of Jeremy Taylor's discussion of "purity of intention." Forty years after encountering this idea Wesley wrote in his Journal, May 14, 1765, "I was struck particularly with the chapter on *intention,* and felt a fixed intention 'to give myself up to God.'" Five years later he reached a second significant point as he became a "man of one Book." In the Journal, under the above date, he says further, "I then saw, in a stronger light than ever before, that only one thing is needful, even faith that worketh by the love of God and man, all inward and outward holiness; and I groaned to love God with all the heart, and to serve him with all the strength."

Curtis believes Wesley entered the experience for which he yearned on December 24, 1744. After quoting the Journal entry, December 23-25, 1744,[63] he observes:

---

61. Olin A. Curtis, *The Christian Faith* (New York: Eaton & Mains, 1905), 373.

62. Ibid., 373-74.

63. "I was unusually lifeless and heavy, till the love feast in the evening; when, just as I was constraining myself to speak, I was stopped, whether I would or no; for the blood gushed out of both my nostrils, so that I could not add another word: but in a few minutes it stayed, and all our hearts and mouths were opened to praise God. Yet the next day I was again as a dead man; but in the evening, while I was reading prayers at Snowfields, I found such light and strength as I never remember to have had before. I saw every thought as well as every action or word, just as it was rising in my heart; and whether it was right before God, or tainted with pride or selfishness. I never knew before (I mean at this time) what it was 'to be still before God.' *Tuesday,* 25. I waked, by the grace of God, in the same spirit; and about eight, being with two or three that believed in Jesus, I felt such an awe and tender sense of the presence of God as greatly confirmed me therein, so that God was before me

To anyone familiar with John Wesley's careful, realistic manner of speech, it is evident that we have here the same sort of testimony to the experience of holiness that we have in his Journal, May 24, 1738, to the experience of conversion. If the one is not quite so near a full definition as the other, it surely is just as expressive of the fact. I find it almost impossible to read Wesley's words in the light of all his later utterance about the doctrine of Christian perfection, and not consider this date, December 24, 1744, as the probable time when he began to love God supremely.[64]

1. *Wesley's Teaching Analyzed*

Curtis devotes six pages to an excellent 11-point analysis of Wesley's teaching, concluding with a personal evaluation.[65] He insists that through constant association with Wesley's writings he has come to a true understanding of the latter's position. Although he considers Wesley's psychology "mixed up" and "crude" in its realism, he can say of the *meaning* of his teaching, "I am as sure of his doctrine of Christian perfection, as sure of its essential import as I am that I walk the earth."[66]

---

all the day long. I sought and found him in every place, and could truly say, when I lay down that night, 'Now I have lived a day.'"

64. Curtis then cites Wesley's letter (CCCLIII) from London, June 19, 1771: "Many years since I saw that 'without holiness no man shall see the Lord.' I began following after it, and inciting all with whom I had any intercourse to do the same. Ten years after, God gave me a clearer view than I had before of the way to attain this, namely, by faith in the Son of God. And immediately I declared to all, 'We are saved from sin, we are made holy, by faith.' This I testified in private, in public, in print; and God confirmed it by a thousand witnesses. I have continued to declare this for above thirty years; and God hath continued to confirm the word of his grace."

Although Curtis' claim that Wesley has left us a witness to the experience of holiness has not gained acceptance among Wesleyan scholars, Peters' observation is surely just: "It is well-nigh impossible to read the public and private record of Wesley's life and thoughts without concluding that he had some inward knowledge of the doctrine he strenuously espoused during his mature ministerial career. '*Now* give yourself up to God,' he wrote Peggy Dale. 'This is all you have to do. And even while you are doing it light will spring up.' 'What you preach to others you have particular need to apply to your own soul,' he said to Joseph Algar. . . . 'Believe, and enter into rest!' 'What a difference,' he told Hester Ann Roe, 'between the *first* love and the *pure* love!' Surely this sort of counsel comes not from merely heresay evidence. Wesley undoubtedly knew experientially what in some measure was this perfect love the preaching of which he so earnestly urged" (Peters, *Christian Perfection,* 213-14).

65. Curtis, *Christian Faith,* 377-84.

66. Ibid., 382-83.

He then summarizes the doctrine in this way:

> According to John Wesley, a sinner has three things the matter with him: First, he is *guilty;* second, he is morally *powerless;* and, third, his inherent and inherited *disposition is wrong.* . . . When a sinner is justified the guilt is canceled. When he is regenerated he receives a nucleus of power, not enough to exterminate his wrong disposition, but enough "to fight it to a standstill." In Christian perfection, there is no such fight with the disposition, "no civil war at all," for the wrong impulse never enters the consciousness as motive. . . . The civil war in the perfect Christian is rendered impossible by love, supreme love toward God and man.[67]

2. *Christian Perfection and Biblical Theology*

But is there for the Wesleyan doctrine of Christian perfection any support in biblical theology? Taking into account the criticism that biblical scholarship in Wesley's day was "arbitrary and fragmentary and superficial," can the scriptural argument for Christian perfection endure the test of modern methods of Bible study? Before answering the question, Curtis enters a protest against the notion that we cannot accept a Christian doctrine until every feature has exact Scripture proof. The Bible must be viewed as the *normative* authority on Christian doctrine. It would be enough, he says, to show that Christian perfection is not in contradiction of any Scripture but harmonizes with the *"trend of emphasis* in the New Testament upon moral love, and is the loftiest ideal belonging to the most normal and most thoroughly developed Christian consciousness."

> If we can make it indubitable that the Bible itself never allows the great saints to rest until they hold and experience this doctrine of supreme love, we will have secured as good a basis for the doctrine as could be secured by any amount of precise scriptural proof.[68]

a. St. John's Doctrine of Love. After quoting 1 John 4:16 to 5:5, he draws up the following "connected points" of Johannine teaching:

> First, in Saint John's conception of God the finality is love. Second, we make entrance into this love of God by being "begotten of God," and this takes place when we believe "that Jesus is the Christ." Third, we are prepared for the day of judgment by having this love of God made perfect in us; and this

---

67. Ibid.

68. Ibid., 385.

perfection of love can be achieved in this life—"because as he is, so are we in this world." Fourth, the marks of this perfect love are that it "casteth out fear," that it makes a man "love his brother also," and that it enables him to "do his commandments," and to have that perfect faith which "overcometh the world."[69]

b. St. Paul's Teaching. In order to avoid not only all personal bias but also all Methodist bias, Curtis makes use of the article of Professor Bartlet, Mansfield College, Oxford, in the *Hastings Dictionary of the Bible.* This article is so comprehensive and clear it should be quoted in its entirety.

> There is a state possible to Christians, corresponding to the ideal of their calling, in which they can be described as "unblamable in holiness" *(amemptous en hagiōsune),* and into which they may be brought by the grace of God in this life. Therein they stand hallowed through and through *(holoteleis),* every part of their being *(holoklēron humōn to pneuma kai hē psuchē kai to sōma)* abiding by grace in a condition fit to bear the scrutiny of their Lord's presence without rebuke *(amemptōs en tē parousia tou kuriou hēmon Jesou Christou tērethein).* Such is the teaching of 1 Thess. 3.13 and 5.23. The fidelity of God to his purpose in calling men to be Christians is pledged to this achievement (1 Thess. 5.24), though there is no definite time, as measured from the initial hallowing of the Spirit in conversion, at which it must needs be accomplished.
>
> God, who begins the good work in the soul, also continues to work at its perfecting *(epitelein)* right up to the day of Jesus Christ (Phil. 1.6); and yet, ere that day dawns, Christians may become already "pure in purpose" (*eilikrineis*—Christ's *katharoi tē kardia,* Matt. 5.8) and "void of offense," and so remain "until the day of Christ" (Phil. 1.10). It is this state of realized sanctification of conduct, or "walk," so as to "please God," that Saint Paul has constantly in view in exhorting his converts to holy living (for example, 1 Thess. 4.1). This is what he means, at times, by his use of *hagiasmos.*
>
> But the conception needs to be carefully guarded and explained by other aspects of his thought. Thus (1) it represents a growth *in* holiness rather than *into* holiness out of something else; (2) it is conceived as realizable by a definite act of faith—claiming and appropriating its rightful experience by an act of will informed by the living energy of the Holy Spirit—rather than as the cumulative result of a slow, instinctive process after conversion; (3) it is not the same as absolute moral perfection or

69. Ibid., 386.

consummation *(teleiousthai),* but is rather the prerequisite to its more rapid and steady realization.[70]

c. *Our Lord's Injunction.* Curtis sees Matt. 22:37-40 as settling forever the entire controversy as to both the ideal of Christian perfection and its possible achievement in the Christian life. "From the Old Testament (Deut. 6.5 and Lev. 19.18) our Lord takes the two items of supreme moment, and lifts them into a Christian primacy of injunction." Against the objection that our Savior did not intend to give an actual commandment but only to suggest a Christian ideal, he answers, "I do not understand how anyone can hold such a view."

> A study of the Saviour's life will show that love toward God and love toward man were the two tests which he used in determining all religious values. And the fact is that to-day, the Christian consciousness surely grasps them as such, making them the final test of life. Every Christian deed *is* Christian, every Christian thought *is* Christian, every Christian feeling *is* Christian, precisely to the extent that it expresses this supreme love. Ignatius clearly apprehended the whole thing when he said: "The beginning of life is faith, and the end is love. And these two being inseparably connected together, do perfect the man of God; while all other things which are requisite to a holy life follow after them. No one making a profession of faith ought to sin, nor one possessed of love to hate his brother. For He that said, Thou shalt love the Lord thy God, said also, And thy neighbor as thyself."[71]

3. *A Psychology of Personal Holiness*

Curtis again expresses his preference for the expression *personal holiness.* "The holiness is *personal* because it is holiness exactly from the standpoint of self-consciousness and self-determination. What you have is holiness in personality."

a. *The Transformed Motive.* In his earlier discussion of conversion he has stated his view that "the motive life of a regenerate man is organized about the motive of *loyalty to Christ.*" This motive, however, is not a simple motive, but is made up of two elements, love and duty. In rare moments these two elements may be in self-consciousness with equal force, but usually the sense of duty is paramount. Typically, the regenerate person is seeking to do his duty. His common remark is, "I will be true; I will not deny my Lord." Although this loyalty is higher than that of the mere mor-

---

70. Ibid., 387-88.

71. Ibid., 388-89.

alist, being loyal to a Person and being rooted in "the enthusiasm of a positive personal affection," it still has some of the same psychological weakness that renders morality ineffective. "Duty always implies a conflict, a civil war. The sense of ought is like a bugle, intended to call the person into battle. And while this moral battle is great, it is less than the highest mood." We see this in a home where all the members are trying to do their duty to each other. "What a dreadful home that would be! Not one day with the simple, rejoicing impulse of dominant love."

The fundamental flaw in the condition of the regenerate man is seen just here. In the struggle to do his duty he cannot organize his inner personal life. The reason of his failure is that when duty is paramount in consciousness, the personal task is done under fear, which can never be an organizing motive.

In personal holiness this motive of loyalty is transformed into the simple motive of pure love. The holy person does not live under "the whip of the ought." He does the things he does *because he loves to do them.* This is not a matter of the *quantity* of love (that is, of endless growth), but rather of *quality.* "Love entirely occupies the self-conscious mood."

> Thus there is a perfect personal organism, because all the man's motivity is nothing but love in a variety of shapes. In the man's personal life there is no antagonism, no civil war whatever. He may be tempted, as we shall see, but he cannot be tempted by his own inorganic condition, by his own depravity.[72]

b. The Exhaustion of Wrong Motive. For Curtis, the old question, "Suppression or eradication?" is inappropriate; his psychological point of view is different from those who raise this question. In Christian perfection the motive of loyalty is transformed.

---

72. Ibid., 389-90. Depravity means that the "basal individual life of a man is *inorganic.* The native characteristics are a clutter of items as unrelated as the odds and ends one finds in an attic." "Every man comes inorganic into the world. . . . No organic man is ever born." This is because man's moral life is cut off from the "blessed holy fellowship" with God for which he was created. Being cut off from God man has individuality but not personality. Personality is found only in communion with God. This communion is reestablished in regeneration, and the organization of personality is begun. But it is not until this personal communion with God is perfected by sanctifying faith, that the organization of the personality is complete (cf. ibid., 199-203). This is the underlying presupposition of Curtis' view of personal salvation.

> The new motive of pure love is not used in a negative conflict, but is used positively; and by this positive use the wrong motives are exhausted. There is no longer any heart-interest in them. They are mere ideas empty of all urgency toward the will. It is not that they are *for the time being* shut out from consciousness; no, the work is profounder than all that, they cease to have any existence as motives. The full use of pure love has exhausted them.[73]

c. The Question of Growth. Is this experience of personal holiness obtained by growth? Curtis answers, first, by reminding us that *growth* is a word we should use with extreme care. To many people growth means a natural, unurged development from an implanted germ.

> Now there is no such unurged development in the Christian life. The whole thing is personally strenuous from conversion until death. But is personal holiness obtained gradually by earnest endeavor? Looking at it in the most comprehensive way, our answer should be in the affirmative; for the crisis itself is profoundly involved in all that has led up to it. Some of the evangelists to the contrary notwithstanding, no man can arbitrarily leap into that faith which is the condition of the divine gift of supreme love. It may, now and then, look like such a leap, but psychologically it is not so. You can leap into self-assertive presumption, but never into real faith.[74]

Nevertheless, John Wesley's insistence upon the final stroke of sanctifying faith is exceedingly important. For there is a great difference between the last phase of the regenerate life and the first phase of supreme love. Only in the latter case does the motive of loyalty *entirely* lose the note of duty; only then does love absolutely fill self-consciousness, so that all the wrong motives of disposition are exhausted.

But why, on the principle of motivity, may a regenerate man, with his motive of loyalty, not simply fight his way into personal holiness?

> My answer is this: To exhaust all wrong motive by a sheer negative fight would require more time than belongs to our earthly life; and even if there were time enough the victory would exalt the element of duty and not the element of love in the motive of loyalty. What we are after is so to escape sin as to escape the bondage of conscience itself, and, like God himself, live the life of moral love.[75]

---

73. Ibid., 390-91.

74. Ibid., 391.

75. Ibid., 391-92.

Curtis, however, can conceive of another way of achieving Christian perfection in love. Theoretically at least, a person might at the beginning of the Christian life grasp the under element of love in his loyalty, *and emphasize that.* He might by self-sacrifice express his love for Christ in a complete manner, and by prayer cultivate a mood of love for Christ. "And so on and on until his love for the Saviour absolutely filled his consciousness, and his entire service was one of rejoicing love, and not one of moral obligation. There are a few of the saints whose experience is at least a hint of this kind of earnest growth into the fullness of love."[76]

d. Falling Away from Personal Holiness. If it is true that the wrong motives of our depraved, inorganic individuality are completely exhausted in their urgency, how is it possible to fall away from personal holiness? The Christian who has been made perfect in love cannot fall in the same way a regenerate person may fall, "by yielding to a motive which springs out of the individuality into consciousness in antagonism to the moral ideal."

But the very essence of the higher life of perfect love is *spiritual self-assertion.* And from this spiritual self-assertion there may come three motives, any one of which may eventuate in personal defeat.

First, there is the threat of *spiritual discouragement.* "A saint in this world, in situations where Christ is not triumphant, can have a sort of discouragement which actually grows out of his supreme love for his Lord; and there is very great peril in such a mood."

Second, there is the danger of *spiritual pride.* There is no experience so lofty in this life as to exempt one from this temptation. Our Lord experienced this temptation, as the Scriptures make clear.

Finally, there is the danger of *spiritual ambition.* A holy man may have the ambition to be a great leader in the church, or a great preacher, growing out of his very love for Christ; and yet there might come such a turn in his affairs that he must choose between his ambition and his Master.

> But beyond all our psychological theorizing we positively know that there are peculiar temptations which are characteristic of the life of personal holiness; and, such temptations once

76. Ibid., 392.

in force, there is ever the possibility of falling away from the experience. The Christian battle is not over until through death we pass into the intermediate state.[77]

77. Ibid., 392-93.

8

Christian Perfection in the Holiness Movement

John Wesley spoke of Christian perfection as "the grand depositum which God has lodged with the people called Methodists." Philip Schaff calls it Methodism's "last and distinctive doctrine." And Frederic Platt identifies it as "preeminently the distinctive doctrine" of Methodism. "The doctrine of Christian perfection has been the one specific doctrinal contribution which Methodism has made to the Church Universal," says Nolan B. Harmon in his *Understanding the Methodist Church.*

> John Wesley called it "the peculiar doctrine committed to our trust." In all else we have been, as we should be, glad and energetic followers in the main stream of Christian belief. But in this one doctrine we stand by ourselves and utter a teaching that reaches up fearlessly and touches the very Scepter of God.[1]

Yet Methodist John L. Peters acknowledges, "In all candor, however, it can hardly be maintained that in the teaching and preaching of the Church the doctrine holds today, anything like the significant place given it by Wesley."[2] While there are many within Methodism who treasure Wesley's doctrine, the proclamation of

---

1. John L. Peters, *Christian Perfection and American Methodism* (Nashville: Abingdon Press, 1956), 196.

2. Ibid.

this truth has largely passed to denominations of the modern holiness movement.[3]

In being transplanted to America and growing up on American soil, the Methodist doctrine has undergone certain modifcations. Nineteenth-century revivalism sharpened the emphasis on "the second blessing" and stressed the urgency and possibility of being fully sanctified *now.* American pragmatism simplified the doctrine, stressing what "works" in Christian experience, sometimes at the expense of a more balanced scriptural presentation. Finally, theological concepts were introduced and incorporated that were not part of the original Wesleyan formulation. The resulting holiness message, while true to Wesley's teaching at most essential points, nevertheless has its own character and shape.

A. A New Blend

Although Christian perfection as understood within the holiness movement derives directly from the message preached by the Wesleys, Melvin Dieter sees it as "a new blend" of Wesleyanism with historic Pietism and American revivalism.[4] Timothy Smith speaks of it as a "synthesis of the Quaker, Pietist, Methodist, and Puritan traditions at work in American religion."[5]

Dieter attaches prime significance to the launching in 1839 of Rev. Timothy Merritt's *Guide to Christian Perfection,* the first magazine in history devoted to the special promotion of holiness. Merritt designed his paper, he explained, for the "encouragement" of the "many" within the Methodist Episcopal church who at that time were demonstrating a new interest in the experience. The *Guide* encouraged pastors to conduct "special meetings of the church" to revive the work of holiness and also published personal testimonies from newly sanctified persons.

---

3. These include the Church of the Nazarene, The Wesleyan Church, the Free Methodist Church, the Church of God (Anderson, Ind.), The Salvation Army, plus a number of smaller groups including several yearly meetings of the Society of Friends (Quakers). Since the 1860s the interdenominational expression of the movement has been the fellowship now known as the Christian Holiness Association.

4. Melvin E. Dieter, *The Holiness Revival of the Nineteenth Century* (Metuchen, N.J., and London: The Scarecrow Press, Inc., 1980), 3.

5. Timothy L. Smith, *Revivalism and Social Reform* (Nashville: Abingdon Press, 1957), 108.

> What Merritt could not have known was that in his call for "specialty" he was most accurately defining a new emphasis, a factor which lent uniqueness to the American holiness revival. As the story of the succeeding history seems to demonstrate, it produced shades of distinction which set it apart from earlier holiness movements within the Christian church in general and from the promulgation of the experience of holiness by the Wesleys in particular. . . . It marked the wedding of the American mind, prevailing revivalism, and Wesleyan perfection in as widespread a popular quest for the beatific vision as the world had known.[6]

The adherents of the holiness revival shared John Bunyan's jail dreams of a Christian existence on the border of heaven itself—a spiritual plateau beyond "the Valley of Shadow . . . out of the reach of Giant Despair . . . out of sight of Doubting Castle."[7] They believed in the present possibility of a life of practical holiness, a "Beulah Land" within the reach of every believer who would utterly consecrate himself to Christ in the faith that God had promised to sanctify him wholly.[8]

"The American milieu in the 19th century comprehended certain cultural moods," Dieter points out, "which encouraged the revival's attempt to adapt Bunyan's dream to everyday Christian experience."[9] Notably these were transcendental philosophy and American idealism.

Transcendentalism was shaping American thought at this time in a remarkable degree. Representing an intellectual effort to transcend the material world, it "created a tendency in American Christianity [to emphasize] the spiritual and ideal side of life."[10] When the transcendentalist spoke of "the normal development, use, discipline, and enjoyment of every part of the body and every faculty of the spirit; the direction of all natural powers to their natural purposes," he was speaking a language that could easily translate into a Wesleyan explanation of entire sanctification as an experience freeing a person to be all that a loving God originally intended him to be.[11]

---

6. Dieter, *The Holiness Revival,* 3.

7. Ibid., 4.

8. Smith, *Revivalism and Social Reform,* 118.

9. Dieter, *The Holiness Revival,* 4-5.

10. Ibid.; cf. Smith, *Revivalism and Social Reform,* 104-05, 113, 142.

11. Dieter, *The Holiness Revival,* 6; Smith writes, "In 1864 a Baptist minister's little volume *The Celestial Dawn,* or *Connection of Earth and Heaven,* wove together

Another factor in the total milieu was the idealism that saw America's destiny and goal to be the creation of a new society free from the evils that had been left behind when immigrants set out for the new world. The conviction of the New England pioneers that their colony was "the place where the Lord . . . [would] create a new Heaven and a new Earth in new churches and a new commonwealth together" had fixed itself generally within the American mind. In their new land Americans were part of a new Israel.

> The inherent optimism in this American dream was readily assimilated with the optimism of perfectionism in the holiness movement; the two were to be traveling companions throughout the nineteenth century—each undoubtedly helping the other along the way. For the holiness advocate it was all part of a grand, divine plan to usher in "the most glorious and last dispensation"—the dispensation of the Holy Spirit.[12]

"Second blessing" witnesses who had entered the "Beulah Land" of perfect love were eager to share their discovery with Christians of all denominations. They were sure that holiness was a revolutionary spiritual force that could counteract and eventually uproot all the evils of society about them, for God had promised the Church a new dispensation of spiritual power.[13] The revival thus became a call to the Church to experience again the outpouring of the Holy Spirit as received by the apostles on the Day of Pentecost, in order that it might fulfill its divine mission to "Christianize Christianity" and "spread scriptural holiness to the ends of the earth."[14]

In summary, the 19th-century holiness movement was the peculiar product of a developing revivalism among persons in whom the principles of Wesleyan perfectionism, Puritanism, and Pietism were at work. Although the doctrine of Christian perfection as understood within the movement did indeed stem from Wesley's teaching, the American milieu gave it an entirely new mood and shape.

---

golden strands from Wesley, Upham, Finney, Wordsworth, and the Catholic mystics to form a magic carpet of evangelical transcendentalism" (*Revivalism and Social Reform,* 143).

12. Dieter, *The Holiness Revival,* 5; cf. Asa Mahan, *Baptism of the Holy Ghost* (New York: W. C. Palmer, Jr., 1870), 72, 140-41; Smith, *Revivalism and Social Reform,* 135.

13. Smith, *Revivalism and Social Reform,* 62, 78, 102.

14. Dieter, *The Holiness Revival,* 8; Smith, *Revivalism and Social Reform,* 49, 51, 58, 75.

B. Phoebe Palmer's "Altar Theology"

One of the most influential personalities in the developing holiness movement was Phoebe (Mrs. Walter C.) Palmer (1807-74). With her physician husband she engaged in holiness meetings in America, Canada, and Great Britain, leading thousands into the blessing. Phoebe was described by John P. Newman, later to be elected a Methodist bishop, as "the Priscilla who taught many 'the way of God more perfectly,'" including Bishops Janes, Hamline, and Peck.[15]

About 1847 Mrs. Palmer developed what came to be known as the "altar theology," using Paul's figure of placing oneself as a "living sacrifice" on God's altar to represent consecration. The altar, she believed, was Christ the Sanctifier himself. The New Testament declares that "the altar sanctifieth the gift." The Christian who is consciously "all on the altar" may at that moment claim the blessing of entire sanctification. In 1848 she published her first book, *The Way to Holiness,* which detailed how she herself had found this "shorter way" to the blessing.

The way to holiness begins with the recognition of the "duty" to be "fully conformed to the will of God, as recorded in his written word."[16] The knowledge that God *requires* holiness *now* is all the seeker needs. "Whether *convicted* or otherwise, *duty is plain. . . . Knowledge is conviction.*"[17] Such apprehension of "simple truth" is a "sufficient plea to take to God—and because of present need, to ask a present bestowment of the gift." "The voice of duty is literally *the voice of God to the soul.*"[18] After "laying all upon the altar" and claiming the blessing, Phoebe herself witnessed: "'Tis done! Thou hast promised to receive me now! Thou dost receive me now! From this time henceforth I am thine—wholly thine! The SPIRIT now bore testimony to [my] spirit of the TRUTH of THE WORD."[19]

Calling herself simply a "Bible Christian," Phoebe Palmer began to teach the "shorter way," emphasizing (1) entire consecration, (2) faith in the written Word, (3) confession.

---

15. Smith, *Revivalism and Social Reform,* 122-23.

16. Phoebe Palmer, *The Way to Holiness* (New York: G. Lane and C. B. Tippett, 1848), 18.

17. Ibid., 19 (italics Palmer's).

18. Ibid., 49 (italics Palmer's).

19. Ibid., 41-42.

> On everyone who will specifically present himself upon the altar . . . for the sole object of being ceaselessly consumed, body and soul, in the self-sacrificing service of God, He will cause the fire to descend. And . . . He will not delay to do this for every waiting soul, for He standeth waiting, and the moment the offerer presents the sacrifice, the hallowing, consuming touch will be given.[20]

It is difficult to assess the subtle distinctions involved in this critical restatement of the Wesleyan approach to entire sanctification. The explicit emphasis upon consecration as a prerequisite is a patent departure from Wesley who stressed instead a "repentance of believers" (the conviction of inbred sin and the believer's utter inability to sanctify himself) as the ordinary precondition of sanctifying faith.[21] For Wesley, entire sanctification is by faith alone, faith understood as "a divine evidence and conviction" produced by the Holy Spirit through the promises of Scripture; although, as Dr. Jack Ford points out, it is inconceivable that Wesley would have said that anyone unwilling to consecrate his life completely to God could expect to receive sanctifying faith.[22]

Mrs. Palmer herself recognized her view of faith as a departure from the commonly held Methodist view. The question is, Does emphasis upon a single statement of faith ("the altar sanctifieth the gift") by the individual, as the basis for claiming the experience of heart holiness, contradict the Wesleyan doctrine of the witness of the Spirit as the ground of assurance? The objection of those who have hesitated to endorse the "altar theology" is the fear that the demand for "naked faith in a naked promise" involves a kind of auto-suggestion that conflicts with Wesley's teaching that the true assurance of heart holiness is the *witness* and *fruit* of the Spirit. Dieter observes:

> The newness, then, essentially was a change in emphasis resulting from a simple, literal Biblical faith and a prevailing mood of revivalism combined with an impatient, American pragmatism that always seeks to make a reality at the moment whatever is considered at all possible for the future.[23]

Eventually the altar theology became one of the common

---

20. Phoebe Palmer, *Guide to Christian Perfection,* 23 (June, 1853), 176; quoted by Dieter in *The Holiness Revival,* 31.

21. See chap. 5.

22. Jack Ford, *In the Steps of John Wesley* (Kansas City: Nazarene Publishing House, 1968), 228-29.

23. Dieter, *The Holiness Revival,* 31.

ways of preaching and teaching in the holiness movement. Mrs. Palmer herself was able to satisfy most of her critics that her teachings were "substantially orthodox, and Wesleyan," but many who taught the Palmer way failed to achieve her balance at essential points. Her "theological syllogism," as Dieter calls it, led to a pattern of teaching into which the ensuing movement often fell, pressing upon seekers a simplistic stereotyped formula that was in danger of precluding an authentic spiritual experience.[24] Dr. H. C. Morrison took note of such spiritual presumption and said: "I sometimes meet people who say when asked if they are sanctified, 'Yes, I have taken it by faith.' Well, where is the witness? 'Brother, you have no right to stop crying to God until the baptism consciously falls.'"[25] Syllogistic holiness is not scriptural holiness.

Furthermore, Mrs. Palmer's insistence on holiness as a present *duty* tended to introduce an element of fear, which at times led to an unscriptural "holiness or hell" teaching, that is, that those who die without a conscious experience of entire sanctification would not be saved.[26]

---

24. Mrs. Palmer herself was at times assailed by doubts and more than once makes the following kind of frank confession: "But you would hardly conceive how often he (Satan) tries to make me think of my faith as mere *intellectual knowledge.* I meet him by saying, it is founded on principles laid down by the eternal Mind, and consequently immovable in faithfulness. . . . I trust Him, and on the authority of *His own word* declare in strongest testimony His faithfulness in fulfilling His promises. The fruits of holiness follow—I dare not doubt it" (*Faith and Its Effects* [New York: Published for the author at 200 Mulberry St., 1854], 112). For further evaluation of the Palmer view see Dieter, *The Holiness Revival,* 28-37; Ivan Howard, "Wesley Versus Phoebe Palmer: an Extended Controversy," *Wesleyan Theological Journal,* 6 (Spring, 1971), 31-40; Smith, *Revivalism and Social Reform,* 125-27. "As late as March 10, 1857, after a long period of praying for guidance, a warm friend of Mrs. Palmer's, Nathan Bangs, appeared at the Tuesday Meeting for the specific purpose of refuting the notion that Christians may believe they have the experience before they have the Spirit's witness to it. Wesley, he said, had considered the faith by which we are sanctified to be 'inseparably connected with a divine evidence and conviction that the work is done.' Hence the 'altar phraseology' was unsound, unscriptural, anti-Wesleyan and no doubt in many cases had caused deception. The importance which Bangs attached to the event is indicated in the written charge he left with his diary that if any of it were ever published, the passage reporting the incident must be included *verbatim*" (Smith, *Revivalism and Social Reform,* 127).

25. Dieter, *The Holiness Revival,* 31-32. Notice that Morrison equates the "witness" with the "baptism" of the Holy Spirit; see pp. 135 ff.

26. Ibid., 37. For Wesley's position see chap. 5. From his Protestant premises Wesley insisted that entire sanctification be preached "always by way of promise; always drawing, rather than driving" (*Sermons,* 2:457).

C. Oberlin Perfectionism

The doctrine of Christian perfection began to find new expression in the late 1830s at Oberlin College in Ohio, where Asa Mahan (1799-1889) was president and Charles G. Finney (1792-1875) spent half of each year as professor of theology.

Committed from its founding to "the broad ground of moral reform in all its departments," Oberlin at once became a center of Christian perfectionism and of Christian reflection aimed at the liberation of Blacks from slavery and racism; of women from male oppression and domination; of the poor from ignorance, alcohol, and economic exploitation; and of American society in general from the social evils that hindered the coming of Christ's kingdom.[27]

The aim of Oberlin teaching seems to have been to find an establishment in grace beyond the ups and downs of the revivalistic pattern. It may be characterized in general as one of several manifestations of the widely prevalent 19th-century quest for Christian holiness. Specifically it was an attempted synthesis of New School Calvinism and the Methodist doctrine of entire sanctification. George Peck, editor of the *Methodist Quarterly Review,* commented that while Finney did not express himself "Methodistically" in his *Views on Sanctification,* "the *thing* which we mean by Christian perfection is truly set forth in that work."[28] Even more "Methodistic" was Mahan's *The Scripture Doctrine of Christian Perfection* (1839), which breathes the spirit of Wesley's *Plain Account.*

A new emphasis found expression, however, in both Finney and Mahan. This was the view that entire sanctification is accomplished by a personal baptism with the Holy Spirit similar to that received by the apostles on the Day of Pentecost. Finney developed this view in his 1838-39 lectures on Christian perfection published in *The Oberlin Evangelist* and Mahan gave it popular form in his 1870 book titled *The Baptism of the Holy Ghost.* Viewing the experience of entire sanctification as accomplished by the "baptism of the Holy Ghost" represents a modification of Wesleyan teach-

---

27. Timothy L. Smith, "The Doctrine of the Sanctifying Spirit: Charles G. Finney's Synthesis of Wesley and Covenant Theology," *Wesleyan Theological Journal* (Spring 1978), 13:93.

28. *Methodist Quarterly Review* (April 1841), 23:308 (footnote 24, Dieter, *The Holiness Revival,* 67).

ing, a modification that came to be generally accepted by the turn of the century both in and beyond holiness circles.

1. *Asa Mahan*

The renewed emphasis on Christian perfection in America—in the *Guide,* in Phoebe Palmer's circle, and in Oberlin perfectionism—was generally along classical Wesleyan lines. Occasional references to the baptism with the Holy Spirit appear, but not as a developed doctrine and only occasionally as identified with entire sanctification. Donald Dayton writes: "The first hints of this teaching occur in Oberlin perfectionism, but the exact development is difficult to trace."[29]

The first appearance of this view in the *Guide to Christian Perfection* was Oberlin professor Henry Cowles' brief article in 1840 titled "Short Sermon—the Baptism of the Holy Ghost." From Acts 1:5 Cowles argues that the blessing promised in the baptism did not include "the grace of conversion, or regeneration" since "the apostles had been converted some years before." Pentecost, he said, produced "love" and fearless witnessing, effecting "a change more striking than even that of their first conversion." In another sermon of that period Cowles refers to the Spirit's "sanctifying agency" and His "purifying our hearts."[30]

The January 1841 issue of the *Guide* carried a sermon by Congregational minister S. S. Smith, titled "Power from on High," from Luke 24:49. Smith writes, "The one hundred and twenty who were baptized with the Holy Ghost on the day of Pentecost, had previously been 'born of God.'" He goes on to say, "Evidently the gift of the Holy Ghost here alluded to [in John 7:39] is the power from on high referred to in the text, and evidently it was not regeneration." This power he understands as transforming "the whole moral character of the recipients," a "sanctifying power" producing "perfect love." He presses the importance of the Spirit's empowerment, saying, "The only power, then, that can render the modern church what the ancient prophets predicted it should be and what the primitive church was, is *the baptism with the Holy*

---

29. Donald Dayton, "Asa Mahan and the Development of American Holiness Theology," *Wesleyan Theological Journal* (Spring 1974), 9:61.

30. J. Kenneth Grider, *Entire Sanctification: The Distinctive Doctrine of Wesleyanism* (Kansas City: Beacon Hill Press of Kansas City, 1980), 70.

Ghost, of which she is now evidently generally ignorant and destitute."[31]

Dayton speaks of "a rising interest in this doctrine in the *Guide to Holiness* in the 1850s"—the name for *Guide to Christian Perfection* after 1846. William Arthur's *Tongue of Fire,* from Britain, was published in 1856 and called for a "new Pentecost" but without associating Spirit-baptism with heart holiness.

> Much of the literature of the revival of 1857-58 spoke of "Pentecost" and the "baptism of the Holy Ghost" without identifying either with the experience of entire sanctification, though it should be noted that the spread of "higher life" teachings was closely associated with this period of the revival.[32]

In 1859 Phoebe Palmer published *The Promise of the Father,* arguing from the Acts 2 quotation of Joel the right of women to preach the gospel. But it was her reports in the *Guide* of her British revival campaigns that reveal her adoption of the new terminology. In her report from the Newcastle revival she writes that she preached "the endowment of power, the full baptism of the Holy Ghost, as the indispensable, aye, *absolute* necessity of all disciples of Jesus."[33]

Even so, Phoebe was still reluctant to publish Mahan's *Baptism of the Holy Ghost* in 1870, arguing that it was too controversial. Mahan's response was that the widespread discussion of the idea indicated that the churches were ready for his book in which "the doctrine of entire sanctification is presented in a form old and yet new." Phoebe finally yielded and the Palmers published the book, which immediately had major impact through several editions. It was widely circulated in both America and Britain, as well as on mission fields around the world, and was translated into German and Dutch.[34]

It is possible to speak of "an increasing crescendo of 'Pentecostal' and 'baptism of the Holy Ghost' language after 1870." In 1871 Finney addressed the Oberlin Council of Congregationalism on "The Baptism of the Holy Ghost," and that same year two Free Methodist women provoked Dwight L. Moody to begin seeking

---

31. Ibid., 67-69.

32. Donald Dayton, "Asa Mahan and the Development of American Holiness Theology," *Wesleyan Theological Journal* (Summer 1974), 9:62.

33. Ibid., 62-63.

34. Ibid., 63.

the blessing by telling him his preaching lacked power. Moody soon found the experience in New York City, and henceforth the teaching became a major theme of his preaching.[35] This was also true of his successor, R. A. Torrey, who wrote an influential book on the subject.[36]

Mahan's book also made a major impact within Methodism. The *Buffalo Christian Advocate* observed that "the author has hit upon just the right time for his work. The church is awakening to the importance of the baptism of power." The *Methodist Recorder* declared the theme "central in the current of all New Testament teaching." And in 1874 Daniel Steele, later professor of N.T. Greek at Boston University, described his own entrance into the blessing of holiness in terms of the "baptism of the Spirit" and urged his Methodist brethren "to cease to discuss the subtleties and endless questions arising from entire sanctification or Christian Perfection, and all cry mightily to God for the baptism of the Holy Spirit."[37]

The significance of Mahan's *Baptism of the Holy Ghost* is that it was the first full-length book on the subject. The author begins by defining both the *pattern* and the *method* of New Testament sainthood.

First, consider the pattern. In Old Testament prophecy we find a distinct revelation of God's ideal for the New Testament saint. He is a redeemed sinner, who under the provisions of "the new covenant" has been cleansed from "all his filthiness and all his idols" and filled with the Spirit.

> In the New Testament, this "new man" is revealed as "after God created in righteousness and true holiness," and as "renewed in knowledge after the image of Him that created him;" as "beholding with open face the glory of the Lord, and being changed into the same image from glory to glory;" . . . as "having been made perfect in love" . . . [and as having Christ] "formed within him, the hope of glory;" . . . constantly growing "into the stature of the fulness of Christ."[38]

---

35. Ibid. Moody's doctrine, however, did not include the idea of heart cleansing but rather stressed the empowering aspect of Spirit baptism.

36. R. A. Torrey, *The Holy Spirit: Who He Is and What He Does and How to Know Him in All the Fulness of His Gracious and Glorious Ministry* (New York: Fleming H. Revell Co., 1927).

37. Donald Dayton, "Asa Mahan and the Development of American Holiness Theology," *Wesleyan Theological Journal*, 9:62.

38. Asa Mahan, *The Baptism of the Holy Ghost* (New York: W. C. Palmer, Jr., 1870), 8-9.

Second, observe the method God employs to produce such Christlike holiness. It is by "'the baptism of the Holy Ghost,' . . . to be sought and received by faith in God's word of promise, on the part of the believer, *after* he has believed. . . ."[39] Citing Acts 19:2, Mahan understands that

> the gift of the Spirit was not expected *in,* but *after* conversion: "Have ye received the Holy Ghost *since* ye believed?" The same fact is referred to and affirmed, Eph. i.13: "In whom ye also trusted, after that ye heard the word of truth, the gospel of our salvation; in whom also, *after* that ye believed ye were sealed with that Holy Spirit of promise."[40]

"In this baptism of power, this 'sealing and earnest of the Spirit,' which is always given, not in conversion, but '*after* we have believed,' 'the promise of the Spirit' is fulfilled."[41]

For Mahan, there are two classes of believers: (1) those who have repented and believed for pardon and eternal life, and (2) those who, *after* conversion, have "received the Holy Ghost." The former have a measure of assurance that God is their Father, but this is mixed with doubts and fears; their spiritual life is weak and best portrayed in the seventh chapter of Romans. With them, however, the Spirit "is ever present, preparing the heart for the promised baptism."[42] The latter class, by contrast, enjoy "absolute assurance and hope" and experience "fellowship with the Father, and with his Son Jesus Christ."[43] By the baptism of the Holy Ghost these persons enjoy "the glorious liberty" of the eighth chapter of Romans.[44]

For Wesley, the Old Testament promise of the Spirit is preeminently, but not exclusively, the promise of full sanctification. The ministry of the Spirit with whom Christ baptized the Church is holistic, from awakening to glorification.[45] The Spirit who was

---

39. Ibid., 13 (italics Mahan's).

40. Ibid., 38 (italics Mahan's).

41. Ibid., 16 (italics Mahan's).

42. Ibid., 17.

43. Ibid., 54.

44. Ibid., 116.

45. Wesley's creed: "I believe in the infinite and eternal Spirit of God, equal with the Father and the Son, to be not only perfectly holy in himself, but the immediate cause of all holiness in us: enlightening our understandings, rectifying our wills and affections, renewing our natures, uniting our person to Christ, assuring us of adoption of sons, leading us in our actions, purifying and sanctifying our

given at Pentecost is "the principle of the conversion and entire sanctification of our lives."

Wesley therefore posits a threefold reception of the Holy Spirit in the ongoing process of salvation—in prevenient grace, in the new birth, and in entire sanctification. *First,* in prevenient grace: "As all merit is in the Son of God, in what he has done and suffered for us, so all power is in the Spirit of God. Therefore every man, in order to believe unto salvation, must receive the Holy Ghost."[46] *Second,* in the new birth: "they all 'received the Holy Ghost' when they were justified. God then 'sent forth the Spirit of His Son into their hearts, crying, Abba, Father.'"[47] *Third,* in entire sanctification: In the instant of sanctifying faith, "God . . . cometh unto them with his Son and blessed Spirit, and, fixing his abode in their souls, bringeth them into the 'rest which remaineth for the people of God.'"[48]

Mahan, on the other hand, limits the promise to the third and final reception of the Spirit. The Spirit is "with" believers from their new birth, but is not "in" them until they receive the baptism of the Holy Ghost.[49] Otherwise, in portraying the ministry of the Spirit Mahan sounds very much like Wesley. Wesley was never willing to limit the *baptism* with the Holy Spirit to entire sanctification, but after his dialogue with Fletcher on the subject could identify Christian perfection with the *infilling* of the Holy Spirit. "I believe one that is *perfected in love,*" he wrote in 1771, "or *filled with the Holy Ghost,* may properly be termed a *father.*"[50]

In general, the holiness movement has followed Mahan in viewing entire sanctification as being wrought by the *baptism* with

---

souls and bodies, to a full and eternal enjoyment of God" (see Sermon, "On Grieving the Holy Spirit," *Works,* 7:486).

46. *Works,* 8:49.

47. *Letters,* 5:215.

48. *Works,* 11:381. Richard S. Taylor also understands "a threefold reception of the Spirit—(1) He is 'received' incognito and non-volitionally in awakening and conviction; (2) He is received as the unidentified Agent of our new birth, when we consciously receive Christ as Savior; (3) He is received consciously and volitionally as a Person in His own right, by a regenerate child of God, to indwell and rule completely as Christ's ever present Other Self" (*Projecting Our Heritage,* ed. Myron F. Boyd and Merne A. Harris [Kansas City: Beacon Hill Press of Kansas City, 1969], 61, fn.).

49. See the Preface of the 1872 revised edition of Mahan's *Baptism of the Holy Ghost* published in London by T. Woolmer, v-vi.

50. *Letters,* 5:229 (to Joseph Benson).

the Holy Spirit. After commenting on Matt. 3:11 and asserting its fulfillment at Pentecost, William McCumber writes:

> Now this question must be raised: Is the baptism with the Holy Spirit a valid promise to believers today? Some sincere and serious students of the Scripture say no, and point to the absence of any command or promise to be "baptized" with the Spirit after the event of Pentecost. This is quite true. However, to those who were already Christians, Paul writes, "Be filled with the Spirit" (Eph. 5:18). If there is no injunction to be baptized with the Spirit, there is plainly an injunction to be "filled." "Filled" is the very term used to describe the results of the outpouring of the Spirit upon the disciples in the Upper Room: "They were all filled with the Holy Spirit." Surely the inner results of being "filled" today will be just what they were then—a cleansing of the heart from sin, with the Spirit indwelling a purified residence and empowering the witness of believers.[51]

2. *Charles G. Finney*

Finney and Mahan embarked on their quest for holiness together, during the winter of 1836-37, when they retreated to New York City to study the Bible and Wesley's *A Plain Account of Christian Perfection,* to see whether the Scriptures do indeed promise the entire sanctification of believers.[52] Mahan apparently found the blessing at that time,[53] but Finney did not profess the experience until about seven years later.[54] The latter's 1838-39 lectures on Christian perfection, published in *The Oberlin Evangelist,* do, however, clearly enunciate entire sanctification as "the promise of the Father" fulfilled by "the baptism of the Holy Ghost" in the Christian dispensation.

These lectures reflect Finney's study of the English Bible and, even more pointedly than Wesley's expositions, relate Christian perfection to Jeremiah's and Ezekiel's prophecies of the new covenant as the Lord's pledge of "an inward holiness brought about by the Spirit of God—the very substance and spirit of the law written in the heart by the Holy Ghost." The Day of Pentecost was "the

---

51. William McCumber, *Holy God, Holy People* (Kansas City: Beacon Hill Press of Kansas City, 1982), 72-73.

52. Asa Mahan, *The Scripture Doctrine of Christian Perfection* (Boston: D. S. King, 1840), 188; Smith, *Revivalism and Social Reform,* 103.

53. Ibid., 189.

54. Smith, "The Doctrine of the Sanctifying Spirit," *Wesleyan Theological Journal* (Spring 1978), 13:105.

commencement of a new dispensation" in which these promises began to be fulfilled in believers.

> "Every individual Christian may receive and is bound to receive this gift of the Holy Ghost at the present moment," he proclaimed. Christians who have been born again do not have the gift "in such a sense as it is promised in these passages of the Holy Scripture, or in a higher sense than he was received by the Old Testament saints . . . of whom it was said that 'they all died in the faith, not having received the promise.'"[55]

The next year in his "Letters to Ministers of the Gospel" Finney urged them to preach this truth he had himself recently found in Scripture. He acknowledged that his instruction to new converts had formerly been "very defective," for he had not seen "that the baptism of the Holy Ghost is a thing universally promised . . . to Christians under this dispensation." This baptism "is the secret of the stability of Christian character." New converts need "to be baptized into the very death of Christ, and by this baptism to be slain, and buried, and planted and crucified, and raised to a life of holiness in Christ."[56]

Finney's position on the Spirit-filled life comes through clearly in a selection of published articles gathered together under the title *Power from on High.*[57] The first selection is a brief recap of his 1871 address to the Oberlin Council on Spirit-baptism. "This baptism with the Holy Ghost," he reiterates, "this thing promised by the Father, this enduement of power from on high, Christ has expressly informed us is the indispensable condition of performing the work which he has set before us."[58]

---

55. Ibid., 103. This is in harmony with Finney's exposition of sanctification in his *Systematic Theology* (1847 and 1851). J. Kenneth Grider says of Finney's treatment in this work: "He teaches that the promises of 'sanctification' were fulfilled by the baptism of the Holy Spirit at Pentecost . . . that 'a promise of sanctification, to be of any avail to us, must be done at some certain time . . . that is, the time must be so fixed . . . as to put us into the attitude of waiting for its fulfillment. . . . The promise of Christ to the Apostles concerning the outpouring of the Spirit on the day of Pentecost, may illustrate the meaning.' In another area of *Systematic Theology,* still treating 'sanctification,' Finney writes: 'They [the Patriarchs] did not receive the light and the glory of the Christian dispensation, nor the fullness of the Holy Spirit. And it is asserted in the Bible, that "they without us," that is without our privileges, "could not be made perfect"'" (*Entire Sanctification,* 67).

56. Ibid., 104.

57. Charles G. Finney, *Power from on High: a Selection of Articles on the Spirit-filled Life* (London: Victory Press, 1944).

58. Ibid., 5.

For Finney, the need for this power is twofold: (1) to enable the Church to fulfill its commission to "disciple all nations,"[59] and (2) to establish in "permanent sanctification" those converted to Christ.

That last phrase is the key to Finney's teaching. "Nothing in the Bible," he says, "is more expressly promised in this life than *permanent sanctification.*" After quoting 1 Thess. 5:23-24 he continues, "This is unquestionably a prayer of the apostle for permanent sanctification in this life, with an expressed promise that he who has called us will do it."[60]

> We learn from the Scriptures that "*after* we believe" we are, or may be, *sealed* with the Holy Spirit of promise, and that this sealing is the earnest of our salvation. Eph. i. 13, 14. This sealing, this earnest of our inheritance, is that which renders our salvation sure. . . . In 2 Cor. i. 21 and 22 the apostle says: "Now He which establisheth us with you is Christ, and hath anointed us, is God, who hath also sealed us and given the earnest of the Spirit in our heart." Thus we are *established* in Christ and *anointed* by the Spirit, and also *sealed* by the *earnest* of the Spirit in our hearts. And this, remember, is a blessing that we receive after that we believe. . . . Now, it is of first importance that converts should be taught not to rest short of this *permanent sanctification,* this sealing, this being established in Christ by the special anointing of the Holy Ghost.[61]

Since "sin consists in carnal-mindedness, in 'obeying the desires of the flesh and of the mind,'"

> permanent sanctification consists in entire and permanent consecration to God. It implies the refusal to obey the desires of the flesh or of the mind. The baptism or sealing of the Holy Spirit subdues the power of the desires, and strengthens and confirms the will in resisting the impulse of desire, and abiding permanently in a state of making the whole being an offering to God.[62]

This seems to be "the *thing* called Christian perfection," as George Peck put it, but the view of entire sanctification as "entire and permanent consecration" reflects the Oberlin doctrine of sin. Reacting against Calvin's doctrine of total depravity, Finney subscribed to a view of moral depravity that locates sin not in the total person but only in the will. "Sin is nothing else than that voluntary, ultimate preference or state of committal to self-pleasing out of

59. Ibid.

60. Ibid., 39.

61. Ibid., 39-40 (italics Finney's).

62. Ibid., 40.

which the volitions, the outward actions, purposes, intentions, and all the things that are commonly called sin proceed."[63]

Entire sanctification accordingly is the elimination of this selfishness to which we are voluntarily committed as free agents. Positively, it is the confirmation of the believer's will in the will of God. Referring to the effort to achieve sanctification by works, Finney says: "To eradicate selfishness from the breast is an absurdity. So the effort to obey the commandments of God in spirit—in other words, to attempt to love as the law of God requires by force of resolution—is an absurdity."

> All such efforts to overcome sin are equally futile, and as unscriptural as they are futile. The Bible expressly teaches us that sin is overcome by faith in Christ. "He is made unto us wisdom, righteousness, sanctification, and redemption." . . . The doctrine of the Bible is that Christ saves His people from all sin through faith; that Christ's Spirit is received by faith to dwell in the heart. It is faith that works by love. Love is wrought and sustained by faith. . . . It is by faith that they "put on the Lord Jesus Christ, and put off the old man, with his deeds." It is by faith that we fight "the good fight," and not by resolution. . . .
>
> This is the victory that overcometh the world, even our faith. It is by faith that the flesh is kept under and carnal desires subdued. The fact is that it is simply by faith that we receive the Spirit of Christ to work in us to will and to do, according to His good pleasure.[64]

When Finney here refers to the "flesh," which must be "kept under," he departs from both Scripture and Wesley. It is not the "flesh" but the *body (soma)* that must be "kept under" (1 Cor. 9:27; cf. Rom. 6:13). By the "flesh" *(sarx)* St. Paul meant the total person "as he is by nature," that is, the creature subjected to sin. The flesh must be "crucified" and done away with (Gal. 5:24; Rom. 8:8-9).[65] The body, however, must indeed be kept from sin's power by its presentation to God (Rom. 6:12-13; 12:1), so that it may be the Lord's (1 Cor. 6:13*b*) and thus the temple of the Holy Spirit (1 Cor. 6:19-20).

In fairness to Finney, however, we must acknowledge that the difference between his and the Wesleyan view is more semantic than substantive. Finney's terminology has been adopted by most

---

63. Ibid., 60.

64. Ibid., 61-62.

65. John Wesley, *Explanatory Notes upon the New Testament,* 545.

advocates of the Spirit-filled life who have gathered since 1876 at the Keswick conventions in England, and this general position has come to be known as the Keswick teaching. Finney insists that a life of spiritual defeat "is no Christian state. For the apostle has distinctly said, 'Sin shall not have dominion over you, because ye are not under the law, but under grace.'"[66] Such has been the characteristic emphasis of subsequent Keswick teachers. The error of the terminology is its abandonment of a scriptural for a Gnostic evaluation of the body (identifying it too closely with sin).[67]

Finney's teaching, therefore, formed a bridge over which holiness teaching passed to those who were Calvinistic in their theological orientation. For this school, the baptism with the Holy Spirit does not cleanse the heart from sin; it is only an empowerment for victorious living and effective witness. While these teachers deny the possibility of sin's destruction prior to death, they do advocate the possibility of a life of victory over "the old nature" for those who put themselves under the direction and control of the indwelling Spirit. But as long as Christians inhabit this mortal body, they must contend with the sin nature.

Another development from the doctrine of Spirit-baptism as essentially empowerment is the Pentecostal Holiness doctrine of the baptism with the Holy Spirit as a third work of grace evidenced by glossolalia.[68] The modern Pentecostal and neo-Pentecostal movements have generally moved away from any doctrine of entire sanctification while making Spirit-baptism and the gifts of the Spirit the true signs of the Spirit-filled life.

D. Daniel Steele

Daniel Steele (1824-1904) was the first major Methodist theologian to embrace the Pentecostal position developed by Mahan and Finney. J. Kenneth Grider refers to Steele as "the most scholarly and most respected holiness movement writer" of this early

---

66. Finney, *Power from on High,* 59.

67. For a discussion of this issue see William M. Greathouse, *From the Apostles to Wesley: Christian Perfection in Historical Perspective* (Kansas City: Beacon Hill Press of Kansas City, 1979), 69-71.

68. "We believe also that the Pentecostal Baptism of the Holy Ghost and fire is obtainable by a definite act of appropriating faith on the part of the fully cleansed believer, and that the initial evidence of the reception of this experience is speaking in other tongues as the Spirit gives utterance" (*Discipline of the Pentecostal Holiness Church* [1937], 12).

period. Founding president of Syracuse University, he became professor of New Testament Greek at Boston University 1884-93, where he also taught systematic theology.[69]

Since Steele fully endorsed the view that Pentecost ushered in the dispensation of the Holy Spirit with its offer of heart holiness for every believer, it is not necessary to outline his complete position. One quotation is sufficient to show his basic agreement with Mahan and Finney:

> We understand that the baptism, the anointing, the fulness, the abiding, the indwelling, the constant communion, the sealing, the earnest, of the Holy Spirit, are equivalent terms, expressive of the state of Christian perfection.[70]

Steele, however, goes beyond his Calvinistic mentors in stressing that the baptism with the Holy Spirit accomplishes, as Grider puts it, "a real, 'Methodist-like' entire sanctification."[71]

> The conclusion is inevitable, that the baptism of the Holy Ghost includes the extinction of sin in the believer's soul as its negative and minor part, and the fulness of love shed abroad in the heart as its positive and greater part; in other words, it includes Christian perfection and entire sanctification.[72]

It appears that Steele is the first holiness writer to cite Acts 15:8-9 as evidence that the Pentecostal baptism accomplishes the heart cleansing Wesley taught as characteristic of true sanctification. He commented on the Acts text "that the Holy Ghost came to Cornelius and his house in his office as Sanctifier, 'purifying their hearts by faith.'"[73] Subsequently this became standard holiness teaching.

Steele also develops a Wesleyan doctrine of the new birth. In *The Gospel of the Comforter* he includes chapters titled "The Spirit's Work in Regeneration," "Two Receptions of the Spirit," "The Witness of the Spirit" and "The Fulness of the Spirit." In this definitive volume Steele endeavors to harmonize the new view with both the New Testament and Wesleyan doctrine.

In the chapter titled "Two Receptions of the Spirit" he writes:

---

69. Grider, *Entire Sanctification,* 75.

70. Daniel Steele, *Love Enthroned* (Apollo, Tenn.: The West Publishing Co., 1951), 70 (quoted by Grider, *Entire Sanctification,* 76).

71. Grider, *Entire Sanctification,* 75.

72. Steele, *Love Enthroned,* 66 (quoted by Grider, *Entire Sanctification,* 75).

73. Ibid., 67 (quoted by Grider, *Entire Sanctification,* 75).

> Jesus on the day of His baptism by John received the Holy Spirit in a manner which indicated that it was a permanent and not a transitory gift, for the Spirit descended and abode upon Him. A second reception of the Holy Spirit took place after His ascension (Acts ii.33).[74]

"As there were two receptions of the Holy Spirit by Jesus," Steele says "so there were two impartations to His disciples, one on the evening of the day of His resurrection and the other on the day of Pentecost."[75] He then tries to bring these two receptions "into harmony with each other and with the apostolical doctrine of the offices of the Spirit in the present dispensation."[76]

Jesus' initial impartation of the Spirit to the disciples (in John 20:22) was of "something real . . . but far less than the fulness of the Spirit" He bestowed at Pentecost.[77]

> Christ's presence in that hour was a slight fulfillment, an earnest of the manifest coming and permanent abiding in them by His representative, the Paraclete. This corresponds to the witness of adoption as stated in Paul's epistles, especially Rom. viii.16 and Gal. iv.6.[78]

Steele fully endorses and explains Wesley's doctrine of the witness of the Spirit, pointing out the distinction between the *direct witness* of the Spirit of God and the *indirect witness* as the human "inference from the discerned presence of the fruit of the Spirit," and the necessary precedence of the direct witness.[79] Fastening on Paul's phrase, "the earnest of the Spirit" (in 2 Cor. 1:22; Eph. 1:14), he writes:

> Those who take a narrow view of the present Christian privilege and of the fruition of the promises after death interpret the earnest only of the fulness of joy in heaven. But I believe that it is a pledge and a foretaste not only of heaven

---

74. Daniel Steele, *The Gospel of the Comforter* (Chicago: The Christian Witness Co., 1917), 147.

75. Ibid., 154-55.

76. Ibid., 155.

77. Ibid.

78. Ibid. Steele quotes Bengel as saying the Johannine bestowment of the Spirit is "the earnest of Pentecost"; and Heinrich Meyer: "It belongs to the peculiarities of the miraculous intermediate condition in which Jesus was, that He, the bearer of the Spirit (John iii. 34), could already impart a special *first fruit,* whilst the *full outpouring,* the *baptism* of the Spirit, remained attached to His exaltation" (ibid., 156).

79. Ibid., 133.

> hereafter, but of a present heaven attainable by faith—even the fulness of the Holy Spirit.[80]

"The direct witness of the Spirit is intermittent in most young Christians," he says. Before the fullness of the Spirit "there are only occasional gleams of light through rifted clouds, followed by sunless intervals where doubts distract and harass the soul." The cry of such young Christians is for what Mr. Wesley called "the abiding witness." Steele then quotes Charles Wesley in verse:

> *O that the Comforter would come!*
> *Nor visit as a transient guest,*
> *But fix in me His constant home,*
> *And take possession of my breast,*
> *And make my soul His loved abode,*
> *The temple of indwelling God!*[81]

This is authentic Wesleyanism. While we truly receive the Holy Spirit at the moment of justification, this is but the beginning of our sanctification and the harbinger of the Spirit's fullness.[82]

> The work of the Holy Spirit in the progressive sanctification of the newborn soul is indirect: in opening the heart to receive the truth, the instrument of purification; in giving vigor to the spiritual life; in strengthening the will to resist temptation, and in diminishing the power of evil habits. It is repressive of depravity rather than totally destructive. The entire eradication of the propensity to sin is by the direct and instantaneous act of the Holy Spirit responsive to a special act of faith in Christ claiming the full heritage of the believer.[83]

By this "distinct and decisive action of the Holy Spirit in the extinction of the proneness to sin" the believer is brought "into the land of rest, in marvelous contrast with his previous wilderness experience, after his regeneration."[84] In this moment of entire sanctification the Comforter is "fully received, or, rather, . . . fully possesses us. . . . He is now the abiding witness," even though "ecstatic joy may come and go as the tides ebb and flow."[85] The fullness of

---

80. Ibid., 134.
81. Ibid., 135.
82. Ibid., 104-10.
83. Ibid., 110-11.
84. Ibid., 111.
85. Ibid., 140.

the Spirit is not ecstatic but ethical. The final evidence of spiritual fullness is not joy but "love enthroned."[86]

E. H. Orton Wiley

H. Orton Wiley (1877-1961) is recognized as the authentic voice of the modern holiness movement. Like Steele, his aim is to synthesize Wesleyan theology and the newer insights of the 19th century. He does indeed adopt the position that entire sanctification is by the Pentecostal baptism with the Holy Spirit but is very careful to preserve the Christocentric nature of the Spirit's work as understood by Wesley. He writes:

> Pentecost marks a new dispensation of grace—that of the Holy Spirit. This new economy, however, must not be understood as in any sense superseding the work of Christ, but as ministering to and completing it. . . . His work as the Third Person of the Trinity is therefore in connection with His offices as the Representative of the Saviour. He is the Agent of Christ, representing Him in the salvation of the individual soul, in the formation of the Church, and in the witnessing power of the Church.
>
> But He is not the Representative of an absentee Saviour. He is our Lord's ever-present other Self. . . . It is through the Spirit, therefore, that our Lord enters upon His higher ministry—a ministry of the Spirit and not merely of the letter.[87]

In this passage and in the discussion that follows, Wiley goes beyond Steele in preserving the Christocentric ministry of the Holy Spirit as well as the reality of His presence in the heart of the regenerate believer. The life we receive in the new birth is "the new life of the Spirit," the very life of Christ within us.[88] "We are regenerated by the life of Christ imparted through the Holy Spirit, . . . 'the Lord and Giver of life.'"[89] By the baptism with the Holy Spirit, the soul's salvation is completed. In explaining the Christocentric nature of this second work, Wiley quotes Dr. P. F. Bresee: "Jesus sought for Himself fellowship, communion and unity with human souls; by this baptism He is enthroned and revealed in man."[90]

---

86. Ibid., 294-98. See also Daniel Steele, *Love Enthroned* (New York: Eaton and Mains, 1902).

87. H. Orton Wiley, *Christian Theology* (Kansas City: Beacon Hill Press of Kansas City, 1952), 2:310-11.

88. Ibid., 322.

89. Ibid., 425.

90. Ibid., 323 fn.

The work of Christ through the Spirit, however, is not only the salvation of the individual but also "the formation of the Church" as the Spirit-filled Body of Christ. For this reason Wiley can speak of Pentecost as the birthday of the Christian Church.

> As Israel, redeemed from Egypt, was formed into a church-state by the giving of the law at Sinai; so also from individuals redeemed by Christ our Passover, the Holy Spirit formed the Church at Pentecost. This was accomplished by the giving of a new law, written upon the hearts and within the minds of the redeemed.[91]

Pentecost produced a unity in the Spirit that before this time was not known or experienced. On that day the Spirit incorporated the 120 "into a single organism under Christ its living Head."

> God did not create men as a string of isolated souls, but as an interrelated race of mutually dependent individuals; so also the purpose of Christ is not alone the salvation of the individual, but the building up of a spiritual organism of interrelated and redeemed persons. . . . The Holy Spirit is therefore not only the bond which unites the individual soul to Christ in a vital and holy relationship; but He is the common bond which unites the members of the body to each other, and all to their living Head. . . .
>
> Prior to Pentecost the mild showers of the Holy Spirit descended upon Israel in drops of saving grace; but in such a manner that each gathered only for himself. This continued until the time of the Incarnation, when Christ gathered into His one Person the full stream of the Holy Spirit for us all. When, after His ascension, He had received of the Father the promise of the Holy Spirit; and when the channels of faith were completed and every obstacle removed, the Holy Spirit on the day of Pentecost came rushing through the connecting channels into the heart of every believer. Formerly there was isolation, every man for himself; now it is an organic union of all the members under their one Head. This is the difference between the days before and after Pentecost.[92]

In pointing out the social as well as the individual nature of the dispensational ministry of the Holy Spirit, Wiley prepares the way for a true synthesis of Wesleyan and Pentecostal views. Wesley affirmed, "There is no religion, but social; no holiness, but social holiness." This insight Wiley preserves by his graphic depiction of the social nature of the Pentecostal baptism. The sanctifying

---

91. Ibid., 329.
92. Ibid., 329-30.

work of the Holy Spirit takes place within the living Body of Christ. The implications of this New Testament truth have yet to be drawn out, but Wiley has given Wesleyan scholars the broad pattern for future investigation.

Bibliography

Because of limited bibliographical data, items from early and medieval centuries, as well as foreign language publications, are not included here except those that have been reprinted in more modern editions. Interested students may pick up from the footnotes the available information concerning sources.

Althaus, Paul. *The Theology of Martin Luther.* Translated by Robert C. Shultz. Philadelphia: Fortress Press, 1966.

Bainton, Roland. *Here I Stand: A Life of Martin Luther.* New York and Nashville: Abingdon Press, 1950.

Baker, Frank. *From Wesley to Asbury.* Durham, N.C.: Duke University Press, 1976.

Baker, John Austin, trans. *Gospel Message and Hellenistic Culture.* Philadelphia: Westminster Press, 1973. (A translation of Jean Daniélou's *Message évangélique et culture hèllènistique.*)

Battifol, P. *Saint Gregory the Great.* Translated by T. Stoddard. London: Burns, Oates, and Washbourne, 1929.

Boehmer, Heinrich. *Road to Reformation.* Philadelphia: Augsburg Press, 1946.

Boyd, Myron F., and Merne A. Harris, eds. *Projecting Our Heritage.* Kansas City: Beacon Hill Press of Kansas City, 1969.

Breen, Q. *John Calvin: A Study in French Humanism.* Grand Rapids: Wm. B. Eerdmans Publishing House, 1931.

Brown, Peter. *Augustine of Hippo.* Berkeley, Calif.: University of California, 1967.

Butler, Cuthbert. *Western Mysticism: The Teaching of Augustine, Gregory, and Bernard.* 3rd ed. New York: Barnes and Noble, 1967.

Butterworth, G. W. *Origen: On First Principles* (a translation of *De principiis*). New York: Harper and Row, 1936.

Cannon, William R. *The Theology of John Wesley.* Nashville: Abingdon-Cokesbury Press, 1946.

Cell, George Croft. *The Rediscovery of John Wesley.* New York: Henry Holt and Co., 1935.

Chadwick, Henry. *Origen: Contra Celsum.* Cambridge: Cambridge University Press, 1953.

———. *Priscillian of Avila: The Occult and the Charismatic in the Early Church.* London: Oxford University Press, 1976.

Chiles, Robert E. *Theological Transition in American Methodism, 1790-1935.* New York: Abingdon Press, 1965.

Clarke, Adam. *Christian Theology, Selected from His Published and Unpublished Writings and Systematically Arranged: With a Life of the Author.* Edited by Samuel Dunn. New York: T. Mason and G. Lane, 1840.

Cochrane, Charles Norris. *Christianity and Classical Culture: A Study of Thought and Action from Augustus to Augustine.* London: Oxford University Press, 1944.

Coke, Thomas. *The Experience and Spiritual Letters of Mrs. Hester Ann Rogers.* London: Milner and Somerby, n.d.

Curtis, Olin A. *The Christian Faith.* New York: Eaton and Mains, 1905.

Daniélou, Jean. *Origen.* Translated by Walter Mitchell. New York: Sheed and Ward, 1955.

de Faye, E. *Origen and His Work.* Translated by Fred Rothwell. New York: Columbia University Press, 1926.

Dieter, Melvin E. *The Holiness Revival of the Nineteenth Century.* Metuchen, N.J.: Scarecrow Press, 1980.

Finney, Charles G. *Power from on High.* London: Victory Press, 1944.

Fletcher, John. *Checks to Antinomianism.* New York: Phillips and Hunt, n.d.

———. *The Works of the Reverend John Fletcher.* London: John Mason, 1839. (Reprint 1974 by Schmul Publishers, Salem, Ohio.)

Flew, R. Newton. *The Idea of Perfection.* London: Oxford University Press, 1934.

Foster, Randolph S. *The Nature and Blessedness of Christian Purity.* New York: Land and Scott, 1851.

Gilson, Etienne. *The Philosophy of St. Thomas Aquinas.* Translated by E. Bullough. 3rd rev. ed. St. Louis and London: B. Herder, 1937.

Goggin, T. A. *The Times of St. Gregory of Nyssa.* Washington, D.C.: Catholic University of America, 1947.

Greathouse, William M. *From the Apostles to Wesley: Christian Perfection in Historical Perspective.* Kansas City: Beacon Hill Press of Kansas City, 1979.

Grider, J. Kenneth. *Entire Sanctification: The Distinctive Doctrine of Wesleyanism.* Kansas City: Beacon Hill Press of Kansas City, 1980.

Hardman, Oscar. *The Christian Doctrine of Grace.* New York: Macmillan Co., 1937.

Harnack, Adolph. *History of Dogma.* Translated by Neil Buchanan. 3rd German ed. New York: Dover, n.d.

Jeremias, Joachim. *Infant Baptism in the First Four Centuries.* Translated by David Cairns. Philadelphia: Westminster Press, 1960.

Kelly, J. N. D. *Early Christian Doctrines.* Rev. ed. New York: Harper and Row, 1978.

Knight, John A. *The Holiness Pilgrimage.* Kansas City: Beacon Hill Press of Kansas City, 1973.

Knudson, Albert. *Doctrine of Redemption.* New York: Abingdon Press, 1933.

Kontzevich, Ivan Michailovich. *Fifty Spiritual Homilies, St. Macarius the Great.* Willits, Calif.: Eastern Orthodox Books, 1974.

Lake, Kirsopp, ed. *The Apostolic Fathers.* 2 vols. New York: Macmillan Co., 1925-30.

Lindström, Harald. *Wesley and Sanctification.* London: Epworth Press, 1950.

McCumber, William. *Holy God, Holy People.* Kansas City: Beacon Hill Press of Kansas City, 1982.

McGiffert, A. C. *A History of Christian Thought.* Vol. 1, *Early and Eastern.* New York: Charles Scribner's Sons, 1932.

Mackinnon, James. *Calvin and the Reformation.* London: Longmans, Green, 1936.

Mahan, Asa. *The Baptism of the Holy Ghost.* New York: W. C. Palmer, Jr., 1870.

———. *The Scripture Doctrine of Christian Perfection.* Boston: D. S. King, 1840.

Miley, John. *Systematic Theology.* New York: Hunt and Eaton, 1894.

Oulton, J. E. L., and Henry Chadwick. *Alexandrian Christianity.* Vol. 2 of Library of Christian Classics. Philadelphia: Westminster Press, 1954.

Outler, Albert. *John Wesley.* New York: Oxford University Press, 1964.

Palmer, Phoebe. *The Way to Holiness.* New York: G. Lane and C. B. Tippett, 1848.

Pelikan, Jaroslav. *The Christian Tradition.* Vol. 1, *The Emergence of the Catholic Tradition (100-600).* Chicago: University of Chicago Press, 1971.

Perkins, Harold William. *The Doctrine of Christian or Evangelical Perfection.* London: Epworth Press, 1927.

Peters, John L. *Christian Perfection and American Methodism.* New York and Nashville: Abingdon Press, 1946.

Pope, William Burt. *A Compendium of Christian Theology.* 2nd ed. New York: Hunt and Eaton, 1899.

———. *Higher Criticism of Theology.* New York: Phillips and Hunt, n.d.

Preus, R. D. *The Theology of Post-Reformation Lutheranism.* St. Louis: Concordia, 1970.

Ralston, Thomas N. *Elements of Divinity.* Nashville: Abingdon-Cokesbury Press, 1924.

Raymond, Miner. *Systematic Theology.* New York: Phillips and Hunt, 1880.

Sangster, W. E. *The Path to Perfection.* New York: Abingdon-Cokesbury Press, 1944.

Simon, John S. *John Wesley, the Master Builder.* London: Epworth Press, 1927.

Smith, Timothy L. *Revivalism and Social Reform.* Nashville: Abingdon Press, 1957.

Souter, A. *Pelagius' Expositions of 13 Epistles of St. Paul.* London: Oxford University Press, 1922-26.

Starkey, Lycurgus. *The Work of the Holy Spirit.* New York: Abingdon-Cokesbury Press, 1962.

Steele, Daniel. *Love Enthroned.* Apollo, Tenn.: West Publishing Co., 1951. Reprint.

———. *The Gospel of the Comforter.* Chicago: Christian Witness Co., 1917.

Stevens, Abel. *Life and Times of Nathan Bangs, D. D.* New York: Carlton and Porter, 1863.

Tappert, Theodore. *Philipp Jacob Spener, Pia Desideria.* Philadelphia: Fortress Press, 1964.

Tollinton, R. B. *Clement of Alexandria: A Study in Christian Liberalism.* 2 vols. London: Williams and Norgate, 1914.

Torrey, R. A. *The Holy Spirit: Who He Is and What He Does.* New York: Fleming H. Revell Co., 1927.

Tuttle, Robert G., Jr. *John Wesley, His Life and Theology.* Grand Rapids: Zondervan Publishing House, 1978.

Tyerman, L. *Life and Times of John Wesley.* London: Hodder and Stoughton, 1876.

———. *Wesley's Designated Successor.* London: Hodder and Stoughton, 1882.

Watson, Richard. *Theological Institutes.* New York: Nelson and Phillips, n.d.

Wesley, John. *Explanatory Notes upon the New Testament.* London: Epworth Press, 1950.

———. *Journal of the Rev. John Wesley.* Edited by Nehemiah Curnock. London: Charles H. Kelly, 1919.

———. *Letters of the Reverend John Wesley.* Edited by John Telford. London: Epworth Press, 1931. (Reprint of 1790 edition.)

———. *The Works of John Wesley.* 14 vols. Kansas City: Beacon Hill Press of Kansas City, 1978. (Reprint of 3rd ed., 1872.)

Wiley, H. Orton. *Christian Theology.* 3 vols. Kansas City: Nazarene Publishing House, 1940-52.

Williams, Charles. *The Descent of the Dove.* New York: Meridian Press, 1956.

Williams, Colin W. *John Wesley's Theology Today.* London: Epworth Press, 1960.

Williams, Norman P. *The Grace of God.* New York: Longmans, Green, 1930.

———. *The Ideas of the Fall and of Original Sin.* London: Longmans, Green, 1927.

Williams, W. W. *Saint Bernard of Clairvaux.* Westminster, Md.: Newman Press, 1952.

Wynkoop, Mildred Bangs. *A Theology of Love.* Kansas City: Beacon Hill Press of Kansas City, 1972.

Subject Index

Index of Persons

Index of Scripture References